AF323722

SERIES ON
ECONOMIC DEVELOPMENT
AND GROWTH VOL. 6

CORPORATE OWNERSHIP AND CONTROL

CORPORATE GOVERNANCE AND ECONOMIC DEVELOPMENT IN SRI LANKA

SERIES ON
ECONOMIC DEVELOPMENT
AND GROWTH   VOL. 6

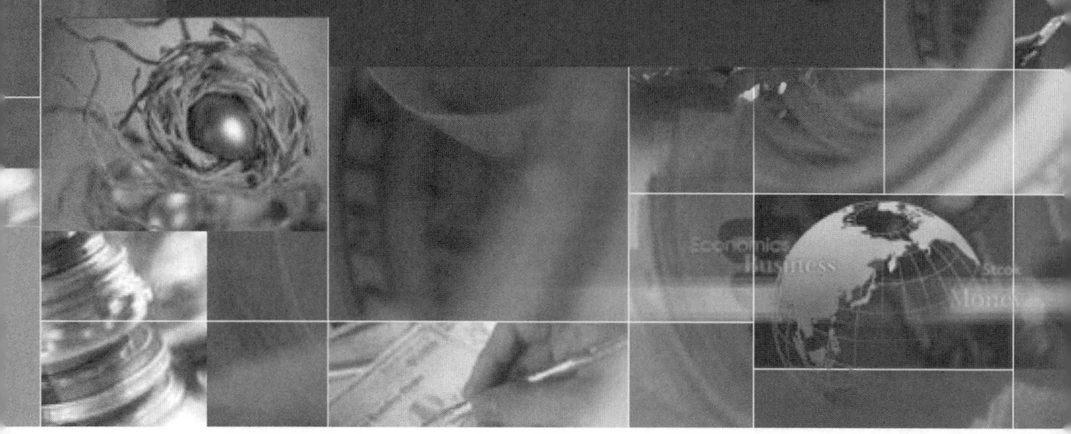

CORPORATE OWNERSHIP AND CONTROL

CORPORATE GOVERNANCE AND ECONOMIC DEVELOPMENT IN SRI LANKA

Shalini Perera

School of Law, Queen Mary, University of London

World Scientific

NEW JERSEY · LONDON · SINGAPORE · BEIJING · SHANGHAI · HONG KONG · TAIPEI · CHENNAI

Published by

World Scientific Publishing Co. Pte. Ltd.

5 Toh Tuck Link, Singapore 596224

USA office: 27 Warren Street, Suite 401-402, Hackensack, NJ 07601

UK office: 57 Shelton Street, Covent Garden, London WC2H 9HE

Library of Congress Cataloging-in-Publication Data
Perera, Shalini.
    Corporate ownership and control : corporate governance and economic development
in Sri Lanka / by Shalini Perera. -- 1st ed.
        p. cm. -- (Series on economic development and growth, v. 6)
    Includes bibliographical references and index.
    ISBN-13: 978-981-283-747-9
    ISBN-10: 981-283-747-7
    1. Corporations--Sri Lanka. 2. Stock ownership--Sri Lanka. 3. Industrial concentration--
Sri Lanka. 4. Sri Lanka--Economic policy--21st century.   I. Title.
    HD2741.P46 2011
    338.6095493--dc22

                                                                        2010044322

British Library Cataloguing-in-Publication Data
A catalogue record for this book is available from the British Library.

Typeset by Stallion Press
Email: enquiries@stallionpress.com

Printed in Singapore by World Scientific Printers.

For my parents, Virgil and Kate Perera

and

my husband, Nuwan

Preface

The governance of companies is of importance to developing countries due to the nexus between effective corporate governance and economic development. Ownership and control of public companies, often in the hands of a few individuals, families or corporate groups in many countries, is the nuclei of corporate governance and often dictates the tenor of the corporate governance debate.

Corporate Ownership and Control: Corporate Governance and Economic Development in Sri Lanka accordingly seeks to discover the implications of corporate ownership and control on the governance of companies in Sri Lanka, an illustrative example, and thereafter, suggests a reform agenda to meet the challenges posed by such structures.

The main purport of the book is to demonstrate that an analysis into the reform of corporate governance in developing countries should begin with a focus on local market structures that define the adaptation and effectiveness of corporate governance. Such analysis also provides an insight into ownership and control structures, the costs and benefits of such local market structures, and a viable reform framework. Above all, the analysis presented can be used to both understand the impact of ownership and control structures on corporate governance and to suggest how corporate governance issues arising from such structures should be resolved.

The book is organised as follows. First, the nexus between corporate governance and economic development, and corporate ownership, control and corporate governance is examined. The focus then shifts to the corporate governance challenge facing developing countries such as Sri Lanka, the illustrative example, by empirical examination of ownership structures of its companies and investigation of the causes of such structures. Thereafter, the focus is on the costs and benefits of controlling shareholder systems and a view is expressed on factors making controlling shareholder systems efficient. Crucially thereafter, the study utilises the findings on ownership structures and their causes to frame a reform agenda to meet the challenges to corporate governance. Finally, the book argues that it is vital to empower a market-based governance mechanism such as a lender to control the costs of controlling shareholders. The conclusions drawn from this detailed analysis of Sri Lanka, applied on a global scale, have the potential to greatly improve the quality of corporate governance of many developing countries.

Acknowledgements

This book grew out of a doctoral thesis I completed at Oxford University.

While I would like to thank everyone who has encouraged and supported me in writing this book, a few deserve special mention. First and foremost, my deepest thanks go to Prof. Dan Prentice and Dr. Linda Yueh, my D. Phil supervisors at Oxford. Prof. Prentice was extremely generous with his time and provided insightful comments on the many drafts. His kindness, humour, patience cannot be overstated and his supervision instilled confidence in a project that at times appeared overwhelming. Dr. Yueh encouraged and supported this publication since its inception and provided extensive comments with respect to almost every part of this book. Quite apart from her generosity with her time, her guidance and exacting standards made me strive even harder on this project.

I have been fortunate in having Jenny Payne and Mindy Chen-Wishart, as my College Advisers at Merton College, Oxford. Their friendship, encouragement and assistance, in particular at difficult times is much appreciated. I would also like to thank Jenny for her valuable comments at the early stages of this work and the many opportunities to discuss corporate law.

Special mention must be made of Prof. John Armour of Oxford University and Prof. Alan Dignam of Queen Mary University of London, my D.Phil examiners, who provided me with insightful comments and suggestions on turning my thesis into a book. I would also like to express my deep thanks to Alan who has been unfailingly helpful and tremendously encouraging of not only this publication but also all my ideas. Queen Mary is a wonderful place to work and his gentle guidance is invaluable.

I would also like to thank a number of colleagues, students and friends at the School of Law, Queen Mary University of London, Oxford University, Columbia University, University of Colombo and elsewhere, for their insightful comments, chance remarks and probing questions which have all contributed directly and indirectly to this publication.

I am also grateful to acknowledge the financial support I received during my doctoral study from the World Bank funded Legal and Judicial Reforms project of Sri Lanka and Merton College, Oxford.

My thanks also to the team at World Scientific/Imperial College Press for being supportive of this publication. Special mention is due to Yvonne Tan Hui Ling, Sandhya Venkatesh and in particular, to Juliet Lee for her support, tireless work, professionalism and most of all her patience.

Last but not least I would like to thank my parents, and my siblings, Priyani, Sriyani and Neville for their encouragement, loving interest and precious support from different corners of the globe. This book is the product of many years of hard work and aspiration. During this time, as always, my husband, Nuwan, guided, supported and inspired my work. I could not have completed this book, or for that matter, much else, without his encouragement and constant support and I am far more indebted and grateful to him than I think he is aware.

Shalini Perera

Contents

Abbreviations

ADB	Asian Development Bank
AG	Attorney General
ALI	American Law Institute
APO	Asian Productivity Organization
ASPI	All Share Price Index
BOI	Board of Investment
BRIPASL	Business Recovery and Insolvency Practitioners Association of Sri Lanka
CACG	Commonwealth Association for Corporate Governance
CalPERS	California Public Employees' Retirement System
CAR	Capital Adequacy Ratio
CBA	Ceylon Brokers' Association
CBSL	Central Bank of Sri Lanka
CEO	Chief Executive Officer
CIPE	Center for International Private Enterprise
COO	Chief Operating Officer
CRIB	Credit Information Bureau of Sri Lanka
CSE	Colombo Stock Exchange
DTI	Department of Trade & Industry (UK)
EBRD	European Bank for Reconstruction and Development
EC	European Commission
ECGI	European Corporate Governance Institute
ECGN	European Corporate Governance Network
EDRC	Economics and Development Resource Centre
EGM	Extraordinary General Meeting
EPF	Employee's Provident Fund
ESOP	Employee Share Option Schemes
ETF	Employee's Trust Fund
GCGF	Global Corporate Governance Forum
GDP	Gross Domestic Product
GOSL	Government of Sri Lanka
HCC	High Court Colombo

ICASL	Institute of Chartered Accountants of Sri Lanka
ICSA	Institute of Chartered Secretaries and Administrators
IFC	International Finance Corporation
IFIs	International Financial Institutions
IMF	International Monetary Fund
IPO	Initial Public Offering
IPS	Institute of Policy Studies (Sri Lanka)
ISS	Institute of Social Studies
LBO	Leveraged Buyout
LPG	Liquefied Petroleum Gas
LSE	London Stock Exchange
LTTE	Liberation Tigers of Tamil Eelam
M&A	Mergers and Acquisitions
MBO	Management Buyout
MD	Managing Director
NLR	New Law Reports
NPL	Non-Performing Loans
OECD	Organization for Economic Co-operation and Development
PERC	Public Enterprises Reform Commission
PVT	Private
ROA	Return on Assets
ROC	Registrar of Companies
S&P	Standard & Poor's
SAPs	Structural Adjustment Programmes
SBE	Specified Business Enterprises
SEC	Securities and Exchange Commission of Sri Lanka
SLAASMB	Sri Lanka Accounting and Auditing Standards Monitoring Board
SLAS	Sri Lanka Accounting Standards
SLAuS	Sri Lanka Auditing Standards
SLFP	Sri Lanka Freedom Party
SLLR	Sri Lankan Law Reports
SLRS	Sri Lankan Rupees
SOE	State-owned Enterprises
SSRN	Social Science Research Network
UK	United Kingdom
US	United States of America
USD	United States Dollar
WB	World Bank

Abbreviations: Companies

Aitken Spence	Aitken Spence & Company Limited (renamed as Aitken Spence Plc)
Apollo Group	Apollo Hospitals Group of India
Asian Hotels	Asian Hotels & Properties Limited (renamed as Asian Hotels & Properties Plc)
Bukit Darah	Bukit Darah Company Limited (renamed as Bukit Darah Plc)
Carson Cumberbatch	Carson Cumberbatch & Company Limited (renamed as Carson Cumberbatch Plc)
Ceylon Theatres	Ceylon Theatres Limited (renamed as Ceylon Theatres Plc)
Ceylon Tobacco	Ceylon Tobacco Company Limited (renamed as Ceylon Tobacco Company Plc)
Colombo Fort Land	Colombo Fort Land & Building Company Limited (renamed as Colombo Fort Land & Building Company Plc)
Commercial Bank	Commercial Bank of Ceylon Limited (renamed as Commercial Bank of Ceylon Plc)
DFCC Bank	Development Finance Corporation of Ceylon/ DFCC Bank Limited
Dialog Telekom	Dialog Telekom Limited (renamed as Dialog Telekom Plc)
Distilleries Company	Distilleries Company of Sri Lanka Limited (renamed as Distilleries Company of Sri Lanka Plc)
E.B. Creasy	E.B. Creasy & Company Limited (renamed as E.B. Creasy & Company Plc)
Hatton National Bank	Hatton National Bank Limited (renamed as Hatton National Bank Plc)

Hemas Holdings	Hemas Holdings Limited (renamed as Hemas Holdings Plc)
John Keells	John Keells Holdings Limited (renamed as John Keells Holdings Plc)
NDB Bank	National Development Bank Limited (renamed as National Development Bank Plc)
Richard Pieris	Richard Pieris & Company Limited (renamed as Richard Pieris & Company Plc)
Sri Lanka Telecom	Sri Lanka Telecom Limited (renamed as Sri Lanka Telecom Plc)

List of Figures

List of Tables

Table of Legislation

Statutes and Rules

Table of Cases

Cases

Introduction

0.1 Objectives and Importance of Study

Globalisation has meant the widening and intensification of links between economies. In the context of the international movement towards privatisation, liberalisation and deregulation, capital flows — both portfolio and foreign direct investment — stimulate economic growth[1] and development. However, developing countries[2] have difficulty in attracting global capital flows,[3] and the critical question to be asked is "what factor best promotes investor confidence, attracts global capital flows and is an essential determinant of economic development in developing countries?". Corporate governance is increasingly identified as fostering economic growth and development by creating a secure environment for investment.[4] The identification of this nexus between corporate governance and economic development has resulted in market forces and development assistance increasingly supporting the reform of corporate governance.

---

[1] R La Porta, L Lopez-de-Silanes, A Shleifer and R Vishny ('LLSV'), Investor Protection and Corporate Governance (2000), 58 *Journal of Financial Economics*, 3; and B Black, The Legal and Institutional Preconditions for Strong Securities Markets (2001), 48 *University of California Los Angeles Law Review*, 781, illustrate a link between the development of capital markets and economic growth.

[2] This study uses the term 'developing' countries or 'developing' economies. Developing countries or economies are poorer states which are in the process of building economies and financial systems and reflect the related terminology used by the International Monetary Fund, *World Economic Outlook: Housing and the Business Cycle* (Washington DC 2008), Statistical Appendix, which classifies countries into two major groups: advanced economies and emerging and developing economies.

[3] International Monetary Fund, *Global Financial Stability Report: Market Developments and Issues* (Washington DC 2002), 20, reports that in 2001 developing countries are estimated to have attracted only 6 percent of the total G7 outflows of capital.

[4] S Claessens, *Focus 1: Corporate Governance and Development* (Global Corporate Governance Forum-World Bank Washington DC 2003), 14–24, indicates a positive correlation between corporate governance and economic development.

However, globalisation, the pressures for convergence of economic systems and the necessity of attracting global capital flows essential for growth and development, have resulted in corporate governance reforms in developing countries being tilted towards transatlantic systems and practices.[5] Corporate governance reforms promoted by market forces and adopted by international financial institutions (IFIs), attempt to ensure the adaptation of a system of corporate governance based on dispersed ownership and prescribe corporate governance practices based on the dispersed ownership model. These reforms are not successful in developing countries due to two interconnected reasons. First, the reforms seek only to minimise the 'agency costs' arising from the separation of ownership and control.[6] Many developing countries' corporate governance concerns further involve minimising costs associated with protecting the minority shareholders from the extraction of private benefits of control by controlling shareholders, while at the same time, providing controlling shareholders with incentives to monitor management. Second, analysis of local market structures, which define with clarity corporate governance concerns and the agency costs within developing countries are largely ignored. For corporate governance to be effective, it must be meaningful in the context in which it is applied. Therefore, reform efforts cannot ignore local market structures that define the adaptation and effectiveness of corporate governance.

Corporate governance systems and practices are shaped and defined by economic, social and political factors within a country such as market structures, the legal system and culture. While it is inevitable that globalisation would bring about a certain degree of uniformity or convergence in corporate governance, it is also inevitable that economic, social and political backgrounds would be a barrier to the hegemony of one system over another.

---

[5] E Berglöf and A Pajuste, Emerging Owners, Eclipsing Markets? Corporate Governance in Central and Eastern Markets, in P Cornelius and B Kogut (eds.), *Corporate Governance and Capital Flows in a Global Economy* (Oxford University Press New York 2003), argue that despite institutional differences, corporate governance codes in Central and Eastern Europe are remarkably similar due to the costs of deviation.

[6] For example, Commonwealth Association for Corporate Governance, *Corporate Governance Principles 1999* (Marlborough 1999), sets out 15 principles of corporate governance primarily for boards of directors of dispersed companies. Further, D Reed, Corporate Governance Reforms in Developing Countries (2002), 37 *Journal of Business Ethics*, 223–233, questions whether the Anglo-American model can generate responsible ownership in developing countries.

The primary thesis advanced by this study is that an analysis into the reform of corporate governance in developing countries should begin with a focus on local market structures, such as ownership and control structures of companies that define the adaptation and effectiveness of corporate governance.[7]

To support this proposition, the focus of this study is on an analysis of the implications corporate ownership and control structures (exemplifying local market structures) have on the governance of companies in Sri Lanka, an illustrative example of a developing country.[8] The study advances three objectives. First, the study illustrates the significant and enlightening nexus between economic development and corporate governance. Second, it defines the corporate governance challenges in Sri Lanka in the light of its ownership and control structures. Third, in order to promote economic development, the study devices an agenda for corporate governance reform in Sri Lanka, based on an analysis of Sri Lanka's corporate ownership and control structures.

This study is mindful that corporate governance cannot be viewed in isolation,[9] while acknowledging that comparisons across countries are difficult due to economic and cultural differences.[10] This study is not meant to be an isolated study of corporate governance in Sri Lanka. While the study's main focus is Sri Lanka, where appropriate, reference is made to developed and other developing countries. However, it is hoped that the single-country focus would identify with clarity, core corporate governance concerns for both Sri Lanka and other developing countries.

There is a need for effective corporate governance systems and practices in developing countries as a part of their market and legal infrastructure to

---

[7] Motivated by the prophesy that global competition in product and capital markets will bring about 'an end of history for corporate law' resulting in the cloning of the Anglo-American model of corporate governance. H Hansmann and R Kraakman, The End of History for Corporate Law (2001), 89 *Georgetown Law Journal*, 439–449.

[8] Country classification in International Monetary Fund, World Economic Outlook Database. WEO Groups and Aggregates Information (April 2009), http://www.imf.org/external/-pubs/ft/weo/2009/01/weodata/groups.htm#oem [5 May 2009].

[9] Isolated in terms of a jurisdictional basis: KJ Hopt and S Prigge, Preface, in KJ Hopt *et al.* (eds.), *Comparative Corporate Governance — The State of Art and Emerging Research* (Oxford University Press Oxford 1998), v.

[10] PK Cornelius and B Kogut, Introduction, in PK Cornelius and B Kogut (eds.), *Corporate Governance and Capital Flows in a Global Economy* (Oxford University Press New York 2003), 1–2.

stimulate economic growth and development. Sri Lanka, as an illustrative example of a developing country is a good context of study first, because it has a positive attitude towards economic development through liberalisation of capital markets and has in the recent past undertaken rigorous programmes of privatisation and capital market liberalisation. However, it is relatively unsuccessful at attracting global private equity flows.[11] Second, despite inheriting English legal principles like many developing countries with a colonial history, particularly commercial laws that were transplanted into its legal system,[12] Sri Lanka, is unreliable in maintaining investor confidence.[13] Third, Sri Lanka's corporate ownership and control structures, its social and political background and institutional capacity, provide fertile ground for an analysis of this nature. Fourth, similar to many other developing countries, corporate governance in Sri Lanka is the subject of increased scrutiny and prescription among IFIs engaged in structural adjustment programmes (SAPs).[14] However, developmental emphasis on corporate governance fails to appreciate that market structures and institutions are embedded in indigenous social, cultural and political processes. Finally, developing country concerns, especially in South Asia, are largely ignored in studies on corporate governance. Sri Lanka, an illustrative developing country in South Asia, is also small enough to lend itself to a study of this nature.

Any scholar, practitioner or policy maker with an interest in corporate law, finance, economic policy and business is aware that corporate governance scholarship attracts a veritable flood of scholarship. This study is an attempt to make a contribution to a technically complex and relatively new area of scholarship. It does so in a number of ways.

First, this study gives a detailed account of the ownership structure of Sri Lankan companies based on original empirical research. Second, it

---

[11] World Bank, *World Development Indicators 2006* (Washington DC 2006), Table 6.1, reports private capital flows into Sri Lanka at 5.2 percent of gross domestic product (GDP), while other lower middle income countries attract over 10.7 percent.

[12] Civil Law Ordinance No. 5 of 1852 as amended, s. 3, states that the law of England be followed with respect to partnerships and corporations.

[13] Sri Lanka was added to the California public employees' retirement system (CalPERS), Permissible Equity Markets (2005). However, its score fell below the permissible threshold of 2.0 in 2006. After a 1-year cure period during which its score improved but was still below 2.0, it was excluded from the list, Wilshire Consulting, *CalPERS Permissible Equity Markets Investment Analysis: Final Report* (California 2007) 19.

[14] Asian Development Bank, *Sri Lanka: Financial Sector Assessment* (Manila 2005), 149, Recommendations.

develops the idea that in the absence of effective enforcement mechanisms and high-quality legal protection for minority shareholders, major lenders may be called upon to monitor the behaviour of controlling shareholders. Third, it uses Sri Lanka to illustrate that a detailed understanding of the context of a particular country needs to be taken into account to develop policy prescriptions for reform. Fourth, it exemplifies that the governance of companies is dependent on a wider context by highlighting the nexus between corporate governance and economic development, the use of a contextual framework[15] of corporate governance and a focus on market structures.

The new paradigm that the study offers is not a simple prescription for reform but an effort to understand the importance of indigenous market structures, such as corporate ownership and control structures of companies, for effective corporate governance.

0.2 Overview of Research Methods

In supporting the thesis presented by this study, both a positive and critical approach is adopted, in that it aims to provide insight into current ownership and control structures in Sri Lanka, the costs and benefits of such structures, and also suggest a substantive and viable framework for reform.

Theoretical debates on corporate governance and economic development, and corporate ownership and control, are analysed in framing the objectives of the study. Empirical research is used to unravel the complex ownership and control structures and measure the costs and benefits of controlling shareholders. A contextual framework of corporate governance is used to understand the context of the study and create a paradigm within the reform context. The study is interdisciplinary and straddles corporate law and corporate finance.

Background statistical information collated from primary sources for the purposes of the study is available with the author.

0.3 Structure of Study

Chapter 1 illustrates and analyses the nexus between economic development and corporate governance, and lays the foundation for the primary

---

[15] The term is used to denote the framework that depicts the variables in corporate governance and the relationship among them.

thesis of this study, that an appropriate model of corporate governance for facilitating economic development should begin with a focus on local market structures which are best able to define the adaptation and effectiveness of corporate governance. It does so, first, by an analysis of the literature relating to corporate governance and economic development and second, by supporting the argument that the appropriate model of corporate governance for facilitating economic development must be both holistic and context dependent.

Chapter 2 further supports the primary thesis of this study that an analysis into reform of corporate governance in developing countries should begin with a focus on local market structures that define its adaptation and effectiveness, by an analysis of the correlation between corporate ownership, control and corporate governance. The first section of the chapter is an analysis of why corporate ownership and control is a good starting point for this study in the context of Sri Lanka, a symbolic example of a developing country. Thereafter, the correlation between corporate ownership, control and corporate governance is subject to analysis.

Chapter 3 characterises the main features of the corporate governance challenge Sri Lanka faces by an examination of corporate ownership and control structures. Empirical data is used to answer questions on the concentrated ownership of companies in Sri Lanka, the significant owners of such companies, whether, these significant owners maintain control in excess of their economic stake and if so the mechanisms used, whether the companies have ultimate controlling owners, and if they are different to the significant owners identified before, and importantly, the specific corporate governance issues identified as a result of the analysis of corporate ownership structures in Sri Lanka.

The objective of Chapter 4 is to analyse the implications for corporate governance in Sri Lanka by an examination of the causes and determinants of ownership and control structures in Sri Lanka. An outline of the evolution of corporate ownership in Sri Lanka is undertaken and probable determinants for the persistence of concentrated ownership are examined. The chapter concludes by drawing implications for corporate governance reform in Sri Lanka in the light of the identified causes and determinants for the persistence of concentrated ownership.

The objective of Chapter 5 is to support the proposition that controlling shareholder systems present a trade-off between its costs and benefits and that such trade-off is dependent not only on functionally good law but also on the regulatory environment, market forces and the ratios between the controlling shareholders' economic and controlling stakes (referred to as the 'trade-off thesis').

Chapter 6 develops a framework for the reform of corporate governance within controlling shareholder systems, which increases the benefits inherent in controlling shareholder systems and also curbs the costs of controlling shareholders, that is, tilts the trade-off balance and creates efficiency among controlling shareholders.

Chapter 7 advances the hypothesis that major lenders are an effective external corporate governance mechanism in controlling the costs of controlling shareholders. The chapter assesses the suitability of lenders as a corporate governance mechanism and thereafter, details a reform agenda based on the legal and institutional preconditions necessary for lenders to be an effective mechanism to control the costs of controlling shareholders.

CHAPTER 1

Corporate Governance and Economic Development: The Nexus

1.1. Introduction

The corporate governance rhetoric is a familiar one. In a time of financial turmoil around the world, governing the modern corporation[1] has never been more important and has captured the attention of not only the companies themselves but also policy makers and reformers. Yet, it seems that the rhetoric glosses over the question of why corporate governance is of such general importance.

Two competing strands of thought exist. On the one hand, and at first glance, the importance of corporate governance to growth and development generally, and economic development in particular, is evident. On the other hand, corporate governance continues to be perceived as being of little importance for economic development. This is primarily due to two factors. First, is the widespread belief that corporate governance serves to protect the interests of shareholders from the misbehaviour of managers in large companies in which management is separate from ownership and shares are traded on stock markets,[2] and therefore, does not serve the interests of the public at large. Second, is the challenging question of the high levels of growth achieved by countries in continental Europe during the post-war period and in Asia in the 1990s while seemingly characterised by poor corporate governance.[3]

---

[1] The words 'corporations', 'companies' and 'firms' are used interchangeably.

[2] N Meisel, *Governance Culture and Development* (OECD Paris 2004), 7, 117.

[3] ibid; the high levels of growth are explained in the study as attributable to the systems of corporate governance that enabled the emergence and prevailing of a 'general interest', particularly among the elites, over the 'potentially conflicting' private interests of different factions of society.

While it is now commonly accepted that property rights,[4] enforcement of contracts[5] and the rule of law[6] are significant factors for economic development, the question which remains to be answered is whether corporate governance and economic development are viewed by the literature as closely correlated as they seemingly appear to be. The question is also raised as to whether policy makers, analysts, international institutions and academics are on the right path in advocating corporate governance as a precondition for economic growth and development.

The objectives of this chapter are twofold. First, it seeks to understand the relationship between corporate governance and economic development. Second, it supports the primary thesis of this study that an analysis into the reform of corporate governance in developing countries should begin with a focus on local market structures that define the adaptation and effectiveness of corporate governance, by presenting a holistic and context-dependent approach to understanding the relationship between corporate governance and economic development.

This chapter seeks to understand the relationship between corporate governance and economic development by a rigorous review of the available evidence on corporate governance and economic development, and an investigation of the conventional wisdom among economists and development scholars that corporate governance is a necessary precondition for economic growth and development in both the descriptive and analytical accounts of the nexus between corporate governance and economic development. Thereafter, to support the thesis of this study, the argument is presented for a more holistic and context-dependent approach to the relationship between corporate governance and economic development.

---

[4] H De Soto, *The Mystery of Capital: Why Capitalism Triumphs in the West and Fails Everywhere Else* (Transworld London 2001); World Bank, *World Development Report 2005: A Better Investment Climate for Everyone* (New York 2004), Chapter 4.

[5] D North, *Institutions, Institutional Change and Economic Performance* (Cambridge University Press Cambridge 1990); R Messick, What Governments Can Do to Facilitate the Enforcement of Contracts (2005), Public Sector Group World Bank, http://siteresources.worldbank.org/INTLAWJUSTINST/Resources/ContractEnforcementCairo.pdf [10 February 2008].

[6] D Kaufmann, A Kraay and M Mastruzzi, Governance Matters IV: Governance Indicators for 1996–2004 (2005), World Bank Policy Research Working Paper 3630, http://ssrn.com/abstract=718081 [5 March 2008]; K Dam, *The Law-Growth Nexus: The Rule of Law and Economic Development* (Brookings Institution Press Washington DC 2006).

Section 1.2 of this chapter surveys the theory and evidence on the relationship between corporate governance and economic development and highlights the emerging consensus on the importance of corporate governance in economic growth and development. This section of the chapter underlines the accepted view among economists and development scholars that corporate governance is a necessary precondition for economic development, especially in the context of developing countries.

Section 1.3 seeks to support the argument that a more holistic and context-dependent approach is essential to understanding the relationship between corporate governance and economic development. The primary line of reasoning put forward to support this argument is that corporate governance cannot be viewed as an isolated and independent phenomenon distinct from the environment in which corporations operate, but rather that the success of corporate governance is contingent upon a number of legal, regulatory, political, and social institutions and market structures, and that therefore, the literature and the reform process needs to encompass such institutions and structures.

1.2. Corporate Governance and Economic Development: The Theory and Evidence

1.2.1. *Economic Development and Corporations*

The concept of development emerged in the post-World War II era and was closely identified with economic development and industrialisation. Through the historic link with industrialisation, corporations have always been directly connected to the development discourse. Over the decades the development discourse has greatly expanded and is now commonly understood to include social, political, cultural components in addition to the economic. As a result of this expansion, development is reframed in different ways such as human development[7] and sustainable development,[8] and it is widely stressed that development is much more than

---

[7] A commonly used index is the human development index, which draws on observed features of living conditions, such as life expectancy, literacy, educational attainment and GDP per capita.

[8] The 2005 UN World Summit Outcome refers to the pillars of sustainable development as economic development, social development and environmental protection. UN Adoption of 2005 World Summit Outcome (2005), A/RES/60/1.

higher income.[9] Such reconceptualisations of development have significant implications for our understanding of the role of corporations in development, although it is with respect to the promotion of economic development that corporations play a key role.

In the year 1000, the rich countries of today were poorer than Asia and Africa at present.[10] In the half century from 1950 to 2000, the developed world grew roughly four times in real per capita income while the developing world grew threefold,[11] and yet in 2008 more than one billion people, one-sixth of humanity, live on less than 50 pence a day.[12] The eradication of this inequity is a key driver of development.

The modern corporation is one of the world's most powerful means for creating wealth and prosperity. However, to fulfil this role corporations must be properly governed. They must have responsible internal governance, operate within competitive markets and help create and support sound public governance structures.

In the years after World War II and during the first stage of development thinking, developmental emphasis was on the proposition that production was the function of both labour and capital. In the post-colonial period many developing countries associated development with industrialisation and adopted interventionist approaches to promote the goal of industrialisation. The first approach adopted in the development process is what became known as import-substitution industrialisation, where efforts were made to achieve industrialisation and development by countries cutting themselves off from international trade and using public expenditure to build infrastructure and to subsidise new industries. The reasons for the failure of import-substitution industrialisation differ from country to country, but from a corporate governance perspective the problems associated with the model were clear. Corporations were not subject to competitive pressures and from a governance point of view the shareholders had little opportunity to exert influence. In many Asian countries, the pursuit of import-substitution industrialisation altered the nature of

---

[9] A Sen, *Development as Freedom* (Knopf New York 1999), 3, famously argues that development should be seen 'as a process of expanding the real freedoms that people enjoy'.

[10] A Madison, *The World Economy: A Millennial Perspective* (OECD Washington 2001), Table 1.3, Level and Rate of Growth of GDP: World and Major Regions, 0-1998 A.D.

[11] A Madison, *The World Economy: Historical Statistics* (OECD Paris 2003).

[12] UNDP, *Human Development Report 2007/2008: Fighting Climate Change: Human Solidarity in a Divided World* (New York 2007), 25.

corporate structures and led to the dominance of large family owned business groups.

The second phase of economic development thinking was the opening of domestic economies to imports, export-led industrialisation and microeconomic reform including privatisation of state-owned industries and reform of financial and labour markets. While the newly industrialising countries of South-East Asia achieved sustained high rates of growth since the 1960s and generated substantial employment, the problems associated with the model from a corporate governance viewpoint became evident during the Asian financial crisis. While dynamic corporations were created during this phase of development, the corporations often operated in repressive political environments with little attention to the promotion of corporate governance.

In the search of new solutions, developmental emphasis turned to weaknesses in developing country governments and institutions,[13] and the new pillar in the third stage of development thinking became institutions.[14] The emphasis on institutions, and in particular legal institutions, intensified after the influential work by a group of economists who conducted cross-country research to determine what legal rules contributed to the development of financial growth.[15] Research into the role of institutions in development is supplemented by research into the role of public governance undertaken primarily by the World Bank Institute.[16] The governance data has been collected since 1996 and reports on six dimensions of governance: 'voice and accountability', 'political stability and absence of violence', 'government effectiveness', 'regulatory quality', 'rule of law' and 'control of corruption'.[17] Corporations continue to be recognised as a significant actor in the current developmental focus on institutions and governance, with emphasis on substantive rules of

---

[13] Following the influential work of North (n. 5) and more recently D Rodik, Institutions for High-Quality Growth: What They Are and How to Acquire Them (2000), 35 *Studies in Comparative International Development*, 59; and M Aoki, *Toward a Comparative Institutional Analysis* (MIT Massachusetts 2001).

[14] Dam (n. 6) 5.

[15] R La-Porta, L Lopez-de-Silanes, A Shleifer and R Vishny (LLSV), Law and Finance (1998), 106 *Journal of Political Economy*, 1113.

[16] For example, World Bank Governance and Anti-Corruption, www.worldbank.org/wbi/governance [25 July 2008].

[17] World Bank, Governance Matters 2008: Worldwide Governance Indicators 1996–2008, http://info.worldbank.org/governance/wgi/index.asp [5 July 2008].

corporate law,[18] corporate social responsibility and the recognition that corporations produce rule-of-law problems.[19]

The present path to economic development with its focus on institutions must pay increased attention to the corporate and financial sector, and the corporate form upon which modern economies are heavily dependent for the conduct of business. This crucial developmental focus must also be on assuring the suppliers of finance of getting a return on their investment, through the better governance of corporations.

1.2.2. *Corporate Governance and Economic Development*

The existing literature on the nexus between corporate governance and economic development suggests that there is an emerging consensus on the importance of corporate governance for economic growth and development. The focus of the studies reviewed is primarily on firm-level and country-level corporate governance measures and law-on-the books. Notably, some studies extend their analysis to the effects of ownership and control on firm valuation, operational performance and the risk of financial crises. While efforts by scholars, to capture the effects of ownership and control structures of corporations, on the governance of such corporations and in turn, on economic development is to be appreciated, gaps can also be identified where further work exploring the nexus between corporate ownership and control, corporate governance and economic development can be undertaken.

The literature reviewed below demonstrates the emerging acceptance of corporate governance as a crucial factor in economic development, primarily since it relates directly to the establishment of long-term productivity and sustained growth. Thus, the argument is that the future of developing countries and financial markets depend on improving governance within and around corporations.

At a microlevel, corporations can promote or impede development through efforts to maximise shareholder value. Corporations can consciously take into account the development impact of corporate activity in making determinations in respect of location, use of technology and also contribute

---

[18] LLSV (n. 15).
[19] Dam (n. 6), 177.

to development through non-business activities such as philanthropy and corporate social responsibility.[20] Effective corporate governance is also proclaimed as having the ability to impact upon development at a macrolevel by enabling access to finance. Global and local flows of capital should lower the cost of capital, resulting in better corporate performance and higher corporate valuation. This in turn should result in favourable treatment of all stakeholders,[21] and create financial stability and stimulate economic growth and development.

The literature identifies several channels through which corporate governance impacts upon economic development, specifically, through the development of the financial sector and increased access to financing, improved firm valuation, better operational performance and the reduction of the risk of financial crises.[22]

(a) *Development of the Financial Sector and Increased Access to Financing*

In making the argument that corporate governance impacts upon the development of the financial sector and increased access to financing, it must be set out at the outset that economists sharply disagree about the role of financial markets in promoting growth.[23]

Yet the idea that financial markets contribute to economic growth and in turn development seems an obvious proposition and is supported by numerous studies, which illustrate that effective financial systems ease external financing constraints facing corporations, and highlight that

---

[20] D Reed and S Mukherjee (eds.), *Corporate Governance, Economic Reforms and Development: The Indian Experience* (Oxford University Press New Delhi 2004), 30.

[21] S Claessens, *Focus 1: Corporate Governance and Development* (Global Corporate Governance Forum-World Bank Washington DC 2003), 1.

[22] International Finance Corporation, *A Corporate Governance Approach Statement by Development Finance Institutions* (Washington DC 2007), lists improving performance, access to capital, improving stakeholder relations, developing capital markets, reducing investment risk and adding value and avoiding reputational risk as reasons why corporate governance matters in emerging markets.

[23] J Robinson, *The Rate of Interest and Other Essays* (Macmillan London 1952); and R Lucas, On the Mechanics of Economic Development (1988), 22 *Journal of Monetary Economics*, 3, argue that financial systems merely respond to economic development adjusting to demands from the real sector.

financial development influences economic growth.[24] Extensive studies have also established that banking and stock market development are good predictors of economic growth.[25]

The law and finance literature shows a positive correlation between shareholder and creditor rights, and banking and capital markets. La Porta *et al.*,[26] find that better creditor rights[27] are rewarded with greater depth of the financial system.[28] Similarly, they find that the better the quality of the shareholder protection,[29] the larger the size of the country's stock market. While other macroeconomic factors and inflation may affect the depth of a financial system, it is undoubted that better quality of shareholder protection and better creditor rights, in other words, a better-governed corporate sector affects the size of a country's financial market and affords greater access to financing. This fact is also supported by the property rights literature which find that in countries with better property rights, corporations have better access to finance and can be expected to contribute to financial development.[30]

Similarly, the argument is made that poor corporate governance (both firm level and country level) stands in the way of countries getting the full benefit of globalisation. Poor governance causes corporations to be valued less by capital markets which inhibits

---

[24] R King and R Levine, Finance and Growth: Schumpeter Might be Right (1993), 108 *Quarterly Journal of Economics*, 717, illustrate that countries with larger initial capital markets grow faster in the future; T Beck, R Levine and N Loayza, Finance and Sources of Growth (2000), 58 *Journal of Financial Economics*, 261; W Carlin and C Mayer, Finance, Investment and Growth (2003), 69 *Journal of Financial Economics*, 191; R Levine, Finance and Growth: Theory, Evidence and Mechanisms, in P Aghion and S Durlauf (eds.), *Handbook of Economic Growth* (North-Holland Elsevier Publishers Amsterdam 2004).

[25] T Beck, A Demirguc-Kunt and R Levine, Law and Firms' Access to Finance (2004), World Bank Policy Research Working Paper 3194, http://ssrn.com/abstract=570365 [10 February 2005]; A Demirguc-Kunt, Finance and Economic Development: Policy Choices for Developing Countries (2006), World Bank Policy Research Working Paper 3955, http://ssrn.com/abstract=923262 [20 July 2008].

[26] LLSV, Legal Determinants of External Finance (1997), 52 *Journal of Finance*, 1131.

[27] Adjusted for the extent to which the rule of law is being enforced in the country.

[28] As measured by the ratio of private credit to GDP.

[29] Adjusted for the efficiency of the judicial system.

[30] S Claessens and L Laeven, Financial Development, Property Rights, and Growth (2002), 58 *Journal of Finance*, 2401.

the ability of entrepreneurs to finance their activities and impedes growth.[31]

There is also evidence that poor corporate governance and underdeveloped financial markets adversely affects growth and development. In a firm-level survey covering 54 countries, Beck *et al.*[32] find that underdeveloped financial and legal systems, and higher corruption affect the growth rates of the smallest companies within their sample. Similarly, Levine and Zervos[33] find that lower stock market development can reduce growth.

(b) *Cost of Capital and Firm Valuation*

Corporate governance is also recognised as affecting access to finance and the development of financial markets by its effect on firm valuation. Higher firm value makes investments attractive to investors and has the ability of lowering the cost of capital and leading to growth and economic development. In contrast, in poor corporate governance environments, external finance is likely to be constrained and costly by the fact that financiers are less willing to provide financing because the environment does not assure them of adequate protection of their investment. Those that do provide financing are likely to charge higher rates and impose conditions or engage in expropriation, driving up the cost of capital.

A well-known line of research that begins with a series of papers by La Porta *et al.*,[34] provide evidence that countries with stronger legal protections of minority shareholders have larger securities markets, less concentrated share ownership and a higher value for minority shares.[35]

---

[31] R Stultz, Corporate Governance and Financial Globalization, National Bureau of Economic Research Reporter (Fall 2005), 13.

[32] T Beck, A Demirguc-Kunt and R Levine (n. 25).

[33] R Levine and S Zervos, Stock Markets, Banks, and Economic Growth (1998), 88 *American Economic Review*, 537.

[34] LLSV (n. 26); LLSV (n. 15); LLSV, Investor Protection and Corporate Governance (2000), 58 *Journal of Financial Economics*, 3; LLSV, Agency Problems and Dividend Policies Around the World (2000), 55 *Journal of Finance*, 1.

[35] LLSV, Agency Problems and Dividend Policies Around the World (2000), 55 *Journal of Finance*, 1, additionally illustrates that better minority shareholder protection is associated with higher dividend payouts in a cross section of firms from around the world.

The La Porta *et al.* study has been expanded with country-specific research illustrating that investors are willing to pay a significant premium for well-governed firms.[36] In comparing the findings of these country-specific studies it is worth noting that the relationship between corporate governance and firm value seems stronger in countries with less developed governance standards. More recent studies have found that better governance is related to higher firm valuation as proxied by Tobin's Q,[37] and that both internal and external governance factors are related to firm value.[38]

The McKinsey Global Investor Opinion Survey on Corporate Governance 2002 illustrates that 15 percent of Western European, 21 percent of Asian and 40 percent of Eastern European and African institutional investors consider corporate governance as more important than a firm's financial issues such as profit, performance or growth potential.[39] Additionally, an overwhelming majority of investors are prepared to pay a premium for companies exhibiting high governance standards, with premiums averaging 12–14 percent in North America and Western Europe, 20–25 percent in Asia and Latin America and over 30 percent in Eastern Europe and Africa.

---

[36] While the correlation between governance attributes and a firm's value in developed markets show weak or no results (for example, S Bhagat and B Black, The Uncertain Relationship between Board Composition and Firm Performance (1999), 55 *Business Lawyer*, 921); it is significantly different in emerging markets, for example, B Black, Does Corporate Governance Matter? A Crude Test Using Russian Data (2001), 149 *University of Pennsylvania Law Review*, 2131; C Bai *et al.*, Corporate Governance and Market Valuation in China (2003), William Davidson Institute Working Paper 564, http://ssrn.com/abstract=393440 [20 July 2008]; W Kim, B Black and H Jang, Does Corporate Governance Predict Firms' Market Values? Evidence from Korea (2006), 22 *Journal of Law, Economics, and Organization*, 366.

[37] L Bebchuck, A Cohen and A Ferrell, What Matters in Corporate Governance? (2005), Harvard Law School John M. Olin Center for Law, Economics and Business Discussion Paper 491; L Bebchuk and A Cohen, The Costs of Entrenched Boards (2005), 78 *Journal of Financial Economics*, 409. Tobin's Q as a measure of performance is calculated by dividing the market value of a company by the replacement value of its assets. Alternatively, return on assets (ROA) may also be used to measure firm valuation.

[38] L Brown and M Caylor, Corporate Governance and Firm Valuation (2006), 25 *Journal of Accounting and Public Policy*, 409.

[39] McKinsey and Company, McKinsey Global Investor Opinion Survey on Corporate Governance 2002: Key Findings, http://www.mckinsey.com/clientservice/organization leadership/service/corpgovernance/pdf/globalinvestoropinionsurvey2002.pdf [5 July 2008].

The correlation between corporate governance and firm valuation is also supported by studies demonstrating that in countries with weaker corporate governance mechanisms,[40] controlling shareholders are able to obtain higher private benefits of control.[41] The benefits obtained by such controlling shareholders exceed their direct ownership stake and is at the expense of minority shareholders. This results in lower firm valuation and higher cost of capital,[42] inhibiting access to finance and growth.

(c) *Improved Operational Performance*

Corporate governance also has the ability to stimulate development by better operational performance through better allocation of resources, efficiency and better management.

Although the evidence is less strong of higher operational performance in countries with better corporate governance, there is evidence to strongly suggest that at firm level, better corporate governance leads not only to improved rates of return on equity and higher valuation, but also to higher profits, sales growth and lower capital expenditures.[43] Klapper and Love[44] using firm-level data from 14 emerging stock markets report that better firm-level corporate governance is highly correlated with better operating performance and higher market valuation.

Claessens,[45] plotting the accounting rates of assets for a sample of publicly listed firms using data from the Worldscope database against an

---

[40] The variables extend to legal origin, rule of law, accounting standards, competition laws, antidirector index, serious crime, labour protection measures etc.

[41] A Dyck and L Zingales, Private Benefits of Control: An International Comparison (2004), 59 *Journal of Finance*, 537.

[42] The economic costs of poor corporate governance due to controlling shareholders and family ownership is illustrated by R Morck, D Wolfenzon and B Yeung, Corporate Governance, Economic Entrenchment and Growth (2004), National Bureau of Economic Research Working Paper 10692, http://papers.nber.org/papers/w10692.pdf [5 November 2005].

[43] P Gompers, L Ishii and A Metrick, Corporate Governance and Equity Prices (2003), 118 *Quarterly Journal of Economics*, 107, use takeover defenses in the 1990s to create a corporate governance index in respect to US companies in the 1990s; also, L Bebchuck, A Cohen and A Ferrell (n. 37).

[44] LF Klapper and I Love, Corporate Governance, Investor Protection, and Performance, in Emerging Markets (2002), World Bank Policy Research Working Paper 2818.

[45] S Claessens (n. 21), Fig. 6.

equity rights index from R La-Porta, L Lopez-de-Silanes, A Shleifer and R Vishny ('LLSV'),[46] finds a less strong relationship between the measure of the quality of the governance framework and firm performance. This is attributed to other factors affecting operational performance, namely, the possibility for reporting bias in worse corporate governance environments which makes it likely that their accounting profits are overstated or that firms in developing countries may face better growth opportunities and therefore, have higher profits.

Claessens also notes that the limited relationship between operational performance and corporate governance measures at country level may reflect the fact that corporate governance in most countries does not concern a conflict between the management and owners leading to poor operating performance.[47] This is supported by the hypothesis that concentrated ownership by providing better monitoring incentives should lead to improved firm performance, although the extraction of private benefits of control by controlling shareholders at the expense of the minority shareholders should lead to lower firm valuation and reduced access to financing. However, empirical studies for both the United States and the United Kingdom suggest that at low levels of ownership concentration, firm performance increases as concentration increases, but then declines as concentration levels keep increasing,[48] and therefore, concentrated ownership may not always result in improved firm performance. It is also important to note that within concentrated ownership structures different owners (parent companies, families, large shareholders) will have different objectives, and it is likely that the identity of the owner will matter for firm performance. Furthermore, performance is also likely to be affected by the industry in question, the stage in the life-cycle of the firm and product market competition.[49]

Recent studies also attempt to identify the exact corporate governance mechanisms most related to improved operating performance. Brown and Caylor using a summary governance score (Gov-Score) based on an Institutional Shareholder Services dataset which is a composite measure

---

[46] LLSV (n. 15).

[47] S Claessens (n. 21), 18.

[48] R Morck, A Shleifer and R Vishny, Management Ownership and Market Valuation: An Empirical Analysis (1988), 20 *Journal of Financial Economics*, 293, as measured by Tobin's Q.

[49] M Maher and T Anderson, Corporate Governance: Effects on Firm Performance and Economic Growth (1999), http://www.ecgi.de/research/accession/cgeu.pdf [20 July 2008].

of 51 factors encompassing eight corporate governance categories, find that good governance, as measured using executive and director compensation is highly associated with good firm performance.[50] Bhagat and Bolton find that while stock ownership of board members and Chief Executive Officer (CEO) chairperson separation is positively correlated with better contemporaneous and subsequent operating performance, board independence is negatively correlated with contemporaneous and subsequent operating performance.[51]

While future research is needed to identify with clarity the governance mechanisms most likely to bring about improved operational firm performance taking into account country-specific variables, and firm-level corporate governance, for purposes of this study, the existing positive correlation between firm-level corporate governance and improved firm performance does illustrate the ability of corporate governance to improve the allocation of resources, create wealth and contribute to growth and development within countries.

(d) *Reduced Risk of Financial Crises*

The quality of corporate governance of individual firms can have economy-wide effects and may actually contribute to the occurrence or the heightening of financial distress. Poor corporate governance permits the expropriation of minority shareholders especially during times of financial distress. Similarly, the disclosure regime is likely to be weak in developing economies and can result in the withholding of bad information or the release of selective information. Further, cross-holdings and pyramid structures within poor governance systems are also likely to cause and increase risk sharing among corporate groups, thereby increasing the chances of conglomerate-level failures.

Evidence of the ability of firm-level governance to minimise the effects of financial distress is illustrated by a study of firms from Indonesia, Korea, Malaysia, Philippines and Thailand, which finds that firm-level differences in variables related to corporate governance, in particular firms

---

[50] L Brown and M Caylor, Corporate Governance and Firm Performance (2004), http://ssrn.com/abstract=586423 [21 July 2008].

[51] S Bhagat and B Bolton, Corporate Governance and Firm Performance (2007), http://w4.stern.nyu.edu/emplibrary/Bhagat_paper_revised.pdf [21 July 2008].

with higher accounting disclosure and higher outside ownership, had better performance during the East Asian financial crisis of 1997–1998.[52]

Country-level evidence that countries with weak corporate governance suffer larger collapses when hit by adverse shocks is presented by Johnson *et al.*,[53] who find that the weakness of legal institutions for corporate governance, particularly the effectiveness of minority protection had an adverse effect on the extent of exchange rate depreciations and stock market declines in the Asian financial crisis. This is primarily due to the fact that in countries with weak investor protection, negative financial events are more likely to adversely affect investor confidence resulting in collapses in currency and stock prices. Country studies by international financial institutions also support the view that poor corporate governance was one of the major contributors to the build up of vulnerabilities in the affected countries that led to the Asian financial crisis.[54] The findings suggest that the weaknesses in corporate governance in the affected countries can be attributed to concentrated ownership structures, government intervention, underdeveloped capital markets and poor investor protection.[55]

The thinking until the present financial crisis was that failures or weakness in corporate governance would not result in a financial crisis in the developed world due to stronger institutional foundations, the size of the financial markets or the fact that weak governance mechanisms were often limited to one or two specific areas of governance, such as audit fraud or inflated reports of stock performance. The present financial crisis has dispelled such myth. Weak corporate governance mechanisms have led to a loss of confidence in the developed world, a slow down in economic growth, and contributed to the current financial

---

[52] T Mitton, A Cross-firm Analysis of the Impact of Corporate Governance on the East Asian Financial Crisis (2002), 64 *Journal of Financial Economics*, 215.

[53] S Johnson *et al.*, Corporate Governance in the Asian Financial Crisis (2000), 58 *Journal of Financial Economics*, 141.

[54] V Capulong, D Edwards and J Zhuang (eds.), *Corporate Governance and Finance in East Asia: A Study of Indonesia, Republic of Korea, Malaysia, Philippines, and Thailand: Volume Two (Country Studies)* (Asian Development Bank Manila 2001).

[55] ibid.

[56] G Kirkpatrick, *Corporate Governance Lessons from the Financial Crisis* (OECD Paris 2009), analyses the failures and weaknesses in corporate governance on the financial crisis, including risk management systems and executive salaries and concludes that the financial crisis can to a certain extent be attributed to the weaknesses and failures of corporate governance arrangements which did not serve their purpose to safeguard against excessive risk taking in a number of financial services companies.

crisis.[56] While it is accepted that macroeconomic causes exist for the current financial crisis,[57] and further evidence and measurement is required with respect to the impact, failures and weaknesses of corporate governance have on corporate collapses within developed financial markets, it is undoubted that deficiencies in corporate governance in the developed world contributed to the loss of investor confidence within particular firms and industries. The linkage of deficiencies in corporate governance in the developed world to the present financial crisis supports the thinking that corporate governance strengthens the overall international financial system and reduces the vulnerability of both developed and emerging markets to financial crises.

1.2.3. *The Emerging Consensus*

The review of the existing literature on corporate governance and economic development illustrates the emerging consensus and positive correlation between corporate governance and economic growth and development, due to the ability of effective corporate governance to facilitate increased access to external financing by firms, lower costs of capital, increase firm valuation, achieve better operational performance by better management and resource allocation, and minimise the risk of financial crises.

Despite clear evidence of the importance of corporate governance to growth in the long run, and economic development, corporate governance continues to be perceived as being of little importance to economic development. The first reason attributed for this misperception is the belief that corporate governance serves to protect the interests of a shareholding class from the misbehaviours of corporate managers and does not therefore affect the lives of the vast majority of the population. This is flawed reasoning. First, the ultimate owners of large companies, not only in the developed countries but also in developing countries[58] (although to a lesser extent) are not the wealthy and the privileged. They are the majority of the population whose pension entitlements are directly linked to investments in the shares of large- and mid-sized companies.[59] Second, financial

---

[57] International Organisation of Securities Commissions, *Report on the Subprime Crisis (Final Report)* (Madrid 2008).

[58] Often by way of state pension funds and investments by commercial and savings banks in stock markets.

[59] D Pitt-Watson, Why Corporate Governance Is Important (2003), 14 *The Edge*, 29.

crises have revealed that shortcomings in corporate governance are not limited to companies and their shareholders. In fact, the repercussions are economy wide.[60] Third, the literature reviewed above,[61] emphatically demonstrates the crucial link between growth, economic development and corporate governance, and effectively rebuts the argument that corporate governance only serves to protect the interests of shareholders of large companies.

The second argument lending support to the view that corporate governance is of little importance for economic development, is based on the challenging question of the high levels of growth achieved by countries in continental Europe during the post-world war period and in Asia in the 1990s while seemingly characterised by poor corporate governance. Krugman[62] asserts that the remarkable period of high growth in output in Asia from the 1960s to the 1990s may have derived more from a mobilisation of the factors of production (i.e., inputs like labour and capital) within the region rather than from productivity growth or efficiency gains. The mobilisation of the factors of production, it may be argued, is less incompatible with strong institutions of corporate governance. Similarly, Miesel[63] explains France's equally paradoxical growth during 1945–1973 when despite having corporate governance institutions below today's standards the country experienced a period of sustained growth,[64] as attributable to a system of governance which enabled the emergence and prevailing of a 'general interest' particularly among France's elites. In short, France's governance culture (particularly public institutions) enabled growth, despite the prevailing and potentially conflicting private interests. Thus, Miesel argues for change in the way we judge the quality of a country's institutions of governance, for while France's corporate governance institutions may well

---

[60] One manner in which this manifests itself is by way of higher operational and reputational risk.

[61] In Section 1.2.2.

[62] P Krugman, The Myth of Asia's Miracle (1994), 73 *Foreign Affairs*, 62–71. Similarly, in p. 63 Krugman claims that the Communist growth rates in the 1950s could be fully explained by the rapid growth in inputs, 'expansion of employment, increases in education levels, and, above all, massive investment in physical capita'. The essential point made by Krugman and excellently illustrated in pp. 67–68 is that economic growth that is based on an expansion of inputs, rather than a growth in output per unit of input is subject to diminishing returns.

[63] Meisel (n. 2).

[64] Significantly called the *Trente Glorieuses* — the 'Glorious Thirty'.

have been below today's standards, it is the society's entire governance culture that affects its long-term development.[65] It could also be argued that while better governance is positively correlated to higher income and growth, the reverse does not always follow.[66]

The evidence surveyed above,[67] clearly demonstrates that effective governance of corporations impacts upon economic development, primarily by creating investor confidence and thereby, directing the flows of investor capital in corporations. This capital in turn, can lead to larger investment, greater growth, the creation of employment and the resultant social and economic development. The increased flows of capital can also stimulate the development of banking systems and financial markets, which are recognised as contributing to growth and development.[68] This in turn, can result in the development of product market competition and the strengthening of the legal institutions increasingly recognised by the academic literature as a major factor in economic development.[69]

The above analysis also reveals that the nexus between corporate governance and economic development is drawn with an initial focus on firm-level and country-level corporate governance measures, particularly law-on-the books. This focus is narrow and does not adequately reflect the governance environment in which corporations exist. Notably some studies extend their analysis to the effects of ownership and control on firm valuation, operational performance and the risk of financial crises. However, further studies on the relationship between the governance culture within a country, the effectiveness of market mechanisms such as

---

[65] Miesel (n. 2), 117–121.

[66] D Kaufmann and A Kraay, Growth Without Governance (2002), World Bank Policy Research Working Paper 2928, http://ssrn.com/abstract=316861 [23 April 2009], examine the finding that a strong positive correlation exists between per capita incomes and the quality of governance across countries. They then go on to adopt an empirical strategy that allows separation of this correlation into (1) a strong positive causal effect running from better governance to higher per capita incomes, and, at first, (2) a weak and even negative causal effect running in the opposite direction from per capita incomes to governance. This second finding is surprising and suggests the absence of a vicious cycle with respect to growth and governance, that is, that higher income does not necessarily lead to better governance.

[67] In Section 1.2.2.

[68] A Demirguc-Kunt and R Levine, Stock Markets, Corporate Finance, and Economic Growth: An Overview (1996), 10 *World Bank Economic Review*, 223.

[69] Dam (n. 6), whose thesis is that institutions and the rule of law in particular provide the keys to unlocking the full growth potential of the developing world.

credit rating agencies and the market for control, the role of politics in business, are necessary to present a holistic picture of the impact of corporate governance on economic development. It is important that the literature extends to external governance mechanisms and country-specific variables such as politics, culture and market structures including corporate ownership and control structures within a jurisdiction, since this would acknowledge the wider contextual framework within which corporations operate and also assist in future efforts at corporate governance reform.

As the wider economic significance of corporate governance becomes increasingly apparent, there has been an explosion of the introduction of codes of best practices for corporations, and the publication of international guidelines[70] advocating good corporate governance. While guidelines and best practices reflect the role good corporate governance can play in promoting economic development, the way ahead may lie not only in promoting firm-level corporate governance, but also in recognising that corporations work within a wider governance framework and that such governance framework is influenced by rules, structures and institutions, those who own and control such corporations, and a country's history and culture.

1.3. Corporate Governance for Economic Development: The Way Forward

The second argument presented in this chapter is that to effectively harness the full potential of the contribution corporate governance makes towards economic development, a more holistic and context-dependent approach must be adopted towards the examination of the relationship between corporate governance and economic development, and also towards future reform. Holistic in the sense that proper account is taken of the environment in which the governance of corporations take place, that is the dynamics of

---

[70] OECD, *Principles of Corporate Governance: 2004* (Paris 2004); and Commonwealth Association for Corporate Governance, *Corporate Governance Principles 1999* (Marlborough 1999), set out principles of corporate governance primarily for boards of directors of dispersed companies; D Reed Corporate Governance Reforms in Developing Countries (2002), 37 *Journal of Business Ethics*, 223–233 questions, whether the Anglo-American model can generate responsible ownership in developing countries.

the corporate governance framework, and context dependent in the sense that there is a focus on specific factors within a jurisdiction, such as market structures, institutions, culture and politics, which define the adaptation and effectiveness of corporate governance. While the nexus between corporate governance and economic development is undoubted, how successfully and widely the benefits of value that good corporate governance can add, depends on the corporate governance framework within a jurisdiction.

To support the argument that a more holistic and context-dependent approach must be adopted in examining the relationship between corporate governance and economic development, this study emphasises that corporate governance cannot be viewed as isolated and independent from other legal, market and social institutions and market structures, but rather that the success of corporate governance is contingent upon a number of different factors within the corporate governance framework. For this purpose, the definition of corporate governance is critically examined and thereafter, a corporate governance framework adopted from within which corporate governance can be analysed and its success promoted to achieve the goal of economic development.

1.3.1. *Corporate Governance*

Although the term corporate governance is relatively new,[71] questions surrounding the governance of firms have been in existence for much longer. Traditionally, corporate governance as its name implies, is about how to properly govern a firm. Originating from the Greek word *'kubernan'* which means 'to steer',[72] governance is, about the power to control, regulate and decide. The most evocative definition is that 'corporate governance deals with ways in which suppliers of finance to corporations assure themselves of getting a return on their investment',[73] which implicitly recognises corporate governance as being concerned with the

---

[71] J Farrar, *Corporate Governance: Theories, Principles and Practice* (2nd edn Oxford University Press Melbourne 2005), 3, claims the first reference was probably made by Richard Eells of Columbia Business School in *The Government of Corporations* (Free Press New York 1962).

[72] *Concise Oxford English Dictionary* (10th edn rev Oxford University Press Oxford 2002).

[73] A Shleifer and R Vishny, A Survey of Corporate Governance (1997), 52 *Journal of Finance*, 737.

conflicts of interest among the various corporate stakeholders. In essence, corporate governance refers to the control of companies and mechanisms to make those in control accountable.[74]

In ensuring that the suppliers of finance get a return on their capital, the focus of traditional Anglo-American governance literature is predominantly on internal governance structures such as shareholders, the board, the management team and their relationships *inter se*. This focus is narrow, ignoring the external environment in which corporations exist. Corporate governance mechanisms include not only legal and formal mechanisms such as the board of directors and management, but also external governance mechanisms such as markets, institutions, legal and regulatory frameworks that influence corporate governance.[75] A broader approach is to define a governance system as 'the complex set of constraints that shape the *ex post* bargaining over the quasi-rents generated by the firm'.[76] This is a more abstract model, in which rules and law play a critical role, but also takes into consideration external constraints imposed by equity and debt markets, institutions and market structures such as corporate ownership and control structures.

1.3.2. *Systems and Practices*

An important distinction made in this study is that, corporate governance 'practices' such as determination of the powers of the board of directors and protection of minority investors, cannot be reformed in isolation without regard to the 'system' of corporate governance, which reflects a country's economic, social and political forces. While macroeconomic policies, structures and social issues are not strictly regarded as part of

---

[74] The Committee on the Financial Aspects of Corporate Governance, *The Financial Aspects of Corporate Governance* (London 1992) para 2.5, 'the system by which companies are directed and controlled'.

[75] J Gordon, The Shaping Force of Corporate Law in the New Economic Order (1997), 31 *University of Richmond Law Review,* 1473–1474, defines corporate governance as the 'mechanisms by which various marketplace signals, particularly from product markets and capital markets, directly influence the makeup of the management team that makes economic decisions for the firm, and in that way, indirectly influence the economic decisions themselves'.

[76] L Zingales, Corporate Governance in P Newman (ed.), *The New Palgrave Dictionary of Economics and the Law* (Macmillan New York 1998), 499.

corporate governance in its traditional sense, they impact on the effectiveness of corporate governance practices.

For this purpose, the following distinction between a 'system' of corporate governance and corporate governance 'practices' is adopted:

> A *system* of corporate governance consists of those formal and informal institutions, laws, values and rules that generate the menu of legal and organisational forms available in a country and which in turn determine the distribution of power — how ownership is assigned, managerial decisions are made and monitored, information is audited and released and profits and benefits allocated and distributed (emphasis added).[77]

> Corporate governance *practices* are those rules that apply to specific financial markets and organisational forms, and that establish the discretion of parties that possess control rights and the information and mechanisms at their disposal to choose management, propose or confirm major strategic decisions, and to determine the distribution of remuneration and profit (emphasis added).[78]

As the definition indicates, a 'system' reflects political and social forces with economic repercussions within a country. As the study later illustrates, systems lie at the heart of divergence in corporate governance. Further, the complementary nature between a 'system' of corporate governance and corporate governance 'practices' must be appreciated to identify and define corporate governance issues. While best practices, are aimed at improving corporate governance regardless of the system, the identification of the system of corporate governance enables practices to be 'best fit'. For example, recognition that controlling shareholder systems with board domination by a controlling shareholder is likely to require more than mere improvement to board practices.

1.3.3. *Systems of Corporate Governance*

'Systems' of corporate governance reflect a country's market structures, political and legal institutions, social forces and financial system

---

[77] P Cornelius and B Kogut, Introduction, in P Cornelius and B Kogut (eds.), *Corporate Governance and Capital Flows in a Global Economy* (Oxford University Press New York 2003), 2.
[78] ibid 3.

and are often categorised according to the ownership structures of companies.

Systems of corporate governance rose to prominence in the midst of the American Great Depression, when an economics and a law professor Adolf Berle and Gardiner Means, respectively at Columbia University, analysing the vast dispersion of share ownership in the United States in the late 1920s, identified that shareholders in large listed companies were so dispersed that they had little control over the management of the corporation.[79] This, they claimed was due to the separation between ownership of the corporation — vested in the hands of dispersed shareholders, and control of the corporation — being vested in the hands of directors and managers. This separation of ownership and control, according to Berle and Means could result in the directors and managers acting in their own interests to the detriment of the dispersed shareholders. The Berle and Means analysis by its force of logic and simplicity, gave rise to corporate law's continued preoccupation with negating the costs arising from the separation of ownership and control.

The Berle and Means analysis that dispersed ownership led to a separation of ownership and control had no application to many nations, because corporate ownership was concentrated in the hands of a few shareholders. This distinction in ownership structures influenced by local market structures, political and legal institutions and social forces contributed to the rise of rival systems of corporate governance.

(a) *Outsider/Arm's Length System (Dispersed Ownership)*

The 'outsider/arm's length'[80] system of corporate governance is based on the Berle and Means finding that large public corporations in the United States are characterised by the separation of ownership and control. The term 'outsider' is used to describe the situation that exists because share ownership is dispersed among a number of investors, while the term 'arm's

---

[79] A Berle and G Means, *The Modern Corporation and Private Property* (Rev edn Harcourt, Brace & World Inc New York 1967), 7, 'quasi public corporation ... has divided ownership into nominal ownership and the power formerly joined to it'.
[80] Term used by E Berglöf, A Note on the Typology of Financial Systems, in K Hopt and E Wymeersch (eds.), *Comparative Corporate Governance: Essays and Materials* (Walter de Gruyter & Co Berlin 1997), 151–164.

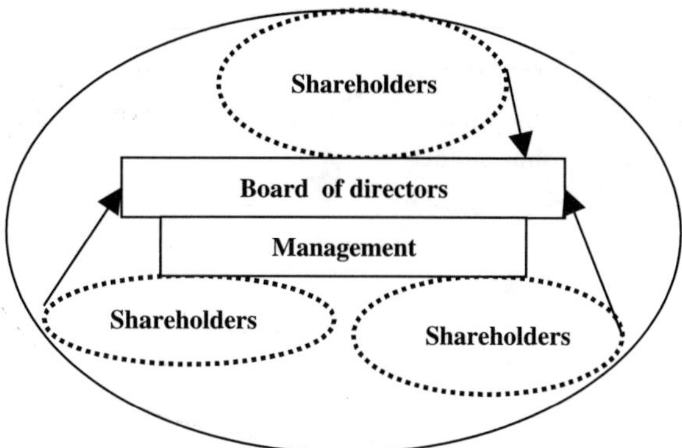

Figure 1.1:   Outsider/Arm's Length System.

length' indicates that shareholders tend to distance themselves from the running of the business and therefore, tend to give managers a free hand to manage the corporation.[81] The 'outsider/arm's length' system is typically characterised by long-term financing through capital markets and therefore, sometimes referred to as the 'market-oriented' system (Fig. 1.1).

(b) *Insider/Control-Oriented System (Concentrated Ownership)*

Recent corporate governance scholarship produced startling revelations. Empirical evidence demonstrates that while the 'outsider/arm's length' system, the basis of the Berle and Means analysis is largely true of the system of corporate governance in the United Kingdom and United States where most large companies are publicly quoted and share ownership dispersed, it is uncommon in a large part of the world. Further, studies even within the United States demonstrate modest concentration of ownership for large American firms.[82] Studies of several wealthy countries also

---

[81] ibid.

[82] M Eisenberg, *The Structure of the Corporation: A Legal Analysis* (Little Brown & Co., Boston 1976); A Shleifer and R Vishny, Large Shareholders and Corporate Control (1986), 94 *Journal of Political Economy*, 461–462. Under the Influence, *Economist* (London 17 November 2001), 57, estimates that founding families influence between 35 and 45 percent of America's 500 largest listed companies depending on how 'influence' is defined.

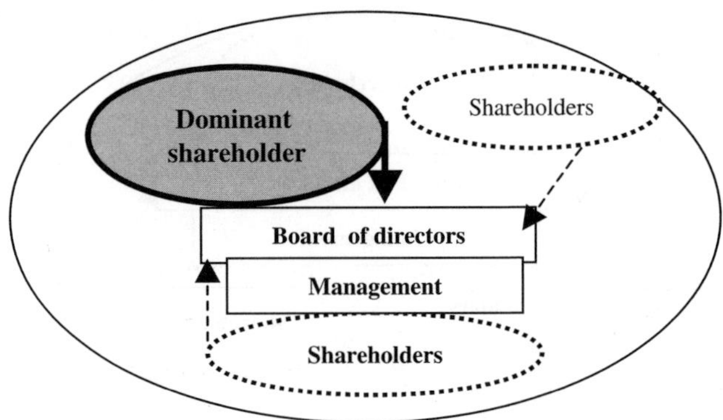

Figure 1.2:   Insider/Control-Oriented System.

demonstrate a significant concentration of ownership.[83] It is also established that ownership is heavily concentrated in developing economies.[84]

Heavy concentration of ownership led to the recognition of an alternative system of corporate governance termed 'insider/control-oriented', where core shareholders exert considerable influence over management decisions (Fig. 1.2). In continental Europe and in large parts of the world, many large businesses have a majority shareholder or core investors owning a substantial portion of the equity. The prevalence of cross-shareholdings also ensures that, corporate control is retained by core investors or by the founding family. The importance of networking between core shareholders explains why this system is sometimes referred to as a 'network-oriented' system.[85]

(c) *The Models*

The 'systems' of corporate governance reflecting a country's market and institutional structures give rise to distinct 'models' of corporate governance in accordance with the nature of the agency conflict that arises

---

[83] European Corporate Governance Network, *The Separation of Ownership and Control: A Survey of 7 European Countries: Preliminary Report to the European Commission* Volumes 1–4 (Brussels 1997); R La-Porta, F Lopez-de-Silanes and A Shleifer, Corporate Ownership Around the World (1999), 54 *Journal of Finance*, 471.

[84] LLSV (n. 15), 1146–1148, Table 7, provides evidence of large shareholders in 47 countries, exploring the hypothesis that countries with poor investor protection have higher concentration of ownership.

[85] L Van den Berghe *et al.*, *Corporate Governance in a Globalising World: Convergence or Divergence? A European Perspective* (Kluwer Boston 2000), 11.

within such system. These models are characterised by the importance they accord to different constituents within the company, due to the system of corporate governance identifying that the costs associated in managing the company under such system, can best be negated by the adoption of a particular model. For example, the 'outsider/arm's length' system views the 'principal-agent' problem of making corporate managers loyal 'agents' for shareholders,[86] as the central problem of corporate governance. The model is primarily concerned with techniques by which the interests of management can be aligned with those of the shareholders, while at the same time minimising the associated costs arising as a result of dispersed ownership structures. This led to the acceptance of the 'shareholder primacy norm'[87] and the resultant 'shareholder-oriented' model becoming a determinant in corporate law and governance evolution during the 20th century.

The alternative corporate governance models discussed in the literature, are the 'manager-oriented' model based on granting discretion to professional managers, the 'state-oriented' model in which the state is proactive in companies especially in welfare states, the 'labour-oriented' model whereby employees have greater participation in the management,[88] or the 'stakeholder' model whereby the interests of constituents such as the environment, workers and community are considered. These models have not worked in isolation. Often arguments are advanced on a mix and match approach.[89]

The prevalence of concentrated ownership systems gives rise to the model of 'owner-managed firms'[90] where the central issue is achieving

---

[86] M Jensen and W Meckling, The Theory of the Firm: Managerial Behaviour, Agency Costs and Ownership Structure (1976), 3 *Journal of Financial Economics*, 305; E Fama and M Jensen, Separation of Ownership and Control (1983), 26 *Journal of Law and Economics*, 301.

[87] Enhancing shareholder value. For a recent explanation, see M Blair, Shareholder Value, Cor-porate Governance, and Corporate Performance: A Post-Enron Reassessment of the Conventional Wisdom, in P Cornelius and B Kogut (eds.), *Corporate Governance and Capital Flows in a Global Economy* (Oxford University Press New York 2003), Chapter 3.

[88] The *Mitbestimmung* law in Germany requiring worker participation in the supervisory boards of large companies.

[89] L Van den Berghe, Redefining the Role and Content of Corporate Governance from the Perspective of Business in Society and Corporate Social Responsibility, in P Cornelius and B Kogut (eds.), *Corporate Governance and Capital Flows in a Global Economy* (Oxford University Press New York 2003), 481–486, argues that 'corporate governance should aim at optimising the (long-term) return to shareholders while satisfying the legitimate expectations of stakeholders'.

[90] E Berglöf and A Pajuste, Emerging Owners, Eclipsing Markets? Corporate Governance in Central and Eastern Markets, in PK Cornelius and B Kogut (eds.), *Corporate Governance and Capital Flows in a Global Economy* (Oxford University Press New York 2003), 267.

a balance between providing incentives to entrepreneurs and protecting minority shareholders.[91] First, there are costs in ensuring that block holders do not expropriate to the detriment of minority shareholders.[92] Second, as large block holders increasingly engage professional managers there are costs involved in monitoring professional managers, similar to the agency problem in dispersed ownership, with the distinction that incentives for providing such monitoring rests with block holders.

1.3.4. *Corporate Governance Framework*

To appreciate the definitional scope of corporate governance, recognise the interaction between the different components of corporate governance and understand the argument presented in this study, that corporate governance cannot be viewed as an isolated phenomenon divorced from other legal, market and social factors within a country, this chapter adopts with modification the 'hierarchical corporate governance framework' proposed by Van den Berghe *et al.* (Fig. 1.3).[93]

First, the above framework illustrates that at its simplest, corporate governance focuses on the operation and composition of the board of directors. In a broader context, corporate governance is viewed as

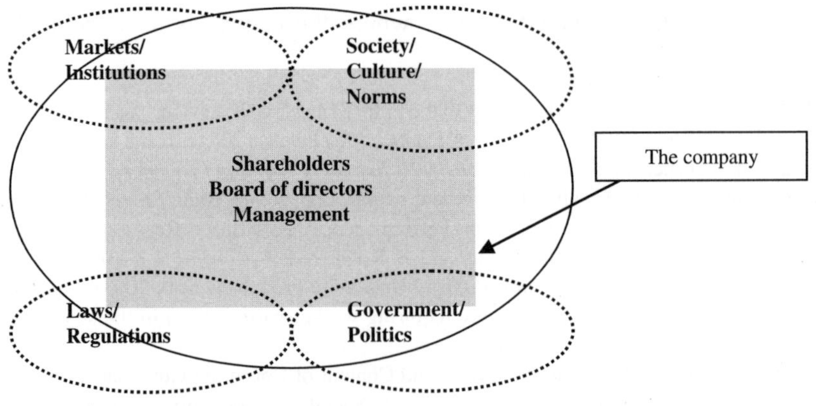

Figure 1.3:   Corporate Governance Framework.

---

[91] ibid.

[92] Shleifer and Vishny (n. 73), 758–760.

[93] Van den Berghe *et al.* (n. 85).

governing the relationships between shareholders, directors and management. In a more holistic approach,[94] the corporate governance framework takes into consideration macroissues such as corporate culture, values of entrepreneurs, the role of government in economic activities, financing through capital markets and competition. The framework will differ from country to country, since it reflects history and culture while also embodying rules and institutions. The framework is also likely to change and develop over time, although the direction of such change is hard to predict.

Second, the framework supports the argument that corporate governance is not an isolated phenomenon but that the success of corporate governance is contingent upon legal, regulatory, political and social institutions and market structures. This in turn lends support to the argument presented in this chapter that a holistic and context-dependent approach is necessary to understand the relationship between corporate governance and economic development. It also supports the view that the appropriate corporate governance model for facilitating economic development must take into account the distinct factors within the contextual and holistic corporate governance framework.

Third, the framework implicitly recognises and illustrates that corporations are shaped by market structures around them,[95] both local and global. The 'system'[96] of corporate governance that emerges from within such framework, gives rise to divergent 'models'[97] of corporate governance due to the distinctive nature of the agency conflict that arises within each system, essentially tying the agency conflict to market structures (corporate ownership and control structures in particular) and both supporting and motivating the primary thesis of this study that an analysis into corporate governance reform must begin with a focus on local market structures that define the adaptation and effectiveness of corporate governance. To illustrate, the lack of finance, poor law enforcement and nepotism within many developing countries often results in an insider/control-oriented system, characterised by concentrated ownership structures and an 'owner-managed'

---

[94] Fig. 1.3.

[95] L Bebchuck and M Roe, A Theory of Path Dependence in Corporate Ownership and Governance (1999), 52 *Stanford Law Review*, 127, argue that corporate structures within an economy are path dependent, that is, likely to depend on initial ownership structures ('structure driven') and corporate rules, which are shaped by ownership structures ('rule driven'), which the economy had at an earlier time.

[96] Section 1.3.3.

[97] Section 1.3.3 (c).

model where the primary agency conflict is between controlling and minority shareholders. A process of corporate governance reform that fails to evaluate the corporate governance framework of market structures and institutions is likely to overlook subtle nuances within the framework such as poor law enforcement. The resulting ill-suited corporate governance reforms, such as a single focus on improving law-on-the-books to meet the agency conflict between controlling and minority shareholders is unlikely to be effective in an environment of poor enforcement and demonstrates why it would be wrong to ignore the contextual and holistic corporate governance framework, which requires attention to market structures and the external governance environment.

Fourth, taking the analysis further, the framework highlights the importance of corporate ownership and control structures as a starting point within the corporate governance framework and also illustrates the nature of the relationship between corporate ownership, control and corporate governance with specific reference to the agency conflict.[98]

1.4. Conclusion

Corporate governance was, until the Asian financial crisis, perceived as important mainly for companies whose shares trade on the stock market. In developing countries the preponderance of small companies, which are not traded on the stock market coupled with family owned, state-owned or foreign-owned companies whose shares are not traded locally, and the ability of some countries to achieve growth without effective corporate governance, illustrate why many doubt the significance of corporate governance for economic development. Yet, corporate governance is not limited to large public-owned companies or companies whose shares are traded on stock markets. Nor is it possible to achieve long-term and sustainable economic development without effective corporate governance. This chapter seeks to dispel such myths by its analysis of the relationship between corporate governance and economic development, and by its argument for a holistic and contextual approach to understanding the relationship between corporate governance and economic development.

This chapter illustrates and analyses the nexus between economic development and corporate governance in two ways. First, by a rigorous

---

[98] This argument is further developed in Chapter 2.

review of the literature on corporate governance and economic development. Second, by presenting and supporting the argument that if corporate governance is to support economic development, it should be approached in a holistic and context-dependent manner.

The important question then is, how does the investigation of the nexus between corporate governance and economic development assist future corporate governance policy? This chapter demonstrates that two points are of value to future policy makers and reformers. First, the general importance of corporate governance to economic development is established, albeit mostly at firm and country level. Second, that corporate governance should be viewed in the context of its internal and external governance framework, taking account of the factors within a country with the ability to affect the proper governance of its corporations. This should enable reform agendas to move away from an exclusive focus on law-on-the-books or institutional development to a more inclusive approach taking into account the environment in which corporations exist.

CHAPTER 2

Corporate Ownership, Control and Corporate Governance

2.1. Introduction

This chapter supports the thesis of this study that an analysis into the reform of corporate governance in developing countries should begin with a focus on local market structures that define the adaptation and effectiveness of corporate governance, by making ownership and control structures of companies (i.e., market structures) its focal point. The objective of this chapter is to analyse the correlation between corporate ownership, control and corporate governance due to (a) the implications of the agency conflict within the firm and (b) the ability of ownership and control structures to illustrate patterns of corporate financing.

The analysis in Chapter 1 by use of a contextual framework highlights the importance of corporate ownership and control not only for our understanding of corporate governance, but also towards understanding the nexus between corporate governance and economic development. This chapter argues that the appropriate model of corporate governance for facilitating economic development must take into account corporate ownership and control structures due to the fact that such structures among the many variables which impact upon corporate governance are best able to define the adaptation and effectiveness of corporate governance. Such a model of corporate governance is also likely to be successful in stimulating economic development due to its capacity to take account of the agency conflicts prevalent within a jurisdiction and its ability to reflect the patterns of financing within the reform agenda. Further, such a model can be used to both understand the impact of corporate ownership and control structures on corporate governance and economic development, and to also suggest how corporate governance issues arising from such ownership and control structures should be resolved to promote economic development.

Section 2.2 of this chapter reinforces the thesis that an analysis into corporate governance in developing countries should begin with a focus on local market structures by an analysis of why corporate ownership and control is a good starting point in the context of Sri Lanka, an illustrative example of a developing country. Section 2.3 examines the concepts of corporate ownership and control and thereafter analyses the correlation between corporate ownership, control and corporate governance.

2.2. Context of Study: Sri Lanka

2.2.1. *Recent Economic History*

Sri Lanka is a tiny island in the Indian Ocean about the geographic size of Ireland, facing the daunting task of moving from its embryonic stage of economic development. At the time of independence, the economy of Sri Lanka was stable and developing, committed to maintaining the welfare measures introduced by the British. Sri Lankans were provided with food subsidies, free health care and free education, contributing to considerable progress in terms of human development.[1] In the period 1948–1956, the country followed open market policies with minimal government intervention in the economy. Plantation companies and foreign banks dominated the corporate sector and the Ceylon Brokers' Association conducted share trading.

The shift towards a command economy occurred after the elections of 1956 with the formation of a new government by the Sri Lanka Freedom Party (SLFP), which nationalised foreign-owned plantations and obtained control of manufacturing and service industries including banking and insurance companies.[2] State corporations dominated the economy with little incentive for private participation. A change of government saw a brief return to a liberalised economy during 1965–1970, and a further change of government saw a return to an inward-looking, closed economy in the period 1970–1977. The plantation sector was acquired by the state under the Land Reform Act[3] and businesses acquired for 'national interest' under

---

[1] The level of social development measured by key indicators, such as life expectancy and adult literacy rates, is well ahead of countries at the same income levels and better than most middle-income countries.

[2] State Industrial Corporation Act No. 49 of 1957.

[3] No. 1 of 1972.

the Business Undertakings Acquisition Act.[4] There was no foreign investment and private sector involvement in corporate affairs was limited to family companies. The financial sector was repressed and the government set up the National Savings Bank to mobilise household savings.

The change of government in 1977 brought economic liberalisation and an outward-looking market economy.[5] The focus was on financial market reform and private sector participation in the economic development of the country.[6] Open market policies encouraged foreign investment and the year 1984 saw the establishment of a public trading floor for securities. In 1995, Sri Lanka embarked on a privatisation programme in the plantation and telecommunication sectors.[7]

In 1999, the private sector comprised of 36,000 registered private companies and 2160 registered public companies.[8] About 75 percent of the public companies were small- or medium sized.[9] Despite privatisation, 75 commercial entities and 15 statutory bodies remain government owned. At the time of economic liberalisation in the early 1980s, there were 63 listed public companies. This number has increased fourfold in the past 20 years,[10] with the privatisation of public corporations and development of capital markets primarily due to inflows of global capital, albeit erratic.[11]

Rapid economic expansion has pushed per capita income over the United States dollars (USD) 1000 mark in 2004 and with high levels of human development Sri Lanka is on the verge of becoming a lower-middle income country.[12] The country has maintained positive growth

---

[4] No. 35 of 1971.

[5] The economy had reached an impasse with economic stagnation and fundamental changes in policy were imperative.

[6] Subject to substantial research by P Athukorala and S Rajapathirana, *Liberalization and Industrial Transformation: Sri Lanka in International Perspective* (Oxford University Press New Delhi 2000).

[7] World Bank, *Sri Lanka: Recapturing Missed Opportunities* (Washington DC 2000), 8.

[8] Listed public companies comprise 29.6 percent of the GDP. Colombo Stock Exchange, *Handbook of Listed Companies 2004* (Colombo 2005).

[9] S Athukorala and B Reid, *Diagnostic Study of Accounting and Auditing Practices in Sri Lanka* (Asian Development Bank Manila 2002), 39.

[10] 236 companies are listed on the Colombo Stock Exchange (May 2007).

[11] Private capital flows to Sri Lanka declined from 13.1 percent of GDP in 1990 to 5.24 percent in 2004. World Bank, *World Development Indicators 2006* (Washington DC 2006).

[12] World Bank Sri Lanka Development Forum, *The Economy, Regional Disparities and Global Opportunities* (Washington DC 2007), vi. The classification is according to World Bank income group country classifications.

Table 2.1:[15] Per Capita GDP (United States = 100).

	1955	1960	1970	1980	1990	2000
Sri Lanka	11.42	10.43	8.96	8.66	10.16	11.78
Hong Kong		23.44	38.71	61.73	84.17	79.26
India	6.21	6.66	6.41	5.98	6.94	7.69
Indonesia		5.43	4.73	9.39	10.59	10.98
Malaysia	14.52	15.28	13.68	24.19	24.53	33.19
Pakistan	6.47	6.39	7.35	7.64	8.06	7.21
Singapore		31.25	36.10	58.85	71.80	85.65
Taiwan	9.5	10.56	16.75	27.37	43.18	55.82
Thailand	7.21	9.04	11.04	11.40	13.68	18.84

despite several adverse shocks, such as a tsunami, increasing oil prices and competition for apparel exports. However, the rate of economic development is not commensurate with its human development achievements.[13]

Further, the economy continues to lag behind the growing economies in Asia, which were at comparable stages at the time of independence in 1948. Table 2.1 shows a comparison of Sri Lanka with other Asian economies in terms of per capita GDP expressed relative to the United States.

In 1955, Sri Lanka's per capita GDP was greater than other major Asian economies except Malaysia. A striking feature of the Sri Lankan economic performance is that relative per capita GDP is not much different from its position in 1955. In fact, there is deterioration in the period in between. Sri Lanka's inadequate economic performance is significant given its initial advantageous starting point.

While many reasons are attributed to the under utilisation of the country's growth potential, among them the ethnic conflict[14] which has permeated economic, social and political life for over 30 years, the underperformance

---

[13] ibid 1.

[14] The violent ethnic conflict manifested itself in the 25-year civil war between the Government of Sri Lanka (GOSL) and Liberation Tigers of Tamil Eelam (LTTE), a terrorist organisation fighting to create an independent state in the North and East. After a 30-month-long military campaign, the Sri Lankan military defeated the Tamil Tigers in May, 2009.

[15] Data extracted from A Heston, R Summers and B Aten, Penn World Table (version 6.2), http://pwt.econ.upenn.edu/php_site/pwt_index.php [13 January 2007].

of Sri Lanka's financial sector is also a primary cause for concern.[16] There is an asset–liability mismatch in the capital structures of both listed and unlisted companies,[17] demonstrating a long-term need for finance through the development of capital markets. There is a need to attract financing not only for the development of capital markets, but also for growth of the entire financial sector if Sri Lanka's growth potential is to be realised.[18] Corporate governance is a key factor in the quest to promote investor confidence, attract capital flows by a secure environment for investment and promote economic growth and development.

2.2.2. *Motivation for Corporate Governance Reform in Sri Lanka*

While economic entities among nations have been interdependent for trade and production from the Middle Ages and concerns about the governance of companies existed since the founding of the first joint-stock companies,[19] for developing countries the impetus for corporate governance reform is its influence in channelling resources to economically viable activities. This is also the overall motivation for corporate governance reform in Sri Lanka. The important nexus between corporate governance and economic development as established,[20] illustrates the ability of corporate governance to fuel economic development and growth. For many developing countries while growth and development are central motivating factors for corporate governance reform, the impetus for corporate governance reform provided by the factors examined below should not be overlooked.

---

[16] International Monetary Fund, *IMF Country Report No. 05/337* (Washington DC 2005), 3, attributes financial sector inefficiencies for Sri Lanka trailing the fast growing economies of Southeast Asia.

[17] Securities and Exchange Commission of Sri Lanka, *Report on the Capital Market Advancement Workshop* (Colombo 1999).

[18] There was a GDP growth of 6 percent in 2005 (3.2 percent in 2003 and 5.5 percent in 2004) with continued expansion in industry and services. The short-term outlook brightened with post-tsunami surge in aid flows. However, the escalation of violence and loss of investor confidence are deep-rooted problems and must be successfully overcome if economic stability is to be achieved. Institute of Policy Studies, *Sri Lanka: State of the Economy* (Colombo 2006), Chapter 1.

[19] CA Mallin, *Corporate Governance* (Oxford University Press Oxford 2003), 11.

[20] Chapter 1.

The following influential factors motivate not only such reform but also this study.

(a) *Financial Stability*

Effective corporate governance creates financial stability and stimulates economic growth by promoting investor confidence and attracting capital flows. The importance of financial systems for economic development is clearly established by recent research.[21] Capital markets are an integral part of a financial system, and provide for savings mobilisation and allocation, risk and liquidity management. Weak or illiquid capital markets are attributed to the lack of investor confidence.[22] Investor confidence is correlated to weaknesses in corporate governance.[23] Together, this evidence provides a positive link from corporate governance to economic development and motivates this study in the context of Sri Lanka, a country desiring financial stability but ranked low in terms of investor confidence.[24]

(b) *Attracting Private Capital*

Private capital is the primary source of funds for economies worldwide.[25] Key factors in attracting private capital are legal and regulatory systems,

---

[21] A Demirguc-Kunt and R Levine, Stock Markets, Corporate Finance, and Economic Growth: An Overview (1996), 10(2) *World Bank Economic Review*, 223–240; R Levine, Financial Development and Economic Growth: Views and Agenda (1997), 35 *Journal of Economic Literature*, 688–726; World Bank, *Finance for Growth: Policy Choices in a Volatile World* (Washington DC 2001), argue that market finance helps economic growth.

[22] LLSV, Law and Finance (1998), 106 *Journal of Political Economy*, 1113–1149.

[23] S Claessens, *Focus 1: Corporate Governance and Development* (Global Corporate Governance Forum-World Bank Washington DC 2003), 14–24, finds positive linkages between investor confidence, corporate governance and development.

[24] Wilshire Consulting, *CalPERS Permissible Equity Markets Investment Analysis: Final Report* (California 2006), added Sri Lanka to its permissible equity markets list in 2005, and in 2006 gave it a 1-year 'cure' period to improve its score before exclusion from the list. It is now excluded from the list. Wilshire Consulting, *CalPERS Permissible Equity Markets Investment Analysis: Final Report* (California 2007).

[25] International Monetary Fund, *Global Financial Stability Report: Market Developments and Issues* (Washington DC 2003), 89, states that 'Since 1990 private capital flows have far exceeded official loans and grants to become the dominant source of external funding for many emerging market countries'.

including effective corporate governance. While global economic integration is rapid, flows of private capital are uneven,[26] with the ability of developing countries to attract private capital limited.[27] Developing countries transforming to market economies have weak capital markets and ineffective corporate governance systems and practices. As a result, the transformation is difficult with weak capital markets ill-equipped to assist liberalisation and the slightest tremors resulting in the flight of international capital. Although no easy solutions are visible, economists, the corporate world and policymakers recognise the potential macroeconomic consequences of weak corporate governance.[28] The need to attract private capital flows also motivates this study into the reform of corporate governance in Sri Lanka, a developing country urgently in need of private capital flows.

(c) *Convergence-Driven Reform*

Economic integration through trade, financial liberalisation and global mergers and acquisitions, results in the interdependence of corporate governance systems and practices across jurisdictions. A consequence of global corporate integration is one of corporate law's interesting debates on whether corporate governance systems will ultimately converge on a single model.[29] The debate has unfortunately fuelled a spate of ill-advised

---

[26] World Bank, *2003 World Development Indicators* (Washington DC 2003), 308, reports that private capital flows (portfolio) to the developing world are negative except for foreign direct investment.

[27] ibid, 307.

[28] Claessens (n. 23), 2; A Krueger, Lessons from the East Asian Crisis (2004), http://www.imf.org/external/np/speeches/2004/021204.htm [26 April 2009].

[29] LA Cunningham, Commonalities and Prescriptions in the Vertical Dimension of Global Corporate Governance (1999), 84 *Cornell Law Review*, 1133; B Cheffins, Current Trends in Corporate Governance: Going from London to Milan via Toronto (1999), 10 *Duke Journal of Comparative and International Law*, 5–6; J Coffee, The Future as History: The Prospects for Global Convergence in Corporate Governance and Its Implications (1999), 93 *Northwestern University Law Review*, 641; J Gordon, Pathways to Corporate Convergence? Two Steps on the Road to Shareholder Capitalism in Germany (1999), 5 *Columbia Journal of European Law*, 219; H Hansmann and R Kraakman, The End of History for Corporate Law (2001), 89 *Georgetown Law Journal*, 439; E Rock, America's Shifting Fascination with Comparative Corporate Governance (1996), 74 *Washington University Law Quarterly*, 367.

Contrast with W Bratton and J McCahery, Comparative Corporate Governance and the Theory of the Firm: The Case Against Global Cross-Reference (1999), 38 *Columbia Journal of Transnational Law*, 213; R Romano, A Cautionary Note on Drawing Lessons from Comparative Corporate Law (1993), 102 *Yale Law Journal*, 2021–2036.

corporate governance reforms in many developing countries based on the shareholder-oriented model,[30] and extending to Sri Lanka.[31] The reforms in Sri Lanka are also related to the past experience of Sri Lanka with historical ties to the Anglo-American model (i.e., English origins of company law) making the movement in this direction appear natural. The limited success of the convergence-driven corporate governance reforms in many developing countries including Sri Lanka motivates this study in devising an agenda for corporate governance reform attentive to local market structures.

(d) *Crisis-Driven Reform*

Regional and global crisis such as the Asian financial crisis, corporate scandals,[32] and the current credit crisis, has led to the dissection of corporate governance systems and practices with IFI,[33] taking a proactive role in advocating adoption of corporate governance practices, with little regard for local market structures.[34] Sri Lanka displays a marked preference for the adoption of best practices and international standards. However, its efforts cannot be attributed to a process of analysis or self-definition, making

---

[30] M Fox and M Heller, Corporate Governance Lessons from Russian Enterprise Fiascoes (2000), 75 *New York University Law Review*, 1720. For failures of corporate law transplants in transition economies, see D Berkowitz, K Pistor and J Richard, The Transplant Effect (2003), 51 *American Journal of Comparative Law*, 163; K Pistor *et al.*, Evolution of Corporate Law and the Transplant Effect: Lessons from Six Countries (2003), 18 *World Bank Research Observer*, 89.

[31] Securities and Exchange Commission of Sri Lanka and Institute of Chartered Accountants of Sri Lanka (ICASL), Rules on Corporate Governance for Listed Companies 2008 (proposed in 2006), with its focus on nonexecutive and independent directors and the minimal requirements to be met by listed companies in respect of the audit committee and the remuneration committees, is likely to have limited success in controlling the costs of controlling shareholders.

[32] In particular, Enron, WorldCom and Parmalat.

[33] For example, World-Bank-sponsored Global Corporate Governance Forum, the Paris-based OECD, Commonwealth Association for Corporate Governance.

[34] D Dunham and S Jayasuriya, Liberalisation and Political Decay: Sri Lanka's Journey from Welfare State to Brutalised Society (2001), Institute of Social Studies Working Paper 352, http://adlib.iss.nl/adlib/uploads/wp/wp352.pdf [10 October 2007], critique the IFIs' approach of treating social and political developments as exogenous variables unrelated to economic policy.

these practices difficult to enforce and of limited success. Blind replication burdens institutions, wastes resources and motivates the framing of an analysis-driven corporate governance reform agenda.

(e) *Structural Adjustment Programmes*

Poor economic performance[35] has resulted in Sri Lanka being placed under the direct influence of the IMF and World Bank. The IFI have imposed liberalising measures, commonly referred to as SAPs,[36] requiring increased attention to corporate governance issues. The imposed standardisation of corporate governance especially by benchmarking an internationally agreed practice against a country practice,[37] are viewed by developing countries as octopus-style surveillance and an attempt at emphasis on shareholder value to ensure that the interests of foreign capital are protected.[38] The resulting short-sighted and ad hoc reforms imposed by SAP motivates this investigation into corporate governance reforms in Sri Lanka with an emphasis on local market structures.

(f) *Pro forma Corporate Governance*

Sri Lanka displays pro forma presence of good corporate governance practices as opposed to actual practice. A survey of 21 percent of the companies listed on the Colombo Stock Exchange (CSE), finds that the average score was 45 percent of the total achievable criteria for good

---

[35] Central Bank of Sri Lanka, *Central Bank of Sri Lanka Annual Report 2002* (Colombo 2003) Key Economic Indicators, reports that annual GDP growth in Sri Lanka has fluctuated between 6.4 percent (1990) and 4.0 percent (2002), even registering a contraction of −1.5 percent (2001).

[36] World Bank, *World Bank Lending Instruments: Resources for Development Impact* (Washington DC 2001), 13, defines 'adjustment lending' as providing 'quick-disbursing assistance to countries with external financing needs, to support structural reforms in a sector or the economy as a whole'.

[37] International Monetary Fund, Reports on the Observance of Standards and Codes, http://www.imf.org/external/standards/index.htm [15 June 2007].

[38] S Soederberg, On the Contradictions of the New International Financial Architecture: Another Procrustean Bed for Developing Countries? (2002), 23 *Third World Quarterly*, 607–615.

corporate governance.[39] While corporate governance practices are on the books and stated as adhered to, scant regard is paid to actual practice either due to unsuitability, lack of motivation, unavailability of an independent verification or enforcement mechanisms,[40] or the fact that existing corporate governance codes are without express legal basis.[41] The resulting lacuna motivates the framing of a corporate governance reform agenda overcoming deficiencies not only in form, but also in practice and enforcement.

2.3. Corporate Ownership, Control and Corporate Governance

2.3.1. *Ownership and Control of Companies*

Ownership in the corporate context is difficult to define due to the concept of a company's separate legal personality.[42] Although shareholders are referred to as 'owners' of a company, it is doubtful whether a company can be 'owned' in any sense. A key aspect of a company is that it exists independent of its members and all assets belong to the company,[43] in contrast to a partnership. However, on application of the 'attributes' or 'incidents' of ownership[44] as accepted by western legal writers to the concept of a

[39] A Cabraal, Corporate Governance in Sri Lanka Fast off the Tracks: But is the Progress Real Progress?, in F Sobhan and W Werner (eds.), *A Comparative Analysis of Corporate Governance in South Asia: Charting a Road Map for Bangladesh* (Bangladesh Enterprise Institute Dhaka 2003), 293–303.

[40] E Wymeersch, The Enforcement of Corporate Governance Codes (2006), 6 *Journal of Corporate Law Studies,* 113, argues that in Europe market-led enforcement, with strengthening of company law, constitutes the best means of developing effective corporate governance practices.

[41] A proposal was in place for corporate governance practices to be formulated as a listing condition. Securities and Exchange Commission of Sri Lanka and the Institute of Chartered Accountants of Sri Lanka (n. 31). This was issued as a code on 1 July 2008.

[42] J Dine, Models of Companies and the Regulation of Groups, in B Rider (ed.), *The Corporate Dimension: An Exploration of Developing Areas of Company and Commercial Law* (Jordon Publishing Bristol 1998), 287, illustrates relationship between a company and corporate personality by drawing parallel to international law and European Community law.

[43] *Macaura, v. Northern Assurance Co Ltd* [1925] AC 619 (HL).

[44] A Honore, Ownership, in A Guest (ed.), *Oxford Essays in Jurisprudence* (First Series Clarendon Oxford 1961), 113, defines 11 leading incidents of ownership as the rights to possess, to use, to manage, to the income of the thing, to the capital, to security, the rights or incidents of transmissibility and absence of term, the prohibition of harmful use, liability to execution, and the incident of residuarity.

company, it is clear that only one of these incidents, the right of transferability, is unequivocally available to a shareholder in a modern company.[45] Company law, principally designed to facilitate 'shareholder-owned' companies, attempts to ensure that at least two other incidents of ownership vest with shareholders, namely the right to control or manage the company and the right to receive income.[46] However, company law sometimes deviates from this facilitating role and permits persons other than investors to assume a degree of control, such as creditors on insolvency.[47]

The etymology of governance is control. Although control is a key concept in governance, it suffers from considerable ambiguity. In the corporate context, there is ambiguity between the concepts of ownership and control due to the indistinctness between the right to control (an incident of ownership) and the actual exercise of control.

The actual exercise of control is distinct from ownership or management of a company.[48] In the corporate context, ownership of all voting shares in a company is likely to result in complete control of a company.[49] However, this is a rare occurrence in many large companies.

The Berle and Means hypothesis of the separation of ownership and control embodies the notion that ownership is, in fact, distinct from control. Their enumeration of the species of control such as control through almost complete control, majority control, control through a legal device, minority control and management control,[50] recognise degrees of control, some unrelated to any economic stakes in the companies, (i.e., control through a legal device such as a pyramid or management control due to a voting power vacuum). It is submitted that actual control can be exerted over a company with no ownership stake such as in the case of a large corporate lender. Thus, actual control as opposed to ownership can be defined as the power to exert influence over the management of a company '... through the *ownership of or power to vote*

---

[45] Sometimes subject to a pre-emption right.

[46] R Kraakman *et al.*, *The Anatomy of Corporate Law: A Comparative and Functional Approach* (Oxford University Press Oxford 2004), 13, by the vesting of voting rights.

[47] ibid 14, or employees.

[48] A Berle and G Means, *The Modern Corporation and Private Property* (Rev edn Harcourt, Brace & World Inc New York 1967), 65–111.

[49] J Farrar, *Corporate Governance: Theories, Principles and Practice* (2nd edn Oxford University Press Melbourne 2005), 41–43, Fig. 4.1 analyses voting control in terms of voting power ranging from 100 percent to 10 percent.

[50] Berle and Means (n. 48), 65–111.

equity interests through one or more intermediary persons, by contract, or otherwise'.[51]

More recently, the derivatives revolution in finance and the growth in share-lending markets ('vote buying') have also illustrated the easy decoupling of economic ownership of a company from its control. This is achieved by emptying the votes of their economic stakes, either through the share-lending market where one investor borrows shares from another, in which case the borrower has voting power but no economic stake, or by the use of an equity swap in which one party acquires the economic stake and the other the voting rights.[52]

2.3.2. *Correlation between Ownership, Control and Corporate Governance*

The focus of this study is on corporate ownership and control structures due to its significance for the governance of companies. Corporate ownership and control structures impact upon the governance of companies in numerous ways, two of which deserve extended analysis. First, ownership and control structures of companies (i.e., the system of governance) intrinsically affect the agency conflict within companies and are correlated to the governance of companies. Second, ownership and control structures reflect the pattern of corporate financing and such financing in turn, impacts on the governance of companies.

The following sections examine the correlation between corporate ownership and control and corporate governance by focussing on the agency conflict and patterns of financing within jurisdictions. This is followed by a brief examination of the importance of corporate ownership and control for corporate theory, for the corporate form, for corporate law, as a potential governance mechanism and finally due to its impact on firm value.

(a) *The Agency Conflict*

Agency relationships are common and universal such as between employer and employee and manager and shareholder. An agency conflict

---

[51] American Law Institute, *American Law Institute Principles of Corporate Governance: Analysis and Recommendations* (Philadelphia 1994), para 1.08 (emphasis added).

[52] H Hu and B Black, The New Vote Buying: Empty Voting and Hidden (Morphable) Ownership (2006), 79 *Southern California Law Review*, 811–816.

occurs whenever the agent acts in the agent's own interest rather than in the interest of the principal,[53] and can be attributed to the incomplete and asymmetric nature of information flows to the principal and the differing goals and preferences of the principal and agent. The conflict invariably gives rise to costs in monitoring the agent and the need for governance.

Various mechanisms are used to motivate the agent to act in the principal's interest rather than in the agent's own interest, such as profit sharing, commissions and incentive schemes. Market mechanisms such as mergers and acquisitions, the stock market and the managerial labour market are used in the corporate context with limited success, as these mechanisms are dependent on the context of the agency relationship and nature of the agency problem.

Broadly, three types of agency conflicts arise in the context of companies.[54] The first between a company's shareholders and its managers, the second between the majority or controlling shareholders and minority shareholders and the third, between the company and outside constituents such as creditors, employees, consumers and society. In the first, the difficulty lies in ensuring that the managers (agents) are responsive to shareholder (principals) interests rather than their own personal interests.[55] In the second, the majority or controlling shareholders and managers share similar interests and the difficulty is in ensuring that the majority or controlling shareholders (agents/principals) and managers (agents) do not act in their own interests to the detriment of minority shareholders (principals). In the third, the difficulty is in ensuring that the company and its shareholders do not act in their own interests to the detriment of society and parties with whom the company has contracted.

The system of corporate governance characterised by ownership and control structures is correlated to the type of agency conflict that arises in companies. For example, the first type of conflict between managers and shareholders is likely to arise in an outsider/arm's length system and the second type of conflict between majority or controlling shareholders and

---

[53] Kraakman *et al.* (n. 46), 22. Agency problems arise when the welfare of one party the 'principal' is dependent on the actions taken by another, the agent.

[54] Kraakman *et al.* (n. 46), 22.

[55] Berle and Means (n. 48), 6–7; Similarly, A Smith, *An Inquiry into the Nature and Causes of the Wealth of Nations* (Regnery Washington DC reprinted 1999), 865, cites Morellet's list of 55 joint-stock companies which all failed from mismanagement not withstanding exclusive privileges to managers.

managers, and minority shareholders in an insider/control-oriented system. The conflict between managers and shareholders arises within the outsider/ arm's length system due to lack of incentive for a minority shareholder to monitor the management, that is, minority shareholders' reluctance to bear the entire costs of monitoring likely to benefit all shareholders.

In the light of the above, large shareholders or blockholders can be viewed as reactionary mechanisms to reduce the agency conflict that arises within an outsider/arm's length system.[56] In countries where the ownership structures are dominated by large shareholders, there is a lower likelihood of the first type of agency conflict between managers and shareholders, except where corporate managers are controlled by large shareholders, giving rise to a conflict between managers and minority shareholders except that in this instance, the managers are acting not in their own interests but in the interests of large shareholders.

The correlation between corporate ownership, control and the agency conflict helps explain differences in corporate behaviour and various approaches taken to minimise the agency conflict. For example, the success of hostile takeovers depends on the stake of a controlling shareholder and the legal and institutional environment in which the company operates.[57] Similarly, scope for large shareholder monitoring depends on the size of the stake of the controlling shareholder. Thus, there is a positive correlation between ownership and control structures and the success of mechanisms designed to control fundamental agency conflicts within corporate governance systems.

There are different degrees of ownership and control within the two identified systems and these distinctions also affect the agency conflict. For example, shareholder distribution can vary from a single shareholder to a number of shareholders and in between there are majority shareholders, large blockholders and blocking minorities. The agency conflict posed by a majority shareholder with control rights commensurate to an economic stake is different to the agency conflict posed by a shareholder whose control rights are in excess of the economic stake. The same holds true for the shareholder's identity, that is, whether the shareholder is part

---

[56] A Shleifer and R Vishny, Large Shareholders and Corporate Control (1986), 94 *Journal of Political Economy*, 461.

[57] E Berglöf and A Pajuste, Emerging Owners, Eclipsing Markets? Corporate Governance in Central and Eastern Markets, in PK Cornelius and B Kogut (eds.), *Corporate Governance and Capital Flows in a Global Economy* (Oxford University Press New York 2003), 267.

of a family, an institutional investor, corporate group or the state. Thus, in family controlled companies, the agency concern is that managers may act solely in the interests of the controlling family.

As illustrated, the nature and magnitude of the agency conflict is moulded by ownership and control structures of companies. The agency conflict, combined with the inherent inability to write perfect contracts or effectively monitor the controllers gives rise to the need for governance of companies. The need for governance is thus inherently linked to the structure of corporate ownership and control. This essential correlation between corporate ownership, control and governance underlies the thesis presented in this study and supports its starting point. The correlation between corporate ownership, control and governance also supports the argument presented in this chapter that the appropriate model of corporate governance for facilitating economic development must take into account corporate ownership and control structures due to the fact that such structures among the many variables which impact upon corporate governance, are best able to define the adaptation and effectiveness of corporate governance.

(b) *Patterns of Financing*

Corporate ownership and control structures reflect the pattern of corporate financing within a country and are of relevance to the governance of companies in two significant ways. First, the pattern of corporate financing reflects inherent financing strengths and weaknesses within a country. Second, mapping the patterns of corporate financing is of importance for the framing of an effective corporate governance reform agenda.

Political forces,[58] legal origin and legal systems, especially investor protection,[59] and rent protection theories[60] are advanced as influencing the formation of corporate ownership and control structures. Similarly, his-

---

[58] M Roe, *Political Determinants of Corporate Governance: Political Context, Corporate Impact* (Oxford University Press Oxford 2002).

[59] T Beck, A Demirguc-Kunt and R Levine, Law and Firms' Access to Finance (2004), World Bank Policy Research Working Paper 3194, http://ssrn.com/abstract=570365 [10 February 2005]; LLSV, Legal Determinants of External Finance (1997), 52 *Journal of Finance*, 1131; LLSV (n. 22).

[60] L Bebchuck, A Rent Protection Theory of Corporate Ownership and Control (1999), National Bureau of Economic Research Working Paper 7203, http://www.nber.org/papers/w7203 [5 November 2005].

torical approaches illustrate that weakness in money and capital markets[61] have also impacted on corporate ownership structures. While factors that influence the formation of corporate ownership and control structures are often indigenous,[62] the link between the availability of financing and ownership structures is undoubted.

Recognition of the link between economic structures and financing gained prominence most recently in the thesis articulated in relation to the Asian financial crisis in the 1990s, where microeconomic structures and the behaviour of agents controlling these structures were held responsible for the crisis.[63] While the thesis has attracted its share of critics,[64] for purposes of this study, the thesis lends support to the intrinsic link between economic structures and financing.

Corporate financing determines who owns and controls a company, its ability to grow and its competitiveness. Countries with greater inequalities in wealth distribution are likely to demonstrate concentrated corporate ownership, such as in Latin America. Similarly, countries with greater reliance on its banking system, illustrated by high interest rates for savings and higher rates of public debt are also likely to have concentrated ownership structures.[65]

The link between corporate structures and a country's financing pattern is reflected within the corporate governance systems and is mapped as follows (Table 2.2).[66]

The analysis reflects the dissimilarities in financing patterns of the corporate ownership and control structures characterised by the two systems of corporate governance. The distinctive features of the two

---

[61] A Murphy, Corporate Ownership in France: The Importance of History (2004), National Bureau of Economic Research Working Paper 10716, http://www.nber.org/papers/W10716 [3 July 2005].

[62] Chapter 3.

[63] L Summers, International Financial Crisis: Causes, Prevention, Cures (2000), 90(2) *American Economic Review Papers and Proceedings*, 1–7.

[64] J Glen and A Singh, Corporate Governance, Competition and Finance: Rethinking Lessons from the Asian Crisis (2004), ESRC Centre for Business Research, University of Cambridge Working Paper 288, http://www.cbr.cam.ac.uk/pdf/wp288.pdf [14 April 2007], claims thesis is deficient as *inter alia*, it is neither compatible with previous success of Asian countries nor explain why India and China with fundamentally worse structures did not have crisis. However, the reason for India and China's insulation from the crisis can be attributed to their lack of capital account convertibility.

[65] The Sri Lankan context is analysed in Chapter 3.

[66] Table 2.2.

Table 2.2: Financing Patterns.

	Outsider/arm's length system (dispersed owners)	**Insider/control-oriented system (concentrated and controlling owners)**
Financing	Capital markets	Wealthy individuals Large companies/corporate groups Banks/financial institutions (Chap. 3) A move from State ownership to privatisation (Chap. 4)
Financial markets	Large, liquid	Small, less liquid (Chaps. 3 and 4)
Relations with banks	Arm's length, diversified	Close, concentrated Possible cross-ownership (Chap. 3)
Companies' capital structure	Mixed debt ratios[67] (mergers and acquisitions markets demonstrate high debt ratios)	High debt ratios (Chap. 7)

systems enable the fashioning of corporate governance reforms taking account of the individual biases. Thus, a corporate governance reform agenda for an insider control-oriented system should consider the high debt ratios of companies and utilise such knowledge in steering the reform agenda such as by strengthening the monitoring role of lenders

---

[67] While the cost of equity finance will be lower in a system in which share ownership is dispersed, as opposed to concentrated, it does not necessarily follow that firms in systems with dispersed share ownership will tend to rely more on equity, rather than debt finance. This is because the institutions (such as well-designed legal rules, effective enforcement, etc.), which enabled share ownership to disperse and thereby, lowered the cost of equity capital, will also facilitate the raising of debt finance in capital markets. This would imply that firms' average leverage would not be markedly different between dispersed and concentrated ownership systems. R Rajan and L Zingales, What Do We Know About Capital Structure? Some Evidence from International Data (1995), 50 *Journal of Finance* 1421– 1428, provide empirical evidence in support of this argument, by reporting similar levels of leverage for US firms (with dispersed share ownership) and Japan, Italy and France (with concentrated share ownership).

as a corporate governance monitor. Similarly, corporate governance reforms within an outsider/arm's length system with capital market financing should focus its reform agenda on strengthening capital market disciplinary devices.

While the most popular explanation for concentrated ownership systems is the weak role of corporate and securities law in protecting minority shareholders,[68] the converse is also true. Concentrated ownership structures give rise to low levels of minority protection and poor enforcement due to the inherent relationship-oriented networks, and economic and political power of large and controlling shareholders.[69] Thus, a focus on ownership and control structures linked to financing patterns within a country, enables the fashioning of a reform agenda with due regard to the disciplinary role of finance.

The discussion above illustrates that financing within a country is intrinsically related to the ownership and control structures of companies. Mapping the patterns of financing in the light of ownership structures reflects the innate strengths and weaknesses of financing within such structures and the acquired knowledge is useful in fashioning a reform agenda. Further, illuminating the interdependence between corporate ownership, control and corporate finance supports both the focus of this chapter (i.e., corporate ownership and control), and the starting point of this study.

(c) *Theories of the Firm*

Ownership and control of companies is also of importance for corporate governance due to theories of the firm which direct that questions regarding the governance of a company can be answered with reference to what a company is ('firm' in the terminology of corporate theorists). While an extended analysis on theories of the firm would digress from the focus of

---

[68] R La-Porta, F Lopez-de-Silanes and A Shleifer, Corporate Ownership Around the World (1999), 54 *Journal of Finance*, 471; LLSV (n. 22); LLSV (n. 59); M Becht and A Röell, Blockholdings in Europe: An International Comparison (1999), 43 *European Economic Review*, 1049; Coffee (n. 59); W Carlin and C Mayer, Finance, Investment and Growth (2003), 69 *Journal of Financial Economics*, 191.

[69] J Zhuang, Some Conceptual Issues of Corporate Governance (1999), Asian Development Bank Economics and Development Resource Centre Briefing Note 13, http://209.225.62.100/Documents/EDRC/Briefing_Notes/BN013.pdf [11 April 2007], 12–15. Ownership concentration is both a symptom and cause of weak corporate governance.

this study, theories of the firm provide a framework for (i) discussion of issues relating to corporate ownership and control and (ii) determining the nature of shareholder interests.

Most theories of the firm, examining why corporate activity is carried out in the form of the firm rather than by means of contracts in the market, can be traced back to the writings of Coase,[70] who submits that the firm is a more efficient mechanism for the carrying out of economic activity due to its ability to reduce transaction cost by 'supersession of the price mechanism'.[71] Other theories of the firm have also attributed the existence of the firm to efficiency reasons.

Two strands of thought on a definition of a firm stand out. The first, identified by Alchian and Demesetz, claim the defining characteristic of a firm to be in 'team use of inputs and a centralised position of some party in the contractual arrangements of other inputs'.[72] Unlike Coase, their theory based on joint production and monitoring requires no authoritarian control. However, transactions involving joint production require careful monitoring so that each actor's contribution can be assessed. The best way to provide such monitoring according to Alchian and Demesetz is to give such actor the following bundle of rights: (i) to be a residual claimant; (ii) to observe input behaviour; (iii) to be the central party common to all contracts with inputs; (iv) to alter membership of the team and (v) to sell these rights which effectively define *ownership* of the firm.[73] Similarly, and more recently, Jensen and Meckling have viewed the firm as a legal fiction, which serves as a nexus of contracting relationships.[74]

However, given that contracts are incomplete,[75] the idea was formulated that firms arise in situations where people cannot write good contracts.[76] Accordingly, two general but distinguishing characteristics of economic

---

[70] R Coase, The Nature of 'The Firm' (1937), 4 *Economica* (ns), 386.

[71] ibid 389.

[72] A Alchian and H Demsetz, Production, Information Costs, and Economic Organization (1972), 62 *American Economic Review*, 777–778.

[73] ibid 783.

[74] M Jensen and W Meckling, The Theory of the Firm: Managerial Behaviour, Agency Costs and Ownership Structure (1976), 3 *Journal of Financial Economics*, 305–311.

[75] Due to uncertainty, asymmetric information, etc. For analysis of the extent to which the incompleteness of contracts can be attributed to their formal nature. L Anderlini and L Felli, Incomplete Written Contracts: Undescribable States of Nature (1994), 109 *Quarterly Journal of Economics*, 1085.

[76] O Hart, *Firms, Contracts, and Financial Structure* (Clarendon Oxford 1995), 1–3.

relationships are (a) that contracts are incomplete and (b) because of this, *ex post* allocation of power matters.[77] This resulted in the second and related definition of the firm characterised as the property rights approach of the firm which views the firm as a set of property rights, that is, a collection of assets that are jointly owned.[78] Ownership is important because it confers the right to make decisions in all contingencies unspecified by the initial contract. The approach is in line with transaction cost logic but differs by focusing on the threshold of physical assets in the economic relationship.

While the theories overlap and interweave in a complimentary manner, important strands of thought, highlighting the relevance of corporate ownership and control to corporate governance can be extracted from the above overview.

In the nexus of contracts theory, set out by Alchian and Demesetz, there is recognition that transactions involving joint production require careful monitoring so that each actor's contribution can be assessed.[79] They use the term 'monitor' to denote the 'specialist *who receives the residual rewards*'.[80] This residual claimant-monitor of the team is then given an entire bundle of rights, which defines the *'ownership'* of the firm.[81] Thus, Alchian and Demesetz's theory of the firm, links the concept of monitoring and governance to corporate ownership.

In the property rights approach of the firm, linkages between ownership and governance are straightforward. In an ideal world, long-term contracts would spell out all the obligations of economic transactions and allocation of power or control is irrelevant. However, according to the property rights approach to the firm, contracts are incomplete.[82] Thus, usage requires that the allocation of these missing aspects reside according to the

---

[77] ibid 3.

[78] S Grossman and O Hart, The Costs and Benefits of Ownership: A Theory of Vertical and Lateral Integration (1986), 94 *Journal of Political Economy*, 691; O Hart and J Moore, Property Rights and the Nature of the Firm (1990), 98 *Journal of Political Economy*, 1119. The genesis of this theory can be found in H Demsetz, Towards a Theory of Property Rights (1967), 57 *American Economic Review*, 347.

[79] Alchian and Demsetz (n. 72), 782. Emphasis added.

[80] ibid 782.

[81] ibid 783.

[82] It is possible to argue that contract incompleteness is not an issue in the light of the ability to renegotiate or revise the terms of contract. But as Hart (n. 76) points out, renegotiation in itself imposes *ex post* and *ex ante* costs due to bargaining and haggling over the terms of the contract and also due to asymmetric information.

ex post allocation of power, that is, with the *owner*. Thus, there is recognition that ownership implies the possession of residual rights of control over that asset, that is, the right to govern.

An analysis of theories of the firm in answering the essential question of 'what is a firm?' brings forth an explanation of how ownership and control is allocated within a firm and the linkages between ownership, control and governance. Governance according to the nexus of contracts approach is tied to 'residual-claimant monitor' and contractual governance.[83] In the property rights approach, governance is linked to the *ex post* allocation of power vested with the owners of the assets and non-contractual governance. Thus, through the use of the 'residual-claimant monitor' and the *ex post* allocation of power, both important strands of thought on a theory of a firm illustrate the essential correlation between corporate ownership, control and governance.

(d) *Core Elements of the Corporate Form*

The 'shared ownership by contributors of capital',[84] and 'allocation of rights of control over the company',[85] are core elements of the corporate form and exemplifies the correlation between corporate ownership, control and governance. Corporate governance is defined,[86] *inter alia*, as the power to control. Since ownership by the contributors of capital embodies an element of control, within the sphere of corporate governance it is only logical to characterise the corporate governance challenge by an examination of ownership and control structures, given that ownership and control are core elements of the corporate form.

(e) *Corporate Control and Corporate Law*

The correlation between corporate ownership, control and corporate governance is manifest in the recognition accorded to corporate control by

---

[83] L Zingales, Corporate Governance, in P Newman (ed.), *The New Palgrave Dictionary of Economics and the Law* (Macmillan New York 1998), 5.

[84] Kraakman (n. 46), 5–15.

[85] P Davies, *Introduction to Company Law* (Clarendon Law Series Oxford University Press Oxford 2002), 9, Chapter 1.

[86] Chapter 1.

corporate law. For example, control is fundamental to the governance mechanisms relating to shareholder meetings, election of corporate management, voting and protection of minority shareholder rights.

(f) *Potential Governance Mechanism*

The correlation between ownership, control and corporate governance is also exemplified by the fact that ownership and control structures are a source of potential governance mechanisms. Thus, the presence of a large shareholder gives rise to the possibility of large shareholder monitoring.[87] Similarly, the likelihood of contests for corporate control, which are greater in dispersed ownership systems, is an important governance mechanism.

(g) *Ownership and Firm Value*

The correlation between corporate ownership, control and corporate governance is corroborated by research establishing a link between corporate ownership structures and firm value.[88] While investors with large economic stakes have strong incentives to maximise the value of their companies, controlling shareholders with control rights in excess of economic stakes have no such compulsion. The link between ownership

---

[87] A Shleifer and R Vishny, A Survey of Corporate Governance (1997), 52 *Journal of Finance*, 737.

[88] S Claessens, S Djankov and L Lang, Corporate Ownership and Valuation: Evidence from East Asia, in A Harwood, R Litan and M Pomerleano (eds.), *Financial Markets and Development: The Crisis in Developing Countries* (Brookings Institution Washington 1999), find that family controlled companies are not valued as highly by markets as companies where control is more widely held; S Claessens *et al.*, Disentangling the Incentive and Entrenchment Effects of Large Shareholdings (2002), 57 *Journal of Finance*, 2741, find that firm value increases with the cash-flow ownership of the largest shareholder, consistent with the positive incentive effect. But firm value falls when the control rights of the largest shareholder exceed cash flow ownership consistent with the entrenchment effect.

Similarly, K Lins, Equity Ownership and Firm Value in Developing Countries (2003), 38 *Journal of Financial & Quantitative Analysis*, 159, finds that firm values are lower when management control rights exceed cash flow rights.

structures and firm value is also of relevance to economic growth[89] and investor protection.[90] The linkage between ownership structures and firm value is also supported by studies on corporate governance and productivity.[91] Due to the predominance of concentrated ownership worldwide,[92] the relationship between corporate ownership and firm value is of importance not only for governance studies but also development studies.

2.3.3. *Correlation between Ownership, Control and Corporate Governance in Sri Lanka*

The established correlation between ownership, control and corporate governance enables this study to define with clarity the agency conflict within companies and reflect financing patterns, in the context of Sri Lanka. Such analysis illustrates the importance of ownership and control structures as a starting point for an analysis of corporate governance and also supports the primary thesis of this study that an analysis into reform of corporate governance in developing countries should begin with a focus on local market structures that defines its adaptation and effectiveness.

(a) *The Agency Conflict*

To understand the integral relationship between ownership, control and corporate governance in Sri Lanka, it is suffice to note that the system of

---

[89] R Morck, D Stangeland and B Yeung, Inherited Wealth, Corporate Control and Economic Growth: The Canadian Disease, in R Morck (ed.), *Concentrated Corporate Ownership* (University of Chicago Press Chicago 2000), find that countries in which billionaire heirs' wealth is large, relative to the GDP, display slower rates of economic growth and spend less on innovation in comparison with countries at similar levels of development.

[90] LLSV, Investor Protection and Corporate Valuation (2002), 57 *Journal of Finance*, 1147, document higher valuation of firms in countries with better protection of minority shareholders and in firms with higher cash flow ownership by controlling shareholders.

[91] L Balasuriya, The Impact of Corporate Governance on Productivity in Sri Lanka, in E Gonzalez (ed.), *Impact of Corporate Governance on Productivity: Asian Experience* (Asian Productivity Organization Tokyo 2004), 366, finds a negative relationship between the degree of concentration of ownership and corporate productivity among eight Sri Lankan companies.

[92] Chapter 1, Section 1.3.

corporate governance in Sri Lanka is 'insider control-oriented'.[93] Pyramidal structures mask true ownership, concentrated among families or family owned corporations. A few shareholders dominate control in many companies. Many shareholders are corporate groups,[94] family owned companies or the state. There is also the presence of foreign institutional investors.[95]

The myriad corporate ownership structures in Sri Lanka are incompatible with Anglo-American corporate governance practices,[96] with costs extending beyond the 'agency costs' of dispersed ownership systems.[97] There are costs in protecting the minority from the extraction of private benefits by block holders, while providing incentives to block holders to monitor management. There are costs in minimising politically motivated state intervention, while protecting the interests of stakeholders. There are costs in avoiding conflicts of interests within group companies[98] and avoiding what is aptly described as 'tunnelling'[99] whereby profits from a group entity is shifted to other group entities by sweetheart deals, excessive rents or by transactions without any apparent justification, to the detriment of minority shareholders. The motivation for this study is that an analysis with its focus on the correlation between ownership, control and corporate governance in Sri Lanka is better able to identify and clarify the agency conflict and its implications for Sri Lanka.

---

[93] Examined in Chapter 3.

[94] E Wymeersch, Do We Need a Law on Groups of Companies?, in K Hopt and E Wymeersch (eds.), *Capital Markets and Company Law* (Oxford University Press Oxford 2003), 573–580, is excellent on typology of group companies.

[95] The Investors Bank & Trust Co, Eaton Vance Asian Small Co Fu, Ohio State Retirement System, Chio State Teachers Retirement System.

[96] Sri Lankan company law and corporate governance practices with English roots was transplanted with little regard for existing corporate structures.

[97] Costs and benefits of ownership structures in Chapter 5.

[98] Wymeersch (n. 94), 574, identifies this as a central issue underpinning groups.

[99] The term tunnelling was coined to characterise the expropriation of the minority shareholders in the Czech Republic — viewed as removing assets through an underground tunnel. S Johnson *et al.*, Tunneling, in K Hopt and E Wymeersch (eds.), *Capital Markets and Company Law* (Oxford University Press Oxford 2003), 611. It is the transfer of resources by controlling shareholder for own benefit or an increase of share of firm through use of dilutive share issues and minority freezeouts.

(b) *Patterns of Financing*

The second factor illustrating the correlation between corporate ownership, control and corporate governance in Sri Lanka and motivating this study is the ability of corporate ownership and control structures to reflect financing patterns.

An investigation into the causes of ownership and control structures in Sri Lanka is undertaken in Chapter 4 and identifies weaknesses in financing as a primary reason for the persistence of concentrated and controlling ownership structures. This integral relationship between ownership structures and financing is of importance from a reform perspective as the desire for financing is a powerful incentive in the reform context. This knowledge motivates a reform agenda in which lenders are proposed as a potential corporate governance mechanism.[100]

Another factor illustrating the correlation between corporate ownership, control and corporate governance in Sri Lanka and motivating this study is the ability of corporate ownership structures to unearth indigenous factors, such as politics and social issues, influencing both financing patterns within a country, and ownership and control structures of companies. Thus, the ethnic conflict in Sri Lanka and its historical roots is reflected in corporate ownership divided along caste and race divisions,[101] and in the lack of trust brought about by life in the midst of conflict, which affects capital market financing.

2.4. Conclusion

To conclude, this chapter supports the thesis of this study that an analysis into reform of corporate governance in developing countries should begin with a focus on local market structures that define its adaptation and effectiveness, by an analysis of the correlation between corporate ownership, control and corporate governance. This relationship is manifold, but in the context of this study, two associations are of importance. The first, that divergent corporate ownership and control structures impact upon the agency conflicts within companies is the first pillar upon which this study is grounded. It guides the examination of ownership and control structures

---

[100] Chapters 6 and 7.
[101] Chapter 5.

of companies in Sri Lanka,[102] and the analysis of the costs and benefits of such structures.[103] The second, that corporate ownership and control structures reflect the inherent financing patterns within a country, is the second pillar upon which this study is grounded. It propels an examination of the determinants of ownership structures in Sri Lanka[104] and a reform agenda utilising knowledge of such financing patterns.[105]

By its focus on the correlation between corporate ownership, control and corporate governance this study understands the roots of corporate governance concerns and highlights its 'causes', rather than making a mere attempt at identifying its 'symptoms'. Further, by its focus on local market structures that define the adaptation and effectiveness of corporate governance this study recognises the broader context in which companies exist.

---

[102] Chapter 3.
[103] Chapter 5.
[104] Chapter 4.
[105] Chapters 6 and 7.

CHAPTER 3

The Separation of Ownership and Control
in Sri Lanka

3.1. Introduction

Corporate ownership[1] is a core feature of the corporate form and under-lies corporate governance.[2] One main element of corporate ownership is the right to control the company.[3] The significance of the distinction between ownership of a company and control of a company came to light when Berle and Means[4] analysing the vast dispersion of ownership in the United States in the late 1920s, called attention to the exceptional fact that shareholders in large listed companies were so dispersed that they had little control over the management of the company. Berle and Means based their image of the modern company on the separation between ownership of the company vested in the hands of dispersed shareholders, and control of the company vested in the hands of professional managers. This separation of ownership and control, according to Berle and Means could result in the directors and managers acting in their own interest to the detriment of dispersed shareholders. The Berle and Means analysis, gave rise to corporate law's subsequent and continued preoccupation with negating the costs arising from the separation of ownership and control.[5]

---

[1] This study uses the term 'ownership' to refer to entitlements to cash flows from the firm whether or not accompanied by control rights.

[2] Chapter 2.

[3] R Kraakman *et al.*, *The Anatomy of Corporate Law: A Comparative and Functional Approach* (Oxford University Press Oxford 2004), 13, identify two key elements in the ownership of a company (a) 'the right to control the firm' and (b) 'the right to receive the firm's net earnings'.

[4] A Berle and G Means, *The Modern Corporation and Private Property* (Rev edn Harcourt, Brace & World Inc. New York 1967), 47–65.

[5] Demonstrated by the volume of scholarship. Significantly, M Jensen and W Meckling, Theory of the Firm: Managerial Behaviour, Agency Costs and Ownership Structure (1976), 3 *Journal of Financial Economics*, 305; S Grossman and O Hart, Take Over Bids, the Free-rider Problem, and the Theory of the Corporation (1980), 11 *Bell Journal of Economics,* 42.

65

In recent years, several studies question the empirical validity of dispersed ownership. Studies in the United States demonstrate modest concentration of ownership even within the largest American firms.[6] Studies of several other developed countries demonstrate a significant concentration of ownership among public companies.[7] In developing economies in Asia and the rest of the world, corporate ownership is heavily concentrated.[8]

The prevalence of concentrated corporate ownership is in contrast to the subsequent scholarship emanating from the United States following the Berle and Means analysis, portraying an image of a corporate world of dispersed ownership. Importantly, concentration of ownership shifts the focus of corporate governance away from its traditional preoccupation with negating management costs arising from the separation of ownership and control, to the costs associated with concentrated ownership structures, the distinction between 'ownership' and 'control' in concentrated ownership

---

[6] A Shleifer and R Vishny, Large Shareholders and Corporate Control (1986), 94 *Journal of Political Economy*, 461–462, find that in a sample of 456 Fortune 500 firms, 354 have at least one shareholder owning at least 5 percent of the firm; R Morck, A Shleifer and R Vishny, Management Ownership and Market Valuation: An Empirical Analysis (1988), 20 *Journal of Financial Economics*, 293, find significant managerial ownership of firms; In Under the Influence, *Economist* (London 17 November 2001), 57, Joe Asrachan of Kennesaw State University in Georgia estimates that founding families wield influence on between 35 percent–45 percent of America's 500 largest listed companies depending on how 'influence' is defined; R Anderson and D Reeb, Founding Family Ownership and Firm Performance: Evidence from the S&P 500 (2003), 58 *Journal of Finance*, 1301, using Standard & Poor's 500 firms from 1992 through 1999, observe that family firms constitute over 35 percent of Standard & Poor's Industrials.

[7] European Corporate Governance Network, *The Separation of Ownership and Control: A Survey of 7 European Countries: Preliminary Report to the European Commission*, Volumes 1–4 (Brussels 1997); LLSV, Law and Finance (1998), 106 *Journal of Political Economy*, 1113; R La-Porta, F Lopez-de-Silanes and A Shleifer, Corporate Ownership around the World (1999), 54 *Journal of Finance*, 471; F Barca and M Becht (eds.), *The Control of Corporate Europe* (Oxford University Press Oxford 2001); M Faccio and L Lang, The Ultimate Ownership of Western European Corporations (2002), 65 *Journal of Financial Economics*, 365; J Grant and T Kirchmaier, Who Governs? Corporate Ownership and Control Structures in Europe (2004), http://ssrn.com/abstract=555877 [15 March 2006].

[8] S Claessens *et al.*, Expropriation of Minority Shareholders: Evidence from East Asia (1999), World Bank Policy Research Working Paper 2088, http://www.worldbank.org/html/dec/Publications/Workpapers/wps2000series/wps2088/wps2088.pdf [10 February 2005]; S Claessens, S Djankov and L Lang, The Separation of Ownership and Control in East Asian Corporations (2000), 58 *Journal of Financial Economics*, 81, report ownership concentration among Asian corporations characterised by family and group control for a sample of 2980 listed companies in nine Asian economies.

structures, the nature of concentrated ownership, the role of ultimate owners, the mechanisms by which ultimate owners increase control in concentrated ownership structures and importantly, the implications of concentrated ownership and controlling shareholder systems for corporate governance.

The objective of this chapter is to characterise the main features of the challenges facing corporate governance in Sri Lanka by examination of the ownership and control structures of its companies. Thus, it is necessary to first, understand the relationship between ownership and control of companies in Sri Lanka and thereafter, evaluate the impact of such ownership and control structures on corporate governance. To achieve this objective, the data is limited to an examination of the ownership and control structures of public companies listed on the CSE with a focus on the 20 largest publicly traded firms in Sri Lanka.[9]

Data on the public companies listed on the CSE and the 20 largest publicly traded firms in Sri Lanka accounting for over 64.32 percent of the market capitalisation[10] provide answers to four key questions. First, how common is the concentrated ownership of companies in Sri Lanka? Second, if the companies have significant owners, who are they? Are they families, the state, institutional investors or other companies? Third, do these significant owners maintain control in excess of their economic stake? If so, do they use their voting rights or develop cross-ownership patterns or do they build control pyramids to maintain control? Alternatively, are they involved in the management of these companies in an attempt to reduce the threat to their control? Fourth, if the companies have ultimate controlling owners, who are they? Are they different to the significant owners identified before? Finally and most importantly, what are the specific corporate governance issues that can be identified as a result of the analysis of corporate ownership structures in Sri Lanka?

This chapter is organised as follows. Section 3.2 examines data, methodology and defines terms. Section 3.3 examines the results of the analysis. Section 3.4 draws upon the analysis of ownership and control structures in Section 3.3 to identify and define the characteristics of the challenges facing corporate governance in Sri Lanka in the light of

---

[9] In terms of market capitalisation as on 24 April 2006. The analysis is restricted to 20 companies due to difficulties in obtaining comprehensive data on a larger sample size.

[10] This is the total value of all securities issued by a company, including debentures, preference and ordinary shares, and bonus and rights issues.

the ownership and control structures of its public listed companies. Section 3.5 concludes.

3.2. Data, Definition of Terms and Methodology

3.2.1. *Corporate Landscape*

Two forms of limited liability companies dominate in Sri Lanka: public and private companies. Among public companies,[11] 252 are listed on the CSE,[12] representing 20 business sectors.[13]

The market capitalisation of listed companies as on 24 April 2006 was Sri Lankan Rupees (SLRS) 701 billion (approximately USD 7 billion) amounting to 29.6 percent of the GDP.[14] However, market capitalisation is highly concentrated among a few large companies. While the average market capitalisation is SLRS 2.7 billion (approximately USD 27 million), the median market capitalisation is SLRS 664 million (approximately USD 6.6 million). In terms of market capitalisation, the 10 largest companies account for over 50.61 percent of the total market capitalisation, while the 20 largest companies account for over 64.32 percent. In contrast, the 100 smallest listed companies in terms of market capitalisation account for only 2.86 percent.[15]

3.2.2. *Data*

The analysis of ownership and control structures of public listed Sri Lankan companies is based on the data of public companies listed on the CSE and the 20 largest companies ranked by market capitalisation. These 20 companies account for over 64.32 percent of market capitalisation of all the listed companies and is a fairly representative sample. However,

---

[11] Of a total of 2160 public companies (11.6 percent). S Athukorala and B Reid, *Diagnostic Study of Accounting and Auditing Practices in Sri Lanka* (Asian Development Bank Manila 2002), 15.

[12] As on 24 April 2006.

[13] Colombo Stock Exchange, *Fact Book 2003* (Colombo 2004), 35–46.

[14] Central Bank of Sri Lanka, *Annual Report 2005* (Colombo 2005), Key Economic Indicators. GDP at current market prices is SLRS Billion 2366.

[15] Statistical information on file with author.

being the 20 largest listed companies, they may presumably have less concentrated ownership than is the norm.

3.2.3. *Definition of Terms*

(a) *Ownership (Cash Flow Rights)*

The definition of ownership or cash flow rights in the text is based on the economic stake held by the shareholder.[16] For example, if a family owns 25 percent of the shares of publicly traded Company A, which in turn has 25 percent of the shares of Company B, and assuming that there are no cross-holdings between Companies A and B or deviations from one-share-one-vote, the family's economic stake in Company B is 6.25 percent, where economic stake is defined as the product of the shareholdings at different levels of the pyramid. Ownership as referred to in the text is also distinct from control, approximated not only to voting power, the most important instrument for obtaining control, but also to 'the power to dispose of the firm's capital, assets and customer relations (goodwill) in anyway not expressly prohibited by existing legislation, regulations or contracts'.[17]

(b) *Control*

The definition of control relies on voting rights and deviations from one-share one-vote, pyramiding schemes, circular holdings and cross-holdings, which are mechanisms used to separate ownership from control. Using the same example as above, and assuming that there are no deviations from one-share one-vote or cross-holdings between the companies, the family's voting rights or control in Company B is 25 percent or the weakest link in the chain of control rights.[18]

---

[16] 'Economic stake' is used to identify bare legal title. Kraakman (n. 3), 55–56, uses the terms 'economic stake' and 'economic ownership'. Economists use the term 'cash flow holdings'.

[17] F Barca, Alternative Models of Control: Efficiency, Accessibility and Market Failures, in J Roemer (ed.), *Property Relations, Incentives and Welfare* (St. Martin's & Macmillan New York & London 1997), 195.

[18] Methodology used by Claessens *et al.* (n. 8), 91; J Franks and C Mayer, Ownership and Control of German Corporations (2001), 14 *Review of Financial Studies*, 943.

(c) *Blockholders*

'Blockholders' are shareholders with an economic stake in excess of 10 percent among the companies in the sample. The cut-off of 10 percent is used since on an one-share one-vote assumption, it provides a significant threshold of votes sufficient to call an extra-ordinary general meeting,[19] an important means of shareholder control.[20] Group companies[21] may also be blockholders.

(d) *Controlling Shareholders*

Controlling shareholders are shareholders with control rights in excess of their economic stakes. This definition is narrowed to shareholders with direct and indirect voting rights in excess of 20 percent in the company, which is usually sufficient to obtain effective control of the company.

(e) *Vertical Groups*

Vertical groups consist of a parent and one or more subsidiaries (Fig. 3.1).[22] The distinction between vertical groups where the subsidiaries are

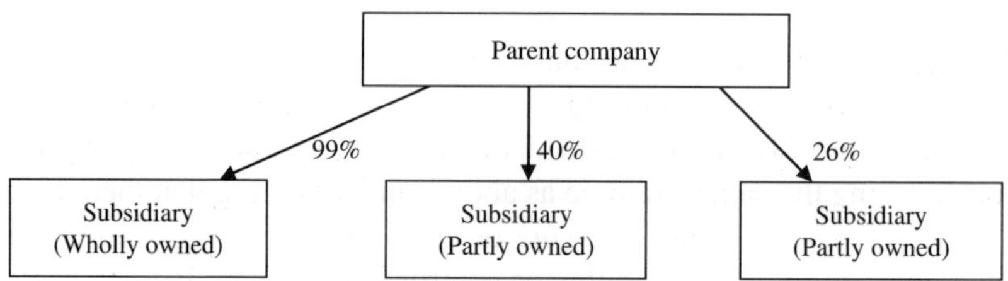

Figure 3.1: Parent and Subsidiaries.

---

[19] Companies Act No. 7 of 2007 s. 134.

[20] However, P Davies, *Gower and Davies' Principles of Modern Company Law* (7th edn Sweet & Maxwell London 2003), 346, recognises that 'the shareholders' meeting is not much of value as a vehicle of shareholders control if the meeting cannot be easily convened'.

[21] Section 3.2.3 (e)–(g).

[22] J Dine, *The Governance of Corporate Groups* (Cambridge University Press Cambridge 2000), 39–40.

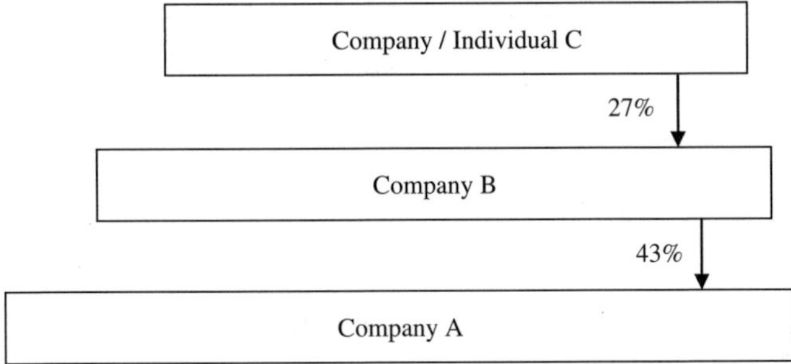

Figure 3.2: Pyramid.

wholly owned and those where they are partly owned is relevant to this study.

Vertical groups can also take the form of 'pyramids', defined as a company, (i) which has a controlling shareholder and (ii) has at least one publicly traded company between it and the controlling shareholder (Fig. 3.2).[23]

(f) *Horizontal Groups*

Horizontal groups consist of companies with cross-shareholdings and circular holdings.[24] Cross-holdings occur where companies with a common board of directors or with boards that have agreed to act in concert, each having a holding of at least 20 percent[25] in the ordinary voting shares of each of the other companies (Fig. 3.3). This can be illustrated as follows:

In circular holdings one company holds 20 percent of the ordinary voting shares of another, which in turns holds 20 percent of the ordinary

---

[23] La-Porta 1999 (n. 7), 477.

[24] Jenkins Committee, *Report of the Company Law Committee* (Cmnd 1749, 1962) [152]; D Prentice, A Survey of the Law Relating to Corporate Groups in the United Kingdom, in E Wymeersch (ed.), *Groups of Companies in the EEC: A Survey Report to the European Commission on the Law Relating to Corporate Groups in Various Member States* (Walter De Gruyter Berlin 1993), 283–284.

[25] Claessens *et al.* (n. 8), 84. Although technically an economic stake of at least 26 percent is required to achieve this form of control, the 20 percent figure is used since control can also be achieved by being a single controlling shareholder though holding only 20 percent economic stake in the company.

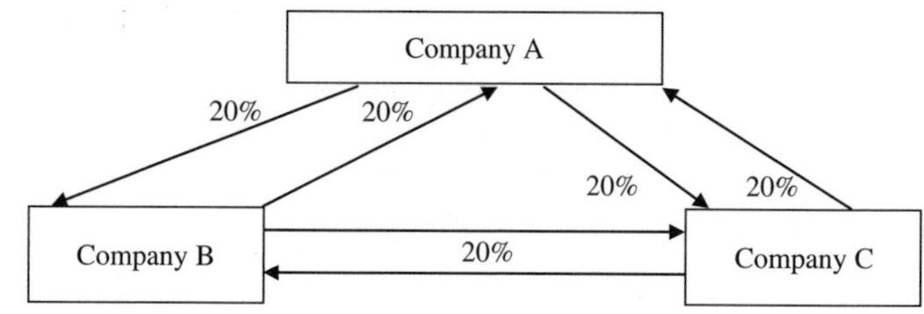

Figure 3.3: Cross-Holding.

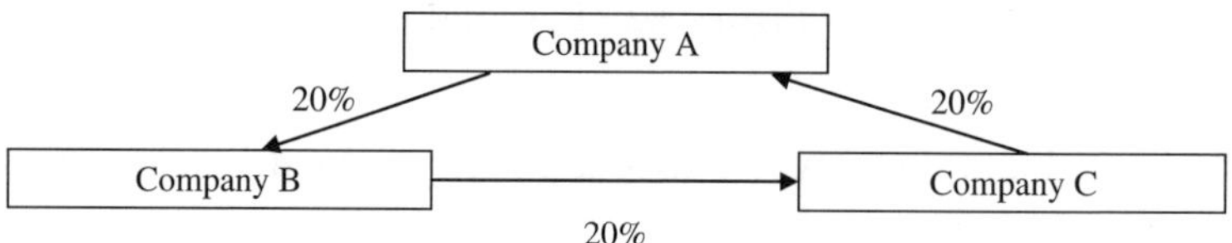

Figure 3.4: Circular Holdings.

voting shares of a third company, which in turn holds 20 percent of the ordinary voting shares of the first company (Fig. 3.4).

In cross-holdings (Fig. 3.3) the board of directors of each company with the assistance of the boards of directors of the other companies, command a majority, and the companies can be operated as a group. In circular holdings (Fig. 3.4) if the directors agree to act in concert there is effective control of each of the companies and group operations.

(g) Subsidiary, Group Companies and Associate Company

A company ('S') is a subsidiary of another if such other company ('H') either (a) controls the composition of its board of directors; (b) is able to control more than half the number of votes; (c) holds more than half of the issued shares and (d) is entitled to receive more than half of the dividends paid[26] or 'S' is a subsidiary of another company which is a subsidiary of 'H'.[27]

---

[26] Companies Act 2007 (n. 19) s. 529.
[27] ibid. Contrast Companies Act 1985 (UK) s. 258 and Companies Act 2006 (UK) s. 1162 (2) which takes into account dominant influence and control.

A group of companies is a parent and subsidiaries.[28] An associate company is an enterprise in which an investor has a significant influence and which is neither a subsidiary nor a joint venture of the investor.[29]

3.2.4. *Methodology*

In the first stage of analysis, concentration of ownership is measured among the companies listed on the CSE. Thereafter, the nature of corporate ownership (i.e., the identity of shareholders with an economic stake) is identified and categorised. To measure concentration of ownership, the economic stake of the largest shareholders in the 252 companies listed on the CSE is examined vis-à-vis the combined economic stakes of the other shareholders. To identify the nature of corporate ownership, data on the individual economic stakes of the 20 largest shareholders in the 20 largest Sri Lankan companies are analysed and grouped into 10 distinct categories of ownership.

In the second stage of the analysis, the relationship between ownership and control in the sample companies is examined. For this purpose, the focus is on blockholders. In many instances, blockholders are other companies. Then, the ultimate owners of these companies are identified. Initially, the focus is on the use of vertical and horizontal groups by blockholders to control a company without acquiring a commensurate economic stake. Group structures are important for the study as they can be replicated and are means of leveraging a shareholder's economic stake in the company.

Thereafter, the focus is on the use of voting rights by blockholders among the sample companies as a mechanism for enhancing control in excess of economic stakes. Finally, affiliations between the management and blockholders among the sample companies are traced as a mechanism for enhancing control in excess of economic stakes.

The primary sources of information are the annual reports and websites of the companies. These include the names of the largest shareholders and the size of their economic stake.[30] Useful other sources

---

[28] Sri Lanka Accounting Standards 2006, Standard 26.5.

[29] ibid, Standard 27.2. Standard 27.6 defines 'significant influence' as an investor holding directly or indirectly 20 percent or more of the voting power of the investee.

[30] CSE Listing Rules 2004, r. 8.7 (g) mandates disclosure of the names of the 20 largest holders of equity, the number of securities and the percentage of capital each of them holds in the annual report to be published before the expiry of 6 months from the close of each financial year.

are the websites of the Registrar of Companies,[31] the CSE,[32] and the Securities and Exchange Commission of Sri Lanka (SEC).[33] All data in the sample is for the years 2005–2006.

3.3. Results

3.3.1. *Coverage of the Sample*

This is represented in Table 3.1.

3.3.2. *Description of the Sample*

The sample of the 20 largest companies ranked by market capitalisation encompass three financial institutions, one utility company with a state ownership stake in excess of 50 percent,[37] four diversified companies with interests in the leisure industry, tea and oil plantations, commodity exports, shipping and energy sectors. One of the companies is a local alcohol

Table 3.1: Coverage of the Sample (As on 24 April 2006[34]).

Stock exchange	Established	Number of listed companies	Market capitalisation[35] (USD)	Number of companies in the sample for second-stage analysis	Share of total market capitalisation of sample
CSE	1985[36]	252	6,825,291,619.15	20	64.32%

---

[31] — Registrar of Companies, http://www.drc.gov.lk [5 December 2004].

[32] — Colombo Stock Exchange, http://www.cse.lk/home/main.jsp [5 December 2004].

[33] — Securities and Exchange Commission of Sri Lanka, http://www.sec.gov.lk/ [5 December 2004].

[34] Colombo Stock Exchange, Market Capitalisation of Listed Companies, http://www. cse.lk/marketinfo/print/marketcap.jsp [24 April 2006].

[35] Definition at (n. 10).

[36] Inception of share trading was in 1896 under the Colombo Share Brokers Association.

[37] Sri Lanka Telecom.

manufacturer. Five are wholly owned subsidiaries of non-resident companies. Four of the sample companies were incorporated over 100 years ago.

The largest company in the sample, Dialog Telekom Limited (Dialog Telekom) is a subsidiary of Telecom Malaysia International, and wholly owned by Telekom Malaysia Bhd. Dialog Telekom operates Dialog GSM the country's largest mobile telecommunications network. The second largest listed company, John Keells Holdings Limited (John Keells), is the largest diversified company on the CSE. It holds key positions in Sri Lanka's tea, food and beverage manufacture, real estate, hotel and banking industries. The third largest listed company, Sri Lanka Telecom Limited (Sri Lanka Telecom), is the country's first telecommunications company and successor to the former government-owned Telecommunications Department privatised in collaboration with Nippon Telegraph and Telecommunications Corporation of Japan.[38]

The fourth largest listed company in terms of market capitalistion, Commercial Bank of Ceylon Limited (Commercial Bank), has been in existence for nearly a century and has consistently maintained its status as the best bank in Sri Lanka.[39] The fifth largest company Carson Cumberbatch & Company Limited (Carson Cumberbatch) is another diversified holding company with business interests in brewing, oil palm plantations, investment holdings and financial services across South East Asia. Lanka IOC Limited (now known as Lanka IOC Plc), the sixth largest listed company is a subsidiary of Indian Oil Company, one of India's Fortune 500 companies. Bukit Darah Company Limited (Bukit Darah), the seventh largest sample company is a subsidiary of Carson Cumberbatch and until recently owned oil palm plantations in Malaysia. These were disposed of during the recent past and the main line of business changed to an investment holding company.[40] The eighth largest sample company is Distilleries Company of Sri Lanka limited (Distilleries Company), a pioneering distillery with secondary interests in cultivation and processing of tea and rubber, insurance, banking, tourism, cargo logistics and manufacturing services. The ninth largest sample company DFCC

---

[38] Subsequently Nippon Telegraph and Telecommunications Corporation of Japan sold their stake in Sri Lanka Telecom.

[39] Rated as best bank in Sri Lanka for 8 consecutive years by *Global Finance Magazine*, New York, Commercial Bank Best bank in Sri Lanka, http://www.combank.net/newweb/ [1 April 2006].

[40] Bukit Darah, *Annual Report 2004–05* (Colombo 2005), 2.

Bank Limited (DFCC Bank), was established as a development bank in the 1950s and is presently a licensed specialised bank. The 10th largest sample company is Asian Hotels & Properties Limited (Asian Hotels) a subsidiary of John Keells involved in the hotel and tourism sectors.

The 11th sample company, Hatton National Bank Limited (Hatton National Bank) is a leading commercial bank, while the 12th sample company, Ceylon Tobacco Company Limited (Ceylon Tobacco), is a member of British American Tobacco Holdings (Sri Lanka) BV. The 13th sample company is Overseas Realty (Ceylon) Limited (now known as Overseas Realty (Ceylon) Plc), a property development company and subsidiary of the Shing Kwan group of Singapore. The 14th sample company is Hemas Holdings Limited (Hemas Holdings), another diversified company involved in healthcare, leisure, transportation and investments. Nestle Lanka Limited (now known as Nestle Lanka Plc), the 15th sample company is a subsidiary of Societe de Produits Nestlé S.A. of Switzerland and engaged in the manufacture and importation of milk and food products.

The 16th and 17th sample companies are Aitken Spence & Company Limited (Aitken Spence) and Richard Pieris & Company Limited (Richard Pieris), respectively, both of which are diversified companies engaged in travel, tourism, plantations, estate management, property development and manufacturing. Ceylon Theatres Limited (Ceylon Theatres), the 18th sample company initially incorporated as a theatre company, is now a diversified holding company engaged in land development, food and beverage sectors and plantations. The 19th sample company, National Development Bank Limited (National Development Bank Limited), provides long-term credit for development projects, merchant banking, venture capital, stock brokering, fund management and property development. The last sample company engaged in tea exports, insurance, pest control, industrial and agro chemicals, plantation management and tourism is James Finlay and Company (Colombo) Limited, (now known as Finlays Colombo Plc) with over 77.21 percent owned by James Finlay and Company Limited, a wholly owned subsidiary of the Swire Group. The group's privately owned parent company, John Swire and Sons, Limited is headquartered in London.

3.3.3. *Concentration of Ownership*

Concentrated ownership cannot be claimed on the basis of an assumption. To challenge the image of a corporate world of dispersed ownership emanating from the writings of corporate governance scholars in the United States in its applicability to Sri Lanka, this section of the study attempts to measure ownership concentration. While it is accepted that an accurate measure of ownership concentration is difficult to achieve due to interactions among block shareholders, an attempt is made to achieve at least an approximation.

To measure concentration of ownership, the focus is on the economic stakes of the largest shareholders in all of the 252 companies listed on the CSE. Largest shareholders are shareholders who hold the most number of shares in a particular company but accounting for less than 1 percent of the total number of shareholders (where the number of shareholders is less than 100 then the shareholding of one shareholder is taken into account). By way of example, if company A, has 500 shareholders who own 100,000,000 shares, the inquiry concerns how many shares as a percentage of the total number of shares, the five largest shareholders (i.e., being 1 percent of the total number of shareholders) own. The inquiry is limited to ordinary voting and non-voting shares[41] in the sample companies.

Figure 3.5 illustrates the enormous concentration of ownership among the listed companies on the CSE. It represents the shareholdings of the total number of shareholders of all the listed companies. Approximately 1 percent of the total number of shareholders' economic stakes average 78.21 percent of the total shares of the 252 listed companies. In other words, a few wealthy shareholders own an average of 78.21 percent of all of the shares of the listed companies. Conversely, approximately 99 percent of the total

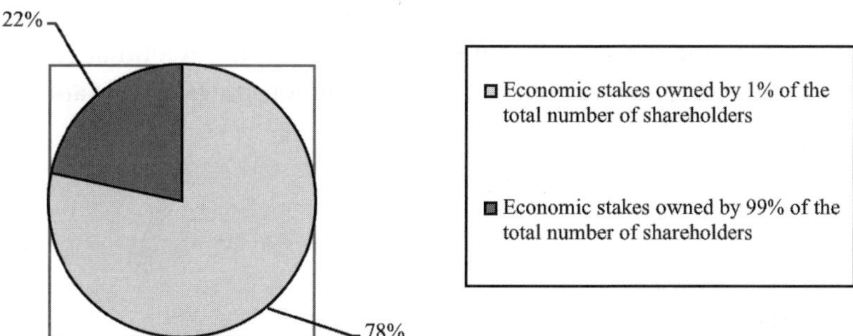

Figure 3.5: Concentration of Ownership.

---

[41] Only 6 of the 252 companies have non-voting ordinary shares in issue. Companies Act 2007 (n. 19) s. 49 allows for companies to vary voting rights.

number of shareholders' economic stakes amount to only 21.79 percent of the sample companies.[42]

The above analysis illustrates that corporate ownership in Sri Lanka is concentrated, in contrast to the image of a corporate world of dispersed ownership as propounded by the literature emanating from the United States. The analysis is also supported by the findings of LLSV,[43] documenting the ownership structures of the 10 largest (by market capitalisation) non-financial companies for a cross section of 49 countries, including Sri Lanka. Their data is on the combined economic stakes of the three largest shareholders.[44] Their findings for Sri Lanka measured by ownership of the three largest shareholders of the 10 largest companies are a mean of 60 percent and a median of 61 percent.[45] The findings of this study, which are more comprehensive due to the coverage of all of the 252 listed companies in Sri Lanka and its focus on 1 percent of the shareholders (i.e., a percentage in contrast to a fixed number), illustrates that concentration of ownership in Sri Lanka is in fact greater than the initial LLSV measurement.[46]

The LLSV analysis also provides useful comparisons of ownership concentration around the world.[47] The average ownership of the three largest shareholders among the 45 sample countries is 46 percent, and the median 45 percent.[48] Ownership concentration is below 30 percent for only the United States, Australia, United Kingdom, Taiwan, Japan, Korea and Sweden.[49] On average Asian countries display greater concentration of ownership. For example, the average ownership concentration for India is 40 percent, for Malaysia 54 percent, for Thailand 47 percent and for Indonesia 58 percent.[50]

It must be noted that while ownership concentration in Sri Lanka is high, it is not significantly different than other countries at similar levels of economic development as the LLSV study demonstrates. For example,

---

[42] Fig. 3.5.

[43] LLSV 1998 (n. 7).

[44] ibid 1146–1147, Table 7.

[45] ibid 1145–1147, Table 7.

[46] The LLSV analysis on the data sets of this study (2006) reveals a median of 63.84 percent and a mean of 61.84 percent.

[47] LLSV 1998 (n. 7), 1147.

[48] ibid 1146.

[49] ibid 1147, Table 7.

[50] ibid.

the average ownership concentration in Egypt is 62 percent, in Mexico it is 64 percent and in Zimbabwe it is 55 percent.[51]

3.3.4. *Nature of Corporate Ownership*

To examine the nature of corporate ownership in Sri Lanka, data on the 20 largest shareholders in terms of their economic stakes in the 20 sample[52] companies is collected (Fig. 3.6). Thereafter, these shareholders are grouped into 10 distinct categories of ownership. The results of the analysis are presented below (Table 3.2).[53]

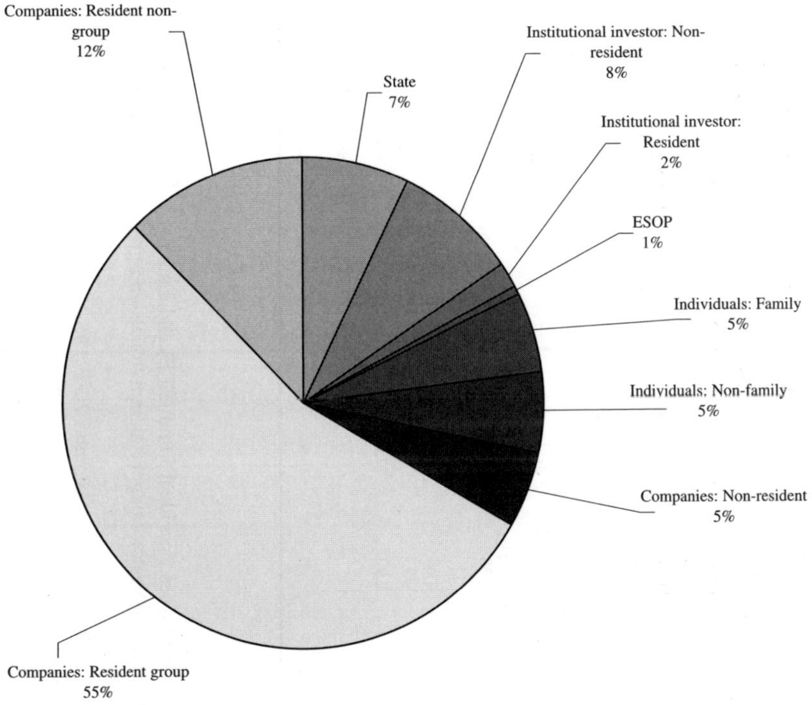

Figure 3.6: Nature of Corporate Ownership.

---

[51] ibid.

[52] Section 3.3.2 describes the sample.

[53] Table 3.2 and Fig. 3.6.

Table 3.2: Nature of Ownership.

Ranking according to market capitalisation[54]	Name of company	Percentage of total market capitalisation	Percentage owned by 20 largest shareholders	Percentage owned by the State	Percentage owned by institutional investors		Employees' share option schemes	Percentage owned by individuals			Percentage owned by companies	
					Non-resident	Resident[55]		Same family (related)	Non-related individuals	Non-resident	Resident group[56] companies	Resident non-group companies
1	Dialog Telekom[57]	22.42	95.93	—	4.43	0.25	2.69	—	—	87.67	—	0.89
2	John Keells[58]	8.38	53.69	—	18.30	—	—	16.35	13.52	—	—	5.52
3	Sri Lanka Telecom[59]	4.63	90.67	49.75	1.99	0.65	—	—	1.36	35.19	—	1.73
4	Commercial Bank[60] (voting)	2.92	77.27	2.03	19.6	1.96	—	—	10.87	—	41.73	1.08
	(nonvoting)		36.84	—	—	—	—	—	8.18	—	10.62	18.04

(Continued)

[54] As on 24 April 2006.

[55] State pension funds (Employees Provident Fund (EPF) and Employees Trust Fund (ETF) and unit trusts. Insurance funds are excluded from the resident institutional investor category as individuals and group companies control them.

[56] Section 3.2.3 (e)–(g) above.

[57] Dialog Telekom, *Annual Report 2005* (Colombo 2005), 95.

[58] John Keells, *Annual Report 2004–2005* (Colombo 2005), 32.

[59] Sri Lanka Telecom, *Annual Report 2005* (Colombo 2005), 84.

[60] Commercial Bank, *Annual Report 2005* (Colombo 2005), 133.

Table 3.2: (*Continued*)

Ranking according to market capitalisation	Name of company	Percentage of total market capitalisation	Percentage owned by 20 largest shareholders	Percentage owned by the State	Percentage owned by institutional investors		Employees share option schemes	Percentage owned by individuals			Percentage owned by companies	
					Non-resident	Resident		Same family (related)	Non-related individuals	Non-resident	Resident group companies	Resident non-group companies
5	Carson Cumberbatch[61]	2.64	96.37	—	—	—	—	0.39	1.40	—	90.48	4.10
6	Lanka IOC Limited[62]	2.09	83.32	—	4.17	0.66	—	—	2.42	75.11	—	0.96
7	Bukit Darah[63]	2.04	96.23	—	—	—	—	—	6.48	—	80.54	9.21
8	Distilleries Company[64]	2.02	83.09	—	7.37	0.50	—	13.29	3.79	—	56.35	1.79
9	DFCC Bank[65]	1.79	90.73	17.8	10.64	1.37	—	—	—	—	44.57	16.36
10	Asian Hotels[66]	1.68	94.82	0.21	—	1.47	—	—	3.78	2.41	83.80	3.15

(*Continued*)

[61]Carson Cumberbatch, *Annual Report 2003–04* (Colombo 2005), 23.

[62] Lanka IOC Limited, *Annual Report 2004–05* (Colombo 2005), 39.

[63] Bukit Darah (n. 40), 9.

[64] Distilleries Company, *Annual Report 2005* (Colombo 2005), 15.

[65] DFCC Bank, *Annual Report 2004–05* (Colombo 2005), 121.

[66] Asian Hotels, *Annual Report 2004–05* (Colombo 2005), 40.

Table 3.2: (*Continued*)

Ranking according to market capitalisation	Name of company	Percentage of total market capitalisation	Percentage owned by 20 largest shareholders	Percentage owned by the State	Percentage owned by institutional investors — Non-resident	Resident	Employees share option schemes	Percentage owned by individuals — Same family (related)	Non-related individuals	Non-resident	Percentage owned by companies — Resident group companies	Resident non-group companies
11	Hatton National Bank[67] (voting)	1.62	68.82	—	—	0.18	—	—	1.46	15.00	26.13	26.05
	(nonvoting)		7.33	—	—		3.88	—	1.38	—	1.11	0.96
12	Ceylon Tobacco[68]	1.56	95.39		0.16	1.18			0.67	92.45	—	0.93
13	Overseas Realty (Ceylon) Limited[69]	1.52				Data not available						
14	Hemas Holdings[70]	1.50	94.90	—	5.15	1.99	—	12.69	0.97	—	70.5	3.60

(Continued)

[67] Hatton National Bank, *Annual Report 2005* (Colombo 2005), 77.

[68] Ceylon Tobacco, *Annual Report 2004* (Colombo 2005), 79.

[69] Annual report is not available.

[70] Hemas Holdings, *Annual Report 2004–05* (Colombo 2005), 71.

Table 3.2: (*Continued*)

Ranking according to market capitalisation	Name of company	Percentage of total market capitalisation	Percentage owned by 20 largest shareholders	Percentage owned by the State	Percentage owned by institutional investors		Employees share option schemes	Percentage owned by individuals			Percentage owned by companies	
					Non-resident	Resident		Same family (related)	Non-related individuals	Non-resident	Resident group companies	Resident non-group companies
15	Nestle Lanka Limited[71]	1.42	94.59	—	0.43	0.42	—	—	1.42	90.82	—	1.50
16	Aitken Spence[72]	1.29	77.16	—	18.27	3.98	—		3.44	—	29.13	22.34
17	Richard Pieris[73]	1.24	90.25	4.97	12.28	1.16	—	5.96	3.84	—	61.38	0.66
18	Ceylon Theatres[74]	1.22	94.98	—	—	—	—	16.6	2.4	—	69.89	6.09
19	National Development Bank[75]	1.19	70.71	14.37	7.24	6.63	2.52	—	—	9.90	—	30.05

(*Continued*)

[71] Nestle Lanka Limited, *Annual Report 2004* (Colombo 2005), 86.
[72] Aitken Spence, *Annual Report 2004–05* (Colombo 2005), 115.
[73] Richard Pieris, *Annual Report 2004–05* (Colombo 2005), 99.
[74] Ceylon Theatres, *Annual Report 2003* (Colombo 2005), 6.
[75] National Development Bank, *Annual Report 2005* (Colombo 2006), 115.

Table 3.2: *(Continued)*

Ranking according to market capitalisation	Name of company	Percentage of total market capitalisation	Percentage owned by 20 largest shareholders	Percentage owned by the State	Percentage owned by institutional investors		Employees share option schemes	Percentage owned by individuals		Percentage owned by companies		
					Non-resident	Resident		Same family (related)	Non-related individuals	Non-resident	Resident group companies	Resident non-group companies
20	James Finlay and Company (Colombo) Limited[76]	1.15	99.56			0.63		12.96	3.6	77.21		5.16
Total		64.32	1692.65	89.13	110.03	23.03	9.09	78.24	70.98	485.76	666.23	155.01
Total excluding subsidiaries with over 50% held by non-resident companies[77] (nonshaded)		35.68	1223.86	89.13	100.84	19.89	6.4	65.28	65.87	62.5	666.23	150.73
Average excluding subsidiaries with over 50% held by non-resident companies			87.41	6.36	7.20	1.42	0.46	4.66	4.70	4.46	47.5	10.76
			100	7.27	8.24	1.62	0.53	5.33	5.38	5.10	54.34	12.31

Companies with over 50 percent held by non-resident companies.

---

[76] James Finlay and Company, *Annual Report 2004* (Colombo 2005), 39.

[77] Text after n. 37.

At this stage of the analysis, no attempt is made to trace the ultimate owners of these shareholdings, beyond identifying group companies as a subcategory. The objective in categorising the nature of corporate ownership is to identify with clarity the vested interests posed by the different ownership categories with respect to corporate governance issues in Sri Lanka.

To avoid distortions in the sample, subsidiaries with over 50 percent holdings by non-resident companies are excluded from this stage of the analysis.[78] This excludes from the sample at the second stage, the largest listed company Dialog Telekom and the 6th (Lanka IOC Limited), 12th (Ceylon Tobacco), 15th (Nestle Lanka Limited) and 20th (James Finlay and Company (Colombo) Limited) sample companies.

The average percentage owned by the 20 largest shareholders in the sample companies is 87.41 percent of the total shareholdings. This is significant given that these are the 20 largest listed companies in Sri Lanka and therefore perceived to have a more dispersed shareholder base.

On the basis of economic stakes, resident companies are among the largest shareholders of the sample companies and account for over 67 percent of the shareholdings. Resident group companies have the largest economic stakes while non-group resident companies have significant holdings at 12 percent. Despite an aggressive privatisation programme, state ownership of the sample companies is relatively high (7 percent), while non-resident institutional investors hold significant stakes in the sample companies (8 percent). An employee share option (ESOP) scheme makes its presence felt in a sample company and account for 1 percent. While resident institutional investors have shareholdings in nearly every one of the sample companies, their holdings are relatively small at 2 percent. On the basis of economic stakes, individual investor holdings among the sample companies account for 10 percent with family stakes amounting to 5 percent.

3.3.5. *The Distinction between Corporate Ownership and Control*

The aim at this second stage of the analysis is to ascertain whether there exists a distinction between corporate ownership and control in Sri Lanka.

---

[78] Overseas Realty (Ceylon) Limited is also excluded due to unavailability of data.

To achieve this objective, it is necessary to first discover whether the shareholders in the sample companies have control rights in excess of their economic stakes; second, understand the mechanisms used to enhance control rights in excess of economic stakes and third, analyse the nature and identity of the controlling shareholders.

The focus is on blockholders (i.e., shareholders with economic stakes in excess of 10 percent),[79] among the 20 largest shareholders. If such blockholder's control rights (i.e., direct and indirect voting rights) exceed 20 percent, such company is identified as having a controlling shareholder.[80] Thereafter, the mechanisms used by blockholders to increase their control rights in excess of their economic stakes are identified. Finally, the findings from the nature of corporate ownership in the sample[81] is contrasted against the nature of controlling shareholders.

(a) *Control Rights of Blockholders*

The objective of this subsection is to ascertain whether the shareholders in the sample companies have control rights in excess of their economic stakes. If such blockholder's control rights exceed 20 percent, the company is identified as having a controlling shareholder.

If such blockholders are companies, an attempt is made to find the ultimate owners of such companies and identify the control that is wielded by such ultimate owners through the use of mechanisms to enhance control in excess of their economic stakes. If such blockholders are individuals, an inquiry is made as to whether such individual relies on investment companies or family members to increase control in excess of the economic stake and identify the control rights wielded by such families.

An analysis of ultimate control of the sample companies requires specific data on the interactions between each of the blockholders and the ultimate ownership data of all shareholders in the sample companies. As this is not feasible for a study of this nature, the analysis is limited to the interactions among the 20 largest shareholders in each company.

---

[79] Text between n. 18 and n. 20.
[80] Text between n. 21 and n. 22.
[81] Table 3.2 and Fig. 3.6.

For clarity, this section of the study is illustrated with charts based on the ownership structures of the sample companies under analysis. The charts also demonstrate the complications in the construction of data and the range of data necessary to identify ultimate control.

The second sample company, John Keells, has a blockholder who does not appear to have any other indirect holdings within the sample of the 20 largest shareholders. There are no deviations from the one-share one-vote rule and no shares with multiple classes of voting rights[82] and therefore, this blockholder does not appear to have any control rights in excess of its economic stake. Since the blockholder's economic stake is 10.09 percent,[83] John Keells cannot be classified as having a controlling shareholder.

The third sample company, Sri Lanka Telecom, has two blockholders, the Government of Sri Lanka and Nippon Telegraph and Telecommunications Corporation of Japan. Although the Government of Sri Lanka's economic stake in Sri Lanka Telecom is represented as 49.50 percent, the collective economic stake of all state actors among the 20 largest shareholders, amounts to 50.39 percent. There are no deviations from the one-share one-vote rule and no shares are issued with multiple classes of voting rights. Therefore, Sri Lanka Telecom has two controlling shareholders, the Government of Sri Lanka with 50.39 percent and Nippon Telegraph and Telecommunications Corporation of Japan with 35.19 percent.[84]

The 10th sample company, Asian Hotels, has one blockholder, John Keells, its holding company with an economic stake of 83.80.[85] John Keells does not appear to have any other indirect holdings within the sample of 20 largest shareholders. Asian Hotels has no deviations from the one-share one-vote rule and no shares with multiple classes of voting rights and therefore, John Keells does not appear to have any control rights in excess of its economic stake. Therefore, John Keells' control of Asian Hotels is proportionate to its economic stake and can be identified as its controlling shareholder.

The 19th sample company, National Development Bank, has a state bank with a holding of 10 percent as a blockholder.[86] However, due to

---

[82] Multiple classes of voting rights are unusual in Sri Lanka.

[83] John Keells (n. 58), 32.

[84] Sri Lanka Telecom (n. 59), 84.

[85] Asian Hotels (n. 66), 40.

[86] National Development Bank (n. 75), 115.

cross-holdings the collective economic stake of this state bank amounts to 14.37 percent.[87] There are no deviations from the one-share one-vote rule and no shares are issued with multiple classes of voting rights. Since the blockholder state bank's total economic stake is below 20 percent, National Development Bank cannot be classified as having a controlling shareholder.

The fourth sample company, Commercial Bank,[88] has two classes of ordinary shares, those with voting rights and those without. Since the analysis is on control rights, the focus is on ordinary voting shares.[89] Commercial Bank has two blockholders, DFCC Bank (ninth sample company) with an economic stake of 29.15 percent and a non-resident institutional investor with an economic stake of 14.69 percent.[90] The non-resident institutional investor, a fund management company has further holdings amounting to a total of 19.1 percent among the 20 largest shareholdings.[91] On the basis of economic stakes among the 20 largest shareholders, DFCC Bank and its group companies have economic stakes amounting to a total of 41.73 percent in Commercial Bank (DFCC Bank 29.15 percent, Sri Lanka Insurance Corporation Limited 9.71 percent, Distilleries Company 2.25 percent and Hatton National Bank 0.62 percent).

A scrutiny of the shareholding of DFCC Bank (ninth sample), and its shareholders is the next step towards revealing the ultimate control of Commercial Bank. DFCC Bank has five blockholders: a state bank with an economic stake of 14.72 percent, Commercial Bank with a shareholding of 13.59 percent, Hatton National Bank with an economic stake of 12.69 percent and two corporate investors with 11.84 percent and 10.21 percent.[92] On the basis of economic stakes, Commercial Bank, Hatton National Bank and group companies have economic stakes amounting to 44.63 percent among the 20 largest shareholders of DFCC Bank.

---

[87] In the light of the National Development Bank of Sri Lanka (Consequential Provisions) Act No. 1 of 2005 read together with provisions of the Banking Amendment Act No. 2. of 2005, National Development Bank can refuse to register a shareholding in excess of 10 percent pending approval of the Monetary Board of the Central Bank of Sri Lanka. The 4.37 percent held by the state bank is subject to such approval.

[88] Fig. 3.7.

[89] Similar to Hatton National Bank.

[90] Commercial Bank (n. 60), 133.

[91] However, only the economic stake of DFCC Bank is under further consideration, as the control stake of the non-resident institutional investor does not exceed 20 percent.

[92] DFCC Bank (n. 65), 121; Fig. 3.7.

A scrutiny of the shareholdings of one of the blockholder corporate investors, a state-owned insurance company privatised in the recent past, (Sri Lanka Insurance Corporation Limited)[93] with an 11.84 percent economic stake in DFCC Bank, reveals that 85 percent of its shareholding is owned by a private company which is in turn controlled by an individual. This individual with 85 percent control of Sri Lanka Insurance Corporation Limited, which has a mere 9.71 percent economic stake in Commercial Bank, controls at minimum (excluding the cross-holdings between DFCC Bank, Commercial Bank and group holdings) 21.55 percent of Commercial Bank, that is, sum of the weakest links in the chain of control, (11.84 + 9.71).[94] The ultimate controlling owner of Commercial Bank is, therefore, an individual investor.

In any event, Commercial Bank is a subsidiary of DFCC Bank and therefore, the ultimate controlling owner of DFCC Bank is the ultimate controlling shareholder of Commercial Bank. The mechanisms used to gain control of Commercial Bank in excess of the economic stakes held by this individual investor, are vertical group structures, namely, a parent–subsidiary relationship enhanced by a pyramid structure.

The ultimate controlling shareholder of DFCC Bank is the same individual investor with control rights in Commercial Bank. Control of DFCC Bank is achieved through the control of each of DFCC Bank's blockholders,[95] that is, Commercial Bank, Sri Lanka Insurance Corporation Limited and Hatton National Bank, in addition to economic stakes in Commercial Bank, Sri Lanka Insurance Corporation Limited and Hatton National Bank. The mechanism used to gain control of DFCC Bank, in excess of the economic stakes of this individual investor, is a vertical group structure of a number of pyramids through each of the blockholders. The cross-holdings below 20 percent of the shareholdings (i.e., between DFCC Bank and Commercial Bank) have helped enhance ultimate control rights of this investor.

Finding the ultimate controlling shareholder in the eighth sample company — Distilleries Company — is relatively simple. There are two

---

[93] Fig. 3.7.

[94] Similarly, Hatton National Bank has a 0.62 percent economic stake in Commercial Bank but control rights far in excess due to cross-shareholdings and pyramiding, that is, Hatton National Bank has an economic stake of 12.69 percent in DFCC Bank, which has an economic stake of 29.15 percent in Commercial Bank.

[95] Fig. 3.7.

blockholders,[96] both public companies, one listed and the other unlisted. Both blockholders (Lanka Milk Foods Limited (now known as Lanka Milk Foods (CWE) Plc and Milford) are part of Stassens Limited, a company controlled by the ultimate controlling shareholder of both Commercial Bank and DFCC Bank. This individual investor uses a vertical group structure enhanced by circular and cross-holdings below 20 percent to retain control of Distilleries Company.

Tracing the ultimate controlling owner of the 11th sample — Hatton National Bank — is more complicated. Hatton National Bank has one blockholder, a non-resident institutional investor. Since this investor appears not to have any other economic stakes in Hatton National Bank, and its economic stake is below 20 percent, this investor is disregarded for purposes of this analysis. Five shareholders of Hatton National Bank among the 20 largest are part of a group of companies with economic stakes amounting to 26.13 percent of the total shareholding of Hatton National Bank.[97] Disregarding the cross-holdings and circular holdings (i.e., horizontal group structures) below 20 percent and on the basis of vertical group structures alone, the ultimate controlling shareholder of Hatton National Bank is the controlling shareholder of the group of companies to which these five shareholders of Hatton National Bank belong. This controlling shareholder is the same individual investor who controls Commercial Bank, Distilleries Company and DFCC Bank. This individual investor uses a vertical group structure enhanced by circular and cross-holdings to maintain control of Hatton National Bank.

The 16th sample company, Aitken Spence, has three blockholders. Two blockholders (Distilleries Company and Sri Lanka Insurance Corporation Limited) belong to the same group of companies with economic stakes amounting to 29.13 percent.[98] On vertical group structures, the ultimate controlling shareholder of Aitken Spence is the same individual who controls Commercial Bank, Distilleries Company, DFCC Bank and Hatton National Bank.

While this individual investor is not a blockholder among the sample companies, he/she has managed through the use of vertical groups and

---

[96] Distilleries Company (n. 64), 15; Fig. 3.7.

[97] Hatton National Bank (n. 67), 77, and two other shareholders among the 20 largest shareholders are also group companies and have economic stakes amounting to 7.51 percent. This increases total control to over 33 percent; Fig. 3.7.

[98] Aitken Spence (n. 72), 115, includes an economic stake of 1.06 percent held by another group company among the 20 largest shareholders of Aitken Spence; Fig. 3.7.

pyramids enhanced through cross-holdings and circular holdings to acquire control rights in the 4th, 8th, 9th, 11th and 16th sample companies, while prima facie not appearing to have any or at most a negligible interest among the sample companies.

Figure 3.7 is based on the ownership and control structures of sample companies numbered 4th (Commercial Bank), 8th (Distilleries Company), 9th (DFCC Bank), 11th (Hatton National Bank) and 16th (Aitken Spence). The analysis is extended to a number of other shareholders (nonblock-holders) to exemplify that ultimate control is enhanced through relatively small economic stakes. Due to the interconnectedness of the sample companies, this analysis also extends to a number of unlisted public and private companies.[99]

Figure 3.8 is based on the fifth sample company, Carson Cumberbatch. The blockholders are two companies.[100] One of the blockholders is the seventh sample company and an associate of the company under analysis.[101] A family controls the other blockholder company, an investment company. This shifts the focus of the inquiry to the associate company (Bukit Darah), the seventh sample, with one blockholder, an investment company controlled by the same family. Thus, the ultimate controlling owner of both the fifth (Carson Cumberbatch) and seventh (Bukit Darah) sample companies is the same family.

The family with minimal holdings in both Carson Cumberbatch and Bukit Darah, has through the use of vertical groups structures, principally pyramid structures further enhanced by cross- and circular holdings, acquired control rights in excess of economic stakes in Bukit Darah and Carson Cumberbatch (Fig. 3.8).

Figure 3.9 is based on the 14th sample company Hemas Holdings (Fig. 3.9). As illustrated,[102] there are four blockholder investment companies with nearly equal economic stakes in Hemas Holdings. Control of these investment companies vests with a family. The actual economic stake of this family in Hemas Holdings amounts to 12.69 percent held among four brothers. However, due to the control of the blockholder investment companies, this family controls in excess of 83 percent of Hemas Holdings.

---

[99] Fig. 3.7 shaded. Distinct arrow lines are for ease of reference.
[100] Fig. 3.8.
[101] Carson Cumberbatch (n. 61), 5.
[102] Fig. 3.9.

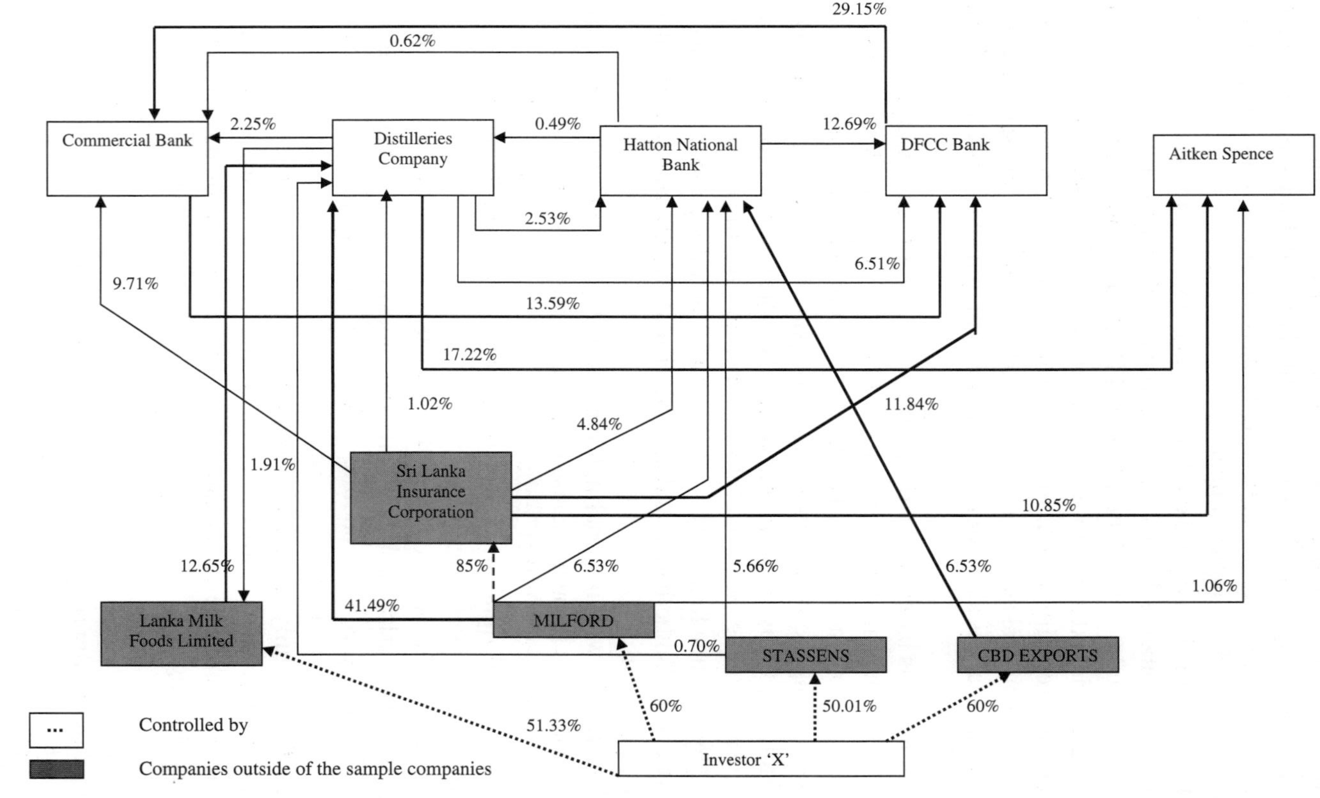

Figure 3.7: Ownership and Control Structures of Commercial Bank, Distilleries Company, DFCC Bank, Hatton National Bank and Aitken Spence.

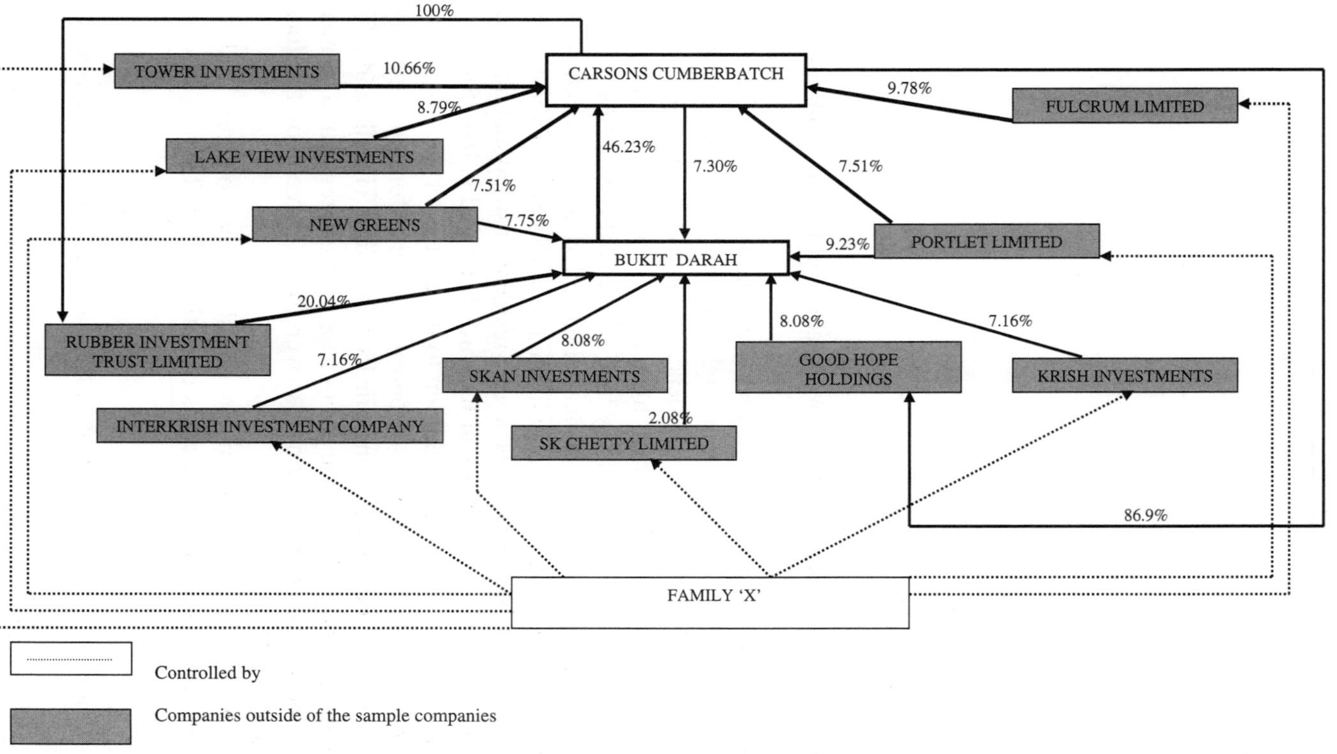

Figure 3.8: Ownership and Control Structures of Carson Cumberbatch and Bukit Darah.

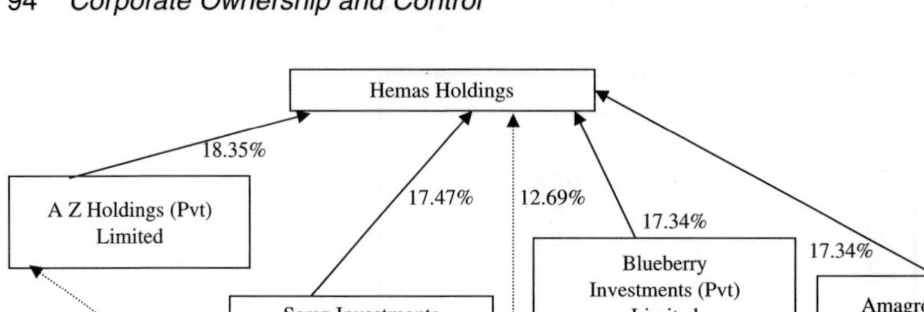

Figure 3.9: Ownership and Control Structures of Hemas Holdings.

There are no deviations from the one-share one-vote and no shares are issued with multiple classes of voting rights to gain control in excess of economic stakes. There is also no evidence of the use of vertical or horizontal group structures.[103] The family maintains its control stake in Hemas Holdings through the use of privately held investment companies.

The 17th sample company Richard Pieris, has three blockholders (Fig. 3.10).[104] As illustrated,[105] an individual controls two of the blockholders. The third blockholder is a non-resident institutional investor without any further control rights in Richard Pieris and is therefore, not subjected to further analysis. In addition to the control of the two blockholders, the individual investor also controls two other foreign-registered companies with significant holdings in Richard Pieris (fourth and fifth largest shareholders). Through the use of four overseas registered companies, this individual investor controls over 61.38 percent of the total shareholdings of Richard Pieris.

There are no deviations from the one-share one-vote rule and no shares are issued with multiple classes of voting rights. There is also no

---

[103] The requirements of a pyramid are not fulfilled, as there is no publicly traded company in between.
[104] Richard Pieris (n. 73), 99.
[105] Fig. 3.10.

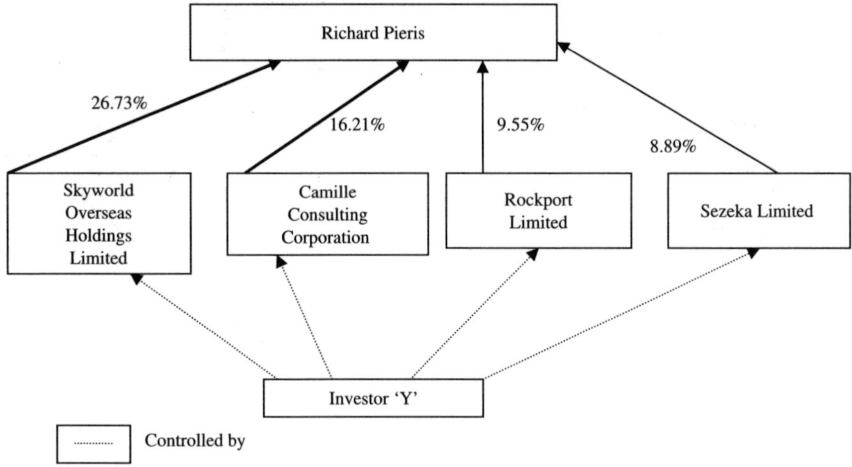

Figure 3.10: Ownership and Control Structure of Richard Pieris.

evidence of vertical or horizontal group structures. Although not listed among the 20 largest shareholders of Richard Pieris, this investor is able to maintain control of the company through the control of four non-resident privately held investment companies.

The 18th sample company, Ceylon Theatres, has three blockholders with economic stakes amounting to 69.89 percent (Fig. 3.11).[106] As illustrated,[107] a family controls the economic stakes of the three blockholders, and an additional 13.3 percent economic stake is held in the names of the family. There is no evidence of the use of any vertical or horizontal group structures or deviations from the one-share one-vote rule and no shares are issued with multiple classes of voting rights. Therefore, this family's control of Ceylon Theatres is commensurate to its economic stake held through privately held investment companies.

The objective of this analysis was to ascertain whether the shareholders in the sample companies have control rights in excess of their economic stakes. As many as 12 of the 14 companies analysed, (i.e., 85 percent), are identified as having a controlling shareholder, that is, a blockholder with control rights (direct and indirect voting rights) exceeding 20 percent. Such

---

[106] Ceylon Theatres (n. 74), 6.
[107] Fig. 3.11.

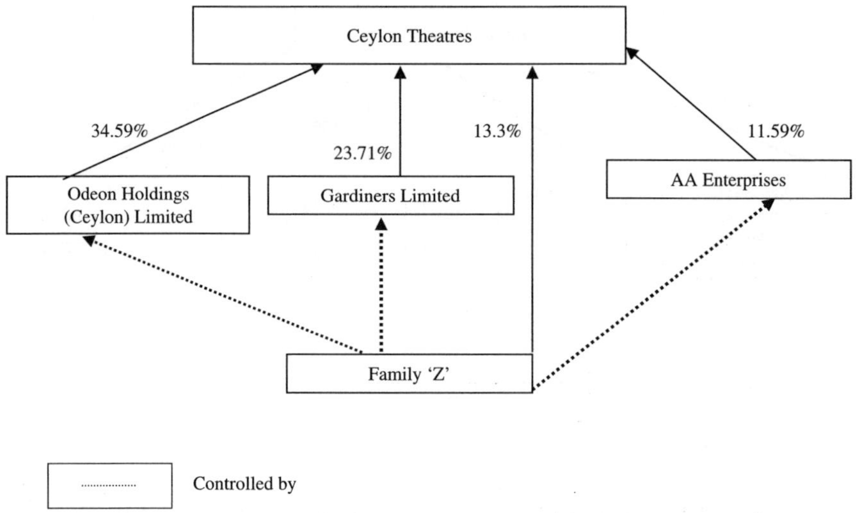

Figure 3.11: Ownership and Control Structure of Ceylon Theatres.

control rights are in excess of the blockholder's economic stakes in the sample companies, which are mostly below 20 percent.

The above analysis on the control rights of blockholders among the sample demonstrates a distinction between ownership (i.e., cash flow rights) and control rights in Sri Lanka with controlling shareholders having control in excess of their ownership stakes.

(b) *Mechanisms to Separate Ownership from Control*

At this stage of the analysis, the use of (i) group structures and (ii) shares with superior voting rights, are evaluated as mechanisms that *separate* ownership from control rights and also *enhance* control rights in Sri Lanka, while (iii) the participation of controlling shareholders in the management of the companies is evaluated as a mechanism to *enhance* control.

(i) Group Structures

There is widespread evidence of the use of vertical and horizontal group structures among the sample companies. Controlling shareholders in 8 of the 14 companies under analysis, use vertical and horizontal group structures as a mechanism to separate ownership from control and obtain control rights in excess of their economic stakes.

A majority of the controlling shareholders use vertical group structures, that is, parent–subsidiary relationships or pyramid structures, to separate ownership or cash flow rights from control rights, and gain control rights in excess of economic stakes. The cross-holdings and circular holdings amongst the companies, in most instances are not large enough to warrant control by themselves without the use of vertical structures. Cross-holdings and circular holdings are used to enhance control rights rather than as a mechanism to obtain control.

Carson Cumberbatch, the fifth sample company is illustrative of a horizontal group structure. Cross-holdings within the horizontal group structure are exemplified by the interconnected relationship between Carson Cumberbatch, Bukit Darah and Rubber Investment Trust (Fig. 3.12).[108] Bukit Darah has an economic stake of 46.23 percent in

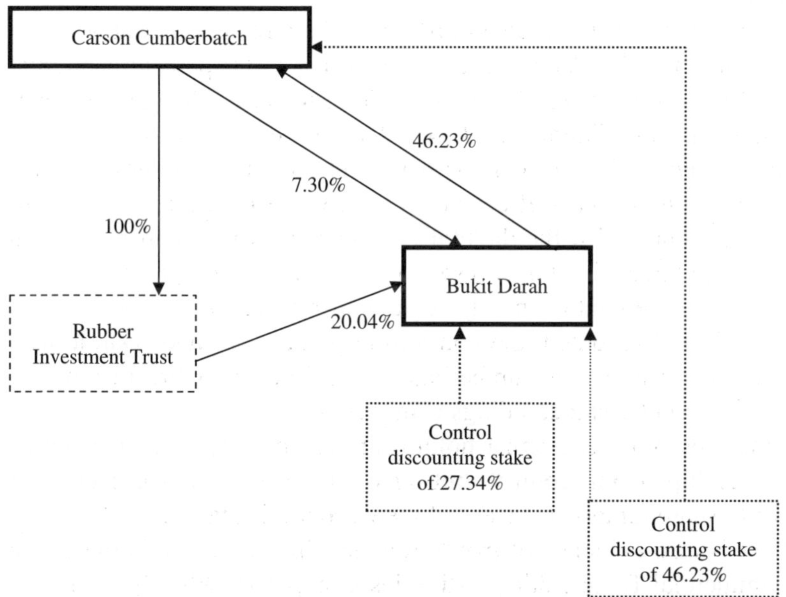

Figure 3.12: Cross-Holdings in Carson Cumberbatch.

---

[108] Fig. 3.12.

Carson Cumberbatch, and Carson Cumberbatch has an economic stake of 7.3 percent in Bukit Darah. Additionally, Rubber Investment Trust has an economic stake of 20.04 percent in Bukit Darah, and is in turn a wholly owned subsidiary of Carson Cumberbatch.

The cross-holding pattern in Carson Cumberbatch has two primary effects: (i) it enables the holders of economic stakes in Bukit Darah to discount the economic stake of 27.34 percent (i.e., 7.3 percent and 20.04 percent) held and controlled by Carson Cumberbatch in Bukit Darah and thereby exercise control over Bukit Darah and (ii) if the other holders of economic stakes in Bukit Darah are also holders of economic stakes in Carson Cumberbatch, these other economic stakeholders are able to exercise control over Carson Cumberbatch in excess of their economic stakes, by discounting the economic stakes held by Bukit Darah in Carson Cumberbatch. In short, the cross-holdings reinforce the control rights of the other shareholders of Bukit Darah.

In this instance, cross-holdings serve to separate ownership from control and enable controlling shareholders to obtain control in excess of their economic stakes.

Carson Cumberbatch is also illustrative of a circular holding horizontal group structure.[109] Carson Cumberbatch has a 100 percent economic stake in Rubber Investment Trust, which in turn, has a 20.04 percent economic stake in Bukit Darah, and Bukit Darah in turn, has a 46.23 percent economic stake in Carson Cumberbatch. The circular holdings in this instance have two primary effects: (i) it enables the operation of the companies as a group and if the directors of the respective companies act in concert, perpetuate director control of each of the companies and (ii) when the 27.34 percent economic stake held by Carson Cumberbatch in Bukit Darah is discounted, the controlling owners of Bukit Darah have control rights over Carson Cumberbatch with little or no direct economic stake due to circular shareholdings (Fig. 3.13).

In the present case, circular holdings have not only separated corporate ownership from control but also enhanced control rights of controlling shareholders in excess of their economic stakes.

There is also evidence of pyramid ownership structures between the 4th (Commercial Bank), 8th (Distilleries Company), 9th (DFCC Bank)

---

[109] Fig. 3.13.

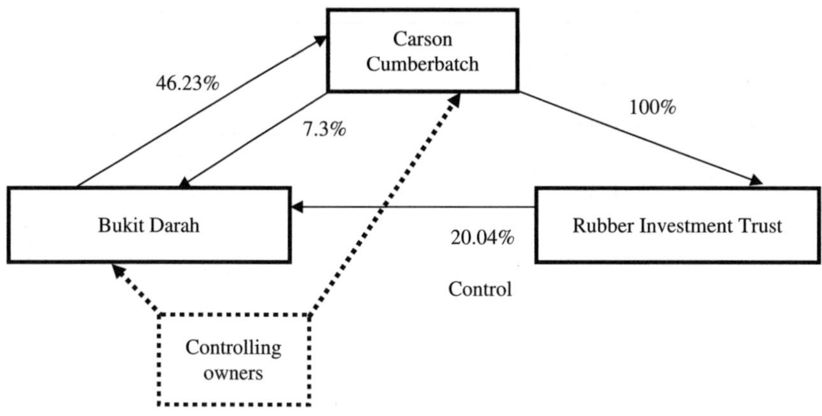

Figure 3.13: Circular Holdings in Carson Cumberbatch.

and 16th (Aitken Spence) sample companies.[110] Pyramid ownership structures separate ownership from control and enable the controlling shareholders to maintain control in excess of economic stakes in nearly all the sample companies.

In contrast to Carson Cumberbatch and Bukit Darah, there is heavy reliance on vertical ownership structures, primarily pyramids among these four sample companies (Fig. 3.14). Although, relatively straightforward than the ownership structures surrounding Carson Cumberbatch and Bukit Darah, the controlling shareholder of this pyramid effectively controls four of the largest companies in Sri Lanka in terms of market capitalisation, even though individually holding negligible economic stakes in each of the companies. An interesting factor is that, in attempting to satisfy the precondition of a controlling shareholder presence in the pyramid structure, no single controlling shareholder is immediately apparent unless the holdings among the vertical group structure companies controlled by this individual investor are amalgamated.

The effect of pyramid structures is that they enable an investor,[111] to separate ownership from control and obtain control rights in a company in which such investor has no significant economic stake. A negative feature of pyramid structures is that they obscure ownership data transparency.

---

[110] Fig. 3.14.
[111] Fig. 3.14.

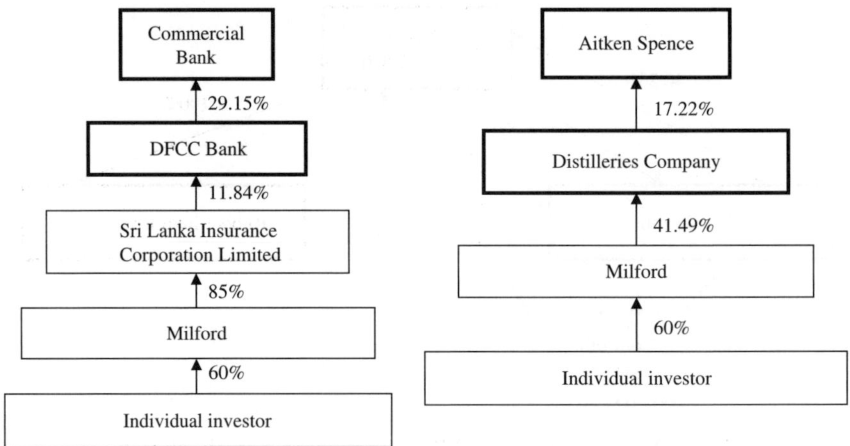

Figure 3.14: Pyramid Ownership Structures.

(ii) Shares with Superior Voting Rights

Among the companies in the sample, two financial institutions, Commercial Bank and Hatton National Bank, have non-voting ordinary shares in issue. While the issue of non-voting shares dilutes ownership, they do not enhance control rights. In the sample, no shares are issued with superior voting rights and the use of shares with superior voting rights is unusual in Sri Lanka.

(iii) Participation in Management

To consider the participation of controlling shareholders in the management of the companies as a control-enhancing mechanism, the focus of the inquiry in this section is on how often an ultimate controlling shareholder is a member of the board of directors of the companies in the sample (Table 3.3). As illustrated below,[112] 12 among the 14 companies under analysis in the sample have one or more controlling shareholders. In all the 12 companies, the controlling shareholders or their nominees are members of the board of directors. In over 75 percent of the companies,

---

[112] Table 3.3.

Table 3.3: Participation in Management.

	Name of company	Controlling shareholder(s) >20%	Is ultimate controlling shareholder(s) or nominee a member of the board of directors?	Is ultimate controlling shareholder the MD/CEO or Chairman/Deputy Chairman of the board of directors?
1	Dialog Telekom	—	—	—
2	John Keells	No	—	—
3	Sri Lanka Telecom	2	Yes	Yes (State nominee is Chairman Nippon Telegraph and Telecommunications Corporation of Japan nominee is CEO)
4	Commercial Bank	1	Yes	No
5	Carson Cumberbatch	1	Yes	Yes [Deputy Chairman]
6	Lanka IOC Limited	—	—	—
7	Bukit Darah	1	Yes	Yes (Chairman and Deputy Chairman)
8	Distilleries Company	1	Yes	Yes (MD)

(Continued)

Table 3.3: (*Continued*)

	Name of company	Controlling shareholder(s) >20%	Is ultimate controlling shareholder(s) or nominee a member of the board of directors?	Is ultimate controlling shareholder the MD/CEO or Chairman/Deputy Chairman of the board of directors?
9	DFCC Bank	1	Yes	No
10	Asian Hotels	1	Yes	Yes Same board as holding company
11	Hatton National Bank	1	Yes	No
12	Ceylon Tobacco	—	—	—
13	Overseas Realty (Ceylon) Limited	—	—	—
14	Hemas Holdings	1	Yes	Yes (Chairman/Deputy Chairman/CEO)
15	Nestle Lanka Limited	—	—	—
16	Aitken Spence	1	Yes	Yes (Chairman)
17	Richard Pieris	1	Yes	Yes (Chairman/CEO)

(*Continued*)

Table 3.3: (*Continued*)

	Name of company	Controlling shareholder(s) >20%	Is ultimate controlling shareholder(s) or nominee a member of the board of directors?	Is ultimate controlling shareholder the MD/CEO or Chairman/Deputy Chairman of the board of directors?
18	Ceylon Theatres	1	Yes	Yes (Chairman/Deputy Chairman/CEO)
19	National Development Bank	No	—	—
20	James Finlay and Company (Colombo) Limited	—	—	—
	Total: 14 Companies analysed	12/14 85.7%	12/12 100%	9/12 75%

▢ Companies with over 50 percent held by non-resident companies.

the controlling shareholders are also the Managing Director (MD) or CEO or chairman or deputy chairman.

Thus, while there is separation of management from ownership (i.e., cash flow rights), separation of control from management is rare. The high percentage of controlling shareholders participating in the management of the companies they control reveals that management participation by controlling shareholders is an important mechanism for enhancing control rights.

Further, the fact that the ultimate controlling shareholder is also the MD or CEO or chairman or deputy chairman in over 85 percent of the sample companies reflects the importance attached to these positions within the board of directors.

The above analysis on the mechanisms that separate corporate ownership from control, demonstrates that controlling shareholders use group structures not only to separate ownership from control, but to also obtain control rights in excess of their economic stakes. Participation of controlling shareholders in the management of the companies they control is a mechanism to enhance control rights and results in significant costs within controlling shareholder systems.

(c) *Nature of Controlling Shareholders*

At this final stage of the analysis, the findings from the nature of corporate ownership[113] are evaluated against the nature of controlling shareholders in Sri Lanka (Table 3.4).

Of the 20 sample companies,[114] 6 are subsidiaries of multinationals and are not a part of this analysis. Of the remainder, two companies (John Keells and National Development Bank) do not have a controlling shareholder. One (Asian Hotels) is a subsidiary controlled by a widely held parent company. Both the Government of Sri Lanka and a foreign company on a 20 percent control stake, have control of Sri Lanka Telecom, the third largest sample company. An individual investor controls five of the sample companies, while another investor controls the 17th sample company (Richard Pieris). A family controls two of the sample companies, Carson Cumberbatch and Bukit Darah. Two families control the 14th and

---

[113] Table 3.2 and Fig. 3.6.
[114] Table 3.4.

Table 3.4: Nature of Controlling Shareholders.

	Name of company	Nature of controlling shareholders
1	Dialog Telekom	—
2	John Keells	N/A
3	Sri Lanka Telecom	State, non-resident company
4	Commercial Bank	Individual
5	Carson Cumberbatch	Family
6	Lanka IOC Limited	—
7	Bukit Darah	Family
8	Distilleries Company	Individual
9	DFCC Bank	Individual
10	Asian Hotels	Resident group
11	Hatton National Bank	Individual
12	Ceylon Tobacco	—
13	Overseas Realty (Ceylon) Limited	—
14	Hemas Holdings	Family
15	Nestle Lanka Limited	—
16	Aitken Spence	Individual
17	Richard Pieris	Individual
18	Ceylon Theatres	Family
19	National Development Bank	N/A
20	James Finlay and Company (Colombo) Limited	—

☐ Companies with over 50 percent held by non-resident companies.
N/A — Not available.

18th sample companies, Hemas Holdings and Ceylon Theatres, respectively. Thus, 85 percent of the sample companies under analysis in this study have a controlling shareholder.

Figure 3.15 assists in the comparison of the findings from the nature of corporate ownership (i.e., based on the 20 largest shareholders among

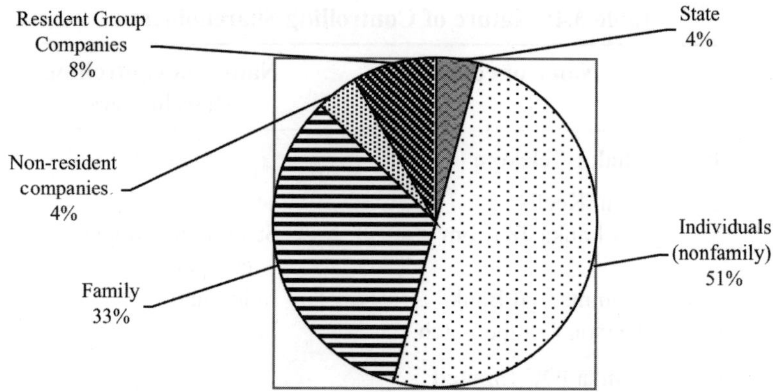

Figure 3.15: Nature of Controlling Shareholders.

the sample companies),[115] against the nature of controlling shareholders in Sri Lanka. The largest shareholders in terms of economic stakes (or cash flow holdings) are resident group companies (55 percent), resident non-group companies (12 percent), non-resident institutional investors (8 percent) and the state (7 percent).[116] In contrast, the ultimate controlling owners for the same sample of companies are individuals (51 percent), families (33 percent) and resident group companies (8 percent).[117]

The identities of controlling shareholders in Sri Lanka are therefore, distinct from the identities of the largest shareholders among the sample. This distinction demonstrates the clear separation of corporate ownership (cash flow rights) and control rights in Sri Lanka and highlights the ability of controlling shareholder systems to obscure the identity of ultimate controlling owners.

(d) *Summary*

The objective at the second stage of the analysis was to determine whether corporate ownership in Sri Lanka is distinct from corporate control. To achieve this objective, it was necessary to establish whether the shareholders in the sample companies have control rights in excess of

---

[115] Fig. 3.6.
[116] Table 3.2.
[117] Fig. 3.15.

their economic stakes, scrutinise the mechanisms shareholders use to enhance control rights in excess of economic stakes and analyse the nature and identity of the ultimate controlling shareholders

The controlling shareholders in the sample companies have control rights in excess of their economic stakes, obtained through the use of vertical and horizontal group structures and enhanced by participation in the management of the sample companies. The identities of the controlling shareholders are also distinct from the identities of the 20 largest shareholders among the sample companies.

As summarised in Table 3.5, the analysis also makes apparent the existence of a distinction between corporate ownership and control in Sri Lanka.

3.4. Corporate Ownership and Control: The Challenges Facing Corporate Governance in Sri Lanka

Differences in the governance of an economy's companies affect its macroeconomic performance, economic growth and development. Since ownership and control structures underlie the governance of companies, this section draws implications for corporate governance in Sri Lanka arising from the analysis of ownership and control structures of its companies.

3.4.1. *Findings*

(a) *Concentration of Ownership*

There is a high degree of ownership concentration in Sri Lanka. Of the 252 companies listed on the CSE, 1 percent of the total number of shareholders, own an average of 78.21 percent of all of the shares of the companies. In contrast, approximately 99 percent of the total number of shareholders, own economic stakes amounting to only 21.79 percent of the companies listed on the CSE.

(b) *Nature of Corporate Ownership*

On the basis of economic stakes, resident companies are the largest shareholders of the 20 sample companies and hold over 67 percent of the

Table 3.5: The Distinction between Ownership and Control in Sri Lanka.

	Name of company	Blockholder(s) >10%	Controlling shareholder(s) >20%	Mechanisms to enhance control in excess of economic stake	Is ultimate controlling shareholder(s) or nominee(s) a member of the board of directors?	Nature of controlling shareholder
1	Dialog Telekom	—	—	—	—	—
2	John Keells	1	No	—	—	—
3	Sri Lanka Telecom	2	2	None	Yes	1. State 2. Non-resident institutional investor
4	Commercial Bank	2	1	Vertical/horizontal group structures	Yes	Individual
5	Carson Cumberbatch	2	1	Vertical/horizontal group structures	Yes	Family
6	Lanka IOC Limited	—	—	—	—	—
7	Bukit Darah	1	1	Vertical/horizontal group structures	Yes	Family
8	Distilleries Company	2	1	Vertical/horizontal group structures	Yes	Individual

(Continued)

Table 3.5: (*Continued*)

	Name of company	Blockholder(s) >10%	Controlling shareholder(s) >20%	Mechanisms to enhance control in excess of economic stake	Is ultimate controlling shareholder(s) or nominee(s) a member of the board of directors?	Nature of controlling shareholder
9	DFCC Bank	5	1	Vertical/horizontal group structures	Yes	Individual
10	Asian Hotels	1	1	Vertical group structure	Yes	Resident group
11	Hatton National Bank	1	1	Vertical /horizontal group structures	Yes	Individual
12	Ceylon Tobacco	—	—	—	—	—
13	Overseas Realty (Ceylon) Limited	—	—	—	—	—
14	Hemas Holdings	4	1	Participation in management	Yes	Family
15	Nestle Lanka Limited	—	—	—	—	—
16	Aitken Spence	3	1	Vertical /horizontal group structures	Yes	Individual

(*Continued*)

Table 3.5: (*Continued*)

	Name of company	Blockholder(s) >10%	Controlling shareholder(s) >20%	Mechanisms to enhance control in excess of economic stake	Is ultimate controlling shareholder(s) or nominee(s) a member of the board of directors?	Nature of controlling shareholder
17	Richard Pieris	3	1	Participation in management	Yes	Individual
18	Ceylon Theatres	3	1	Participation in management	Yes	Family
19	National Development Bank	1	No			
20	James Finlay and Company (Colombo) Limited					
Total: 14 companies analysed		14/14 100%	12/14 85%		12/12 100%	

▢ Companies with over 50 percent held by non-resident companies.

shareholdings. Resident group companies have the largest economic stakes at 55 percent, other non-group resident companies have significant holdings of 12 percent. State ownership of the cash flow rights of the sample companies is at 7 percent, while non-resident institutional investors hold a significant 8 percent of the shareholdings among the sample companies. Individual investor holdings account for a total of 10 percent and of these, families have economic stakes amounting to 5 percent. The holdings of resident institutional investors are relatively small at 2 percent.

(c) *Distinction between Corporate Ownership and Control*

Corporate ownership in Sri Lanka is distinct from corporate control. This conclusion is grounded on an examination of the control rights of blockholders, the mechanisms that separate ownership from control and the identity of controlling shareholders contrasted against the identity of the largest shareholders among the sample companies.

(i) Control Rights of the Blockholders

Of the companies analysed, over 85 percent are identified as having a controlling shareholder. Although an exact measurement of control rights is not undertaken and is not necessary for a study of this nature, the control rights of the blockholders are excessive in comparison to their economic stakes.

(ii) Mechanisms to Separate Ownership from Control

Controlling shareholders in 8 of the 14 companies under analysis use vertical and horizontal group structures as mechanisms to separate ownership from control. A majority of the controlling shareholders use vertical group structures, that is, parent–subsidiary relationships or pyramids to separate ownership from control and obtain control rights in excess of their economic stakes. Cross-holdings and circular holdings are used to enhance control rights rather than as a mechanism to obtain control rights.

Shares with superior voting rights are not a popular mechanism to separate ownership from control in Sri Lanka. In contrast, in over 85 percent of the companies with controlling shareholders, the controlling shareholders or their nominees, are members of the board of directors. In over 75 percent of these companies, the controlling shareholders are also the MD or CEO or chairman or deputy chairman. This is indicative of the fact that there is no separation of *management* from control in Sri Lanka.

(iii) Identity of Controlling Shareholders

The ultimate controlling owners among the same sample of companies are individuals and families, controlling over 51 percent and 33 percent of the sample companies, respectively. Thus, controlling shareholders in Sri Lanka (individuals and families) are distinct to the largest shareholders (resident group and non-group companies) in terms of economic stakes.

3.4.2. *The Challenges facing Corporate Governance in Sri Lanka*

The primary objective of this chapter is to characterise the challenges facing corporate governance in Sri Lanka by an examination of the ownership and control structures of its companies.

The findings emphasise the important characteristics of corporate ownership and control in Sri Lanka.[118] These findings are of utmost importance in identifying the challenges facing corporate governance as the characteristics of corporate ownership and control, determine the form of the agency conflict in corporate governance.[119] The discussion below defines the agency problem and the main features of the challenge facing corporate governance in Sri Lanka by reference to the characteristics of its corporate ownership and control structures.

(a) *Concentration of Ownership*

The first finding is the high degree of ownership concentration in Sri Lanka. The concentration of corporate wealth has the ability to negatively affect the legal and institutional framework and the manner in which

---

[118] Section 3.4.1.

[119] Chapter 2. Further, corporate ownership and control also throw light on the patterns of financing within a country.

economic activity within the country is conducted.[120] It could result in a barrier to any future policy reform. This is a policy challenge facing the reform of corporate governance in Sri Lanka.

Concentration of ownership as a starting point may provide monitoring incentives and long-term planning coupled with reputational benefits that lead to better corporate performance and competitiveness. However, it may also lead to the pursuit of goals that lie in the interests of the blockholders, and not in the interests of the minority shareholders such as expropriation of corporate assets and entrenchment of blockholders in positions of corporate management.

At this stage of the analysis, the agency conflict is between the blockholder and minority shareholders. It is also likely that this agency problem will extend between the blockholder and other corporate constituencies due to the concentration of corporate wealth in the hands of a few.

(b) *Nature of Corporate Ownership*

The second finding of the analysis is that companies are among the largest blockholders. This finding underscores the lack of financing within the country,[121] and demonstrates the need to develop capital markets and attract global capital flows into the country.[122] This is another challenge facing the formulation of an agenda of corporate governance reform in Sri Lanka.

With group companies as the largest blockholders, the agency conflict at this stage can now be defined with clarity as between corporate groups and minority shareholders. In the light of group affiliation, the beneficial aspects of concentrated corporate ownership, that is, monitoring and long-term planning will be tailored to suit group interests,[123] and the reputational focus shifts from that of an individual owner to a corporate entity. Further, the agency conflict between corporate groups and minority shareholders also gives rise to the specific agency problem of tunnelling. Business groups in many developing countries are also found

---

[120] Claessens *et al.* (n. 8), 110, by undue influence.

[121] Identified as a primary cause of the prevailing ownership structures in Sri Lanka, Chapter 4.

[122] This is reinforced by findings that non-resident institutional investor's economic stakes amount to only 8 percent of the shareholdings among the sample companies.

[123] Other benefits from group affiliation are flexibilities in intragroup financing, the reduction of transaction costs, economies of scale in production etc.

to have undue political influence, giving rise to ancillary corporate governance challenges such as unfair trade practices and monopolies.[124]

(c) *Distinction between Corporate Ownership and Control*

The presence of controlling shareholders changes the paradigm in different ways. The agency conflict shifts between controlling shareholders and minority shareholders. Further, the presence of two or more blockholders unconnected to the controlling shareholder extends the agency conflict between a controlling shareholder and other blockholders.

The nature of the agency problems arising from this two-pronged agency conflict between controlling shareholders and minority shareholders, and controlling shareholders and blockholders, differs according to the identity of the controlling shareholders and the mechanisms used by such controlling shareholder to separate ownership from control.

The primary agency problems arising due to the agency conflict between controlling shareholders and minority shareholders are the extraction of private benefits of control by controlling shareholders to the detriment of the minority, the ability of controlling shareholders to gain positions of management in companies controlled by them and the resultant entrenchment and in certain instances, the spill-over effects of certain interfamily feuds into the corporate sector.

The identification of individuals and families as ultimate controlling shareholders implies that any monitoring or long-term planning by such controlling shareholders depends on the controlling shareholders' involvement in the management of these companies and on other companies within the control of these controlling shareholders. However, the reputational benefits of an identified blockholder will not be available in a controlling shareholder scenario as the ultimate controlling shareholder is often invisible due to the opaque controlling structures.

The concentration of corporate control in the hands of a few families or individuals also creates powerful incentives and the ability to lobby government agencies and officials for preferential treatment on contracts

---

[124] In the context of India, T Khanna and Y Yafeh, Business Groups in Developing Countries: Paragons or Parasites? (2005), European Corporate Governance Institute Finance Working Paper 92, http://ssrn.com/abstract=787625 [10 January 2006].

and obtain non-market-based financing.[125] This is enhanced by the political influence and connections wielded by wealthy families and powerful individuals. This is another challenge facing corporate governance in countries with families and individuals as controlling owners.

The findings suggest that the primary mechanism used to separate ownership from control is the use of vertical and horizontal group structures. The findings also suggest that the most popular mechanism used to separate ownership from control and for controlling shareholders to obtain control rights in excess of their economic stakes are pyramids. Morck and Yeung, identify control pyramids as 'one feature of an institutionally deficient economy'.[126] Control pyramids enable a handful of wealthy families or individuals govern the greater part of a country's corporate wealth. This is because pyramids allow families and individuals to control corporate assets worth vastly more than their own wealth. By permitting control pyramids, most countries entrust the governance of their corporate sectors to a few wealthy families and individuals. This means that the governance of companies within a country may ultimately not be entrusted to the most able people in the country and this is another challenge facing corporate governance in Sri Lanka.

Pyramids also affect the agency conflict between controlling shareholders and minority shareholders, by recreating the same incentive agency problems as in widely held companies, with the only difference being that in pyramids, it is the corporate insiders (i.e., controlling shareholders) spending the outside (minority) shareholders' funds. However, agency problems within pyramids in Sri Lanka are likely to be worse than in widely held companies. This is because widely held companies that are severely mismanaged suffer share price declines. These, in turn, trigger shareholder lawsuits, hostile takeovers etc. These, disciplining devices are unlikely to be effective in Sri Lanka with its weak capital markets, poor enforcement mechanisms, concentrated corporate ownership and controlling shareholder system. This is another challenge facing corporate governance in Sri Lanka.

The findings suggest a lack of separation of management from ownership, which results in an agency conflict between the management and the

---

[125] Claessens *et al.* (n. 8), 109.

[126] R Morck and B Yeung, Special Issues Relating to Corporate Governance and Family Control (2004), World Bank Policy Research Working Paper 3406, http://econ.worldbank.org/files/38739_wps3406.pdf [10 May 2005], 3.

minority shareholders. The difference between this agency conflict (i.e., management and minority) and the agency conflict in widely held companies is that here the management is comprised of and controlled by controlling shareholders. The resultant agency problem in this scenario occurs when controlling shareholders in positions of management utilise such positions to engage in tunnelling. Another agency problem is the likely entrenchment of controlling shareholders in management positions who are unlikely to be ousted even in the event of mismanagement. Positions of management also enable controlling shareholders to make corporate decisions in the interest of group companies within their control.

On the one hand, the agency conflict between controlling shareholders and blockholders also gives rise to a number of agency problems, such as board disputes, which affect the performance and proper functioning of companies. On the other hand, blockholders may play a monitoring role and help constrain the controlling shareholders.

Control in excess of economic stakes among controlling shareholders in Sri Lanka also poses challenges for corporate governance. Control without a commensurate economic stake (i.e., cash flow right) suggests that controlling shareholders have little actual wealth tied up in the companies they control. This negatively affects the beneficial aspects of monitoring and planning ideally expected from a blockholder. Controlling shareholders and blockholders also stifle capital markets by affecting the liquidity of shares with concentrated and controlling shareholdings.

The above discussion, demonstrates that the characteristics of corporate ownership and control in Sri Lanka, inform and determine the form of the agency problem and the wider policy issues facing corporate governance in Sri Lanka. It is the different agency problems that arise due to the distinct agency conflicts between the different corporate constituencies that characterise the main features of the corporate governance challenges facing Sri Lanka.[127]

3.5. Conclusion

This chapter provides a factual basis for this study. An analysis into the reform of corporate governance in developing countries should begin with

---

[127] For a cost–benefit analysis of the corporate governance challenges facing Sri Lanka, see Chapter 5.

a focus on local market structures, such as corporate ownership and control structures that define the adaptation, efficiency and effectiveness of corporate governance. This chapter applies this thesis in practice, by examining the corporate ownership and control structures in Sri Lanka and thereafter, characterising the main features of the challenges facing corporate governance in Sri Lanka.

The greatest challenge in corporate governance is to minimise the agency conflicts and resulting agency problems. This involves a balancing of conflicting interests among different corporate constituencies. This chapter by its examination of the corporate ownership and control structures in Sri Lanka and characterisation of the main features of the challenges facing corporate governance in Sri Lanka takes the first step towards meeting such challenges.

CHAPTER 4

Determinants of Ownership and Control Structures in Sri Lanka

4.1. Introduction

The analysis in Chapter 3 reveals that there is a high degree of corporate ownership concentration in Sri Lanka with approximately 1 percent of the total number of shareholders' economic stakes averaging 78.21 percent of all of the shares of the listed companies. Group companies are the largest blockholders of all of the shares of the listed companies and control is leveraged in excess of economic stakes through pyramids and cross-shareholdings, and individuals and families are the ultimate controlling shareholders.

With respect to corporate ownership and control, Sri Lanka is no different from several Asian and Western countries.[1] It is an established fact in contemporary corporate governance literature that corporate ownership of companies is dispersed in the UK and the US, while concentrated in most other countries. Concentrated ownership, family businesses and corporate groups are common and voting rights frequently exceed the economic stakes of the controlling owners via pyramid structures and cross-holdings among many Asian companies.[2] These range from the *Keiretsus* in Japan and *Chaebols* in Korea to family businesses in India, like the Tatas, Birlas and Ambanis.

Explanations for the existence of different ownership structures among countries is dominated by the scholarship of LLSV who argue that ownership concentration is an adaptive response to poor investor protection.[3] In

---

[1] Chapter 3 reviews the literature on ownership and control around the world.

[2] S Claessens, S Djankove and L Lang, The Separation of Ownership and Control in East Asian Corporations (2000), 58 *Journal of Financial Economics*, 81, conduct a survey of ownership structures in nine Asian countries and find that voting rights exceed cash flow rights in all.

[3] LLSV, Law and Finance (1998), 106 *Journal of Political Economy*, 1113–1152.

their view, in the absence of adequate investor protection, large investors seek to protect their investments by the direct exercise of control through blockholdings.[4] A second explanation is the 'political' thesis advanced by Roe, who claims concentrated ownership is a defensive stance adopted by vulnerable shareholders in left-leaning 'social democracies.'[5] Social democracies reportedly press managers to unite with employees and not with distant shareholders. Owners must, therefore, seek other means to control managers and the chosen alternative is block ownership. Bebchuk offers another related explanation by advancing the 'rent protection' model of shareholder ownership, which claims that when the private benefits of control are high, publicly traded companies tend to have blockholdings.[6] In fact, concentrated ownership may persist simply owing to path dependencies.[7]

However, the determinants for the evolution and persistence of different ownership structures are often indigenous. A recent overview,[8] in an attempt to find explanations for the different ownership structures around the world, examines the historical evolution of ownership structures in 11 countries. Papers in this study argue that weaknesses in money and capital markets brought about concentrated ownership structures in France,[9] political relationships between dominant families and the spirit of entrepreneurship exhibited by dominant families explain the persistence of concentrated ownership in India,[10] estate taxes and state intervention brought

---

[4] ibid 1145.

[5] M Roe, Political Preconditions to Separating Ownership from Corporate Control (2000), 53 *Stanford Law Review*, 539; M Roe, *Political Determinants of Corporate Governance: Political Context, Corporate Impact* (Oxford University Press Oxford 2002).

[6] L Bebchuck, A Rent Protection Theory of Corporate Ownership and Control (1999), National Bureau of Economic Research Working Paper 7203, http://www.nber.org/papers/w7203 [5 November 2005].

[7] L Bebchuck and M Roe, A Theory of Path Dependence in Corporate Ownership and Governance (1999), 52 *Stanford Law Review*, 127.

[8] R Morck (ed.), *A History of Corporate Governance Around the World: Family Business Groups to Professional Managers* (University of Chicago Press Chicago 2005).

[9] A Murphy, Corporate Ownership in France: The Importance of History (2004), National Bureau of Economic Research Working Paper 10716, http://www.nber.org/papers/W10716 [3 July 2005].

[10] T Khanna and K Palepu, The Evolution of Concentrated Ownership in India: Broad Patterns and a History of the Indian Software Industry, in R Morck (ed.), *The History of Corporate Governance Around the World: Family Groups to Professional Managers* (University of Chicago Press Chicago 2005).

about a resurgence of concentrated ownership in Canada,[11] and cultural inertia, a long culture of family businesses and top-down reformers view of capital markets only as a source of funds, overlooking their role as disciplinary institutions, is attributed to the failure of the Chinese Corporations Law of 1904 and the illiquid Chinese stock markets in the 20th century.[12] In contrast, Franks *et al.* find the main cause of ownership dispersion in the UK was acquisitions, which occurred in the absence of investor protection in the first half of the 20th century due to reliance on informal relations of trust between directors and shareholders.[13] As Becht and De-Long[14] document in their study on ownership evolution in the US, powerful families established some of the largest corporations in the US and pyramidal groups were the norm at the beginning of the 20th century. However, activist judges aided by progressive politicians and a free press, ended the reign of the 'robber barons'.

The indigenous determinants of different ownership structures are of importance not only for their own intrinsic value but also because of the valuable insights such ownership evolution patterns provide for the framing of an effective corporate governance agenda. The objective of this chapter is to analyse the implications for corporate governance in Sri Lanka by an examination of the determinants of ownership and control structures in Sri Lanka. The rest of the chapter is organised as follows. Section 4.2 provides an outline of the evolution of corporate ownership in Sri Lanka. Section 4.3 examines probable causes and determinants for the persistence of concentrated ownership, group structures and control rights in excess of ownership

---

[11] R Morck *et al.*, The Rise and Fall of the Widely Held Firm: A History of Corporate Ownership in Canada, in R Morck (ed.), *A History of Corporate Governance Around the World: Family Business Groups to Professional Managers* (University of Chicago Press Chicago 2005).

[12] W Goetzmann and E Koll, The History of Corporate Ownership in China: State Patronage, Company Legislation, and the Issue of Control, in R Morck (ed.), *A History of Corporate Governance Around the World: Family Business Groups to Professional Managers* (University of Chicago Press Chicago 2005).

[13] J Franks, C Mayer and S Rossi, Ownership: Evolution and Regulation (2003), European Corporate Governance Institute Finance Working Paper 92, http://ssrn.com/abstract=354381 [10 January 2006]; J Franks, C Mayer and S Rossi, Spending Less Time with the Family: The Decline of Family Ownership in the UK (2004), European Corporate Governance Network Finance Working Paper 35, http://ssrn.com/abstract=493504 [25 July 2005], that is, by issuance of equity in the process of acquisitions.

[14] M Becht and J De-Long, Why Has There Been So Little Blockholding in America?, in R Morck (ed.), *A History of Corporate Governance Around the World: Family Business Groups to Professional Managers* (University of Chicago Press Chicago 2005).

in Sri Lanka. Section 4.4 concludes by drawing implications for corporate governance reform in Sri Lanka in the light of the identified causes and determinants for the persistence of concentrated ownership.

4.2.　An Outline of Ownership Evolution in Sri Lanka

4.2.1.　*Introduction*

Large companies almost everywhere in the world begin their lives as family companies and family firms predominate in countries whose industrial history is short.[15] The evolution of corporate ownership is best traced in countries whose industrial histories are long. However, Sri Lanka, the focus jurisdiction of this study, has an industrial history, which is relatively short. The ownership structures of Sri Lankan companies have had a small window of opportunity to evolve during the short space of two generations.

On the one hand, family ownership is a dominant theme in the business history of Sri Lanka. While listed Sri Lankan companies are linked to prominent families, the shareholdings of these families are on the wane. On the other hand, business groups linked to *nouveau-rich* entrepreneurs are on the rise. More interesting than the nature of ownership is the process by which it came about. The economic policies followed by successive Sri Lankan governments after independence, including the policy of 'Ceylonisation', nationalism, the establishment state-owned enterprises (SOEs) and subsequent privatisation programme can be identified as being among the forces of change.

The next four subsections by briefly tracing the industrial history of Sri Lanka, establish that concentrated ownership structures have evolved and persisted in Sri Lanka over several decades, but that (a) the identity of owners have changed significantly for companies established in the late 19th century; (b) founding families have managed to retain ownership stakes, albeit minor, in the indigenous companies established just prior to independence and (c) the establishment of SOEs followed by an active privatisation agenda led to higher levels of concentrated ownership.

---

[15] For example, the *chaebol* in South Korea. For a detailed discussion, see K Chung and Y Wang, Republic of Korea, in M Capulong, D Edwards and J Zhuang (eds.), *Corporate Governance and Finance in East Asia: A Study of Indonesia, Republic of Korea, Malaysia, Philippines and Thailand* (Asian Development Bank Manila 2001).

4.2.2. *Pre-Independence: Pre-1948*

While organised economic activity has existed in Sri Lanka for hundreds of years, it was relatively fragmented until the arrival of the trading powers of Europe in the early part of the 16th century. Being an agricultural society, trading did not receive prominence in the early Ceylonese kingdoms. With the rise of the spice trade, the Ceylonese kings were content with taxes and tributes and left the trading to the Moorish traders settled in the coastal areas of the country. It was with the advent of the British, followed by the loss of monopoly of the East India Company, that trading houses and produce and exchange brokers owned and managed by foreign nationals such as George Steuart & Company, Clark Spence & Company (later to become Aitken Spence and Company Limited), E. John & Company (later to become John Keells), Cumberbatch & Company (later to become Carson Cumberbatch), Chas P. Hayley & Company (later to become Hayleys Limited and thereafter, Hayleys Plc) came to be established. Some of the early businesses were branches of the UK companies, such as James Finlay and Company (Colombo) Limited (now Finlays Colombo Plc). Imperial commerce dominated the economy and local statutes were based on UK corporate legislation.[16]

Many of these early proprietorships and partnerships established in the late 19th century with listings on the CSE today, are the holding companies of diversified business groups. Originally established as trading and agency houses, these early companies ventured into the plantation industry during the tea and rubber boom years in the early part of the 20th century.[17] Commodity brokerage firms traditionally carried out share trading as part of their general commodity trading under an institutional set-up devised by the Colombo Share Brokers' Association established in 1896.[18] The activities of the share market in the form of direct dealings among brokers and plantation companies accounted for over 90 percent of all

---

[16] The joint stock company was first introduced in Ceylon (the former name for Sri Lanka) in 1853 by virtue of the Civil Law Ordinance No. 5 of 1852. The Joint Stock Companies Ordinance No. 4 of 1861 is based on the Joint Stock Companies Act 1856 (UK) while the subsequent Companies Ordinance No. 51 of 1938 is based on the Companies Act 1929 (UK).

[17] A Wright, *Twentieth Century Impressions of Ceylon* (Lloyd's Great Britain Publishing Company London 1907), 425–449.

[18] ibid 368; Colombo Stock Exchange, Introduction to the CSE, http://www.cse.lk/static/introduction_to_the_cse.htm [20 April 2009]; P Athukorala and S Jayasuriya, *Macroeconomic Policies, Crises, and Growth in Sri Lanka, 1969–90* (World Bank Washington DC 1994), 39.

shares listed for trading. Some of these plantation ventures obtained listings on the London Stock Exchange (LSE) and became known as sterling companies,[19] while others with listings with the Colombo Share Brokers' Association (later known as the Ceylon Brokers' Association), became known as rupee companies.[20]

Ownership and control separated from the original founding families in many of these early colonial companies with the obtaining of listings with the Ceylon Brokers' Association. In some instances, post-independent Sri Lankan companies amalgamated with, or acquired a controlling interest in these early trading companies resulting in ownership remaining concentrated but transferred to a Sri Lankan family. In other instances, the policy of 'Ceylonisation' after independence led to the selling out and retirement of many of the original founders and their heirs from these trading companies. Another reason for the disappearance of the original founders and their heirs from these companies is attributed to the speculative nature of their investment. The early pioneers ventured out to Ceylon as speculators[21] and therefore their stay in the country was short-lived.

Table 4.1 traces the history of seven colonial companies established in the 19th century.[22] Presently, as reflected in the final column of Table 4.1, none of the colonial companies' shares are held by any of the founding families or their heirs.

4.2.3. *Independence: 1948*

It is documented that the indigenous private sector and entrepreneurship at the time of independence in 1948 was weak.[23] A small number of indigenous business enterprises came into prominence in a supportive economic atmosphere. In contrast to the companies depicted in Table 4.1,

---

[19] For example, the Grand Central Ceylon Rubber Estates belonging to Carson Cumberbatch.

[20] — History of Ceylon Tea: Foundation Laid for a Plantation Enterprise, http://www. historyofceylontea.com/Tea_Feature/Foundation_%20Laid_for_a_Plantation_Enterprise. htm [20 April 2009].

[21] ST Villiers, *Mercantile Lore* (Ceylon Observer Press Colombo 1940), 1–5.

[22] The sample is representative of companies formed in the pre-1900 era and in existence today as holding companies of diversified business groups.

[23] G De Silva, Development of Entrepreneurship in Sri Lanka (1982), 12 *Central Bank of Sri Lanka Staff Studies*, 45.

Table 4.1: Historical Shareholdings of Seven Colonial Companies.[24]

Company	Established	Limited liability company	Publicly listed	Significant change in shareholding	Shareholding by founding family (2005)
Cargills (Ceylon) Limited	1844 as a partnership by two Scotsmen William Milne and David Sime Cargill[25]	1946	1946	1981 Acquisition of controlling interest by Ceylon Theatres, (family owned)	Nil
Carson Cumberbatch	1860 as agent for London Assurance	1913 Carson & Company 1947 merger between Carson & Company and Cumberbatch	1967	1986 acquisition of controlling interest by Sri Krishna Corporation, (family owned)	Nil

(Continued)

[24] *Sources*: Annual reports of the respective companies; Colombo Stock Exchange Historical milestones, http://www.cse.lk/home/main.jsp [3 June 2005]; Villiers (n. 21), 47–247; various issues of *Lanka Monthly Digest*.
[25] The founder of Burmah Oil Company, T Corley. *Cargill, David Sime (1826–1904), Oxford Dictionary of National Biography* (Oxford University Press Oxford 2004).

Table 4.1: (*Continued*)

Company	Established	Limited liability company	Publicly listed	Significant change in shareholding	Shareholding by founding family (2005)
Aitken Spence	1868 as a partnership by two Scotsman, Thomas Clark and Patrick Gordon Spence	1950	1983	2000–2003 acquisition of a controlling stake by Distilleries Company and Sri Lanka Insurance Corporation Limited	Nil
John Keells	1870 by Englishman George and Edwin John	1948 as John Keells Limited	1974 as John Keells Limited 1986 as John Keells Holdings Limited	Dispersed	Nil

(*Continued*)

Table 4.1: (*Continued*)

Company	Established	Limited liability company	Publicly listed	Significant change in shareholding	Shareholding by founding family (2005)
Brown & Company	1875 by James Brown from Aberdeen	1892	1970	2005 Cooray family exits after sale to Taprobane Fund	Nil
Hayleys Limited	1878 by Chas P. Hayley	1952 as Hayleys Limited	1954	Trustees of Jayasundara Trust	Nil
E.B. Creasy & Company Limited	1878 by Edward B. Creasy	1929	1968	Colombo Fort Land & Building Company Limited	Nil

many of the companies established in the era just prior to independence by Sri Lankan entrepreneurs continue to remain in the hands of the founding families. A striking feature is the close connections these entrepreneurs had to the colonial ruling classes and the accolades they received from the government of the time.

Table 4.2 traces the history of five[26] Sri Lankan companies established in the period just prior to independence. The table illustrates that ownership of these companies have remained with the founding families. Even

Table 4.2: Historical Shareholdings of Five Pre-Independence Companies.[27]

Company	Established	Publicly listed	Shareholding by founding families (2005)
Ceylon Theatres	1928 by Sir Chittampalam A Gardiner, Dr. C.V.S Corea, E.V.R Samarawickrema and A.L. Thambiayah	1928	Gardiner family: Minority holding
Richard Pieris	1940 by brothers Richard and Percy Pieris, Evelyn Fonseka and Walter Rutnam	1951	5.36% (directly)
The Finance Company Limited	1940 by Senator Kotelawala	1960	2.93% (direct) 48.6% (indirectly)
Hemas Holdings	1948 by Sheikh Hasannally Esufally (MBE)	2003	12.69% (directly)
Associated Motorways Limited	1949 by Sir Cyril de Zoysa	1969	8.94% (directly) 46.73% (indirectly)

---

[26] Sample is representative of family owned companies established around the time of independence. They remain today as holding companies of some of Sri Lanka's largest business groups.

[27] *Source*: (n. 23).

where there have been acquisitions by other families or companies, the founding families have struggled to retain at minimum a minority shareholding in these companies.

4.2.4. *Post-Independence*

The post-independent economy of Ceylon underwent several phases of major structural changes. In the first phase, from late 1950s through 1960s, a programme of nationalisation was launched. While this programme was not based on any clear formulation of economic policy, it was perceived as the only means for the removal of the foreign ownership of certain industries after independence. The State Industrial Corporations Act[28] and the Government-Sponsored Corporations Act[29] were enacted to enable the government to establish industrial undertakings and corporations. Thus, the Ceylon Petroleum Corporation was formed in 1961 to compete with foreign-owned oil companies. In 1963, the entire oil industry was vested as a monopoly in this corporation. Similarly, private passenger transport was nationalised and vested in the Ceylon Transport Board in 1958. This phase of economic development in Sri Lanka saw the creation of monopolies for the benefit of SOE and ownership of many corporations and industries vesting with the government.

In the second phase from the late 1960s through the early 1970s, controversial land acquisition laws were imposed and an import substitution economy was promoted. New public enterprises were promoted, further monopolies created and the extensive use of the Business Undertakings Acquisition Act[30] enabled the acquisition of businesses by agreement or compulsion. The single most important act of acquisition during this period was acquisition of all privately owned plantations that exceeded 50 acres and thereafter, in 1975 the acquisition of foreign-owned plantations. This resulted in state-owned plantations being managed by either the Janatha Estates Development Board or the Sri Lanka State Plantation Corporation. At the end of this phase, the size of the public sector measured by government expenditure as a percentage of GDP had grown from

---

[28] No. 49 of 1957.
[29] No. 19 of 1955.
[30] No. 35 of 1971.

23.1 percent in the period 1950–1959 to 28.8 percent in the period 1970–1979.[31]

Economic activities such as banking, plantations, large-scale industries, transport, insurance, telecommunication, postal services, ports, electricity, import and distribution of petroleum, roads, health and education were either under public sector monopoly or undertaken by SOEs. The size of the SOEs sector as a share of the GDP increased from 5.7 percent in 1961 to 12.2 percent in 1974 and to above 15 percent in 1977.[32] With nationalisation it became necessary for many of the plantation companies to venture into property development, tourism, freight forwarding and other service sectors. With the plantation companies' core assets in the tea and rubber industry now vested with the government, diversification became a necessity and led to the formation of a number of group-affiliated companies. Thus, nationalisation directly contributed to the rise of the business group form in Sri Lanka.

By 1960, listed companies in Ceylon had grown to accommodate listings by industrial, financial and commercial companies. However, the market for equities was practically nonexistent and the annual share turnover declined from Sri Lankan Rupees (SLRS) 19.8 million (approximately USD 198,000) in 1960 to SLRS 7 million in 1976 (approximately USD 7000).[33] Further, restrictions on foreign exchange remittances halted trading by foreign companies and only a tiny minority of Sri Lankans owned shares in listed companies.[34] In the period 1960–1977, there were only 12 new share issues with a value of about SLRS 230 million (approximately USD 230,000). In contrast, in the period 1980–1984 there were 87 new issues of shares with a total value of SLRS 2307 million (approximately USD 2.3 million) and by the late 1980s the number of listed companies on the CSE rose to over 170.

Despite economic liberalisation in 1977, brought about by a change of government and historical momentum, the share of the public sector in the

---

[31] Central Bank of Sri Lanka, *Annual Report 2003* (Colombo 2004) Special Statistical Appendix, Table 5.

[32] Athukorala and Jayasuriya (n. 18), 47, citing study by W Lakshman (ed.), *Public Enterprises in the Economic Development of Sri Lanka* (National Institute of Business Management Colombo 1979).

[33] ibid, citing Ceylon Brokers's Association *Rupee Company Year Book* (Colombo 1977).

[34] H Karunatilake, *The Banking and Financial System of Sri Lanka* (Center for Demographic and Socio-Economic Studies Colombo 1987).

economy remained high in the 1980s, especially in the light of large-scale infrastructure projects undertaken with foreign assistance. While the government continued to be monopolistic and active in certain spheres of the economy, the reforms of 1977 created an environment conducive to private sector growth.

4.2.5. *Privatisation*

The necessary legislation for privatisation was enacted in 1987 with the Conversion of Government Owned Business Undertakings into Public Corporations Act[35] and the Conversion of Public Corporations or Government Owned Business Undertakings into Public Companies Act[36] and streamlined thereafter with the Public Enterprises Reform Act.[37] Cajoled by the Washington Consensus,[38] the first wave of privatisation[39] took place in the late 1980s with the restructuring and divestiture of less complex commercial entities. Thereafter, in the 1990s, privatisation was pursued aggressively with reforms in the utilities and services sector. By mid-1990s, 43 enterprises in the industrial sector were privatised. By 1997, the number rose to 75 with the privatisation of several plantation companies and large utilities such as telecommunications and gas.[40]

The period of nationalisation, the creation of monopolies for the benefit of SOEs and the prevalence of the state in the corporate sector, followed by a period of aggressive privatisation in the late 1980s and early 1990s would potentially have resulted in dispersed ownership of corporate entities, if the methods of privatisation utilised in Sri Lanka were different. However, in the Sri Lankan context, the prospect of issuing all

---

[35]No. 22 of 1987.

[36] No. 23 of 1987.

[37] No. 1 of 1996.

[38] Washington Consensus is a specific set of 10 economic policy prescriptions that are considered to constitute a standard reform package promoted for crisis-wracked countries by the IMF, World Bank and US Treasury.

[39] Alternatively called 'peoplisation' in an attempt to appease public resentment towards privatisation.

[40] Public Enterprises Reform Commission Past Divestitures, http://www.perc.gov.lk/past-divt.html [5 June 2005]; R Salih, Privatisation in Sri Lanka, in G Joshi (ed.), *Privatisation in South Asia: Minimizing Negative Social Effects through Restructuring* (ILO New Delhi 2000), 178.

the shares of a privatised company to the public was not viable due to requirements of technological modernisation and management expertise in the restructuring of the SOEs.

The most widely used approach to privatisation in the late 1980s was the sale of a majority of shares (around 50 percent) to a corporate investor on the basis of open tenders and bidding.[41] However, sale of a majority block of shares to investors was a concern, as there was a need to appease public and worker opposition to privatisation. Therefore, of the remaining equity, around 30 percent was offered to the public on an equitable basis,[42] 10 percent was gifted to the employees based on their service periods and 10 percent retained by the Government of Sri Lanka (GOSL).

While this approach to privatisation with a large majority shareholder with a 50–80 percent shareholding contained various advantages,[43] it also meant the rise of concentrated ownership structures whereby a single investor obtained a majority stake in enterprises which had previously enjoyed state patronage and a monopolistic stranglehold on the economy, as in the case of the privatisation of the Colombo Gas Company in 1995[44] and Ceylon Oxygen Limited in 1990.[45]

---

[41] This approach was used in over 80 percent of transactions. S Ranaraja, *Case Study of Privatised Enterprises in Sri Lanka* (ILO special collection on Sri Lankan Publications ILO Colombo 2001), 9.

[42] S Kelegama, Privatization in Sri Lanka: An Overview, in A Bennett (ed.), *How Does Privatization Work? Essays on Privatization in Honour of Professor V.V. Ramanadham* (Routledge London 1997), 169, note 6, explains this equitable basis as 'all applicants, irrespective of the number of shares they have applied for, in the first instance, get 100 shares each. Thereafter, all applicants for 200 or more shares get another 100 and so on. Usually the authorities do not go beyond the second slab, and all investors get the same number of shares, that is, between 100 and 200 shares.'

[43] ibid 169, lists the over 50 percent incentive given to the core investor, the public sale of shares and capital market development as advantages.

[44] The assets and liabilities of Colombo Gas Company were absorbed by Shell Gas Lanka Limited in which Shell International BV/Royal Dutch has a 51 percent stake and GOSL a 49 percent stake.

[45] Ceylon Oxygen Limited was initially a fully owned subsidiary of British Oxygen Company International Limited, nationalised in the 1970s and incorporated as a limited liability company in 1989 in preparation for privatisation. Norsk Hydro AS of Norway acquired 60 percent on divestiture and 30 percent was offered to the public and 10 percent gifted to the employees. Recently, Actis, a private equity investor acquired a 96 percent stake and took the company private, Actis Takes Sri Lanka Gas-maker Private Signifying the End of an Era, http://www.lankabusinessonline.com/fullstory.php?nid=748141097 [4 June 2007], *Lanka Business Online.*

In the period from June 1986 to March 2004, 98 divestitures of SOEs took place. Of these, 40 former SOEs have obtained listings on the CSE. The ownership of these entities has evolved from 100 percent state ownership to a couple of significant shareholders obtaining an economic stake in excess of 79 percent. Table 4.3 and Fig. 4.1 illustrate the present significant shareholdings of privatised enterprises with listings on the CSE. The privatisation programme undertaken by the government in the post-1977 period has resulted in 12 percent of the total number of shareholders of these entities holding 79.99 percent of the total shareholdings in the privatised entities.

A study commissioned in 2000 by the Federation of International Stock Exchanges and Organization for Economic Co-operation and Development (OECD)[46] finds that while privatisation has dramatically increased the number of shareholders in many countries, the large numbers of shareholders created by privatisations involving share issues have not created 'stable ownership structures'[47] that is, by the large number of small shareholders. Conversely, the privatisation programme in Sri Lanka by the issue of a large block of shares to a single investor contributed to the evolution and persistence of concentrated ownership among listed companies. Thus, the process of privatisation in the context of Sri Lanka is one of the key determinants of its present corporate ownership and control structures.

Further, the method of privatisation has also led to the rise of business groups in the post-privatisation economy. As the government divested majority shares of the SOEs by way of block-sale/tender, often to a corporate investor, the privatised enterprises became affiliated to business groups. As the shaded text in Table 4.3 illustrates business groups have majority holdings in 22 of the 40 privatised entities with subsequent listings on the CSE. As of January 2005, of the 243 companies listed on the CSE, 60 percent were companies affiliated to a business group, 11.1 percent had affiliations to multinationals and 3 percent were controlled by the state.[48]

---

[46] M Boutchkova and W Megginson, Privatization and the Rise of Global Capital Markets (2000), 29 *Financial Management*, 31.

[47] ibid 71.

[48] Approximate numbers calculated using company websites and company annual reports.

Table 4.3: Significant Shareholdings of Privatised Enterprises in Sri Lanka.[49]

Privatised enterprises with subsequent CSE listing	Number of significant shareholders (holding over 1 million shares)	Significant shareholders as a percentage of total shareholders	Percentage of total holding held by significant shareholders	Majority acquisition by
Agalawatte Plantations Limited	3	0.03%	81.27%	Mackwood Plantations (Private) Limited
Asian Hotels Corporation Limited[50]	1	0.15%	93%	John Keells
Balangoda Plantations Limited	4	0.02%	70.07%	Stassens Limited
Bogala Graphite Lanka Limited	1	0.05%	80.27%	Graphit Kropfmuhl AG
Bogawantalawa Plantations Limited	3	0.02%	92.15%	Metropolitan Resource Holdings Limited (Ambani family)
Capital Development & Investment Company Limited	2	2%	99.52%	75.6% National Development Bank 23.92% Bank of Ceylon (government bank)

(*Continued*)

[49] *Sources*: Various annual reports and company websites. Complete data is not available for four of the companies.

[50] The majority shares in Asian Hotels Corporation, now renamed as Asian Hotels, were purchased by blue-chip conglomerate John Keells in September 2003: 2003 — One of The Best Years for Trans Asia Hotel, http://www.dailynews.lk/2004/06/08/bus02.html [8 June 2004], *Daily News*.

Table 4.3: (*Continued*)

Privatised enterprises with subsequent CSE listing	Number of significant shareholders (holding over 1 million shares)	Significant shareholders as a percentage of total shareholders	Percentage of total holding held by significant shareholders	Majority acquisition by
Ceylon Glass Company Limited	1	0.01%	83.76%	Gujarat Glass Limited (India)
Ceylon Leather Products Limited	2	0.11%	68.2%	—
Ceylon Oxygen Limited[51]	1	0.02%	70.85%	Norsk Hydro A.S Norway
Colombo Dockyard Limited[52]	7	0.17%	81.33%	51% Onomichi Dockyard Company Limited
Dankotuwa Porcelain Limited[53]	5	0.19%	78.37%	50% International Ceramic Inc, Japan 40% Employees' Trust Fund
Distilleries Company	6	0.04%	71.63%	Stassens Limited

(*Continued*)

[51] Nortrade Norsk Hydro, http://www.nortrade.com/Companies/ShowCompany.aspx?id=1827&p=5 [7 July 2005].

[52] Colombo Dockyard Limited, a subsidiary of Onomichi Dockyard Limited (Zosen) Japan, acquired 51 percent in the formerly state-owned dockyard at the Colombo port. Colombo Dockyard Limited, Our Partners, http://www.cdl.lk/Our%20Partner.htm [15 July 2005]; Board of Investment, Japanese Investments, http://www.boi.lk/InvestorSite/content.asp?content=japan&SubMenuID=58#5 [25 July 2005].

[53] Dankotuwa Porcelain Limited, Who We Are, http://www.dankotuwa.com/about_us.htm [10 March 2005].

Table 4.3: (*Continued*)

Privatised enterprises with subsequent CSE listing	Number of significant shareholders (holding over 1 million shares)	Significant shareholders as a percentage of total shareholders	Percentage of total holding held by significant shareholders	Majority acquisition by
Elpitiya Plantations Limited	2	0.02%	92.01%	Aitken Spence
Hapugastenne Plantations Limited	3	0.01%	91.76%	57.7% James Finlay and Company (Colombo) Limited
Horana Plantations Limited	3	0.03%	85.56%	Ceyexxe Plantations Limited/Ceylon Theatres
Hotel Services Ceylon Limited	1	0.08%	97.33%	—
Hunas Falls Hotels Limited[54]	1	0.03%	46.89%	Hayleys Limited
Kahawatte Plantations Limited	2	0.01%	87.93%	MJF Group of Companies

(*Continued*)

[54] Hayleys Limited and Jetwing Group (Sri Lanka) acquired the major stake holdings. Hunas Falls — A Paradise on the Misty Mountains, http://www.sundayobserver.lk/2002/01/13/fea10.html [13 January 2002], *Sunday Observer*. As much as 25 percent of the Jetwing Group is owned by Hayleys. Jet-Wing, About Us, http://www.jetwing.com/about_us.html [19 March 2005].

Table 4.3: (*Continued*)

Privatised enterprises with subsequent CSE listing	Number of significant shareholders (holding over 1 million shares)	Significant shareholders as a percentage of total shareholders	Percentage of total holding held by significant shareholders	Majority acquisition by
Kegalle Plantations Limited	2	0.02%	74.5%	63.67% Richard Pieris[55] / RPK Management Services (Private) Limited
Kelani Tyres Limited[56]	—	—	—	Associated Motorways Limited/CEAT Limited
Kelani Valley Plantations Limited[57]	2	0.01%	74.33%	71% Hayleys Limited/ DPL Plantations (Private) Limited

(*Continued*)

[55] Richard Pieris, *Annual Report 2004–05* (Colombo 2005).
[56] Former Tyre Corporation of Sri Lanka, Board of Investment, Indian Investments, http://www.boi.lk/InvestorSite/content.asp?content=india&SubMenuID=59#4 [10 March 2005].
[57] Dipped Products Limited, *Annual Report 2004–05* (Colombo 2005).

Table 4.3: (*Continued*)

Privatised enterprises with subsequent CSE listing	Number of significant shareholders (holding over 1 million shares)	Significant shareholders as a percentage of total shareholders	Percentage of total holding held by significant shareholders	Majority acquisition by
Kotagala Plantations Limited	5	0.03%	89.27%	51% Lankem Tea & Rubber Plantations Limited (subsidiary of Lankem Ceylon Limited, a subsidiary of E. B. Creasy & Company Limited)
Lanka Ceramic Limited	—	—	—	Ceylon Theatres
Lanka IOC Limited	—	—	—	Indian Oil Corporation
Lanka Milk Foods (Co-operative Wholesale Establishment) Limited[58]	4	0.10%	62.36%	51% Stassens Limited

(*Continued*)

---

[58] Lanka Milk Foods (CWE) Limited, established in 1981 by the Government-owned Co-operative Wholesale Establishment. In 1991, Stassens Limited purchased 51 percent. Lanka Milk Foods (CWE) Limited, About Us, http://www.lankamilkfoods.com/lmf/about_lmf.htm [25 March 2005].

Table 4.3: (*Continued*)

Privatised enterprises with subsequent CSE listing	Number of significant shareholders (holding over 1 million shares)	Significant shareholders as a percentage of total shareholders	Percentage of total holding held by significant shareholders	Majority acquisition by
Madulsima Plantations Limited	3	0.01%	79.33%	Stassens Exports Limited
Malwatte Valley Plantations Limited	3	0.02%	78.99%	—
Maskeliya Plantations Limited	2	0.012%	80.64%	RPK Management Services (Private) Limited/ Richard Pieris Group
Namunukula Plantations Limited	3	0.02%	79.79%	John Keells
National Development Bank	14	0.21%	59.37%	National Development Bank
Pelwatte Sugar Industries Limited	3	0.10%	86.65%	Master Divers (Private) Limited
People's Merchant Bank Limited	4	0.03%	74.2%	Subsidiary of People's Bank

(*Continued*)

Table 4.3: (*Continued*)

Privatised enterprises with subsequent CSE listing	Number of significant shareholders (holding over 1 million shares)	Significant shareholders as a percentage of total shareholders	Percentage of total holding held by significant shareholders	Majority acquisition by
Sathosa Motors Limited	1	0.07%	59.67%	Formerly part of Co-operative Wholesale Establishment
Sri Lanka Telecom	38	0.15%	91.82%	Nippon Telegraph and Telecommunications Corporation of Japan/ Government of Sri Lanka
Statcon Rubber Company Limited	—	—	—	—
Tea Small Holder Factories Limited	4	0.36%	71.96%	John Keells
Trans Asia Hotels Limited	3	0.2%	90.51%	93% John Keells (2005)

(*Continued*)

Table 4.3: (*Continued*)

Privatised enterprises with subsequent CSE listing	Number of significant shareholders (holding over 1 million shares)	Significant shareholders as a percentage of total shareholders	Percentage of total holding held by significant shareholders	Majority acquisition by
Udapussellawa Plantations Limited	3	0.02%	91.58%	James Finlay and Company (Colombo) Limited 56.8%
United Motors Lanka Limited	4	0.12%	86.5%	—
Watawala Plantations Limited	2	0.01%	76.56%	Estate Management Services (Private) Limited and Tata Tea Limited

Privatised enterprises with a majority stake acquired by a resident business group.

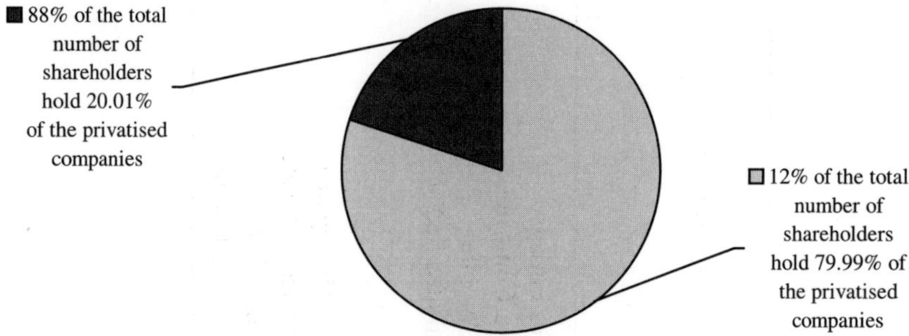

Figure 4.1: Ownership Concentration of Privatised Companies after Colombo Stock Exchange Listing.

4.3. Determinants for the Persistence of Concentrated Ownership in Sri Lanka[59]

4.3.1. *Introduction*

The evolution of concentrated ownership structures among companies in Sri Lanka is a direct result of the economic policies followed by post-independent Sri Lankan governments. Section 4.2 makes the argument that the drive towards nationalisation, the establishment of SOEs and subsequent economic liberalisation in 1977, followed by aggressive privatisation of SOEs in the 1980s and 1990s resulted first, in concentrated ownership structures and second, in a move away from family ownership of companies to ownership of companies by business groups.

Concentrated ownership in the guise of business groups or families have persisted in varying degrees in Sri Lanka for nearly a century, and thus, the focus in this section is on identifying probable determinants for the persistence of concentrated ownership structures and business groups in Sri Lanka. This chapter illustrates that the lack of entrepreneurship in a

---

[59] It should be noted that concentrated ownership of shares in listed companies is, internationally, the norm. The only real exceptions are the UK and the US. While it is indeed plausible that even in the absence of the factors examined in this section of the study, concentrated ownership may persist owing to path dependencies, the identified factors are indigenous factors intensifying and contributing to the rigidity of corporate ownership and concentrated structures in Sri Lanka. Therefore, an examination of why concentrated corporate ownership tends to persist is of importance in the context of reform.

liberalised economy, the lack of developed market intermediaries, high budget deficits, low levels of public float among the companies listed on the CSE and high interest rate spreads contributed to the stifling of the free flow of funds into capital markets in Sri Lanka. The inability of capital markets to attract domestic savings and investment is a primary factor for the persistence of concentrated ownership among companies in Sri Lanka. Further, the lack of external funds and the high cost of market intermediation within capital markets have also indirectly contributed to the rise of group structures with their ability to draw upon internal funds.

4.3.2. *Determinants for the Persistence of Concentrated Ownership and Business Groups in Sri Lanka*

(a) *Entrepreneurship*

Corporate finance is generated from three sources: the capital market, banks and self-financing. While Sri Lanka has deficiencies in all the three channels of financing, its economy has suffered due to the lack of entrepreneurship and the resultant averseness to self-financing. Jennings[60] in 1951 laments on the lack of entrepreneurship among individuals in Ceylon and identifies two traditions as probable explanations. The first according to Jennings, is the anxiety for posts in the public sector, which he attributes to a 'desire for 'security'-a safe and comfortable job, a substantial dowry, a fairly high salary, and a pension to sweeten those declining years ...',[61] and the second to the tradition of land as a main source of income. These traditions as the figures below demonstrate, though minimal today, remain entrenched in Sri Lankan society. In 2004, public sector employees made up over 13 percent of the total labour force,[62] while the average share of GDP at current factor cost prices for agriculture, forestry, fishing and hunting was 46.6 percent in the period 1950–1954, 25.6 percent in 1989, 20.7 percent in 1999 and 19.0 percent in 2003.[63] The State as the biggest capitalist for over three decades has also stifled the development of individual entrepreneurship as

---

[60] Sir I Jennings, *The Economy of Ceylon* (2nd edn Oxford University Press Madras 1951), 32–37.

[61] ibid 33.

[62] Central Bank of Sri Lanka (n. 31) Special Statistical Appendix, Table 57.

[63] ibid Table 2; Athukorala and Jayasuriya (n. 32), 30, Table 3.4.

evident by the size of the public sector as a share of GDP which increased from 17.2 percent in 1960 to 24 percent in 1977.[64]

The lack of corporate entrepreneurship coupled with mistrust for financial innovation resulted in fewer companies being set up in post-independent Sri Lanka.[65] Entrepreneurial individuals were the landed gentry with self-financing resources, which enabled the affluent entrepreneurs and their descendants to retain shareholdings in family controlled businesses. The retention of shareholdings in family controlled businesses also ties in with the Sri Lankan intergenerational mentality of asset ownership and contributed to the persistence of concentrated ownership.

The lack of entrepreneurship also resulted in the rise of business groups able to fill this self-financing void in the economy of Sri Lanka by identification and exploitation of promising business opportunities with in-house capital and management skills.[66] For example Fig. 4.2, representative of many diversified business groups in Sri Lanka, shows a timeline of the entry of John Keells into various new businesses from 1870 to 2004: brokering at the turn of the century, hospitality in the 1970s, food,

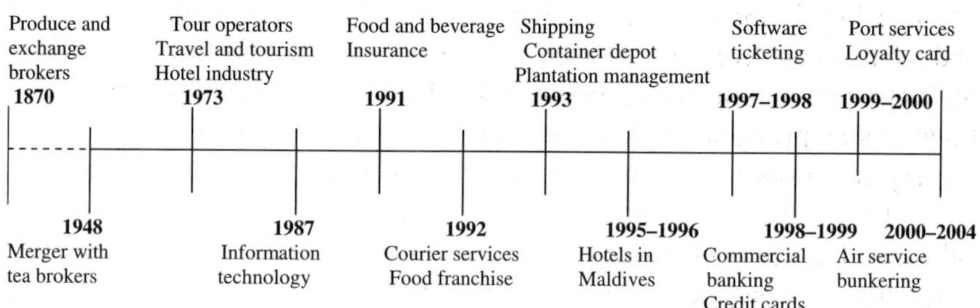

Figure 4.2: Timeline of John Keells.[67]

---

[64] H Karunatilake, *The Economy of Sri Lanka* (Center for Demographic and Socio-Economic Studies Colombo 1987).

[65] Institute of Research for Development *Measurement of the Contribution of Informal Sector/Informal Employment to GDP in Developing Countries* (Paris 2006), 15. Sri Lanka's informal sector including agriculture, accounts for 11 percent of its GDP, comparable to developing countries in Asia. While this is evidence of small-scale entrepreneurship among Sri Lankans, there is an inability to take this to the next level, which may be due to constraints in financing.

[66] T Khanna and K Palepu, Is Group Affiliation Profitable in Developing Countries? An Analysis of Diversified Indian Business Groups (2000), 15 *Journal of Finance*, 867–869. Business groups are a private sector response to institutional voids in society.

[67] John Keells, *Annual Report 2003–04* (Colombo 2004), 109–110.

insurance and information technology in the 1980s, plantation management, banking, shipping and financial services in the 1990s. Thus, the ability of business groups in Sri Lanka to provide something akin to venture capital to other companies within the group in the absence of self-financing and lack of entrepreneurial spirit contributed to the persistence of concentrated ownership structures.

(b) *Market Intermediaries*

Despite financial market liberalisation in Sri Lanka, there is a paucity of market intermediaries. This is exacerbated by the limited market size and lack of market competition making the available market intermediaries costly in providing entrepreneurs with the necessary finance, monitoring and institutional support. In developed nations, market intermediaries are the link between issuers and investors, providing liquidity to capital markets and access to investors.

In the years after independence, foreign banks dominated Sri Lanka's commercial banking sector. Of the 12 commercial banks only two were indigenous.[68] Post-independent commercial banks providing financing to the plantation sector and foreign trade in Colombo were not a source of capital market funds. The three savings banks at the time of independence, the Ceylon Savings Bank, the Post Office Savings Bank and the National Savings Movement were merged in 1972 to form the National Savings Bank. The incorporating Act[69] mandates National Savings Bank to invest at least 60 percent of its deposits in government securities. Since its inception National Savings Bank has surpassed this threshold, investing about 95–97 percent of its funds in government securities.[70] Sri Lanka's first development bank DFCC Bank was established in 1955 to encourage greater equity financing.

An analysis of Fig. 4.3 illustrates the embryonic development of mutual funds, investment banks and venture capitalists (excluding the government-controlled pension funds) in Sri Lanka who make up less than 2 percent of the assets of financial system. Further, those that exist in the

---

[68] This was an improvement from the pre-independent position where eight of the nine banks in Colombo were foreign — *Ferguson's Ceylon Directory for 1930* (Lake House Colombo 1930), 647–648.

[69] National Savings Bank Act No. 30 of 1971, s. 39(3).

[70] Athukorala and Jayasuriya (n. 32), n. 11.

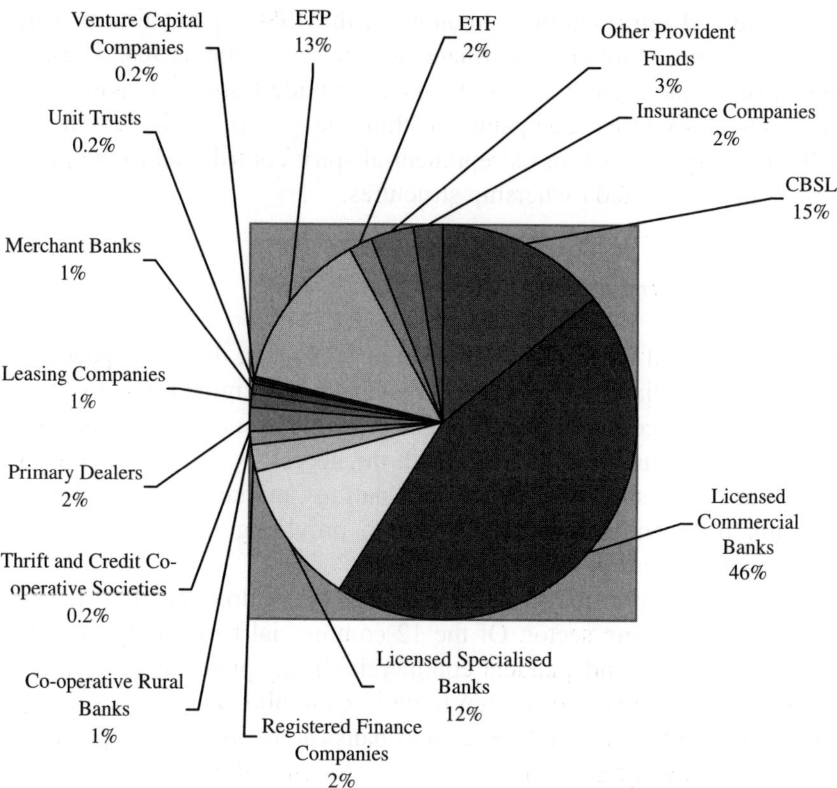

Figure 4.3: Assets of Financial Market Intermediaries as a Percentage of the Financial System (2004).[71]

market are inadequately supervised[72] or state controlled. Although contractual savings institutions in Sri Lanka have substantial financial sector assets, in reality, the two state controlled contractual savings funds, the Employees' Provident Fund and Employees' Trust Fund with assets in excess of 15 percent of the financial system, invest their funds predominantly in

---

[71] Central Bank of Sri Lanka, *A Guide to Financial Services in Sri Lanka* (Colombo 2004).

[72] The Central Bank of Sri Lanka supervises licensed commercial and specialised banks, registered finance companies, the EPF, primary dealers and leasing establishments. Rules are drafted for registration of market intermediaries such as brokers, underwriters, investment managers, under the Securities and Exchange Commission of Sri Lanka Act No. 36 of 1987; Securities and Exchange Commission of Sri Lanka Market Intermediaries, http://www.sec.gov.lk/ [12 September 2005].

government securities.[73] Licensed commercial banks with control of over 46 percent of the assets of the financial system use 44 percent of their funds to grant loans and advances.[74] Investments in other assets (such as shares) including fixed assets are reported to amount to 25 percent of the total use of funds.[75] Of the 14 licensed specialised banks with assets amounting to 12 percent of the total assets of the financial system, the largest savings bank (National Savings Bank) utilises over 62 percent of its funds on treasury bills and bonds and 10.1 percent on loans and advances,[76] while the two specialised banks, the DFCC Bank and the National Development Bank utilise 60 percent[77] and 65 percent[78] of their respective funds on loans and advances. Thus, reliance by market intermediaries with access to finance, on interest-bearing activities such as loans and advances deprives the equity market of capital and liquidity. This is heightened by the under-developed nature of venture capital, private equity, unit trusts and merchant banking, which in turn, creates a paucity of finance and contributes to the persistence of concentrated ownership among listed companies.

Further, the reliance on interest bearing activities such as loans and advances as a source of income by significant market intermediaries can among other reasons be attributed to the high interest rate spread.[79] The high interest rate spread has also meant high costs of financial intermediation. In an underdeveloped capital market like Sri Lanka, where banks are the key financial intermediaries, high interest rate spreads cause higher costs of financing and make it prohibitive for potential borrowers to expand existing business or undertake new investments.

---

[73] As much as 91.8 percent of the ETF portfolio is invested in government securities. Employees' Trust Fund, ETF Investments, http://www.lanka.net/etf/investment.html [5 July 2005]. As much as 70 percent of the EPF portfolio is invested in treasury bonds. EPF Investments, http://www.epf-cbsl.lk/ [5 July 2005].

[74] Central Bank of Sri Lanka (n. 31), 128, Chart 8.1.

[75] ibid.

[76] National Savings Bank, *Annual Report 2004* (Colombo 2005).

[77] NDB Bank, *Annual Report 2004* (Colombo 2005).

[78] DFCC Bank, *Annual Report 2005* (Colombo 2005).

[79] Measured by difference between lending rate and deposit rate. The interest rate spread in Sri Lanka at 6.99 on average, is comparatively high in comparison to other Asian countries (Bangladesh 6.94; Malaysia 3.41; Nepal 3.5; Thailand 4.5), World Bank, *World Development Indicators 2002* (Washington DC 2002). A general idea can also be obtained by a comparison of commercial banks' weighted average deposit rate with the weighted average prime-lending rate — Fig. 4.8.

The possible connection between concentrated ownership and weakness of market intermediaries is recognised by Khanna and Palepu who attribute concentrated ownership and the presence of business groups in India to 'institutional voids' and the 'absence of specialised intermediaries in capital markets'.[80] Underdevelopment of financial intermediaries increases costs for emerging market companies to acquire finance, technology and management talent. In this context, a new investment is most likely to be pursued by a business group with its reputation, access to internal finance and ability to adapt to external market failures. The likelihood of a business group pursuing a new investment also increases if external capital is costlier than internal capital finance.

Further, as Khanna and Palepu[81] point out, in India because business groups are public companies the ability of a group to use internal capital to fund the ongoing activities of another affiliated member is limited. Therefore, the most important role for the group's internal capital is to launch new ventures in which other group affiliates and significant owners have an opportunity to acquire ownership stakes. This reliance on internal financing strengthens the concentration of corporate ownership and ensures that ownership remains in the hands of business groups and individuals.

(c) *Budget Deficits*

Fiscal mismanagement in Sri Lanka is a key factor in the persistence of concentrated ownership structures. High budget deficits have necessitated high returns on government securities with minimum risks. To help bridge budget deficits of between −10.8 and −8.0 percent of the GDP over the years 1998–2004,[82] the government utilised the domestic debt market, which is in fact, greater than its external debt market.[83] Domestic debt at 13.7 percent of the GDP in 1950, reached an all time high of 59.8 percent in 2002. In 2003,

---

[80] Khanna and Palepu (n. 66), 867.

[81] Khanna and Palepu (n. 66), 868–869.

[82] Central Bank of Sri Lanka (n. 31) Special Statistical Appendix, Table 5.

[83] ibid 112–113 and Chart 6.6. Note that Sri Lanka has the highest government debt as a percentage of its GDP among South Asian nations at 105.5 percent. Asian Development Bank, *Key Indicators 2005: Labour Markets in Asia: Promoting Full, Productive and Decent Employment* (Manila 2005).

it remained at 57.9 percent of the GDP.[84] Domestic borrowings are primarily met by the issuance of treasury bills and treasury bonds,[85] accounting for over 72 percent of the capital market, as illustrated by Fig. 4.4.

The dominance of government securities in the capital market is due to the attractive rates of interest on treasury bills and bonds. For example, in 2000, the 1-year treasury bill yield was 18.2 percent.[86]

The comparison in Fig. 4.5 of the interest rates on 1-year treasury bills[87] and the dividend yield[88] of the listed companies on the CSE[89] for the period 2000–2004 demonstrates that interest rates on treasury bills are consistently

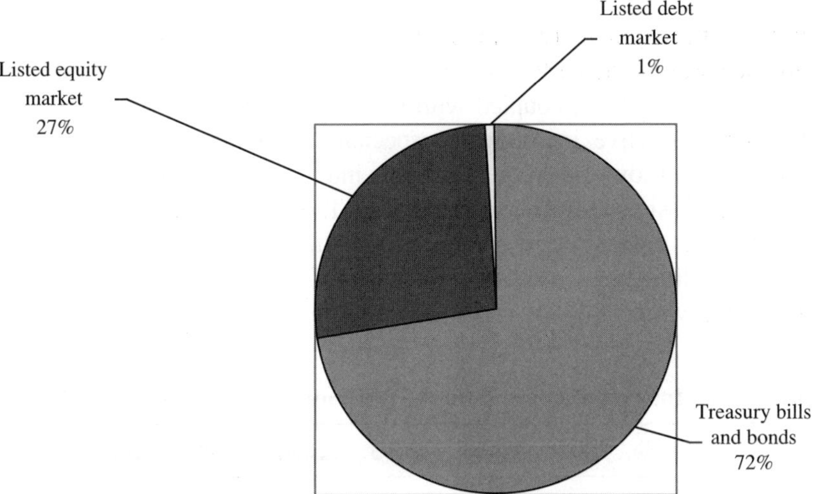

Figure 4.4: The Sri Lankan Capital Market (2003).[90]

---

[84] ibid Special Statistical Appendix, Table 6.

[85] With Treasury bills and bonds, the investor acquires the credit risk of the government. Bills are of a shorter maturity period than bonds.

[86] Central Bank of Sri Lanka, Historical Information on Treasury Bill Auctions, http://www.lanka.net/centralbank/billdata.xls [5 February 2005].

[87] Central Bank of Sri Lanka (n. 31) Special Statistical Appendix, Table 8.

[88] Measure of the percentage of dividend that an investor may receive based on the stock's current market price.

[89] Colombo Stock Exchange (n. 86), 13, Fig. 5.

[90] Central Bank of Sri Lanka, *Public Debt Management & Debt Profile of Sri Lanka* (Colombo 2004) Table 16; Colombo Stock Exchange, *Annual Report 2004* (Colombo 2005), 13; Central Bank of Sri Lanka (n. 31) Special Statistical Appendix, Table 6.

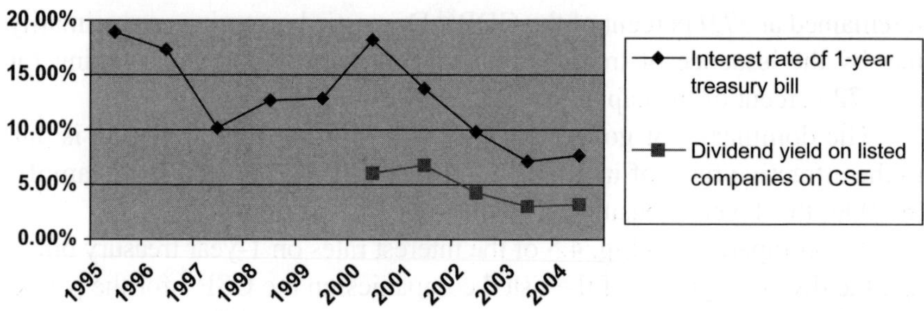

Figure 4.5: Interest Rates on Treasury Bills and Dividend Yields.

higher than the average dividend yield of companies listed on the CSE. This divergence was particularly high in 2000. With consistent higher rates of return on treasury bills, coupled with the fact that they are sovereign risk make them attractive investments especially to domestic investors, and diverts capital inflows from equity markets into the government debt market.

The discussion is further expanded in Table 4.4 to encompass stock price appreciation, as return on equity investment comprises both capital growth and dividend yield. As reflected in Table 4.4 during the period 2001–2006, while the all share price index[91] (ASPI) return was at

Table 4.4: Interest Rates and the ASPI Growth: From 2001 to 2007.[92]

	2007	2006	2005	2004	2003	2002	2001
ASPI annual growth (%)	(6.66)	41.63	27.56	41.88	30.30	31.26	38.74
Average weighted fixed deposit rate (%)	15.49	11.5	9.25	7.67	7.11	10.17	13.47
364-day treasury bill rate (%)	19.96	12.96	10.37	7.65	7.24	9.91	13.74

[91] 'The ASPI measures the movement of share prices of all the listed companies. The ASPI is based on market capitalisation. Weighting of shares is conducted in proportion to the issued ordinary capital of the listed companies, valued at current market price (i.e., market capitalisation). Colombo Stock Exchange, Colombo Stock Exchange Glossary, http://www.cse.lk/static/Glossary.htm [20 April 2009].

[92] Source: ibid 16–17, Fig. 2.

35.2 percent on average, the interest rates were between 7 percent and 13 percent. However, stock price appreciation by itself is often insufficient to attract investor capital, especially long-term domestic investors, who may view the share market as a speculative and risky investment in view of the more secure and high returns, albeit not as high as the stock price appreciation, offered by treasury bills and fixed rate deposits. The negative correlation between interest rates and the share market return is clearly demonstrated in 2007, when high rates of interest coupled with the security situation in the country resulted in a negative return of the ASPI.[93]

The attraction of the non-bank sector, that is, pension funds, savings institutions, insurance and finance companies, institutional investors and private investors to the high yields offered by treasury bills and bonds is evident in Figs. 4.6 and 4.7 illustrating the ownership of treasury bills and treasury bonds.

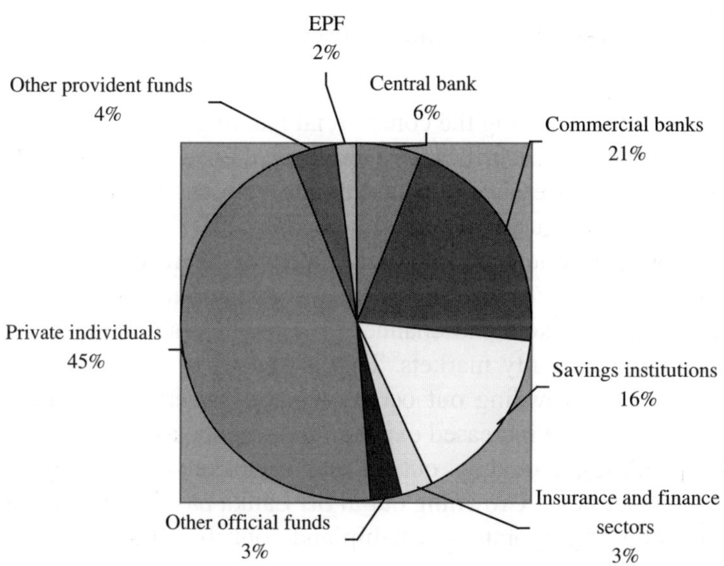

Figure 4.6: Ownership of Treasury Bills (2003).[94]

---

[93] Colombo Stock Exchange, *Annual Report 2007* (Colombo 2007), 16.

[94] Central Bank of Sri Lanka (n. 88), 26, Table 16; Central Bank of Sri Lanka (n. 31) Special Statistical Appendix, 108–109.

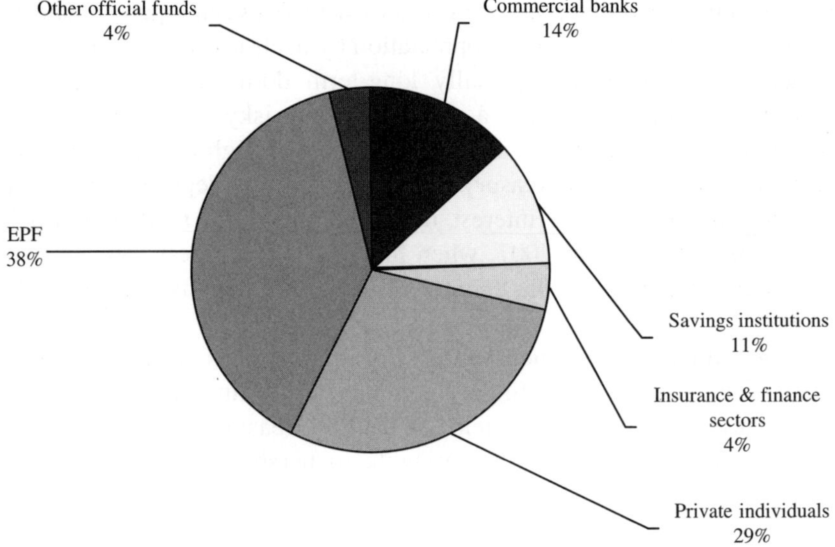

Figure 4.7: Ownership of Treasury Bonds (2003).[95]

The preference among the commercial banking and non-banking sector for government securities is also strengthened by a perception of greater security in treasury bills and bonds, reflecting a lack of investor education and immaturity of capital markets.

High budget deficits and attractive rates of interest on treasury bills and bonds contribute to the dominance of government securities in Sri Lanka's capital markets and channel investment funds into government securities than to equity markets. This is known in economic theory as 'crowding out'. Crowding out occurs when a government expands its' borrowing to finance increased expenditure, or cuts taxes (i.e., engages in deficit spending), crowding out private sector investment by way of higher interest rates.[96] Crowding out in Sri Lanka has, in turn, constrained the dispersion of corporate ownership and contributed to the persistance of concentrated ownership structures.

---

[95] ibid.

[96] There is disagreement among macroeconomists on the exact behaviour of financial markets to increased government borrowings, because it is possible that government spending could stimulate the market. However, if increased borrowings are to service debt payments, market stimulation is not possible.

Constraints on the dispersion of corporate ownership and the resultant concentrated ownership structures is also exacerbated by the fact that global capital flows to emerging countries have been constrained in the recent past.[97] For many emerging markets, the greatest potential benefits of open capital markets arise from capital inflows. Theoretically, capital inflows to emerging markets are anticipated since capital is relatively scarce in emerging markets and therefore, the return to capital investment should be higher on average, than in countries with established flows of capital. However, paradoxically forecasts for capital flows to emerging markets are subdued and are identified as tending to flow from poor to wealthy countries instead of the other way around.[98] While a detailed analysis on global capital flows would take away from the focus of indigenous factors which contribute towards concentrated corporate ownership, the subdued nature of global capital flows to emerging markets in general and the tendency of capital flows to be uneven across emerging markets may also constrain the dispersion of corporate ownership in emerging markets and result in the persistence of concentrated ownership structures.

(d) *Public Float*

Concentrated ownership also persists among the listed companies in Sri Lanka due to the low levels of public floatation, that is, the number of shares of a listed company that are available for trading by the public not including those shares that are closely held by officers, directors and the other so-called insiders.[99] Listing rules and continuing listing requirements set by stock exchanges specify the market capitalisation of shares and the minimum percentage of shares to be distributed to the public.[100]

---

[97] International Monetary Fund, *World Economic Outlook: Crisis and Recovery* (Washington DC 2009), Fig. 1.13.

[98] B Block and K Forbes, Capital Flows to Emerging Markets: The Myths and Realities (2004), Conference on the Myths and Realities of Globalization, http://web.mit.edu/-kjforbes/www/Shorter%20Articles/CapitalFlowsToEmergingMarkets-Myths&Realities.pdf [21 April 2009, 10].

[99] J Smullen and N Hand, *Dictionary of Finance and Banking* (Oxford University Press Oxford 2005).

[100] London Stock Exchange Listing Rules 2003 (UK) specify that to obtain a listing on the London Stock Exchange the expected aggregate value of shares must be at least £700,000, r. 3.16 (a); and subject to exception, 25 percent of such shares must be distributed to the public, r. 3.19.

The listing rules of the CSE require that to obtain a listing on the main board '25% of the issued capital must be held/offered to the public'.[101] However, if a company obtaining a listing requests a waiver of the public float requirement, the CSE may exercise its right of discretion under the listing rules[102] and in consultation with the Securities and Exchange Commission of Sri Lanka, waive such requirement. While the waiver of the public float requirement encourages new listings, it also results in companies with low public floats obtaining listings by way of offers for subscription/sale. A case in point is the Dialog Telekom Initial Public Offering in June 2005 whereby, 712,336,293 shares amounting to a mere 9.6 percent of the 7,403,434,913 issued and fully paid share capital were offered to the public. The largest initial public offering at the time in Sri Lanka, Dialog Telekom obtained a listing on the CSE and commenced trading on 28 July 2005 as the largest market capitalised company on the first day of trading, with the following shareholding structure: 87.67 percent held by its Malaysian holding company TM International (L) Limited, 9.62 percent by the public, 2.70 percent by an Employee Share Option Trust and 0.01 percent by the subscribers to the share issue.[103] The low levels of public floatation among other listed companies is illustrated by Table 4.5, where only three of the nine companies obtaining listings on the CSE by way of subscription in 2002 and 2003 made offers to the public in excess of 25 percent of their issued share capital.

While waivers of the public float requirement are often granted in issues with large market capitalisation, this by itself does not ensure the distribution of shares to 'the public' or motivate companies to increase their public float. Further, the absence of a continuing listing requirement of a public float in the listing rules of the CSE has meant that companies, which initially obtained listings by meeting the public float requirement, are subsequently free to dilute public holdings. Minority shareholders, in general, have been indifferent to such dilutions.

It is doubtful whether encouraging new listings by waiving the requirement of a public float is a healthy option for emerging equity markets. Concentrated ownership of listed companies is inevitable in a low public float equity market. Low public float stifles the mergers and acquisitions

---

[101] Colombo Stock Exchange Listing Rules 2004, r. 1.6–1 d(iii).

[102] ibid, r. 1.1 and 1.3.

[103] Dialog Telekom, *IPO Prospectus 2005* (Colombo 2005), 77–78.

Table 4.5: Shares of Listed Companies Offered to and Subscribed by the Public in 2002/2003.[104]

Name of company	Number of ordinary shares offered to and subscribed to by the public[105]	Issued ordinary shares[106]	Number of ordinary shares offered to and subscribed to by the public as percentage of the issued ordinary shares (in %)
Touchwood Investments Limited	800,000	2,227,200	35.9
E-Channelling Limited	6,667,000	10,468,407	63
Tess Agro Limited	2,500,000	13,300,000	18.7
Lanka Hospital Corporation Limited	20,555,000	156,612,518	13.1
Sri Lanka Telecom	216,583,000	1,804,900,000	11.9
Ceylon Leather Products Limited	2,500,000	12,500,000	20
Ceylon Hospitals Limited	4,500,000	19,500,000	23
Hemas Holdings	12,000,000	78,000,000	15.3
HNB Assurance Limited	10,000,000	25,000,000	40

market, an important management monitoring mechanism. It locks in minority shareholders and affects market liquidity. The limited number of shares available for trading among the public also results in price volatility as a result of speculative trading.

---

[104] Years based on date of issue to the public.

[105] Central Bank of Sri Lanka, *Annual Report 2002* (Colombo 2003), 269, Table 10.28; Central Bank of Sri Lanka (n. 31), 253, Table 10.26.

[106] Colombo Stock Exchange, *Handbook of Listed Companies 2004* (Colombo 2005).

Thus, in Sri Lanka the low levels of public floatation, the granting of waivers of public float requirement and the absence of a continuing listing requirement with regard to maintaining a public float has contributed to the persistence of concentrated ownership among companies listed on the CSE.

(e) *Interest Rates on Deposits*

A further cause for the persistence of concentrated ownership among companies in Sri Lanka is the high rates of deposit interest offered by the banking sector. The average dividend yield on shares is consistently lower than the average deposit rate offered by commercial banks. This is evident in a comparison of the commercial banks' weighted average deposit rate with the dividend yield for listed companies for the period 2000–2004 as illustrated by Fig. 4.8. The high rates of deposit interest coupled with public perception of shares as high risk, low liquidity investments, is successful in diverting public savings from equity markets into bank deposits.[107]

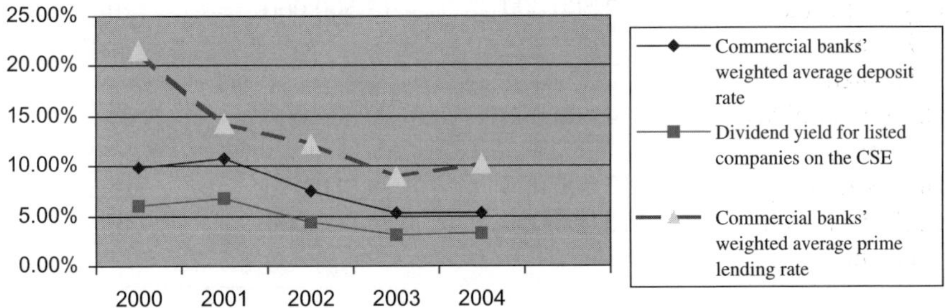

Figure 4.8[108]: Comparison of the Commercial Banks' Weighted Average Deposit Rate with Dividend Yield.

---

[107] Table 4.4 illustrates the negative correlation between interest rates and share market return in 2007. While external factors such as investment risk (due to the security situation in 2007) may affect stock market returns, it is also plausible that the high interest rates on deposits could also negatively impact upon stock market returns.

[108]Central Bank of Sri Lanka (n. 31) Table 123; Colombo Stock Exchange (n. 86), 13, Fig. 5.

It is accepted that for companies to obtain capital there must be 'savings somewhere in the system'.[109] Therefore, increased savings per se within a country is not a cause of concern for purposes of this study, if a substantial portion of such savings are channelled into the equity market thereby, achieving broad-based ownership of listed companies, at least among financial intermediaries with monitoring capabilities such as banks, financial institutions, venture capitalists, unit trusts, pension funds and institutional investors.

However, in the context of Sri Lanka, high deposit interest rates attract demand, time and savings deposits[110] into banks, which are then channelled back into the economy primarily as loans and advances.[111] This heavy reliance on interest bearing activities as a major source of income by commercial banks can *inter alia* be attributed to the high interest rate spread.[112] A negative implication of a high interest rate spread and heavy reliance on interest bearing activities by banks is, that the banking sector as a key financial intermediary is not effective in channeling funds from the banking sector into equity markets[113] and contributes to the persistence of concentrated ownership among companies in Sri Lanka. The lack of or high cost of external financing offered by banks and other financial institutions as illustrated by the high interest spread has also resulted in companies in Sri Lanka engaging in internal financing leading to the rise of group structures among companies.

Berle and Means,[114] writing in the 1930s, notes that the shift of ownership from the smaller owners back to the high income class in the United States is dependent on two conditions, 'the treatment of the small

---

[109] M Roe, The Institutions of Corporate Governance (2004), Harvard Law and Economics Discussion Paper 488, http://ssrn.com/abstract=612362 [3 August 2005, 23]. It is possible for global capital flows to overcome the paucity in savings if the investment risk within a jurisdiction is low.

[110] Central Bank of Sri Lanka, *Bulletin-January 2005* (Colombo 2005) Table 71, reports that in September 2004, over 75.7 percent of demand, time and savings deposits with commercial banks were owned by individuals.

[111] Central Bank of Sri Lanka (n. 31), 128, Chart 8.1.

[112] Fig. 4.8 and (n. 79).

[113] The merchant banking sector accounted for 1 percent of the total assets of the financial sector (Fig. 4.3); Central Bank of Sri Lanka, *Annual Report 2005* (Colombo 2005), 132, reports that leasing and lending have become main lines of business for merchant banks due to lack of opportunities in the equity and debt markets for investment banking.

[114] A Berle and G Means, *The Modern Corporation and Private Property* (Rev edn Harcourt, Brace & World Inc New York 1967), 61–62.

investor by those in control of corporate affairs, and the existence of other fields for the investment of his savings'. In its application to the Sri Lankan context, it can be concluded that a shift of ownership from the blockholder to small investors is unlikely to occur primarily due to the availability of alternative forms of lucrative investments.

4.4. Implications for Corporate Governance in Light of the Causes for the Persistence of Concentrated Corporate Ownership

The common threads running through the discussion in the previous section demonstrate that concentrated ownership structures in Sri Lanka persisted in the post-independence years primarily due to constraints in financing within Sri Lanka. Market-based finance is diverted into banks, savings institutions and government securities, while financial intermediary-based finance is underdeveloped, expensive and diverted into interest bearing activities than into equity markets. The constraints in financing are further exacerbated by the relaxed requirements with regard to public floatation and cultural inhibitions such as the lack of entrepreneurship.

The objective of this study is to discover the implications of corporate ownership and control on the governance of companies in Sri Lanka and thereafter, suggest a reform agenda to meet the challenges posed by such ownership and control structures.

First, this chapter by its analysis of the determinants of ownership concentration in Sri Lanka identifies the paucity of finance as both a cause and a consequence for the persistence of concentrated ownership structures, that is, concentrated ownership arises and persists due to constraints in financing, while concentrated ownership structures, such as large shareholders and business groups, are responsible for the loss of confidence in equity markets, thus hindering the flows of finance.

The finding that constraints in financing is both a cause and a consequence for the persistence of corporate ownership and control patterns in Sri Lanka supports the second pillar of this study, which is that corporate ownership and control structures reflect the pattern of corporate financing within a country and reflects inherent financing weaknesses.

Second, this chapter by its analysis of the determinants for the persistence of ownership concentration in Sri Lanka and the finding that constraints in financing are both a cause and a consequence for the persistence of concentrated ownership structures, lends itself to the framing of a reform agenda to meet the challenges posed by such concentrated ownership structures. The knowledge that constraints in financing contribute to the persistence of concentrated ownership structures enables the framing of a reform agenda which addresses not only just the symptoms of concentrated ownership structures (i.e., private benefits of control, entrenchment etc), but also the root cause of such concentrated ownership structures. Thus, this chapter by its analysis, identifies the demand for finance by companies in Sri Lanka as a powerful incentive in the reform of corporate governance and signals that the actors capable of filling the financing void may best be equipped to monitor and guide the reform of corporate governance in Sri Lanka.

Further, the recognition of the interactive relationship between constraints in financing and corporate ownership structures also makes it implicit that corporate ownership structures cannot be instantly changed or removed by corporate governance reform agendas.

This chapter by its analysis of the determinants of corporate ownership structures in Sri Lanka and the resultant implications for corporate governance in the light of such analysis, also supports and applies the primary thesis of this study that an analysis into the reform of corporate governance in developing countries should begin with a focus on local market structures and institutions, such as corporate ownership and control structures that define the adaptation, efficiency and effectiveness of corporate governance.

CHAPTER 5

Controlling Shareholder Systems
and Corporate Governance

5.1. Introduction

The system of ownership and control of Sri Lankan companies discussed in Chapters 3 and 4 is not dissimilar to the system of ownership and control of public companies in Asia, South America or continental Europe. It is accepted that public companies in many countries outside the UK and the US have a shareholder or group of shareholders with voting control and without corresponding equity holdings (i.e., cash flow rights).

5.1.1. *Ownership and Control*

A large volume of literature provides evidence of shareholders with voting control but without corresponding cash flow rights. La Porta *et al.*, surveying ownership structures of 27 developed economies using a 20 percent control threshold, find that only 36 percent of large companies on average in these developed economies are widely held.[1] Claessens *et al.*[2] examine 2980 publicly traded companies in Asia using a 10 percent blockholder to define control, and determine that widely held companies in their Asian sample companies account for less than 3 percent of companies on average, excluding Japan and Korea. On a 20 percent control threshold, widely held companies still account for less than 20 percent of the companies in Asia, except in Japan, Korea and Taiwan. Faccio and

---

[1] R La-Porta, F Lopez-de-Silanes and A Shleifer, Corporate Ownership around the World (1999), 54 *Journal of Finance*, 471.

[2] S Claessens, S Djankove and L Lang, The Separation of Ownership and Control in East Asian Corporations (2000), 58 *Journal of Financial Economics*, 81.

Lang ascertain the controlling shareholders of 5232 companies in 13 Western European countries using a 20 percent control threshold and find that only 37 percent of the companies are widely held in Western Europe.[3] Barca and Becht survey ownership structures of large companies across Europe and find that the widely held company is not representative of Europe.[4]

Franks and Mayer find that in their sample of German companies, family holdings account for 33 percent of ultimate shareholdings (i.e., control rights) as against the 20.5 percent of actual ownership (i.e., cash flow rights). Similarly, banks in Germany control 12 percent as against the 5.8 percent of actual ownership recorded.[5]

In Belgium[6] and Italy,[7] corporate ownership and control is similar to that in Germany. In France, at the end of 1995, the sum of all known or identified voting blocks (i.e., control rights) amounted to around 40 percent, while the largest voting blockholder holds 20–30 percent in economic stakes (i.e., cash flow rights) in the 40 largest listed companies in terms of market capitalisation.[8] In Spain, in 1995, the difference between voting rights (i.e., control rights) and economic stakes was relatively low at about 4 percent, while indirect ownership for the largest

---

[3] M Faccio and L Lang, The Ultimate Ownership of Western European Corporations (2002), 65 *Journal of Financial Economics*, 365; J Grant and T Kirchmaier, Who Governs? Corporate Ownership and Control Structures in Europe (2004), http://papers.ssrn.com/sol3/papers.cfm?abstract_id=555877 [15 March 2006].

[4] M Becht and C Mayer, Introduction, in F Barca and M Becht (eds.), *The Control of Corporate Europe* (Oxford University Press Oxford 2002), 1.

[5] J Franks and C Mayer, Ownership and Control of German Corporations (2001), 14 *Review of Financial Studies*, 943–947 and Table 1.

[6] M Becht, A Chapelle and L Renneboog, Shareholding Cascades: The Separation of Ownership and Control in Belgium, in F Barca and M Becht (eds.), *Ownership and Control: A European Perspective* (Oxford University Press Oxford 2001), 71, Table 3, find that in 1995 the largest shareholding in Belgium was 44.75 percent, while the ultimate voting block was 55.77 percent.

[7] M Bianchi, M Bianco and L Enriques, Pyramidal Groups and the Separation between Ownership and Control in Italy (1999), http://ssrn.com/abstract=293882 [15 March 2006], 18–19 and Table 12, find that in 1996 in Italy, on average one unit of capital allowed an ultimate control of 1.95 units.

[8] L Bloch and E Kremp, Ownership and Voting Power in France, in F Barca and M Becht (eds.), *The Control of Corporate Europe* (Oxford University Press Oxford 2002), 106, Fig. 1; S Boubaker, Ownership-control Discrepancy and Firm-value: Evidence from France (2005), http://ssrn.com/abstract=740756 [10 March 2006].

shareholder on average was 8 percent higher than the direct ownership figure.[9]

In the developing world, controlling shareholders without corresponding equity holdings are more extensive. A study of the 325 companies listed on the Brazilian Sao Paulo Stock Exchange in 1996 demonstrates that the largest shareholder has on average 41 percent of the equity capital, while the five largest together have 61 percent, and violation of the one share-one vote rule with the use of non-voting shares is common. Further evidence illustrates that individuals indirectly control over 70 percent of the voting control of companies with economic stakes amounting to only 13 percent.[10]

The results are similar in Turkey and Thailand. In Turkey, of the 94 companies analysed, families control 68 companies with an average controlling stake of 52.05 percent. This is double the average direct cash flow rights of families, which is 23.60 percent.[11] In Thailand, of the 270 companies surveyed, the largest shareholders in 82.59 percent of the companies (i.e., 233 companies) were also the controlling shareholders owning at least 25 percent of the votes.[12] Single families control over 57.41 percent of these Thai companies.[13]

5.1.2. *Family Control*

A common feature in developing countries with controlling shareholders is that controlling shareholders are wealthy families who have achieved control in excess of their economic stakes through the use of pyramids. Families are dominant controlling shareholders in both Turkey[14] and

---

[9] R Crespi-Cladera and M Garcia-Cestona, Ownership and Control of Spanish Listed Firms, in F Barca and M Becht (eds.), *The Control of Corporate Europe* (Oxford University Press Oxford 2002), 207, Tables 4, 6, 8 and Fig. 2.

[10] S Valaderes and R Leal, Ownership and Control Structure of Brazilian Companies (2000), http://ssrn.com/abstract=213409 [5 March 2006], Table 6.

[11] I Demirag and M Serter, Ownership Patterns and Control in Turkish Listed Companies (2003), 11 *Corporate Governance: An International Review*, 40–45, Table 2.

[12] Y Wiwattanakantang, The Equity Ownership Structure of Thai Firms (2001), http://ssrn.com/abstract=271358 [5 March 2006], 23.

[13] ibid 12.

[14] Demirag and Serter (n. 11), 47.

Thailand.[15] Anderson and Reeb,[16] in a study using S&P's ('Standard and Poor's') 500 firms from 1992 through 1999, observe that family firms constitute over 35 percent of S&P's industrials and on average families own nearly 18 percent of their firms' outstanding equity.[17] They suggest that family control is more extensive than these ownership levels suggest, since in companies where the family does not have outright majority ownership, their control of board seats is 2.75 times greater than their cash flow rights.

La Porta *et al.*, in their study covering corporate ownership and the incidence of family control (inferred if the largest shareholder is a family and if such family's stake is greater than a 20 percent voting control threshold) among the 20 largest publicly traded companies in 27 wealthy economies, find that 30 percent of the companies are family controlled and that family control is least important in the UK, where no family controls more than 20 percent of the votes of the 20 largest publicly traded companies.[18] In contrast, in Mexico all of the top 20 companies are family controlled by this definition.[19] Italy has 15 percent of its most successful 20 companies controlled by families, Belgium has 50 percent family control of its companies and Sweden 45 percent. Similarly, Khanna and Palepu find that the majority of companies listed on the Bombay Stock Exchange in India are associated with diversified business groups controlled by families.[20]

5.1.3. *Group Affiliation*

Another common feature of controlling shareholder systems, especially in Asia, is group affiliation. Khanna and Palepu note that the 'diversified

---

[15] Y Wiwattanakantang (n. 12), 12–23.

[16] R Anderson and D Reeb, Founding Family Ownership and Firm Performance: Evidence from the S&P 500 (2003), 58 *Journal of Finance*, 1301–1302.

[17] Reference to any firm with a dominant shareholder as a family firm, detracts from their argument.

[18] La-Porta (n. 1), 501, Table 5; M Burkart, F Panunzi and A Shleifer, Family Firms (2003), 58 *Journal of Finance*, 2167 argue that 'Most firms in the world are controlled by their founders, or by the founder's families and heirs'.

[19] La-Porta (n. 1), Table 5.

[20] T Khanna and K Palepu, Developing Country Business Groups, Foreign Investors and Ccorporate Governance (1999), National Bureau of Economic Research Working Paper 6955, http://papers.nber.org/papers/w6955.pdf [29 April 2005].

business group remains the dominant form of enterprise throughout most developing countries'.[21] These range from *Keiretsu*[22] in Japan, to *Chaebols*[23] in Korea. Similarly, as recently as a decade ago, six mining finance houses with group affiliation dominated the economy of South Africa.[24] Khanna and Palepu in a study of business groups classify about a fifth of companies in Chile, about two-thirds in Indonesia, and about half in Korea, as group affiliated.[25] Sometimes the apex company is itself widely held or is a financial institution or the state. In most Asian countries, notably India and China,[26] the state is an important controlling shareholder.

5.1.4. *Impact of Controlling Shareholder Systems*

The most visible effect of widespread prevalence of controlling shareholder systems on corporate governance is the shift of corporate governance scholarship from dispersed ownership systems to controlling shareholder systems, alternatively termed 'controlling minority structures'.[27] This shift within the corporate governance scholarship highlights new corporate governance concerns within controlling shareholders systems, distinct from those prevalent in dispersed shareholder systems.

---

[21] T Khanna and K Palepu, Why Focussed Strategies May Be Wrong for Developing Countries (1997), 75 (4) *Harvard Business Review*, 41.

[22] Companies with no single controlling shareholder but each holds a small stake in one another, and these stakes collectively amount to control blocks and each company is controlled by the professional managers of all the other companies in the group.

[23] Pyramidal structures with extensive reciprocal holdings and intercorporate ownership links.

[24] S Maherbe and N Segal, South Africa: After Apartheid, in C Oman (ed.), *Corporate Governance in Development: The Experiences of Brazil, Chile, India and South Africa* (Center for International Private Enterprise/OECD Paris 2003), 161.

[25] T Khanna and Y Yafeh, Business Groups and Risk Sharing around the World (2005), 78 *Journal of Business*, 301–309, Table 2.

[26] W Goetzmann and E Koll, The History of Corporate Ownership in China: State Patronage, Company Legislation, and the Issue of Control, in R Morck (ed.), *A History of Corporate Governance Around the World: Family Business Groups to Professional Managers* (University of Chicago Press Chicago 2005).

[27] L Bebchuk, R Kraakman and G Triantis, Stock Pyramids, Cross-ownership and Dual Class Equity: The Mechanisms and Agency Costs of Separating Control from Cash-flow Rights, in R Morck (ed.), *Concentrated Corporate Ownership* (University of Chicago Press Chicago 2000), 445–446.

In Chapters 1 and 2, the argument is made that ownership structures are an important starting point for a study on corporate governance due to the implications of the agency conflict within the corporate form. The prevalence of controlling shareholder systems worldwide has meant that the traditional 'agency' conflict between shareholders and managers, the core of the corporate governance debate over the past three decades, is replaced by a different form of 'agency problem'[28] in the form of 'opportunism of controlling shareholders vis-à-vis shareholders'.[29]

Controlling shareholders as defined in Chapter 3, obtain positions of control within a company without a commensurate economic stake. Once in control, they are often immune from challenges to their control due to entrenched positions of control. The unfettered control rights of controlling shareholders raise common corporate governance concerns of expropriation and mismanagement in controlling shareholder systems. While expropriation and mismanagement by controlling shareholders lead to a fall in company value and productivity, the wider consequences are discouragement of investment, thin capital markets, inefficient allocation of resources, and slower growth of the economy.[30] Studies on the Asian financial crisis attribute the ineffectiveness of the mechanisms preventing the expropriation of minority shareholders to the precipitation of the crisis.[31]

Controlling shareholders with unfettered control rights over a majority of companies raise corporate governance concerns for not only the company and its minority shareholders, but for the entire economy. This is more so in developing countries such as Sri Lanka, the focus jurisdiction of this study, where unsupported local market mechanisms, weak legal

---

[28] R Gilson and J Gordon, Doctrines and Markets: Controlling Controlling Shareholders (2003), 152 University of Pennsylvania Law Review, 785, describe the divergent interests of the controlling shareholders and non-controlling shareholders as an 'agency problem'.

[29] R Kraakman *et al.*, *The Anatomy of Corporate Law: A Comparative and Functional Approach* (Oxford University Press Oxford 2004), 215, Chapter 2.1, include descriptions of the three principal-agent problems, that is, the opportunism of controlling shareholders vis-à-vis minority shareholders; the opportunism of managers vis-à-vis shareholders and opportunism of the firm vis-à-vis other stakeholders, such as creditors and employees.

[30] R Morck, D Wolfenzon and B Yeung, Corporate Governance, Economic Entrenchment and Growth (2004), National Bureau of Economic Research Working Paper 10692, http://papers.nber.org/papers/w10692.pdf [5 November 2005], 31–36.

[31] S Johnson *et al.*, Corporate Governance in the Asian Financial Crisis (2000), 58 *Journal of Financial Economics*, 141.

protection and poorly functioning institutions are incapable of meeting the challenges of entrenched controlling shareholders.

There is thus, a need to frame an agenda for the reform of corporate governance taking into account the agency problems arising not only from controlling shareholder systems but also from the specific features of such controlling shareholder systems such as family control or group affiliation.

The *first step* in framing such reform agenda is an analysis of the implications for corporate governance of not only controlling shareholder systems but also of the different features within such system. For example, private benefits of control, a cost of the controlling shareholder system, may not incur the same cost in family controlled companies as among non-family-controlled business groups. Neither will it be static across jurisdictions with different institutional and market backgrounds.

5.1.5. *Why are Controlling Shareholders Efficient in One Jurisdiction and Not in Another?*

The empirical realities of widespread controlling shareholder systems described earlier[32] pose an interesting dilemma. Does the prevalence of public companies in countries other than the UK and the US, with shareholders in effective voting control but without corresponding economic stakes, mean that all such countries suffer from the alleged debilitating effects of controlling shareholder systems? Is the corporate governance of public companies in Canada with a controlling shareholder system comparable to the governance of public companies in Thailand or India or Sri Lanka with similar shareholding structures? What explains the investor perception that corporate governance of public companies in Canada[33] is better than in Sri Lanka, though both countries may have public companies with a controlling shareholder or have control leveraged in excess of economic stakes by the use of pyramids or cross-holdings? In short, the inquiry must move to what factor or factors contribute towards making controlling shareholder systems efficient in one country and not another?

---

[32] Section 5.1.1.

[33] World Bank, Doing Business in 2006: Protecting Investors, http://www.doingbusiness. org/ExploreTopics/ProtectingInvestors/ [5 June 2006], demonstrates an investor protection score of 8.3 for Canada and 5.3 for Sri Lanka.

Therefore, the essential *second step* in framing an agenda for the reform of corporate governance is to extend the analysis to the factors that contribute towards making controlling shareholders efficient in some jurisdictions, but not in others. The answer to this question is pivotal in the reform context.

5.1.6. *Framework of the Chapter*

The primary objective of the chapter is to support the thesis that controlling shareholders systems present a trade-off[34] between its costs and benefits (i.e., that some of the benefits pay for its costs) and that such trade-off is dependent not only on functionally good law but also on the regulatory environment, market forces and the ratios between the controlling shareholders' economic and controlling stakes (hereinafter referred to as the 'trade-off thesis'). The identification of these specific institutional, legal and market conditions help formulate a reform agenda.

The trade-off thesis is presented through a two-step analysis. The *first step* is an analysis of the costs and benefits of controlling shareholder systems and the identification of the different factors that affect such costs and benefits.

The *second step* is the formulation of an answer to the question of what makes controlling shareholders efficient in some jurisdictions. The analysis starts with the recognition of the trade-off between the costs and benefits of controlling shareholder systems, followed by a reframing of the factors that determine the point of trade-off in light of the cost-benefit analysis undertaken in the first step of the analysis. It is the factors that determine the point of trade-off that shape the efficiency of controlling shareholders.

The strategy of the analysis is to answer the following questions. First, what form do the costs of controlling shareholder systems take, and what factors affect such costs? Second, do controlling shareholder systems have any benefits and what factors affect such benefits? Third,

---

[34] Gilson and Gordon (n. 28), 785–786, use the word 'trade-off' to explain the compromise between controlling shareholder systems and widely held systems — that is, the preference by non-controlling shareholders for controlling shareholders, as long as the costs of private benefits of control do not exceed the benefits of monitoring. The terminology is used more recently in R Gilson, Controlling Shareholders and Corporate Governance: Complicating the Comparative Taxonomy (2005), European Corporate Governance Institute Law Working Paper 49, http://ssrn.com/abstract=784744 [8 January 2006].

does the existence of both costs and benefits within controlling shareholder systems result in a 'trade-off' or do controlling shareholder systems equal expropriation and other costs only and should therefore be dismantled? Fourth, in the light of the cost-benefit analysis what factors affect such controlling shareholder trade-off?

The analysis is undertaken and the thesis applied in the context of the focus jurisdiction of this study, Sri Lanka. The chapter proceeds as follows. Section 5.2 analyses the distinct costs of controlling shareholder systems, generally and in Sri Lanka. Section 5.3 analyses the benefits of controlling shareholder systems, again generally and in Sri Lanka. Section 5.4 sets out the implications for corporate governance by a cost-benefit analysis. Section 5.5 sets out the controlling shareholder trade-off and its implications for corporate governance reform.

5.2. Costs of Controlling Shareholder Systems

As discussed, the widespread existence of controlling shareholder systems entails a shift in the agency conflict. Managers in controlling shareholder systems, unlike in dispersed shareholder systems, are accountable to the controlling shareholder who has the ability to provide focussed monitoring due to the incentives available and the avoidance of collective action problems. However, the presence of controlling shareholders also presents new costs. Theoretically, controlling shareholders can exert their unfettered control rights to expropriate private benefits of control or entrench themselves in positions of power.

This section of the chapter analyses the potential costs of controlling shareholder systems identified as private benefits of control, tunnelling among group companies, political influence, the abuse of market power and anti-competitive practices and entrenchment.

The costs associated with controlling shareholder systems become potentially more significant when investors other than controlling shareholders are of a different type. For example, if the controlling shareholder is an equity holder, there is incentive to force the firm to take on too much risk, while other stakeholders, such as creditors bear all the costs of failure.[35] Similarly, the size of the economic stakes held by investors

---

[35] M Jensen and W Meckling, The Theory of the Firm: Managerial Behaviour, Agency Costs and Ownership Structure (1976), 3 *Journal of Financial Economics*, 305.

other than controlling shareholders, is also significant as other large but non-controlling shareholders may have a constraining effect on the costs incurred by controlling shareholders.

5.2.1. *Private Benefits of Control*

The main focus of the literature on investor protection and its role in the development of financial markets is on the private benefits that controlling shareholders extract from the companies they control.[36] The term invoked to refer to these agency costs is 'private benefits of control',[37] and take place when 'some value, whatever the source, is not shared among all the shareholders in proportion of the shares owned, but it is enjoyed exclusively by the party in control'.[38]

The literature identifies private benefits of control as a value some shareholders attribute to simply being in control. These include non-financial benefits, such as the prestige of public recognition as the founder,[39] or the 'driving force' behind a company. However, the pure pleasure of command is hard to justify in all cases. Traditional sources of private benefits of control are the perquisites enjoyed by top executives,[40] who are most likely, the controlling shareholders. This is the most visible but, not the most important way, in which corporate resources can be expropriated for the advantage of the controlling party.

Hofstetter[41] in his recent study on companies with controlling shareholders categorises private benefits of control as 'internal' and 'external'.

(a) *Internal Benefits of Control*

Internal benefits of control are benefits a controlling shareholder can extract from the company using the position of an insider (often as a

---

[36] LLSV, Investor Protection and Corporate Governance (2000), 58 *Journal of Financial Economics*, 3–13; A Dyck and L Zingales, Private Benefits of Control: An International Comparison (2004), 59 *Journal of Finance*, 537; Gilson and Gordon (n. 28).

[37] Distinct from expropriation, which implicitly means the expropriation of the minority by the majority and is not dependent on a party being in control.

[38] Dyck and Zingales (n. 36), 541.

[39] Gilson (n. 34).

[40] Jensen and Meckling (n. 35).

[41] K Hofstetter, One Size Does Not Fit All: Corporate Governance for "Controlled Companies" (2005), http://www.hertig.ethz.ch/LE_200506_files/Papers/Hofstetter_Corporate_Governance_2005.pdf [10 February 2006].

member of a company's organ, such as the board of directors),[42] other than in arms-length transactions. Such extractions take the form of (i) outright theft by siphoning off cash and other assets without business justification; (ii) transfer of assets to controlling shareholders (self-dealing) or to companies controlled by controlling shareholders,[43] under terms which violate arms-length principles such as the payment of excessive salaries to controlling shareholders in management positions, transfer pricing in corporate groups, or unsecured low interest loans to controlling shareholders or to companies controlled by controlling shareholders; (iii) allocating business opportunities to related parties that arise as a result of the activities of the company; (iv) use of insider information in connection with the sale or purchase of shares in the market[44] and (v) implementing transactions in the interests of controlling shareholders that do not affect the company directly but open the company to risk (e.g., tax evasion schemes for the benefit of controlling shareholders).

In corporate groups, it is fairly easy for a controlling shareholder to choose to exploit these internal opportunities through group-affiliated companies with no advantage to the remaining shareholders. This is because in corporate groups, it is difficult to demarcate what belongs to the company and what belongs to its shareholders (i.e., companies within the group). This is the case when shareholder assets and company assets are jointly put to work, as is common in corporate groups. In such scenarios, the opportunity and probability for the extraction of internal private benefits of control are likely to be higher.[45]

In family controlled companies the role of non-financial internal benefits of control are likely to be larger and the use of insider information in connection with sale or purchase of shares in the market is likely to be common. Further, when the controlling shareholder is a family, internal private benefits of control are likely to be larger because the family is likely to be directly involved in the management of the firm as directors and executive officers which gives them discretion over company decisions and facilitates the extraction of private benefits of control.

----

[42] ibid 16.

[43] S Johnson *et al.*, Tunneling, in K Hopt and E Wymeersch (eds.), *Capital Markets and Company Law* (Oxford University Press Oxford 2003).

[44] Hofstetter (n. 41), 16.

[45] Discussion in Section 5.2.2.

If the controlling shareholders are financial institutions, internal benefits of control are likely to take the form of increased high interest borrowings by the companies under control of such financial institutions.

(b) *External Benefits of Control*

In situations encompassing external benefits of control, the controlling shareholders are acting as shareholders and in that capacity have greater discretion to create value for themselves as shareholders, which is not shared among the other shareholders.

This includes the use of voting rights to make choices that might be detrimental to minority shareholders, such as an alteration to the company's articles of association, its capital structure, board of directors or a decision to merge the company. Similarly, controlling shareholders can sell their shares in the market or as a block,[46] or choose to increase their stake in the company and thereby, adversely affect the minority shareholders (e.g., dilutive share issues), or engage in a freeze-out at a discounted price.[47]

Conceptually the above activities appear to be within the inherent rights of any shareholder, although they may be less than desirable for a minority shareholder. Unlike in internal benefits of control situations where the shareholders are acting as insiders and subject to fiduciary obligations, in external benefits of control situations, the controlling shareholders have greater capacity to create value for themselves subject only to market forces or specifically designed legal or regulatory rules.

(c) *Measuring Private Benefits of Control*

By their very nature, private benefits of control are difficult to observe and difficult to measure. A way to measure private benefits of control is to estimate the value the market attaches to control rights. If this value is positive, the market believes that the controlling party obtains benefits over and above those that are shared with the other shareholders.

---

[46] Gilson (n. 34) recognises this as a sale of control.
[47] ibid 787.

Dyck and Zingales,[48] using a method pioneered by Barclay and Holderness,[49] measure private benefits of control in 39 countries based on values of privately negotiated transfers of controlling blocks in publicly traded companies. Based on 3993 control transactions between 1990 and 2000, they find that the value of corporate control (i.e., block premium as a percent of the company's equity)[50] is on average 14 percent of the equity value of a company and range between −4 percent in Japan (i.e., the market finds negative value in the controlling block) to +65 percent in Brazil.[51]

Interestingly, Dyck and Zingales conclude that the premium paid for control is higher when the buyer is from a country that is not only less protective of its investors, but also that non-legal market factors such as diffused ownership of the press, stronger product market competition and higher tax compliance are related to lower block premiums.[52] The findings imply that the buyer pays a premium for the ability to extract private benefits of control, easier in countries less protective of its investors and lacking market and institutional structures.

Dyck and Zingales also make the following theoretical predictions about the effects of private benefits of control[53]: (i) that in countries where a controlling party can appropriate private benefits of control, there would be a general reluctance to take companies public; (ii) when such companies do go public, the controlling party is more likely to retain control and (iii) where private benefits of control are larger, the government is more likely to sell a company through a private sale than through a share offering. In a similar prior analysis, Nenova[54] documents high control

---

[48] Dyck and Zingales (n. 36).

[49] M Barclay and C Holderness, Private Benefits of Control of Public Corporations (1989), 25 *Journal of Financial Economics*, 371.

[50] Dyck and Zingales (n. 36), 551, Table II. The block premium is computed as the difference between the price per share paid for the control block and the price on the Exchange two days after the announcement of the control transaction, divided by the price on the Exchange after the announcement (i.e., the premium paid for the block) and multiplied by the proportion of the economic stakes represented in the control block.

[51] ibid Table III. As to whether corporate control transactions are capable of accurately capturing private benefits of control is debatable, as corporate control transactions are affected by information inequalities, systemic overpayment and other institutional deficiencies.

[52] ibid 538.

[53] ibid 538–539.

[54] T Nenova, The Value of Corporate Votes and Control Benefits: A Cross-country Analysis (2003), 68 *Journal of Financial Economics*, 325.

premia in countries where minority shareholder protection is poor and capital markets are underdeveloped.

5.2.2. *Private Benefits of Control in Sri Lanka*

Private benefits of control are difficult to observe and measure. However, the existence of private benefits of control demonstrates the nature of agency costs in Sri Lanka and therefore, an investigation is undertaken by the use of two representative examples. A larger sample is necessary to obtain an exact measurement and more definitive conclusions.

The method pioneered by Barclay and Holderness,[55] and used by Dyck and Zingales,[56] measuring the difference between the price paid by the acquirer for a controlling block and the price quoted in the market the day after the sales announcement, is applied to two control transactions in Sri Lanka. If there exists a difference between the price paid by the acquirer for a controlling block and the price quoted in the market the day after the sales announcement, it represents an estimate of the private benefits of control enjoyed by the controlling party. However, it should be noted that a sample of two control transactions cannot be claimed to be statistically significant and the weight attached to these transactions should be adjusted accordingly.

In the first example, on 04 April 2006, Janashakthi Insurance Company Limited (now known as Janashakthi Insurance Company Plc), a diversified group of companies with principal business activities in insurance, dairy industry, finance and investments, agriculture and property development bought 40 percent of the equity stake of Central Securities Limited, an investment fund listed on the CSE, promoted and managed by Central Finance Company Limited (now known as Central Finance Company Plc).[57] The price per share for the control block was SLRS 40 while the price after the announcement of the transfer was SLRS 37.25.[58] The price premium paid per share for the controlling block over the post announcement price in this case was 7.38 percent.

---

[55] Barclay and Holderness (n. 49).

[56] Dyck and Zingales (n. 36).

[57] Sri Lanka's Janashakthi Group Agrees to Buy Central Securities Ltd (4 April 2006), *Lanka Business Online*.

[58] Colombo Stock Exchange Stock Market Statistics 07-04-2006 (8 April 2006), *Daily News*.

A more accurate measure of the value of the private benefits of control is the total premium paid, divided by the equity value of the firm.[59] In this example, Janashakthi Insurance Company Limited paid a 7.38 percent premium relative to the post announcement price for 40 percent of the company's equity, producing an estimate of private benefits of control as a percentage of equity of 2.95 percent.

In the second example, on 08 July 2005, the Gardiner family with a 26 percent economic stake in Galle Face Hotels group,[60] bought a further 35 percent equity stake of Ceylon Hotels Corporation (now known as Ceylon Hotels Corporation Plc), a company engaged in the management of a number of local inns mostly catering to the local tourists.[61] The purchase was on an all or nothing basis from a state-run bank.[62] The price per share for the control block was reported to be SLRS 610.57, while the price the day after the announcement of the transfer was SLRS 568.25.[63] The price premium paid per share for the controlling block over the post announcement price was 7.45 percent.

As a measure of the value of the private benefits of control, the total premium paid is divided by the equity value of the company. In this example, the Gardiner family paid a 7.45 percent premium relative to the post announcement price for 35 percent of the company's equity, producing an estimate of private benefits as a percentage of equity at 2.61 percent.

While by no means conclusive or statistically significant, the above two examples illustrate that control transactions in Sri Lanka attract a premium indicative of the existence of private benefits of control. On the basis of these two examples, on average, private benefits of control as a percentage of equity amount to around 3 percent. This implies that in Sri Lanka on average private benefits of control as measured by control

---

[59] Dyck and Zingales (n. 36), 544–551.

[60] A large economic stake in the hands of a controlling shareholder can effectively reduce the value of the acquiring stake and could also affect the measurement of the control transaction and private benefits of control.

[61] Galle Face Hotels Group Takes Control of Ceylon Hotels Corp (8 July 2005), *Lanka Business Online*.

[62] Bank of Ceylon Plans to Sell Off Stakes in Ceylon Hotels Corp (6 July 2005), *Lanka Business Online*.

[63] Colombo Stock Exchange Stock Market Statistics 11-07-2005 (12 July 2005), *Daily News*.

transactions is relatively low.[64] In the survey conducted by Dyck and Zingales,[65] other countries where private benefits of control are 3 percent of the value of equity or less, are Australia, Canada, Finland, France, Hong Kong, Japan, Netherlands and New Zealand. Yet, the low level of premium in the two transactions under analysis in Sri Lanka should not be considered as being comparable to the findings of the studies with respect to Australia, Canada, Finland, France, Hong Kong, Japan, Netherlands and New Zealand, where private benefits of control as a percentage of equity amount to around 3 percent. First, only two transactions were measured in Sri Lanka over a short period of time. Thus, the findings cannot be statistically significant. Second, the two transactions also achieved a high level of publicity, which may also have contributed to the low level of premium. Third, other factors such as the presence of other large shareholders, speculative trading etc were not discounted. Thus, the two transactions can only be taken as indicative of the existence of private benefits of control in Sri Lanka.

Further, on application to Sri Lanka of the theoretical predictions,[66] as to the existence of private benefits of control made by Dyck and Zingales,[67] it is evident that (i) in Sri Lanka, there is a general reluctance to take companies public;[68] (ii) when they do go public, the controlling party is more likely to retain control;[69] and (iii) the government is more likely to sell a company through a private sale than through a share offering.[70] Thus, the

---

[64] Other explanations may be present for the low premium (of 3 percent of equity) such as the presence of other large shareholders or that in Sri Lanka control transactions attract speculative trading which persists for longer than 2 days. Alternatively, benefits may also be extracted prior to the sale.

[65] Dyck and Zingales (n. 36), 550.

[66] Text between n. 53 and n. 54.

[67] Dyck and Zingales (n. 36), 538.

[68] From 1928 to 1976 there were 59 listed companies, which increased to 133 by 1989 and 205 by 1999 and finally 252 in 2005. Colombo Stock Exchange, Year-to-Date Listings, http://www.cse.lk/home/main.jsp [10 July 2006], in contrast to the 2160 registered public companies.

[69] Evidenced by the large number of listings by way of introduction. In 2003, 1/3 of all new listings were by way of introduction (i.e., without requirement of a public issue). Colombo Stock Exchange, *Fact Book 2003* (Colombo 2004).

[70] During 1989–1999, 62 out of a total of 83 privatisation transactions involving sale of control were conducted by way of a private sale, tender or split transaction with the control sold through a private sale. World Bank, 1988–1999 Privatization Transaction Data: Sri Lanka, http://rru.worldbank.org/Documents/Privatization/PrivatizationData.xls [10 July 2006].

accuracy of the theoretical predictions reaffirms the existence of private benefits of control in Sri Lanka.

While the measurement of private benefits of control in Sri Lanka is not conclusive given that only two control transactions were measured, the existence of a control premium in a low liquidity market and the applicability of the theoretical predictions pinpoint not only to the existence of private benefits of control in Sri Lanka, but also to the low levels of investor protection and lack of institutional and market structures in line with the Dyck and Zingales argument.[71]

5.2.3. *Private Benefits of Control in Group Scenarios: Tunnelling*

Tunnelling is the intercorporate transfer of resources among companies.[72] Although tunnelling does not require a control pyramid to take effect, its likelihood is greater among companies in a pyramid. Within a pyramid tunnelling takes place to the advantage of the controlling shareholder, that is, owners of pyramidal groups tunnel resources from companies where they have small economic stakes (but large control rights) to companies where they have larger economic stakes.

Johnson *et al.* distinguish between two forms of tunnelling.[73] First, controlling shareholders can simply transfer resources from a company for their own benefit through self-dealing transactions such as sale of assets above or below the market price, give each other high or low interest loans or loan guarantees, expropriate corporate opportunities etc., which are in fact, internal private benefits of control in groups. Second, controlling shareholders can increase their own share in a company through dilutive share issues, minority freeze-outs and other kinds of transactions that discriminate against minority shareholders, which are in fact, external private benefits of control within groups.

While some forms of tunnelling, such as outright theft, are illegal in many jurisdictions, in certain jurisdictions tunnelling in the form of expropriation of corporate opportunity or transfer of assets from a company to

---

[71] Private benefits of control are higher where a country is less protective of its investors, Dyck and Zingales (n. 36), 538–539.

[72] Johnson *et al.* (n. 43).

[73] ibid 612.

its controlling shareholder at below market value takes place consistent with both statutes and judicial principles.[74]

Tunnelling reduces returns to minority shareholders of companies lower down the pyramid structure and diminishes investor confidence in markets. Illicit transfers of assets and clouding of financial accounting, reduces transparency and affects company valuation, and hinders equity market growth. The presence of tunnelling also reflects poor investor protection.

Families control large companies throughout most of the world and these families achieve control through pyramid structures within business groups.[75] When controlling families manage many companies in the form of pyramids, tunnelling assumes the form of intercorporate business transactions. The opportunity for tunnelling within family controlled group structures is exacerbated by the presence of family members on the board of directors of these companies. This is recognised by Morck *et al.*, in their claim that in family controlled pyramids, entrenched controlling shareholders in positions of management have the ability to not only tunnel corporate resources, but also 'raise a corporate veil against outsider monitoring'.[76]

(a) *Measuring Private Benefits of Control in Group Scenarios:*
    Tunnelling

Johnson *et al.* provide detailed examples of several cases of tunnelling in Europe, involving intrabusiness group transactions and suggests that tunnelling is common in countries where investor protection is low and that it is severe in times of financial crisis.[77] However, due to the illicit nature of tunnelling, evidence and measurement of tunnelling remains illusive.

A study by Bertrand *et al.* attempts to quantify tunnelling among Indian business groups (family controlled pyramids) and whether they correlate to controlling shareholders' ownership in each company within the group.[78] They trace the spread of earnings shocks through a business group, and find evidence of tunnelling occurring via non-operating

---

[74] ibid name this as 'legal tunnelling'.

[75] Text after n. 12.

[76] Morck, Wolfenzon and Yeung (n.30).

[77] Johnson *et al.* (n. 43).

[78] M Bertrand, P Mehta and S Mullainthan, Ferreting Out Tunneling: An Application to Indian Business Groups (2002), 117 *Quarterly Journal of Economics*, 121.

components of profit (such as miscellaneous and non-recurring items).[79] They find that groups (especially those lower on the pyramid) are less sensitive to industry shocks to their profitability, than stand-alones. For example, a shock resulting in a one-rupee[80] decrease, leads to about a one-rupee increase in earnings for a stand-alone company, while for a group it only results in a 0.75 rupee increase. This suggests a dissipation of rupees 0.25.[81] However, group companies on average are sensitive to shocks affecting other companies within the group. This sensitivity is larger for companies in which the group has lower economic stakes.[82] They interpret this result as evidence that positive shocks to companies lower down the pyramid are tunnelled to companies in upper levels of the pyramid. This serves the interest of the controlling shareholders to the detriment of the minority shareholders with economic stakes in only the tunnelled company.[83]

Other studies identifying tunnelling are by Bae *et al.*, who find that in Korea, within-group takeovers rarely raise the value of the bidder, but do raise the value of the other group members. Intra-*chaebol* acquisitions thus tunnel wealth away from companies whose economic stakes are more in the hands of public shareholders towards companies, whose economic stakes are in the hands of controlling shareholders.[84] Morck and Nakamura, suggest that growth patterns of some of the Japanese pre-war *zaibatsu*[85] reflect among other things, the importance attached to private benefits of control by large shareholders.[86] These findings are consistent with the occurrence of tunnelling.

---

[79] ibid 123–124, 142–143. Interestingly, they examine whether market prices incorporate tunnelling and imply that the market may penalise tunnelling.

[80] Unit of Indian currency.

[81] Bertrand, Mehta and Mullainthan (n. 78), 132–133.

[82] ibid 136–139.

[83] T Khanna and Y Yafeh, Business Groups in Developing Countries: Paragons or Parasites? (2005), European Corporate Governance Institute Finance Working Paper 92, http://ssrn.com/abstract=787625 [10 January 2006], 24, question whether the explanation is plausible for negative shocks.

[84] K Bae, J Kang and J Kim, Tunnelling or Value Added: Evidence from Mergers by Korean Business Groups (2002), 62 *Journal of Finance*, 2695.

[85] Family controlled conglomerates.

[86] R Morck and M Nakamura, A Frog in the Well Knows Nothing of the Ocean: A History of Corporate Ownership in Japan, in R Morck (ed.), *The History of Corporate Governance around the World: Family Business Groups to Professional Managers* (University of Chicago Press Chicago 2005).

The effect of tunnelling on firm performance and valuation is less clear. Studies of Indian group companies provide statistical evidence that companies affiliated with the most diversified business groups outperform unaffiliated firms.[87] This is attributed to the ability of diversified groups to add value by replicating the functions of institutions that are missing, such as inadequate information, imperfect contract enforcement, weak regulatory structure.[88] More generally, tunnelling should result in a negative impact on firm performance and valuation.

5.2.4. *Private Benefits of Control in Group Scenarios: Tunnelling in Sri Lanka*

The fact that controlling shareholders in Sri Lanka predominantly use corporate group structures (i.e., pyramids and cross-shareholdings) to increase their control stakes in excess of their economic stakes,[89] suggests that propensity to tunnel is higher in Sri Lanka. However, the mere existence of groups is not necessarily correlated to tunnelling. Group structures may be motivated by reasons other than control and may simply be holding companies.

While it is impracticable in a study of this nature to attempt to measure the prevalence of tunnelling among group companies in Sri Lanka, evidence of tunnelling can be illustrated by anecdotal evidence. Distilleries Company,[90] a group company listed on the CSE has more than 65 percent of its net worth invested in its' group companies.[91] These investments yield a rate of return of less than 0.60.[92] This minimal rate of

---

[87] T Khanna and K Palepu, Is Group Affiliation Profitable in Developing Countries? An Analysis of Diversified Indian Business Groups (2000), 15 *Journal of Finance*, 867, using Tobin's-*Q* as a measure of performance, calculated by dividing the market value of a company by the replacement value of its assets.

[88] ibid 887–888.

[89] Chapter 3.

[90] Eighth sample company in Chapter 3.

[91] Distilleries Company, *Annual Report 2004* (Colombo 2004), 19, SLRS 5,627,414,000, SLRS 20,000,000 and SLRS 548,904,000 (a total of SLRS 6,196,318,000) are set out as investments in subsidiaries, jointly controlled entities and associates, respectively. The balance sheet sets out the total equity as SLRS 9,570,097,000.

[92] ibid 21, 30, n. 5 to financial statements sets out a nil figure for dividend received from subsidiaries and SLRS 37,425,000 as dividend received from associate company.

return fuels speculation that investments by Distilleries Company in its group companies are indicative of tunnelling.

Carson Cumberbatch,[93] another company listed on the CSE is similar. Carson Cumberbatch has more than 73 percent of its net worth invested in other companies within its group.[94] Yet these investments in 2005 yielded a zero percent rate of return,[95] giving rise to the speculation that investments made by Carson Cumberbatch in its group companies were intracorporate transfer of resources (i.e., tunnelling) for the advantage of the controlling shareholders, with larger economic stakes in the subsidiary and associate companies of Carson Cumberbatch. These investments made by Carson Cumberbatch, with a zero rate of return are detrimental to the minority shareholders of Carson Cumberbatch, who do not have economic stakes in the other group companies.[96]

Perhaps due to the illicit nature of tunnelling, evidence of tunnelling beyond anecdotal evidence is scarce. However, the evidence does give rise to speculation that some form of tunnelling exists among group companies in Sri Lanka.

In line with the argument presented by Johnson *et al.*[97] that tunnelling is common in countries where investor protection is low, the anecdotal evidence of tunnelling in Sri Lankan is indicative that investor protection is likely to be poor and that institutional and market mechanisms necessary to curb tunnelling are missing.

5.2.5. *Political Influence*

Companies with controlling shareholders have greater motivation to be politically influential. This is because the close ties that controlling

---

[93] Fifth sample company in Chapter 3.

[94] Carson Cumberbatch, *Annual Report 2004–05* (Colombo 2005), 33, SLRS 1,490,539,409 and SLRS 125,237,418 (total of SLRS 1,619,776,827) are set out as investments in subsidiaries and associates, respectively. The balance sheet sets out the total equity as SLRS 2,200,679,591.

[95] ibid, n. 5 to financial statements sets out a nil figure for dividend received from associate companies.

[96] Also illustrative of tunnelling in Sri Lanka is the payment of excessive management fees to groups companies. Minority Shareholders of Maskeliya Plantations Threaten Court Action (8 July 2007), *Sunday Times*.

[97] Johnson *et al.* (n. 43).

shareholders in the form of wealthy families and business groups in many developing countries enjoy with governments bring about greater likelihood of political favouritism and rent seeking, than in widely held companies with dispersed shareholders. This is detrimental to other widely held companies in the economy and reflects corruption. While political influence and anti-competitive practices are also prevalent in systems with dispersed share ownership, the prospect of controlling shareholders in the form of business groups, families and wealthy individuals, seeking to exert political influence is greater than managers in dispersed systems, who may not have the same form of family and historical background to support the close political connections or the vested interests of controlling shareholders.

The commonness of politically connected firms around the world is highlighted in a study by Faccio, who assembles a data set of 20,202 publicly traded companies in over 47 countries, and finds political connections to be fairly widespread in 35 of the 47 countries surveyed.[98]

The value of being politically connected can take pecuniary and non-pecuniary forms such as relaxed regulatory oversight, preferential tax treatment and preferential status in relation to government contracts. Faccio in a related study argues that politically connected companies differ sharply from those not connected, in that politically connected companies have higher leverage, greater market power, lower taxes, and that such differences become stronger when the political link is through owners than directors. It follows then that the likelihood of such political link being made through an owner is higher in controlling shareholder systems due to the prominence given to controlling shareholders as opposed to salaried directors or managers. Therefore, political influence is likely to be higher in controlling shareholder systems than in dispersed shareholder systems.

Political influence has a greater role to play in the context of business groups within controlling shareholder systems. Many business groups, whether run by wealthy families or not, form and survive due to government policies. In India, for example, some business groups were formed

---

[98] M Faccio, Politically Connected Firms (2006), 96 *American Economic Review*, 369, identifies a company as closely connected with a politician if at least one of its large shareholders (anyone controlling at least 10 percent of voting rights) or one of its top officers is a member of parliament, or is closely related to a top politician or party.

to receive favourable treatment from the 'License Raj'.[99] Groups with the ability to influence governments receive favourable tax treatment, oppose positive reforms or institutional change, and in extreme instances, act as power brokers.[100] Business groups in the form of control pyramids are in superior positions to use political connections to further business interests, because of the greater discretion in the use of companies lower down a control pyramid to return favours.

Further, groups run by wealthy families are preferable trading partners for most corrupt politicians as only a few families run the business groups, and as such, politicians need maintain relationships with only a few influential individuals. Family controlled groups are also more likely to return past favours because of longer continuity of the families in the management of such groups.[101]

However, close relationships between the government and business groups do not necessarily always operate to the detriment of the economy or other companies. Governments can attack or attempt to dismantle groups,[102] and it is suggested that government support of business groups may in fact, help preserve the social equilibrium as in the case of Malaysia, where government support of Malay business groups forced the transfer of assets from the economically dominant Chinese to the numerically dominant, poorer Malays[103] (however, such transfers were costly to the Chinese and probably inefficient). Similarly, it can also be suggested that the relationship between the government and family businesses with controlling shareholders are joint efforts at 'nation building' as in the case of Japan or South Korea.

However, the ability of controlling shareholders to wield political influence is reflective of the institutional deficiencies within society, which permits such factors to influence economic decisions. Additionally, to preserve their privileged positions under the *status quo*, the controlling

---

[99] T Khanna and K Palepu, The Evolution of Concentrated Ownership in India: Broad Patterns and a History of the Indian Software Industry, in R Morck (ed.), *The History of Corporate Governance Around the World: Family Groups to Professional Managers* (University of Chicago Press Chicago 2005), 283.

[100] For example the Japanese *zaibatsu*, the Mitsui and Mitsubishi groups.

[101] R Morck and B Yeung, Special Issues Relating to Corporate Governance and Family Control (2004), World Bank Policy Research Working Paper 3406, http://econ.worldbank.org/files/38739_wps3406.pdf [10 May 2005].

[102] Undertaken in many developing countries as part of nationalisation programmes.

[103] Khanna and Yafeh (n. 83), 32.

elites arguably use their political connections to stymie the institutional development of capital markets and erect a variety of entry barriers. This restricts the governance of a country's corporate sector to a collection of elite controlling shareholders who can bias capital allocation to their advantage and also reduce the pace of innovation. These effects, in turn, impede the development of capital markets, further distort capital allocation and generally retards growth.

5.2.6. *Political Influence in Sri Lanka*

In Sri Lanka, businesses have historically had their fortunes closely aligned with the government of the day. During the British period of colonisation, merchant capitalism depended to a great extent based on political patronage. A noteworthy example of the embodiment of such political patronage and merchant capitalism was *Muhandiram* (an honorary headman) Tudugalage Don Philip Wijewardene (1844–1903), who was perhaps the most successful timber dealer in the late 19th century. He was the chief contractor to the government and contracted to supply timber for the breakwater for the port of Colombo.[104]

The link between the government of the day and commercial entities persisted with the establishment of the British agency houses and plantation companies (subsequently dismantled and nationalised in the post-independence period).[105] 'European colonialism was a system of political and economic domination',[106] and beneath the formally organised colonial firms with international trading links was a layer of enterprises controlled by business communities, which extended to wealthy families with political connections. At the time of independence, Sri Lankans in power were a capitalist elite. Notable are the Senanayake–Kotelawala–Wijewardena

---

[104] M Roberts, Elite Formation and Elites, 1832–1931, in M Roberts (ed.), *Sri Lankan Collective Identities Revisited* (Marga Institute Colombo 1997), 201, citing A Wright, *Twentieth Century Impressions of Ceylon* (Lloyd's Great Britain Publishing Company London 1907).

[105] Under the first phase of the Land Reform Act No. 1 of 1972.

[106] M Moore, Ethnicity, Caste and the Legitimacy of Capitalism, in M Roberts (ed.), *Sri Lanka-Collective Identities Revisited* (Marga Institute-Sri Lanka Centre for Development Studies Colombo 1998), 63.

families that produced the first three prime ministers of Ceylon (as it was then named), with business interests in plantations, graphite mining and newspaper ownership.[107]

Subsequent economic policies in the post 1950s through the 1970s, such as the nationalisation of foreign businesses and plantations coupled with the growth of the state sector resulted in most economic activity vesting in state hands. In such an environment, political connections and patronage of some form were important for business success.

As Moore points out, of the 50 wealthiest businessmen in the mid-1980s in Sri Lanka, five were descendants of the political elite at the time of independence.[108] Further, the period after 1977 gave rise to the prominence of family controlled business groups with close connections to the government as reflected by the privatisation process in the late 1980s and 1990s.[109]

As set out above, politics and business lead an intertwined existence in Sri Lanka[110] and contributed to the rise of a wealthy entrepreneur class presently occupying positions of control among Sri Lankan companies. While political connections of controlling shareholders *ipso facto* do not give rise to costs within controlling shareholder systems, it does give rise to speculation that companies with controlling shareholders, with close relationships to politicians, wield political influence not available to other companies within the economy. This results in an unfair competitive advantage to companies controlled by politically connected individuals.

An unobserved factor in the context of Sri Lanka and other developing countries is that political connections are not necessarily only based on familial relationships. The small size of the economy and the

---

[107] Sir J Kotelawala, *An Asian Prime Minister's Story* (George Harrap London 1956); ______ *Ferguson's Ceylon Directory for 1930* (Lake House Colombo 1930).

[108] Moore (n. 106) Table 2, 76, note 20, names Upali Wijewardena (Upali Group), Ranjit Wijewardena (Lake House Printers and Publishers), CA Harischandra (Harischandra Mills), Mallory Wijesinghe (Bartleets) and Lalith Kotelawala (Ceylinco Group).

[109] S Ranaraja, *Case Study of Privatised Enterprises in Sri Lanka* (ILO Colombo 2001), 13, states that 'The private sector was perceived as scrambling to curry political favour in return for advantages in gaining control of state enterprises …'.

[110] Contrast Faccio (n. 98), surveying 18 Sri Lanka companies on the Worldscope database, finds no political connection either through ownership or directorship. This may not be a strictly accurate analysis since political influence can be obtained from connections other than blood ties.

interconnectedness among the elite class and politicians ensures beneficial treatment to those with the 'right' connections.[111]

Further, in the light of the perceived prevalence of corruption in
Sri Lanka,[112] it is likely that close ties enjoyed among the government,
wealthy individuals and business groups are more likely than not detrimental to other companies and stakeholders, rather than welfare enhancing.[113]

While an exact measurement of the political influence wielded by
controlling shareholders in Sri Lanka is difficult to obtain due to the
opaque nature of such connections, the historical context analysed above,
the presence of descendants of political elites among the wealthy entrepreneurs of today, the rise of family controlled business groups in the
post-privatisation period and the perception of high levels of corruption in
Sri Lanka illustrate not only the interconnections between politicians and
wealthy entrepreneurs and a presumption of favouritism, but also the lack
of legal and regulatory structures, and market mechanisms to constrain
such influence.

While political influence can be costly to any economy, its impact is
greater in a controlling shareholder or large shareholder system due to its
emphasis on personal relationships.[114] It is also likely to have a greater
impact in Sri Lanka, which is less protective of its investors, and deficient
both institutionally and in market mechanisms, in meeting the challenges
of corporate corruption.

5.2.7. *Market Power and Anti-Competitive Practices*

Another identified cost of controlling shareholder systems is the concentration of wealth and market power in the hands of a few wealthy

---

[111] However, Sri Lanka is one of the few countries in the world, with its constitution
containing an article restricting members of parliament from holding directorships.
Constitution of the Democratic Socialist Republic of Sri Lanka 1978, Art. 66 (e).

[112] Transparency International, *Transparency International Corruption Perception Index
2002* (Berlin 2002), Sri Lanka scores 3.7 out of a top score of 10.

[113] M Faccio, The Characteristics of Politically Connected Firms (2006), http://ssrn.com/
abstract=918244 [18 August 2006], submits that the distinction between politically
connected and non-connected companies are greater when the company operates in a
country with a high degree of corruption.

[114] ibid 4, 16.

individuals or business groups within an economy. Market power is easily assembled in controlling shareholder systems by control of a number of companies either individually or through a group form. Market power in countries with inadequate regulatory structures can give rise to the emergence of monopolies and other anti-competitive practices, either preventing the entry of rivals into markets or forcing their exit.

The general perception that business groups and family controlled companies are likely to harm competition is best illustrated by the actions of President Roosevelt during the Great Depression in the United States, who sought to dissolve business groups by taxing intercorporate dividends.[115] However, empirical evidence on the market power wielded by business groups and controlling shareholders is scarce.

Like most identified costs of controlling shareholder systems, the actual cost of the market power wielded by controlling shareholders depends on the context, that is, the regulatory environment, institutions and market mechanisms. Market power in the hands of controlling shareholders leads to anti-competitive practices only when the regulatory regime is poor. If the regulatory regime does not tolerate anti-competitive practices, competition between wealthy families and business groups can give rise to a healthy competitive environment, resulting in increases in efficiency.[116]

5.2.8. *Market Power and Anti-Competitive Practices in Sri Lanka*

In the Sri Lankan context, there is anecdotal evidence to illustrate that market power in the hands of controlling shareholders gives rise to anti-competitive practices and monopolies rather than increases in efficiency. The poor legal and regulatory environment further aggravates the situation.

Many of the recent examples arise as a result of the privatisation process, where the government sold controlling stakes in SOEs (e.g., sale of a 35 percent stake in Sri Lanka Telecom, the fixed telephony operator,

---

[115] R Morck, How to Eliminate Pyramidal Business Groups: The Double Taxation of Intercorporate Dividends and Other Incisive Uses of Tax Policy (2004), National Bureau of Economic Research Working Paper 10944, http://ssrn.com/abstract=629586 [5 December 2005], 8–15.

[116] This is an important argument in the reform context as competition (i.e., product market, market for corporate control) is a suggested mechanism to ensuring good corporate governance. F Allen, Corporate Governance in Emerging Economies (2005), 21 *Oxford Review of Economic Policy*, 164.

to Nippon Telegraph and Telecommunications Corporation of Japan, and 51 percent of the Colombo Gas Company to the Dutch company, Shell Overseas International BV/Royal Dutch), which had hitherto enjoyed monopolistic market positions, to private entrepreneurs, thereby creating market control positions. Many of these control stakes were sold with assurances of monopolistic positions with little regard for consumer welfare or long-term efficiency. The government's apparent willingness to sustain monopolies and impose regulatory restrictions hindering competition after privatisation is apparent in the cases of Sri Lanka Telecom and Shell Gas Lanka Limited.[117]

The ill effects of the privatisation process in terms of anti-competitive practices are apparent in the LPG[118] and telecommunications sectors in Sri Lanka[119] where there is abuse of the dominant market positions with negative effects on competitors and consumers.

Increased market power in certain industries also gives controlling shareholders positions of political and social influence such as the newspaper industry in Sri Lanka, which is largely under the control of the Wijewardene family.[120] The close family control and involvement found in three of Sri Lanka's leading media institutions, the Lake House (founded by Wijewardene and subsequently taken over by the government), the

---

[117] M Knight-John and P Athukorale, Assessing Privatization in Sri Lanka: Distribution and Governance, in J Nellis and N Birdsall (eds.), *Reality Check: The Distributional Impact of Privatization in Developing Countries* (Center for Global Development Washington DC 2005), 389, 405, state that in the case of the privatisation of the Colombo Gas Company the contract specified that Shell Gas Lanka Limited would solely undertake liquefied petroleum gas (LPG) business for an exclusive 5-year period. In the case of Sri Lanka Telecom, Nippon Telegraph and Telecommunications Corporation of Japan received a 5-year monopoly to provide international telephony.

[118] ibid 389, 416, argue that the decrease in LPG prices when another supplier entered the market in 2001–2002, consequent to the ending of Shell Gas Lanka Limited's 5-year exclusive period, suggests that lack of competition contributed to earlier price increases.

[119] S Jayasuriya and M Knight-John, Sri Lanka's Telecommunications Industry: From Privatization to Anti-competition (2002), University of Manchester Center on Regulation and Competition Working Paper 14, http://www.competition-regulation.org.uk/publications/working_papers/wp14.pdf [14 August 2006] argue that Sri Lanka Telecom privatisation would have better results in terms of prices and access if monopoly was granted on international telephony and the regulatory regime more effective.

[120] Described as an '88-year-old Wijewardene nexus' in L Brady, Colonials, Bourgeoisies and Media Dynasties: A Case Study of Sri Lankan Media, http://www.ejournalism.au.com/ejournalist/brady2521.pdf [5 November 2005], 3.

Upali Group and Wijeya Newspapers, places the Wijewardene family and a number of elite families related through blood or marriage at the epicentre of a political and media dynasty in Sri Lanka. Market power over the newspaper industry enables members of this family to influence not only politics but also expand their reach into other forms of media such as radio and television.

Excessive market power in the hands of controlling shareholders and resultant anti-competitive market practices are primarily due to the concessions granted by the government during the privatisation process and the poor regulatory structure in Sri Lanka.[121] Market power is more likely to be abused by way of anti-competitive practices in Sri Lanka, due to the opaque nature of control pyramids and cross-holdings used by controlling shareholders to increase their control stakes in excess of their economic stakes, the lack of a regulatory framework to meet such challenges, and the lack of effective market-based mechanisms, such as consumer group lobbies.

5.2.9. *Entrenchment*

The essence of controlling shareholder systems is the ability of controlling shareholders to secure control rights without a commensurate economic stake. The control rights of a controlling shareholder provide a certain degree of insulation from the pressures of other shareholders and the market, and gives rise to 'entrenchment'[122] by such controlling shareholders. Entrenchment protects positions of power and enables controlling shareholders to escape the wrath and scrutiny of other investors when they take value-distorting decisions. Thus, control rights allow for entrenchment by controlling shareholders,[123] which in turn affects firm value (both positively and negatively) and economic growth.

---

[121] R Samarajiva and A Dokeniya, Regulation and Investment: Sri Lanka Case Study (2004), World Dialogue on Regulation Discussion Paper 303b, http://www.regulateonline.org/content/view/207/31/ [12 July 2006], 11, Table 2.3, report that the telecom regulatory environment (market entry, regulation of anti-competitive practices) in the period 1997–2002 were either unsatisfactory or poor.

[122] *Concise Oxford English Dictionary* (10th edn rev Oxford University Press Oxford 2002), 'to be established so firmly that change is difficult'.

[123] Large shareholdings also create entrenchment. However, in controlling shareholder systems, the entrenchment is without a commensurate economic stake and is therefore, arguably undeserved.

Entrenchment is most visible when a controlling shareholder destroys value or refuses to go along with value-enhancing proposals, although it will be disputed as to whether the actions of the controlling shareholder destroys or enhances value. Hofstetter,[124] identifies three possible entrenchment scenarios: (i) in a corporate crisis; or (ii) in connection with succession to a corporate position or (iii) in connection with a strategic decision.

An important aspect of entrenchment is that it can lock in control, especially in family controlled companies where a founder may bequeath control to an incompetent offspring.[125] Entrenchment makes investors helpless in the face of mismanagement by incompetent offspring, while the only constraining effect on the value decreasing actions of such offspring is the effect on firm value and the resultant share price decline.

Unlike in dispersed ownership systems where severe mismanagement results in stock price declines, controlling shareholder systems are insulated to a great degree from hostile takeovers, pressures from institutional investors, and other market-based disciplinary devices. In controlling shareholder systems, hostile takeovers are not possible as control rights are often enhanced to exceed 50 percent by the use of pyramids or cross-shareholdings. Further, it is not in the nature of institutional investors to take an active role if their holdings are insignificant, as they are, in many controlling systems. Shareholder lawsuits are unlikely to be successful if enforcement of investor protection measures is poor and market disciplinary forces are likely to be minimal as control stakes are not commensurate with equity stakes.

Minority shareholders in controlling shareholder systems also have difficulties exiting mismanaged companies, not only because of the resultant decline in share prices but also because of the low investor demand for noncontrol or minority stakes within such systems. In effect, 'voice' and 'exit' are poor options in controlling shareholder systems and aggravates entrenchment by controlling shareholders.

---

[124] Hofstetter (n. 41), 18.

[125] N Bloom and J Van-Reenen, Measuring and Explaining Management Practices Across Firms and Countries (2006), Centre for Economic Performance Working Paper 716, http://cep.lse.ac.uk/pubs/download/dp0716.pdf [5 July 2007], find poor management practices are more prevalent when product market competition is weak and/or when family owned firms pass management control down to the eldest sons.

Theory predicts that where private benefits of control are large, entrepreneurs are more reluctant to go public[126] and more likely to retain control when they go public,[127] demonstrating a cyclic link between private benefits of control and entrenchment. As a result, few companies in controlling shareholders systems will go public and equity markets in countries characterised by such systems continue to remain underdeveloped.

Studies have also found varying degrees of entrenchment dependent on the type of controlling owner. For example, families may more easily entrench themselves,[128] and companies controlled by founders are found to be less likely than the average firm to be taken over.[129] Using data for Canadian public corporations, Morck *et al.* argue that family controlling shareholders have a vested interest in preserving the value of existing capital,[130] and therefore, inherited corporate control is more likely to be entrenched and impede growth.

In a later study, Claessens *et al.*,[131] find the entrenchment effect to be greatest in family controlled companies and somewhat less for state-controlled companies, but not to be significant when the controlling shareholder is a widely held company or a financial institution. This is plausible as families are more likely to be directly involved in management giving them discretion over company decisions and leading to entrenchment.

---

[126] Dyck and Zingales (n. 36), 571.

[127] ibid; L Bebchuck, A Rent Protection Theory of Corporate Ownership and Control (1999), National Bureau of Economic Research Working Paper 7203, http://www.nber.org/papers/w7203 [5 November 2005].

[128] R Morck, D Stangeland and B Yeung, Inherited Wealth, Corporate Control and Economic Growth: The Canadian Disease, in R Morck (ed.), *Concentrated Corporate Ownership* (University of Chicago Press Chicago 2000), 319, submit that families manipulate their countries' political systems to entrench themselves.

[129] R Morck, A Shleifer and R Vishny, Characteristics of Targets of Hostile and Friendly Takeovers, in A Auerbach (ed.), *Corporate Takeovers: Causes and Consequences* (National Bureau of Economic Research/University of Chicago Press Chicago 1988), 101, find that companies where founders are present are more likely to be targets of friendly bids.

[130] Morck, Stangeland and Yeung (n. 128), in their study of heir-controlled Canadian firms show low industry-adjusted financial performance, labour capital ratios, and that research and development spending is relatively low compared to firms of similar age and size.

[131] S Claessens *et al.*, Disentangling the Incentive and Entrenchment Effects of Large Shareholdings (2002), 57 *Journal of Finance*, 2741–2744.

Further, participation by controlling shareholders in the management of the companies, especially family controlled companies, are associated with greater entrenchment and valued less by investors.[132]

Constraining entrenchment by controlling shareholders is difficult. Franks *et al.*[133] describe how for a short time in the 1950s and 1960s the corporate landscape of Britain began to resemble continental Europe. Companies responded to an unregulated takeover market by introducing dual class shares, voting right restrictions and pyramids. But these takeover defences were met with opposition from large institutional investors and the LSE, concerned about interference with the takeover process, the ability of management to entrench itself behind takeover defences, and the withdrawal of voting rights. It is noteworthy that it was not only specifically designed legal or regulatory rules that successfully prevented entrenchment by British corporate insiders but also market forces in the guise of institutional investors with sufficient interests to warrant corporate monitoring.

5.2.10. *Entrenchment in Sri Lanka*

Evidence of entrenchment by controlling shareholders, the institutional deficiencies and difficulties faced by market-based disciplinary devices in Sri Lanka is demonstrated by a typical example.

Lanka Hospital Corporation Limited (owners of Apollo Hospitals and now known as Lanka Hospital Corporation Plc) was formed as a joint venture with the Apollo Hospitals Group of India (Apollo Group) holding 35 percent of shares and the rest divided between the International Finance Corporation (IFC) (private-sector arm of the World Bank), the National Development Bank, the Sri Lanka Insurance Corporation Limited and several local investors. The issue arose in July 2006 when Sri Lanka Insurance Corporation Limited increased its economic stake in Lanka Hospital Corporation Limited from 20 percent to 36.07 percent.

---

[132] Y Yeh and T Woidtke, Commitment or Entrenchment? Controlling Shareholders and Board Composition (2005), 29 *Journal of Banking & Finance,* 1857–1882, suggest that board affiliation is a reasonable proxy for the degree of agency costs in family controlled companies.

[133] J Franks, C Mayer and S Rossi, Spending Less Time with the Family: The Decline of Family Ownership in the UK (2004), European Corporate Governance Network Working Paper 35, http://ssrn.com/abstract=493504 [25 July 2005], 24.

Sri Lanka Insurance Corporation Limited controlled by business tycoon Harry Jayawardene became the largest shareholder of Lanka Hospital Corporation Limited. The 16 percent purchase triggered the Takeovers and Mergers Code,[134] and required a mandatory offer to be made to the remaining shareholders.

At the time of the acquisition, Apollo Group held 32.6 percent of shares and controlled a further 4 percent in the Sri Lankan joint venture, while Property Development Limited (subsidiary of a state bank) held a 13.6 percent stake, another Sri Lankan investor 5 percent, and the rest dispersed.[135]

Reflective of entrenchment and political influence by controlling shareholders in Sri Lanka, the Reddy family of India (controlling shareholders of the Apollo Group) expressed concern on the proposed mandatory offer to the Indian High Commissioner in Sri Lanka, who raised the matter with the Sri Lankan government. The Sri Lankan government, displaying an obvious bias towards the Indian investor made a declaration to the effect that the mandatory offer was perceived to be a hostile offer which the state bank subsidiary, Property Development Limited, will not take up.[136] The Board of Investment of Sri Lanka, also under pressure, made a statement that any new owners other than the principal investor will not enjoy the same investment benefits, which meant the company forgoes the tax holiday granted, pays import duty on goods imported, and pays the current market price for the land.[137]

The above scenario is reflective of government interference in capital markets at the behest of foreign controlling investors attempting to safeguard their entrenched positions. The non market-based actions of the Reddy family of India and the Apollo Group are demonstrative of entrenchment by controlling shareholders in Sri Lanka and affected the value of Lanka Hospital Corporation Limited to the detriment of its minority shareholders.[138] In this scenario, the necessary law was in place

---

[134] Takeovers and Mergers Code 1995 (amended 2003).

[135] Harry Jayawardene Now Eyes Apollo Hospital (21 July 2006), *Daily Mirror*.

[136] Rohitha to Save Apollo from Harry (7 August 2006), *Daily Mirror*.

[137] BOI Says Any New Owners of Apollo Will Lose Special Benefits (9 August 2006), *Daily Mirror*.

[138] Reverse political pressure resulted in assurances to the hostile bidder from the Board of Investment that the concessions were to the company and not to the Reddy family. Subsequently, Apollo Group of India exited the company after failing to stave off the hostile bid.

and was triggered against entrenchment by controlling shareholders (i.e., a mandatory offer), but was subdued by the controlling shareholders through political influence.

5.2.11. *Conclusion*

This section of the chapter analysed the potential costs of controlling shareholder systems identified as private benefits of control, tunnelling among group companies, the abuse of political influence, the rise of market power and anti-competitive practices and entrenchment. The analysis illustrates that while the costs of controlling shareholder systems are influenced by (a) the identity of controlling shareholder, (e.g., political influence is more significant in controlling shareholder systems with family controlled companies) and (b) the mechanisms used to enhance control rights in excess of economic stakes, (e.g., tunnelling is more likely to be an issue in pyramid group structures than in companies with enhanced voting rights), the primary constraint on the potential costs of controlling shareholder systems is the legal and regulatory environment and effective market forces.

The analysis also extends to an examination of the costs of controlling shareholders in Sri Lanka. Although exact measurements are not undertaken, the sampling of anecdotal evidence demonstrates the existence of identified costs in Sri Lanka. The identification of these costs in Sri Lanka assists this study in two ways. First, it is useful not only for the trade-off argument, which follows, but also in the light of the identification that not all controlling shareholder systems give rise to the same agency costs. Second, the identification of the nature of the agency costs in Sri Lanka and the factors that influence such costs enable the framing of reforms to better meet the associated challenges of such controlling shareholder system.

5.3. Benefits of Controlling Shareholder Systems

The following sections analyse the potential benefits of controlling shareholder systems, generally and in Sri Lanka. Specifically, the analysis identifies factors that influence these benefits.

5.3.1. *Limiting the Classic Agency Problem*

In widely held firms, the 'classic agency problem', as identified by Jensen and Meckling,[139] occurs when professional managers, 'the agent' acts to maximise his or her personal benefit than the interests of the principal, 'the shareholders'. Morck and Yeung use the term 'other people's money' agency problem,[140] to distinguish it from other forms of agency problems, within controlling shareholder systems.[141] One of the advantages of concentrated ownership is that shareholders with a large part of their wealth tied up in the company are unlikely to allow the occurrence of the 'other people's money' agency problem.[142]

However, while this is true of concentrated ownership systems with large shareholders whose control rights are proportionate to their economic stakes,[143] it is unlikely in controlling shareholder systems for a simple reason, namely that the controlling shareholders have very little of their own wealth tied up in the companies they control. Such control is exercised in excess of their economic stakes through pyramid structures and cross-holdings, further distancing actual ownership. Therefore, while controlling shareholder systems have the potential to eliminate the 'other people's money' agency problem, there is a shift of the agency problem from professional managers to controlling shareholders within such system. The difference is that, it is the controlling shareholder, rather than the professional manager, who extracts value for personal benefit.[144] Thus, the actual economic stake of the controlling shareholder in the company basically recreates the same incentive incompatibility problems that occur in widely held firms and is a variant of the 'classic agency problem'.

---

[139] Jensen and Meckling (n. 35).

[140] Morck and Yeung (n. 101).

[141] Kraakman *et al.* (n. 29), 22.

[142] A Shleifer and R Vishny, Large Shareholders and Corporate Control (1986), 94 *Journal of Political Economy*, 461, explore a model in which large minority shareholders provide a monitoring role.

[143] ibid, argue that large shareholders with wealth tied up in the company are unlikely to allow too much leeway to professional managers in managing the company. Similarly, J Kang and A Shivdasani, Firm Performance, Corporate Governance, and Top Executive Turnover in Japan (1995), 38 *Journal of Financial Economics*, 29, demonstrate that firms with large shareholders are more likely to replace managers in response to poor performance than firms without them.

[144] Morck and Yeung (n. 101), 6.

Despite the new agency problem created by controlling shareholders, one of the benefits of controlling shareholder systems is its inherent potential to limit the 'classic agency problem'. Such limitation, through the potential policing role of controlling shareholders is dependent on two factors found within the controlling shareholder system. The first is the type of controlling owner, that is, family, group or individual, and the second, the mechanisms used by the controlling shareholders to increase their control stakes in excess of their economic stakes.

For example, studies that measure the relative agency costs between shareholders and managers, and between controlling family shareholders and minority shareholders, find that the agency conflict is not as severe in the latter with founder-CEO.[145] This indicates that controlling shareholder systems have the ability to limit the 'other people's money' or 'classic agency problem', when controlling shareholders are part of a family and the founder serves as CEO or chairman, because of a desire to preserve capital. However, Bennedsen *et al.*,[146] using a data set from Denmark to examine the determinants of family succession and its influence on firm performance, find that family successions have a negative impact on firm performance, and profitability falls by at least six percentage points around CEO transitions, implying that familial succession to positions of management results in poor firm performance.

In contrast, some studies in developing countries seem to suggest that, group-affiliated firms outperform non-group companies.[147] This seems to suggest that group structures similar to family controlled companies have the ability to limit the 'classic agency problem'.

The mechanisms used by the controlling shareholders to increase their control stakes in excess of their economic stakes, are also credited with

---

[145] R Amit and B Villalonga, How Do Family Ownership, Control, and Management Affect Firm Value? (2004), http://wgfa.wharton.upenn.edu/VillalongaAmit121004.pdf [20 July 2006], find that family ownership creates value only when the founder serves as the CEO of the family firm or as its chairman with a hired CEO.

[146] M Bennedsen *et al.*, Inside the Family Firm: The Role of Families in Succession Decisions and Performance (2005), Center of Industrial Economics University of Copenhagen Working Paper 13, http://www.econ.ku.dk/CIE/Discussion%20Papers/2005/2005-13.pdf [16 July 2006].

[147] Khanna and Yafeh (n. 83) Table 1; Khanna and Palepu (n. 87); T Khanna and K Palepu, The Future of Business Groups in Developing Countries: Long-run Evidence from Chile (2000), 42 *Academy of Management Journal*, 268, portray groups as a welfare-enhancing response to imperfect markets.

influencing the agency problem within controlling shareholder systems. Controlling shareholders use group structures and superior voting rights to separate ownership from control and participate in the management of the companies they control to enhance control rights.[148] While control in excess of ownership obtained through the use of group structures or superior voting rights implies that controlling shareholders have little of their own wealth tied up in the companies they control, the participation of controlling shareholders in the management of the companies they control can provide monitoring and planning that dispersed shareholders cannot provide, and thereby, contain the 'classic agency problem' between managers and shareholders.

Controlling shareholders limit the 'classic agency problem' by providing monitoring and long-term planning and the following sections analyse the extent to which the use of monitoring and long-term planning by controlling shareholders limit the 'classic agency problem'.

(a) *Monitoring*

The most obvious but often underestimated advantage of an ownership structure with controlling shareholders is that controlling shareholders have interests closely aligned with other equity holders as a class, that is, profitability and improved performance.[149] The aligned interests, together with the controlling shareholder involvement in the management of the company, give rise to the potential for an effective monitoring role to be played by controlling shareholders in limiting the 'classic agency problem'.

While small shareholders do not have a sufficient stake in the company to absorb the costs of monitoring the management, it is assumed that controlling shareholders, if in possession of large equity stakes will perform a monitoring function.

In family companies, firm specific know-how and entrepreneurial talent, support the monitoring role of controlling shareholders, especially when the founders are also the controlling shareholders. In corporate groups, parent companies with controlling stakes in subsidiary companies engage in a monitoring role to take advantage of group value maximisation.

---

[148] Chapter 3.

[149] Hofstetter (n. 41).

The type of controlling shareholder (i.e., whether family or group) and the involvement of the controlling shareholder in the management of the company is likely to influence the monitoring role of the controlling shareholders. However, the monitoring advantages of controlling shareholders are primarily dependent on the controlling shareholder having enough incentive to avoid expropriation of the minorities, and thereby, decreasing the value of the company. Therefore, a controlling shareholder will engage in a firm value decreasing expropriation, if the controlling shareholder's economic stake in the company is small and if the ratio between the controlling shareholder's economic stake and control stake is large.[150]

Thus, the first important determinant of the strength of the monitoring role of a controlling shareholder is the size of the economic stake of the controlling shareholder. The greater the economic stake in the hands of the controlling shareholder, the greater the incentive to add value to the company and engage in monitoring as it would result in a direct increase in personal wealth and lower the motivation to reduce the wealth of the company by extraction of private benefits. This determinant reasserts the correlation between corporate ownership and control, the separation of which led to the classic agency problem.

While a controlling shareholder has opportunity to monitor and influence corporate decisions through the use of voting power and in most instances as a member of the board of directors of the company, effective monitoring by a controlling shareholder resulting in increased corporate value is likely to occur only if the economic stakes of the controlling shareholders are equal to or greater than their control rights. This is supported by a study by Claessens *et al.*[151] distinguishing between the 'incentive' and 'entrenchment' effects of large shareholders and finding that corporate value[152] is higher when large shareholders own a greater economic stake, consistent with a positive incentive effect. However, corporate value falls when control rights of the large shareholder exceed the economic stake, consistent with an entrenchment effect.[153] In other words, the larger the difference between economic stake and control rights, the lower the corporate value.

---

[150] Claessens *et al.* (n. 131).

[151] ibid 2743–2755, using data for 1301 publicly traded companies in eight Asian economies.

[152] Market value of assets divided by book value of assets (market-to-book asset ratio) as a measure of firm valuation.

[153] Claessens *et al.* (n. 131), 2755.

The second important determinant of the monitoring ability of controlling shareholders is whether the economic stakes of the controlling shareholders exceed the median economic stakes of the other shareholders. A recent survey of listed Taiwanese companies finds that it is only when the economic stakes of the largest shareholders are greater than the median economic stakes that the positive incentive effects will outweigh the negative entrenchment effects.[154] Interestingly, this study also finds that where the largest shareholder enhances voting rights through cross-holdings, is involved in the management of the company or controls the board of directors, there is a negative influence on corporate value.[155] This may be attributed to the ease with which expropriation is possible in these situations.

(b) *Long-term Planning*

Another argument in favour of controlling shareholders is that controlling shareholders are often long-term investors and this provides them with the opportunity to devise and implement long-term strategies for the companies.

However, Morck *et al.*,[156] find that Canadian family controlled companies' underinvest in research and development relative to other peer firms of similar size and age, which they attribute to family companies avoiding risks to ensure a corporate inheritance for the heirs. While a controlling shareholder will engage in long-term planning due to large equity stakes which demand a more committed role, it is sometimes just as easy for a controlling shareholder with control rights in excess of economic stakes to engage in short-term asset stripping.

Thus, while the identity (e.g., family or group) of the controlling shareholders may influence long-term planning, it is likely that the size of the economic stake and the ratio between the economic stake and control stake held by controlling shareholders will determine whether controlling shareholders engage in short-term asset stripping leading to a decline in firm value, or long-term planning leading to potential firm value growth.

---

[154] Y Yeh, Do Controlling Shareholders Enhance Corporate Value? (2005), 13 *Corporate Governance: An International Review*, 313–322.

[155] ibid, using market value of the assets divided by the book value of the assets (market-to-book ratio of assets) to measure firm value.

[156] Morck *et al.* (n. 128).

5.3.2. *Limiting the 'Classic Agency Problem' in Sri Lanka*

This section applies the former analysis to Sri Lanka, that is, that controlling shareholders have the potential to limit the 'classic agency problem' through monitoring and long-term planning only if (a) the economic stakes of the controlling shareholders are equal to or greater than their control rights and (b) the economic stakes of the controlling shareholders are greater than the median economic stakes of the other shareholders.

With respect to the first requirement, there is a sharp divergence between economic stakes and control rights among controlling shareholders in Sri Lanka, with control enhanced by the use of pyramid structures and cross-holdings among companies.[157] This sharp divergence between economic stakes and control rights theoretically gives rise to an agency problem whereby controlling shareholders are able to act to the detriment of the minority shareholders without significantly affecting the value of their own shareholdings. The fact that controlling shareholders have very little of their own wealth invested in the companies they control, also implies that they are unlikely to engage in monitoring or long-term planning to limit the 'classic agency problem'. The significant levels of participation by a number of controlling shareholders in the management of the companies they control as CEO or directors,[158] can be attributed either to the controlling shareholders wishing to engage in monitoring and long-term planning through management positions or alternatively, use management positions to enjoy private benefits of control.

In Sri Lanka, the stronger argument in support of the significant levels of participation is likely to be due to the second requirement of the combined economic stakes of controlling shareholders in many family companies being greater than the median economic stakes of other shareholders in Sri Lanka.[159] This is evident where many controlling

---

[157] Chapter 3.

[158] Chapter 3, of the 12 companies analysed all had an ultimate controlling shareholder or nominee as a member of the board of directors while 75 percent had the ultimate controlling shareholder as MD, CEO, chairman or deputy chairman.

[159] The economic stake of the family controlling Hemas Holdings is 12.69 percent. The median economic stakes of the 20 other largest shareholders is 1.67 percent. Hemas Holdings, *Annual Report 2004–2005* (Colombo 2005).

shareholders serve as CEOs and directors, and are able to bear the costs of increased monitoring of managers and engage in long-term planning and therefore, limit the 'classic agency problem' where professional managers act in their own interest.

The identity of the controlling shareholders and the mechanisms used by them are useful pointers in determining which side of the cost-benefit divide controlling shareholders in Sri Lanka find themselves. Studies suggest that family ownership creates value only when the founder serves as CEO of the family company or as its chairman with a hired CEO.[160] In Sri Lanka individuals and families control a significant proportion of the companies with non-founder Chief Executive Officers or Chairman.[161] This suggests that family ownership may not create any value in Sri Lanka. Further, the fact that many ultimate controlling shareholder families and individuals use groups, that is, pyramids and cross-holdings, to enhance control rights has meant extra layers of insulation from corporate failures and market discipline for the ultimate holding companies and controlling shareholders.

To summarise, controlling shareholders in Sri Lanka, by participation in the management of the companies they control and holding large economic stakes in the companies they control, have greater likelihood in limiting the 'classic agency problem' and preventing the opportunistic behaviour of professional managers. However, the divergence between economic stakes and control rights, their identity as families and individuals, and the use of pyramids and cross-holdings to increase control rights in excess of economic stakes theoretically, raises the alternative agency problem of controlling shareholders vis-à-vis minority shareholders.

5.3.3. *Trust and Reputation*

Trust and reputation are increasingly gaining importance as non-standard mechanisms that support the financing and growth of an economy,[162] and

---

[160] Amit and Villalonga (n. 145).

[161] Individuals control over 51 percent of the 20 largest listed companies, while families control 33 percent.

[162] F Allen, Corporate Governance in Emerging Economies (2005), 21 *Oxford Review of Economic Policy*, 164–175.

are credited with the ability to overcome the lack of effective legal and contractual enforcement and underdeveloped institutions.[163]

Trust and reputation mooted as virtues of controlling ownership systems play an important role in family controlled companies than with any other controlling owner scenario.[164] Relationships based on trust with the labour force, other shareholders and stakeholders are evident in family controlled companies. A connection with the controlling family builds trust between businesses in economies where trust is otherwise scarce,[165] and facilitates economic transactions in institutionally deficient economies.

Family control also brings about a degree of co-operation and reputation with the transfer of knowledge and skill from business to business and generation to generation. Khanna and Palepu[166] attribute the hard-earned reputation of some families as the key to the success of family businesses.

Similarly, being part of a successful group of companies or having a high profile controlling shareholder with recognised business acumen also brings an aura of trust and reputation to controlling shareholder systems. Employees, shareholders and stakeholders of companies are more willing to compromise on salary or price in return for job security, higher trading volumes or prestige offered as part of a family controlled company or company with a high-profile controlling shareholder. This is likely to be more important in countries with poor regulatory systems and mechanisms for enforcing contracts, in which business groups fill institutional voids.[167]

However, managers, employees and suppliers contracting at the 'pleasure' of the family or controlling shareholder pay the price for trust and

---

[163] A Greif, Contract Enforceability and Economic Institutions in Early Trade: The Maghribi Traders' Coalition (1993), 83 *American Economic Review*, 525, hypothesises that trade organizations in the 11th century developed institutions based on reputation, implicit contractual relations and coalitions; A Gomes, Going Public without Governance: Managerial Reputation Effects (2000), 55 *Journal of Finance*, 615, argues that managerial reputation can replace governance in an Initial Public Offering; J Franks, C Mayer and S Rossi, Ownership: Evolution and Regulation (2003), European Corporate Governance Institute Finance Working Paper 92, http://ssrn.com/abstract=354381 [10 January 2006], attribute trust and reputation to the development of a securities market in the UK in the early 20th century.

[164] ibid, Franks, Mayer and Rossi; Franks, Mayer and Rossi (n. 133).

[165] Morck and Yeung (n. 101), 10–11.

[166] Khanna and Palepu (n. 99).

[167] Khanna and Palepu (n. 21), 48–49, the Tata conglomerate.

reputation within controlling shareholder systems. While family values and blood ties enable family controlled companies to appear reputable and trust-worthy, in reality, actual governance may be replete with intrafamilial disputes. Similarly, a high-profile controlling shareholder may foster an aura of trust, but may also create personality clashes and strife in the boardroom.

Khanna and Yafeh[168] in answer to the question of why investors continue to invest in situations where their investment is likely to be abused, provide the explanation that group reputation is sufficient to account for investor interest. Sociologists emphasise that social ties, which facilitate economic transactions and network structures such as business groups, serve social purposes.[169]

However, trust and reputation are likely to be an important determinant in ownership systems with large shareholders whose interests are aligned with minority shareholders, than in systems with controlling shareholders obscured beneath layers of corporate ownership. Thus, the beneficial aspects of trust and reputation in a controlling shareholder system tend to be dependent on the economic stake of the controlling shareholders.

5.3.4. *Trust and Reputation in Sri Lanka*

In developing countries, such as India, Malaysia and Sri Lanka, trust and reputation play a role in facilitating economic transactions and attracting investment into companies, evidenced by the importance attached to the ethnicity, caste or social backgrounds of business groups, controlling families or individuals.

The battle lines in the biggest challenge, which Sri Lanka faced in the recent past, the ethnic conflict between the 'Liberation Tigers of Tamil Eelam' (LTTE) in the North and the Sinhalese in the South, were drawn along ethnicity,[170] and ethnic origins play an important role in the business environment. In many respects, the conflict is a consequence of a certain trajectory of economic development as state-led development in the

---

[168] Khanna and Yafeh (n. 83), 27.

[169] M Granovetter, Business Groups and Social Organization, in N Semelser and R Swedberg (eds.), *The Handbook of Economic Sociology* (2nd edn Princeton University Press Princeton 2005).

[170] J Goodhand, *Aid, Conflict, and Peacebuilding in Sri Lanka* (Centre for Defence Studies, King's College London 2001), 24, labels it as 'complex political emergency' a crisis of the state than an ethnic crisis.

post-colonial period operated within a framework of dominant nationalism which favoured one ethnic group over the other.[171] It is also undoubted that the cost of war has obvious and wide-ranging economic repercussions,[172] such as lost income due to forgone investment.

The importance attached to ethnicity is also evident in the caste system, which lingers within the business community in Sri Lanka and affect decisions in ways few speak about. The underlying caste system can be traced back to the times of the ancient kingdoms of Ceylon, where family origins determined professions. Sri Lanka has two caste systems reflecting the minority Tamil and majority Sinhalese cultures.[173] Various regional differences add another layer of complexity. Sri Lankans with landowner or tenant farmer ancestors are near the top of the hierarchy (*Goyigama*). Those whose relatives once worked in trade groupings, such as alcohol brewers, jewellery makers, laundry men and fishermen, make up the middle (*Karava*, *Salagama* and *Durawa*). Descendants of such groups as beggars, mat weavers and funeral drummers are near the bottom.

Moore in an excellent anthropological analysis of the new corporate sector in Sri Lanka, claims that 'most large quoted companies are controlled, substantially or completely, by members of two particular non-*Goyigama* indigenous minorities',[174] the Sinhalese *Karava*, *Salagama* and *Durava* ('KSD'[175] group) and Sri Lankan Tamils. Using data from 13 quoted (nonstate) companies controlled by Sri Lankans that earned the largest post-tax profits in 1991, Moore finds that five of these companies are effectively controlled by members of the *Karava*, *Salagama* and *Durava* group, four by Tamils, one by a *Karava*, *Salagama* and *Durava* group-Tamil combination, one by a mixed non-*Goyigama* Sinhalese caste, and one by a *Goyigama* member.[176]

Moore's previous analysis of the main caste and ethnic groups representation at the top levels of business in the 1980s validate these

---

[171] For example, requests by the Tamils for the Mahaweli irrigation project to cover traditional Tamil areas were rejected and new settlers were overwhelmingly from the Sinhalese community.

[172] For an excellent analysis, A Arunatilake, S Jayasuriya and S Kelegama, The Economic Cost of the War in Sri Lanka (2001), 29 *World Development* 1483.

[173] Human Rights Watch, *Caste Discrimination: A Global Concern* (2001 London) Part IV.

[174] Moore (n. 106), 90.

[175] Acronym used by M Roberts, *Caste, Conflict and Elite Formation: The Rise of a Karava Elite in Sri Lanka*, 1500–1931 (Cambridge University Press Cambridge 1982).

[176] Moore (n. 106) fails to define control, which detracts from this analysis.

findings.[177] The Sinhalese *Goyigama* caste make up 37 percent of the total population in 1981, but representation among 50 most wealthy businessmen in the early 1980s is at 26 percent. In contrast, the Sinhalese- *Karava*, *Salagama* and *Durava* Group make up just 7 percent of the total population in the same period, but its representation among the 50 most wealthy businessmen in early 1980s is at 28 percent. Sri Lankan Tamils make up 13 percent of the total population, while their representation among the 50 wealthiest businessmen in early 1980s is at a comparable 12 percent.

Moore's explanation for the prominence of business minorities is relevant when considering the benefits of the trust and reputation argument presented in this section. He focuses on the ways in which 'social linkages that can exist between individuals within small communities'[178] contribute to business success. Two concepts central to such social linkages are information and trust. In Sri Lanka, where business is intermingled with politics, and the judiciary is ineffective as a mechanism of contract enforcement, business success is dependent on social linkages, and therefore trust and business reputation mooted as a virtue of controlling ownership systems play a central role in the prominence of minorities in business. In effect, the reliance on ethnic and social networks is an important feature of entrepreneurship in Sri Lanka and a substitute for institutional voids.[179]

Another feature that illustrates the importance of trust and reputation in Sri Lanka is that one can almost always identify corporate ownership and control in terms of the individual or family with which it is associated. Despite stock market listings and the veil of incorporation, there is failure to adequately disguise the identities of large shareholders. This inability to depersonalise companies implies that trust and reputation has the capacity to act as a constraining influence on large shareholders.

To summarise, the constraining role of trust and reputation is dependent to a large extent on the size of the economic stake held by the controlling shareholder. However, if the investing public do not identify the controlling shareholder to be a large shareholder or the ultimate owner, then trust and business reputation fails to act as a constraining influence.

---

[177] ibid 69, Table 2.

[178] ibid 70.

[179] Reliance on social networks for entrepreneurship is a feature in not only Asia (such as the Japanese Mitsui family, Marawi's in India) but also in the West as evidenced by the Rothschild family.

5.3.5. *Controlling Shareholders as Private Investment Vehicles*

Many developing countries are missing vital market intermediaries, such as venture capitalists, investment bankers and pension funds,[180] making it costly for developing country companies to acquire necessary finance and technological support. Further, companies in developing countries are constrained in not being able to share the risks of their investments with other market intermediaries.

As established, controlling shareholders in developing countries use corporate groups as mechanisms to leverage control in excess of their ownership. However, an overlooked feature of corporate groups is their capacity to act as private investment vehicles in terms of both debt and equity.[181] Controlling shareholders in developing countries are in positions to harness corporate groups to act as private investment vehicles using group business reputation to obtain financing in weak capital and debt markets.

More generally, corporate group structures are able to provide internal financing to companies within the group and fund new ventures.[182] However, where families control corporate groups, they prefer to raise debt finance rather than equity finance because they are relatively averse to increases in equity due to issues of succession and dilution of control.[183]

Friedman *et al.*[184] in a study on propping[185] and tunnelling by entrepreneurs who control publicly traded companies, hypothesise that in some conditions (such as a moderate shock) entrepreneurs use private funds to prop the companies they control and indirectly benefit minority shareholders. The strongest evidence of such propping is from Japan where banks

---

[180] Chapter 4, where lack of market intermediaries is identified as a primary reason for the prevalence of controlling ownership structures in Sri Lanka.

[181] E Berglof and E Perotti, The Governance Structure of the Japanese Financial Keiretsu (1994), 36 *Journal of Financial Economics*, 259, argue that concentrated ownership in Japanese *keiretsu* plays the role of internal capital markets; Khanna and Yafeh (n. 83), 15, 21.

[182] Khanna and Palepu (n. 87) support this proposition in Indian by finding that while firm performance initially declines with group diversification, there is a subsequent increase once group diversification exceeds a certain level; Khanna and Palepu (n. 147).

[183] S Chang, *Financial Crisis and Transformation of Korean Business Groups* (Cambridge University Press Cambridge 2003) with respect to the Korean *chaebol*.

[184] E Friedman, S Johnson and T Mitton, Propping and Tunneling (2003), 31 *Journal of Comparative Economics*, 732, suggest that in countries with weak investor protection, outside investment is in the form of debt rather than equity.

[185] Prop or propping is defined as the transfer by controlling shareholders or large shareholders of private resources into companies with minority shareholders.

provide capital to companies within the same industrial group experiencing liquidity shortfalls.[186] Friedman *et al.* suggest that propping may explain why many companies in developing countries with weaker corporate governance have a higher ratio of debt to total assets.[187] However, according to their model if the negative shock is large, it is likely that the controlling shareholder will engage in tunnelling rather than propping.[188]

A related study by Khanna and Yafeh[189] covering a sample of 12 emerging economies, find that in nearly all countries[190] group-affiliated companies are larger than unaffiliated companies, and that in many developing countries group-affiliated companies outperform other companies. However, their findings do not validate the importance of risk sharing among groups. While they find substantial evidence of risk sharing among Japanese, Korean and Thai corporate groups, there is little evidence of it elsewhere. This study casts doubt on the importance of controlling shareholders as private investment vehicles, at least with respect to the provision of risk sharing.

Despite the ambiguity of contrasting studies, evidence suggests that corporate groups make up for missing institutions in developing countries, and controlling shareholders are able to utilise such groups as private investment vehicles. Private investment capabilities of controlling shareholders can also be beneficial in a hostile takeover scenario if a potential acquirer is a raider and would produce less cash flow benefits and expropriate more than the incumbent controlling shareholder.

However, the ability of controlling shareholders to act as private equity investors depends on the actual economic stake held by such controlling shareholders, because a controlling shareholder is unlikely to want to commit to an investment in a company in which its economic stake is in the minority.

5.3.6. *Controlling Shareholders as Private Investment Vehicles in Sri Lanka*

The evidence suggests that tunnelling occurs after a large negative shock and presumably, at other times, entrepreneurs use private funds to prop up

---

[186] Friedman, Johnson and Mitton (n. 184), 733, fn. 4. But this leads to non-performing loans and a weak-banking sector in Japan.

[187] ibid Table 1.

[188] ibid 748.

[189] Khanna and Yafeh (n. 25).

[190] With the exception of Turkey.

the companies they control and indirectly benefit minority shareholders. An illustrative example of related-party transactions among group companies with controlling shareholders provides evidence as to whether controlling shareholders in Sri Lanka use group structures as private investment vehicles to prop the companies they control.

Aitken Spence, the 16th largest listed company according to market capitalisation[191] has two blockholders, Distilleries Company and Sri Lanka Insurance Corporation Limited, both controlled by the same individual investor. The annual report of Aitken Spence under related-party transactions show long-term borrowings from Sri Lanka Insurance Corporation Limited amounting to approximately 11 percent of all long-term borrowings,[192] which is significant and indicative of some form of propping by the controlling shareholder. However, further analysis demonstrates that Aitken Spence has an unquoted investment in Milford Holdings (Private) Limited, the shareholding company of Aitken Spence, privately owned and controlled by the same controlling shareholder with control stakes in both Distilleries Company[193] and Sri Lanka Insurance Corporation Limited. This unquoted investment in shares of Milford Holdings (Private) Limited amounts to over 55 percent of all long-term investments made by Aitken Spence including investment properties.[194] Thus, in contrast to what initially appears to be propping, there is overwhelming evidence, demonstrating that Aitken Spence, a company with 49.56 percent of its shares held by the public,[195] has invested 55 percent of its long-term investment portfolio in a private company under the control of its controlling shareholder. This raises concerns of tunnelling rather than propping, contrary to the model proposed by Friedman *et al.*[196]

The above example, although of limited value, is suggestive that companies in Sri Lanka are more prone to tunnelling than propping in the absence of any negative shocks,[197] presumably because the actual economic stakes of the controlling shareholders are small and also because the weak investor protection environment and limited market discipline facilitates the transfer of resources between group companies.

---

[191] Chapter 3.

[192] Aitken Spence, *Annual Report 2004–05* (Colombo 2005), 110.

[193] Holding company of Sri Lanka Insurance Corporation Limited.

[194] Aitken Spence (n. 192), 99.

[195] ibid 73.

[196] Friedman, Johnson and Mitton (n. 184).

[197] Propping is not without its wider costs to the economy, the banks and the parent company.

However, these findings need further investigation for more definitive conclusions.

Like most benefits of controlling shareholder systems, the ability of controlling shareholders to act as private equity investment vehicles depend on the size of such shareholder's economic stake as large economic stakes are likely to result in some form of propping, while smaller economic stakes are likely to give rise to tunnelling. The mechanisms used by the controlling shareholder to leverage control rights in excess of economic stakes are also important, as it is likely that a group structure within a controlling shareholder system is likely to facilitate either propping or tunnelling due to the ease of resource transfers within group companies.

5.3.7. *Conclusion*

This section of the chapter analysed the potential benefits of controlling shareholder systems, identified as limiting the 'classic agency problem' by increased monitoring and long-term planning, the facilitation of business on a trust and reputation basis in developing countries with institutionally deficient markets, and the capacity of controlling shareholders to act as private equity investment vehicles.

The enjoyment of the benefits of controlling shareholder systems is primarily dependent on the size of the economic stake held by controlling shareholders both in relation to their own control stakes and the economic stakes of other shareholders. The mechanisms used by controlling shareholders to gain control rights in excess of their economic stakes and the identity of the controlling shareholders also influence the extent and nature of these benefits.

The analysis is extended to an examination of the potential benefits of controlling shareholders in Sri Lanka. Although exact measurements are not undertaken, the analysis demonstrates that controlling shareholders in Sri Lanka are able to limit the 'classic agency problem', facilitate business transactions through the use of trust relationships and reputation which is in itself a constraint on self-serving behaviour, and in some instances prop companies facing financial difficulties.

The analysis of the benefits of controlling shareholder systems in Sri Lanka assists this study in two ways. First, it identifies the nature of the potential benefits, which is useful for the trade-off argument that follows. Second, the identification of the nature of the benefits and the factors that influence potential benefits (i.e., primarily the size of the economic stake) in Sri Lanka is useful for a reform agenda.

5.4. The Implications of a Cost-Benefit Analysis of Controlling Shareholder Systems for Corporate Governance

The analysis in Sections 5.2 and 5.3 makes clear that controlling shareholder systems embody both costs and benefits. These distinct costs and benefits give rise to three important implications for corporate governance.

First, the *benefits* to be derived from controlling shareholder systems is primarily dependent on the size of the economic stake in the hands of the controlling shareholder and the divergence between their economic stakes and control rights. The higher the economic stake the more likely that the controlling shareholder is involved in monitoring, long-term planning and reputation building.

It should be noted that the costs associated with controlling shareholders are similarly correlated to the size of the controlling shareholders' economic stake and the divergence between their economic stakes and control rights. However, the ability to extract such costs is primarily dependent on effective legal and regulatory environment within the system together with market forces. Therefore, the size of the controlling shareholders' economic stake and the divergence between their economic stakes and control rights is not the primary or sole determinant for controlling shareholders seeking to extract costs from a controlling shareholder system.

Second, the *costs* associated with controlling shareholder systems are less dependent on the economic stakes of the controlling shareholders. It is likely that controlling shareholders with control rights far in excess of their economic stakes are more likely to engage in tunnelling or derive private benefits of control. However, the primary constraint on the behaviour of controlling shareholders is the legal and regulatory environment together with market forces. For example, internal private benefits are constrained by an effective legal and regulatory environment, while external private benefits, tunnelling and entrenchment are constrained by disciplinary market forces, such as creditors, stock price declines, hostile takeovers, investor activism, transparency and reputation.

Third, the overriding inference from the existence of both costs and benefits within controlling shareholder systems is the resultant *'trade-off'* between these costs and benefits. Thus, a controlling shareholder may provide monitoring, but this may be outweighed by the private benefits of control extracted by this controlling shareholder.

The next section examines the first and second of these identified implications. Section 5.5 examines the controlling shareholder trade-off.

5.4.1. *The Benefits of Controlling Shareholder Systems are Dependent on the Size of the Economic Stake of the Controlling Shareholders and the Divergence between their Economic Stakes and Control Rights*

The pronouncement that the *benefits* of controlling shareholder systems are dependent on the economic stakes of controlling shareholders and the divergence between their economic stakes and control rights, emanating from the cost-benefit analysis above, is supported by the theoretical studies of Grossman and Hart[198] and Harris and Raviv[199] who predict a negative relationship between the deviation of control from economic stakes and firm value. Similarly, Bebchuck *et al.*,[200] argue that separation of control rights from economic stakes create agency costs which are larger than the costs associated with a controlling shareholder with a majority economic stake in the company.

The relationship between large shareholdings and firm value is formalised in studies on managerial ownership. An inverse 'U-shaped' relationship is found between managerial equity ownership and firm valuation for a cross section of Fortune 500 firms.[201] One interpretation is the 'entrenchment hypothesis', which predicts that a company's per-formance improves with higher managerial ownership, but that after a point managers become entrenched and pursue private benefits at the expense of outside investors.[202] A decline in company performance is predicted when managers are protected against the discipline of the

---

[198] S Grossman and O Hart, One-share, One-vote, and the Market for Corporate Control (1988), 20 *Journal of Financial Economics*, 175.

[199] M Harris and A Raviv, Corporate Governance: Voting Rights and Majority Rules (1988), 20 *Journal of Financial Economics*, 203.

[200] L Bebchuk, R Kraakman and G Triantis (n. 27), 295.

[201] R Morck, A Shleifer and R Vishny, Management Ownership and Market Valuation: An Empirical Analysis (1988), 20 *Journal of Financial Economics*, 293.

[202] ibid 294–295.

market by their ability to block value enhancing takeovers through large ownership stakes.[203] The non-linear relationship also offers limited support for the 'convergence of interests hypothesis', which suggests that agency costs should fall and performance should improve as the management stake rises,[204] as found within the 0–10 percent ownership range.

The entrenchment hypothesis can be adapted and applied to controlling shareholders, that is, that a company's performance improves with larger economic stakes held by controlling shareholders,[205] but that after a point the controlling shareholders become entrenched and pursue private benefits at the expense of outside investors. This behaviour is more likely among controlling shareholders with relatively small economic stakes.

A study specifically in relation to controlling shareholder systems, by Claessens *et al.*, using data for 1301 publicly traded companies in eight East Asian countries, find that while positive incentive effects (i.e., positive as there is an increase in relative firm value as measured by the market-to-book-ratio of assets) are associated with an increased economic stake in the hands of one or few shareholders, while negative entrenchment effect on firm value is found when the largest shareholder's control rights exceed its economic stake (hereinafter the 'Claessens hypothesis').[206]

The negative effect of entrenchment on firm value is also found when the largest shareholder's economic stake is less than the median economic stake held by the rest of the shareholders.[207] There is evidence that family control is an important determinant in the negative relationship between control rights and market valuation,[208] supported by evidence on firm performance in Canada.[209]

---

[203] R Stulz, Managerial Control of Voting Rights: Financing Policies and the Market for Corporate Control (1988), 20 *Journal of Financial Economics*, 25.

[204] Morck, Shleifer and Vishny (n. 201), 294.

[205] LLSV, Investor Protection and Corporate Valuation (2002), 57 *Journal of Finance*, 1147, find that higher cash flow ownership by controlling shareholder improves valuation especially in countries with poor investor protection.

[206] Claessens *et al.* (n. 131), 2743.

[207] Yeh (n. 154).

[208] S Claessens, S Djankov and L Lang, Corporate Ownership and Valuation: Evidence from East Asia, in A Harwood, R Litan and M Pomerleano (eds.), *Financial Markets and Development: The Crisis in Developing Countries* (Brookings Institution Washington 1999), 159; Morck, Shleifer and Vishny (n. 201), 295, 310–311, find market valuation to be lower when an older firm is run by founding families than when it is run by officers unrelated to the founder.

[209] Morck, Stangeland and Yeung (n. 128), 319.

Mechanisms to enhance control in excess of economic stakes such as cross-holdings or participation in management are also found to lead to conspicuous decreases in firm value, especially in family controlled companies.[210]

5.4.2. *Application to Sri Lanka*

This section tests and applies the first implication derived from the above cost-benefit analysis, that the *benefits* of controlling shareholder systems in Sri Lanka are dependent on the economic stakes of controlling shareholders and the divergence between their economic stakes and control rights.

Many publicly traded Sri Lankan companies have a controlling shareholder with a sharp divergence between economic stakes and control rights, with control enhanced by the use of pyramid structures, cross-holdings and participation in management.[211] If the negative effect of entrenchment is a feature of the controlling shareholder system in Sri Lanka, then in line with the 'Claessens hypothesis', the value of companies in Sri Lanka should drop in proportion to the divergence between the controlling shareholders' economic stakes and controlling rights. Large economic stakes in the hands of a few shareholders should result in an increase in firm value, consistent with the positive incentive effect.

To examine the relationship between company valuation and ownership structures and the application of the 'Claessens hypothesis' to Sri Lanka, the sample companies in Chapter 3, are analysed according to the actual economic stake of the controlling owner, and thereafter, according to the divergence between ownership and control rights among the controlling shareholders or family, ranging from zero to over 40 percent. The market-to-book[212] values for all but one of the companies[213] under analysis were obtained from a survey conducted by Media Services (Private) Limited.[214] The results are as set out in Table 5.1.

Company valuation measured by the market-to-book ratio generally increases with the share of economic stake in the hands of the controlling

---

[210] Yeh (n. 154), 322; Yeh and Woidtke (n. 132).

[211] Chapter 3.

[212] Current share price/net asset value per share (book value).

[213] Distilleries Company.

[214] The LMD 50 Share Profile, *The Lanka Monthly Digest's 50 Sri Lanka's Leading Listed Companies (Special Issue)* (December 2005), 44–45.

Table 5.1: Corporate Ownership, Control and Valuation in Sri Lanka.

Name of Company	Market-to-book value	Economic stake of controlling shareholder/family (in %)	Divergence between ownership and control (in %)
Dialog Telekom			
John Keells	1.8	11.38	1.23
Sri Lanka Telecom	1.0	49.50	0.25
Commercial Bank	1.3	29.15	12.58
Carson Cumberbatch	1.7	46.23	44.25
Lanka IOC Limited			
Bukit Darah	4.4*	—	—
Distilleries Company	1.3	41.49	14.86
DFCC Bank	1.4	13.53	31.04
Asian Hotels	—	—	—
Hatton National Bank	0.6	7.17	26.47
Ceylon Tobacco			
Overseas Realty (Ceylon) Limited			
Hemas Holdings	2.7	83.35	0
Nestle Lanka Limited			
Aitken Spence	1.2	17.22	11.91
Richard Pieris	3.0	61.38	0
Ceylon Theatres	—	—	—
National Development Bank	1.0	10	4.37
James Finlay and Company (Colombo) Limited			

☐ Controlling shareholder is a multinational.

* Change from previous year of over 1000%.

shareholder, who in most cases also happens to be the largest shareholder. This is consistent with the positive incentive effect of large economic stakes on company valuation. While company value is greatest when the conomic stakes of the controlling shareholders are over 50 percent, company value is slightly higher at the 10–20 percent economic stake threshold than the 20–40 percent and 40–50 percent ranges.

Figure 5.2 suggests that the larger the wedge between the economic stakes and control rights, the lower the company valuation. Companies with no or very little separation between ownership and control rights have the highest values. Companies with separation between 20 percent and 40 percent, that is, when the control rights exceed the economic stakes between 20 percent and 40 percent, have the lowest values. Companies with a divergence between the economic stakes and control rights at above 40 percent appear to increase in value. However, given the small sample size, that is, only one of the companies under analysis fell into this category and the actual economic stake of the controlling shareholder in this company was also above 40 percent, may explain the increase in corporate value despite the large wedge between the economic stake and control stakes of the controlling shareholder. This suggests that a controlling shareholder with a majority economic stake may not be as costly to corporate valuation as a controlling shareholder whose economic stake is in the minority.

Figures 5.1 and 5.2 reinforce the 'Claessens hypothesis' in Sri Lanka. Positive incentive effects associated with increased economic stakes in the hands of the large shareholders who may also be controlling shareholders is reflected by an increase in company value and as the control rights of the controlling shareholder increases relative to the economic stakes, corporate value falls, indicative of a negative entrenchment effect.

While larger sample size, together with other control factors that affect corporate value such as the age of the company, sales growth, and capital spending relative to sales and growth prospects, will draw definitive

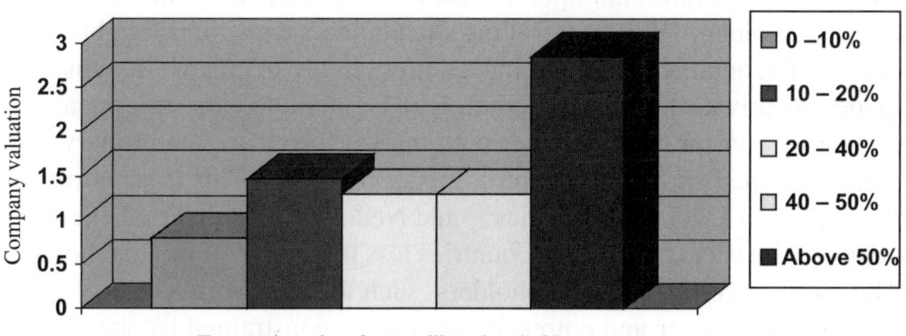

Figure 5.1: Company Valuation and Economic Stake of the Controlling Shareholder/Family.

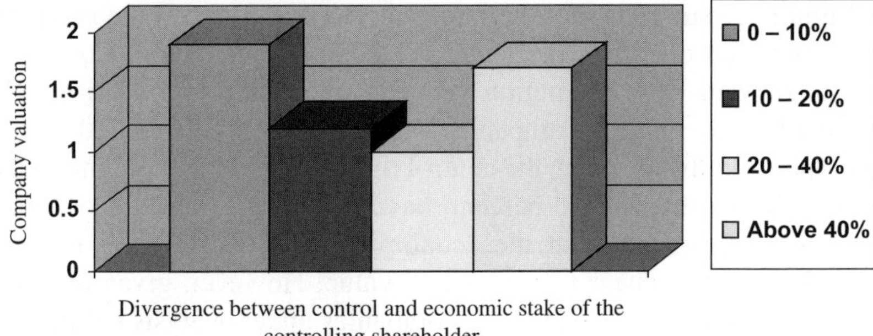

Figure 5.2: Company Valuation and Divergence between Control and Economic Stake of the Controlling Shareholder/Family.

conclusions, for purposes of this study, the above analysis suggests that the *benefits* of controlling shareholders in Sri Lanka are mainly dependent on the size of the economic stakes of controlling shareholders and the divergence between their economic stakes and control rights.

5.4.3. *Costs Associated with Controlling Shareholder Systems are Contingent upon the Legal and Regulatory Environment, and Market Forces*

The second implication arising as a result of the costs-benefit analysis in Sections 5.2 and 5.3 is that *costs* of controlling shareholder systems are not primarily conditional upon the actual economic stakes of the controlling shareholders. While controlling shareholders with control rights far in excess of economic stakes are indeed more likely to engage in tunnelling or derive private benefits of control, it is submitted that the legal and regulatory environment together with market forces are the primary constraints on the behaviour of controlling shareholders. This is supported by the studies of Dyck and Zingales[215] and Nenova[216] that private benefits of control are easier to extract in countries less protective of its shareholders. The costs of controlling shareholders, such as tunnelling, political influence, market power and entrenchment can be constrained by specifically

---

[215] Dyck and Zingales (n. 36).
[216] Nenova (n. 54).

drafted legal rules and an effective regulatory environment assisted by disciplinary market forces.

The proposition advanced by Gilson that the appropriate distinction is not between controlling shareholder systems and dispersed shareholder systems but rather between countries with functionally good law which support both dispersed and 'efficient' controlling shareholder systems and countries with functionally bad law which support 'inefficient' controlling shareholder systems,[217] also lends support to the view that the costs of controlling shareholder systems are dependent on the regulatory environment and effective market forces.

It is important to clarify that the argument proposed is not the sceptical view of controlling shareholder systems supported by the 'law and finance' literature that all controlling shareholder systems are associated with poor legal and regulatory environments or poor capital markets, but, rather, that the costs of controlling shareholder systems can be constrained by functional laws and regulations which expose controlling stakes to disciplinary market forces.

5.4.4. *Application to Sri Lanka*

This section tests and applies the second implication derived from the cost-benefit analysis in Sections 5.2 and 5.3 that the *costs* of controlling shareholder systems are for the most part contingent upon the legal and regulatory environment and market forces. The hypothesis tested in Sri Lanka is that the existence of private benefits of control, tunnelling, the abuse of market power, and anti-competitive practices by controlling shareholders is due to the lack of specifically designed legal rules, ineffective regulatory environment and weak market forces.

This is illustrated by an example concerning three companies: Colombo Fort Land & Building Company Limited (Colombo Fort Land) which since October 2002 has been on the default board[218] of the CSE for failure to comply with the listing rules; E.B. Creasy & Company Limited (E.B. Creasy), a company ranked 112th on the CSE in terms of market capitalisation,[219] and Lankem Ceylon Limited (now known as Lankem

---

[217] Gilson (n. 34).

[218] Colombo Stock Exchange (n. 69), 83.

[219] ibid 92.

Ceylon Plc), a company ranked 98th in terms of market capitalisation.[220] Four of the six directors comprising the board of directors of E.B. Creasy are also members of the board of directors of Colombo Fort Land.

Colombo Fort Land with an economic stake of over 48.41 percent in E.B. Creasy in the years 2001–2002[221] increased its stake to 52.4 percent by 2005 and together with its associate companies a controlling stake in excess of 75 percent of E.B Creasy.[222] E.B. Creasy in turn, holds a controlling stake in excess of 78 percent in Lankem Ceylon Limited.[223]

On 6 August 2004, Lankem Ceylon Limited issued a 'one for two' bonus share issue[224] under which E.B. Creasy, which held 9,366,697 shares of Lankem Ceylon Limited, was entitled to receive approximately 4.5 million bonus shares. At the annual general meeting of E.B. Creasy held in late 2005, the Kuwaiti investor Al-Nakib who, together with his brother control 14.5 percent of E.B. Creasy, alleged that E.B. Creasy, which acquired 4.5 million bonus shares of its subsidiary Lankem Ceylon Limited, had manipulated the funds by transferring the bonus shares among its group companies.[225] The annual general meeting reportedly turned stormy with allegations of the Kuwaiti investor being called a 'troublesome foreigner' and a threat to throw out another minority shareholder.[226] E.B. Creasy's MD was quoted stating that the bonus shares in question were sold to Colombo Fort Land, its holding company.[227] If such transfers were done at below market prices, such transaction would be detrimental to the interests of the minority shareholders of E.B. Creasy, who are not shareholders of Colombo Fort Land.

Al-Nakib had previously instituted action[228] against E.B. Creasy, its directors and other respondents, including Colombo Fort Land. The

---

[220] ibid.

[221] Last available Colombo Fort Land, *Annual Report 2001–02* (Colombo 2002), 36.

[222] D Edirimuni, E.B. Creasy, AGM Turns Stormy (4 December 2005), *Sunday Times*.

[223] On 31 March 2004, E.B. Creasy held an economic stake of 78.06 percent in Lankem which fell to 48.41 percent by 31st March 2005. Lankem Ceylon Limited, *Annual Report 2004–2005* (Colombo 2005), 81.

[224] Colombo Stock Exchange (n. 69), 70.

[225] D Edirimuni (n. 222).

[226] ibid.

[227] ibid, however, in a statement the MD states that the 4.5 million bonus shares were disposed of. E.B. Creasy Says Shareholders Should Not Abuse AGMs (18 December 2005), *Sunday Times*.

[228] *Al-Nakib v. E.B. Creasy* [Commercial HCC 9/2005].

petitioners, Al-Nakib and his brother, alleged abuse of power by the directors of E.B Creasy, and contended that the directors were conducting the affairs of the company in a manner gravely prejudicial to the interests of the E.B Creasy and oppressive to the petitioners as minority shareholders under sections 210 and 211 of the Companies Act.[229] The petitioners, also claimed that Colombo Fort Land on account of its own financial predicament and those of its subsidiaries, (i.e., Muller and Phipps (Ceylon) Limited, and Pettah Pharmacy Limited), is systematically siphoning off funds from E.B Creasy to keep itself and its subsidiaries afloat, with the active connivance and participation of the directors of E.B Creasy.[230] Commercial High Court (Colombo), being satisfied that the material facts of the petition were prima facie established, issued Order Nisi conditioned to take effect in the event of the respondents not showing cause against it. The court further granted the equitable interim relief restraining E.B. Creasy from advancing further monies by way of loans to Colombo Fort Land until the final determination of the application.[231] Al-Nakib contends that the present transfer of the bonus shares is in violation of this interim order.

Since financial accounts of Colombo Fort Land are not available after 2001, it is difficult to comment on whether the said transfer of the bonus shares took place for valuable consideration or not. If the bonus shares of Lankem Ceylon Limited were transferred to the parent company of E.B. Creasy, (i.e., Colombo Fort Land) for market value in an arms-length transaction, there is no cause for concern. If, however, the transfer is at undervalue, it is detrimental to the interests of E.B. Creasy and its shareholders without economic stakes in Colombo Fort Land. It is also illustrative of the costs of the controlling shareholder system in Sri Lanka and the intracorporate transfer of wealth within a corporate group to the detriment of the minority shareholders of one of the subsidiaries.

Figure 5.3 illustrates that the control rights of Colombo Fort Land in E.B. Creasy are far in excess of the economic stakes held by Colombo Fort Land through cross-holdings and pyramiding. Despite the 3:2 ratio between control rights and economic stakes, E.B. Creasy may benefit

---

[229] The remedy for oppression and mismanagement under Companies Act No. 17 of 1982.

[230] Plaint in *HCC 9/2005*. (Note: Statement of claim is referred to as a Plaint in Sri Lanka.)

[231] Leave to proceed in the appeal filed by Creasy in the Supreme Court was refused on 13 February 2006. Accordingly, the Commercial High Court of Colombo matter is due to be disposed of by written submissions.

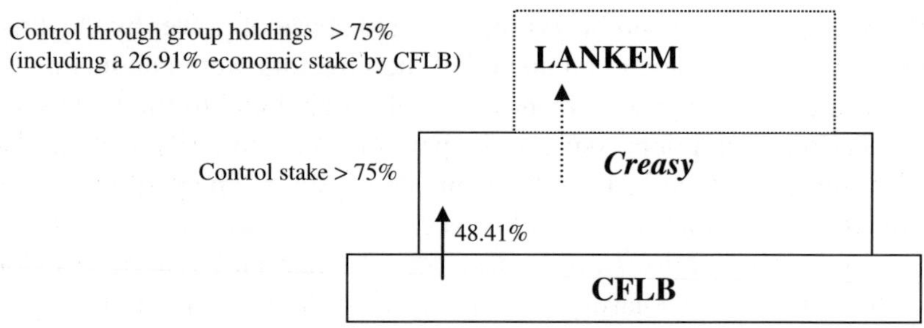

Figure 5.3:   Shareholding of Colombo Fort Land Group.

from monitoring and long-term planning on account of the high economic stake of Colombo Fort Land. However, this benefit must be weighed against the potentials costs of alleged tunnelling and internal private benefits of control. These costs, exclusively beneficial to controlling shareholders, if proved, outweigh any potential benefits of monitoring, or long-term planning.

The example illustrates that deficiencies in the regulatory and legal framework and the lack of market pressure, contributed to the costs of the controlling shareholder system in Sri Lanka. It is also alarming that the holding company Colombo Fort Land has been on the default board[232] of the CSE for noncompliance with the listing rules due to nonpublication of audited annual accounts for nearly 3 years and continues to trade on the default board of the CSE without audited accounts being presented. The lack of transparency and inadequate disclosure especially with regard to related-party transactions in corporate groups is also a cause of concern. Further, the fact that trading has continued at high values in 2005[233] despite these allegations, is indicative of the lack of disciplinary market pressure within the system.

It also highlights the deficient remedies available to a shareholder in such scenario. Arguably, minority shareholders of E.B. Creasy can bring an action under sections 210, 211 of the Companies Act[234] and possibly an action for contempt of court. Whether the alleged tunnelling amounts to

---

[232] Colombo Stock Exchange, Listing Rules 2004, r. 10.1.

[233] Colombo Stock Exchange, E.B. Creasy High-low Prices Quarterly (2004–05), http://www.cse.lk/listings/highlowprices_table.jsp?symbol=EBCR [10 January 2006].

[234] Companies Act No. 17 of 1982; Companies Act No. 7 of 2007 s. 224–33, embodies a statutory derivative action.

oppression or mismanagement in terms of sections 210 and 211 is debateable given the restrictive judicial interpretation of these sections.[235]

The example also raises concern about internal mechanisms of governance, the general meetings of companies, especially annual general meetings at which the consideration of the accounts, balance sheets and reports of the directors and auditors are deemed normal agenda items.[236]

The above analysis implies that in the context of Sri Lanka, the *costs* of controlling shareholder systems are contingent upon the legal and regulatory environment and market forces. However, the analysis goes further in illustrating weaknesses in the legal and regulatory framework in constraining conflicts within controlling shareholder systems. Corporate norms are ignored especially at shareholder meetings. Market forces fail to act as a disciplining device due to the lack of information, minimal intervention of dispersed minority shareholders, and short-term trading. Disclosure and transparency standards are de facto derisory. There is a lack of shareholder lawsuits due to the limited remedies available to minority shareholders. Further, the delay and costs in pursuing corporate litigation, is made worse by the lack of effective regulatory enforcement.

5.5. The Controlling Shareholder Trade-off

5.5.1. *Introduction*

The initial reaction of academia to the empirical reality of controlling shareholder systems was sceptical and biased.[237] Dispersed ownership systems were seen as the ultimate goal of corporate governance evolution.[238] As

---

[235] The term oppression is defined as including '"burdensome", "harsh" and "wrongful" acts' and on a balance of probability the affairs of the company must be conducted in a manner oppressive to the minority shareholder when 'all the events are considered as part of a continuing story as opposed to individual events, in isolation', *Ratnam et al. v. Jayatilake* [2002] 1 SLLR 409, 415–6.

[236] Companies Act 1982 (n. 234), Article 53, Table A.

[237] For example, Morck and Yeung (n. 101). In contrast, J Franks and C Mayer, Capital Markets and Corporate Control: A Study of France, Germany and the UK (1990), 5 *Economic Policy*, 189, recognise the trade-offs between controlled ownership systems as they prevail on the continent and the widely held system in the UK in the context of takeovers.

[238] H Hansmann and R Kraakman, The End of History for Corporate Law (2001), 89 *Georgetown Law Journal*, 439.

Gilson submits,[239] the preference for widely held systems was evident in the World Bank and IMF responses to the Asian financial crisis.

This view is supported by the growing 'law and finance' literature, which seeks to reveal links between the quality of legal regimes and corporate governance systems.[240] The implications to be drawn from the 'law and finance' studies are that controlling shareholder systems are more likely to exist in countries with 'weak' legal systems and poor investor protection because weak legal systems are prone to abuse by controlling shareholders. It follows that where minority shareholders are not protected by the legal system from controlling shareholders, extraction of the private benefits of control and tunnelling is rampant. Entrenchment is a feature of such system as controlling shareholders would not part with control through public offerings, as they risk losing any future extraction of private benefits. Illiquid equity markets characterise such corporate governance systems.

However, recent scholarship argues that concentrated ownership exists in countries with both good and bad investor protection,[241] and furthermore, countries with controlling shareholder systems experience different levels of private benefit extraction,[242] and possibly entrenchment and tunnelling, without any reference to the level of investor protection within such country.

If one is able to separate controlling shareholder systems from the association with poor investor protection and weak legal systems (i.e., in contrast to the 'law and finance' literature), it can be argued that all controlling shareholder systems do not essentially lead to the same levels of private benefits of control extraction, tunnelling or entrenchment. As Berle and Means recognised in their seminal work, '…the interests of the minority owners run parallel to those of the controlling majority and are in the main protected by the self-interest of the latter'.[243]

---

[239] Gilson (n. 34) 7–8.

[240] LLSV, Legal Determinants of External Finance (1997), 52 *Journal of Finance*, 1131; LLSV, Law and Finance (1998), 106 *Journal of Political Economy*, 1113; La-Porta *et al.* (n. 1); LLSV (n. 36); C Himmelberg, R Hubbard and I Love, Investor Protection, Ownership, and the Cost of Capital (2002), World Bank Working Paper 2834, http:// econ.worldbank.org/files/34858_wps2834.pdf [12 April 2006].

[241] M Roe, *Political Determinants of Corporate Governance: Political Context, Corporate Impact* (Oxford University Press Oxford 2002), 9, '…even in nations with good legal structures generally and, by measurement, good shareholder protection — such as in Germany and Scandinavia — ownership *did not* separate from control.'

[242] Dyck and Zingales (n. 36), 588–590.

[243] A Berle and G Means, *The Modern Corporation and Private Property* (Rev edn Harcourt, Brace & World Inc New York 1967), 62.

It is useful to seek an answer to the question of whether controlling shareholder systems deserve the blanket ostracism of recent years? Controlling shareholder systems have inherent monitoring mechanisms, motivate efficiency and are credited with improved firm performance when coupled with economic stakes.[244] Studies in the mid-1990s investigating concentrated ownership in the form of institutional investors argue that shareholder activism increases in direct proportion to ownership concentration.[245] The implication to be gleaned from such studies for controlling shareholder systems is that economic stakes in the hands of controlling shareholders commensurate to controlling stakes (making them large shareholders) has the ability to increase shareholder activism and thereby, limit the 'classic agency problem'. Further, private benefits of control can be nonfinancial in nature, that is, business reputation of a controlling shareholder, in which case the behaviour of such shareholders may not be detrimental.

If controlling shareholder systems are not per se detrimental to corporate governance and bring about different levels of costs and benefits within different jurisdictions, it must mean that factors within such jurisdictions are tilting the balance, that is, making controlling shareholder systems more worthy in certain jurisdictions, while bringing out its worst in others.

5.5.2. *Controlling Shareholder Trade-off*

In seeking to answer the question of what makes controlling shareholders efficient in one jurisdiction and not in the other, the concept of a *trade-off* is important. This is because the factors that determine the point of trade-off between the *costs* of and *benefits* of controlling shareholder systems are what contributes towards making controlling shareholder systems efficient in one jurisdiction and not in the other.

The primary objective of this chapter is to support the trade-off thesis, that is, controlling shareholder systems present a trade-off between its costs and benefits and that such trade-off is dependent *not only* on

---

[244] LLSV (n. 205).

[245] J Coffee, Liquidity v. Control: The Institutional Investor as a Corporate Monitor (1991), 91 *Columbia Law Review*, 1277; B Black and J Coffee, Hail Britannia? Institutional Investor Behavior Under Limited Regulation (1994), 92 *Michigan Law Review*, 1997.

functionally good law but also on the regulatory environment, market forces and the ratios between the controlling shareholders' economic and controlling stakes.

Controlling shareholder systems embody both costs and benefits.[246] In recent times, Gilson and Gordon have conceptualised the 'trade-off' prevalent in controlling shareholder systems due to its inherent costs and benefits.[247] They claim that controlling shareholders are at a cross road between the principal-agent problem arising from the separation of ownership and control, which the controlling shareholder has the ability to overcome with better monitoring, and the agency problem between controlling and non-controlling shareholders, which produces the potential for private benefits of control.[248]

The divergent interests between the controlling and non-controlling shareholders result in a trade-off, because the controlling shareholder has to bear liquidity,[249] diversification[250] and monitoring costs, and thus some costs of controlling shareholder systems such as private benefits of control (pecuniary or nonpecuniary) are likely to occur. Thus, from a minority shareholder point of view, it is a trade-off between better monitoring and the potential for a controlling shareholder to extract private benefits of control, engage in tunnelling or seek entrenchment. In fact, Gilson claims that '[p]ublic shareholders will prefer a controlling shareholder as long as the benefits from reduction in managerial agency costs exceed the private benefits that the controlling shareholder will extract'.[251]

Gilson takes his taxonomy further by claiming that the trade-off gives rise to a distinction between systems with *inefficient* controlling shareholders where the private benefit extraction exceeds the value of monitoring, and systems with *efficient* controlling shareholders, where the benefits of monitoring exceed the cost of private benefits.[252] In effect, controlling shareholder systems where the costs related to such system

---

[246] Sections 5.2–5.4.

[247] Gilson and Gordon (n. 28).

[248] ibid 785.

[249] Constraints on other investments if controlling shareholder is to maintain a large investment in one company. Coffee (n. 245), 1281 — 'Investors that want liquidity may hesitate to accept control.'

[250] Constraints on controlling shareholder's entry into other areas of investment related to the business if the investment in the current venture is large.

[251] Gilson (n. 34), 13.

[252] ibid 14.

outweigh the benefits of such system and vice versa. This aspect of the trade-off thesis is useful in framing a corporate governance agenda.

While there is merit in this distinction, it is difficult to unqualifiedly accept Gilson's subsequent claim that the controlling shareholder trade-off framework implies a varying relationship between functionally good law and efficient controlling shareholders and functionally bad law and inefficient controlling shareholders.[253] It is submitted that while functionally good law may constrain controlling shareholders, it is unlikely by itself to bring about changes to ownership structures. Gilson fails to define 'functionally good law' or 'functionally bad law', but if taken in the ordinary sense of the word as 'working or operating in the context in which it is placed',[254] it would imply that there is a varying relationship between an effective legal system and controlling shareholders.

For purposes of this study, Gilson's trade-off hypothesis is modified and extended by the cost-benefit analysis.[255] The implications drawn from the cost-benefit analysis posit that the *costs* of controlling shareholder systems are for the most part dependent on the legal, regulatory and market forces within a jurisdiction and that the *benefits* of controlling shareholder systems are primarily dependent on the size of the economic stake of the controlling shareholders and the ratio between the economic and control stakes of the controlling shareholders. Therefore, the controlling shareholder trade-off hypothesis articulated by Gilson should be reframed as implying a varying relationship not only between functionally good law (i.e., legal and regulatory environment) and efficient controlling shareholders, and functionally bad law and inefficient controlling shareholders, but also as a varying relationship between market forces within a country coupled with the size of the economic stake of the controlling shareholders and the ratio between the economic and control stakes of the controlling shareholders. This is the trade-off thesis articulated and supported by this chapter.

In the light of the cost-benefit analysis and the reframed trade-off thesis, the answer to the question of what makes controlling shareholders efficient in one jurisdiction and not in the other, is that such efficiency is

---

[253] ibid 13, 14–19.

[254] *Concise Oxford English Dictionary* (10th edn rev Oxford University Press Oxford 2002).

[255] Sections 5.2–5.4.

conditional on not only legal and regulatory conditions with a country but also on market forces and size of the economic stake of controlling shareholders and the ratio between their economic stakes and control rights. Thus, just as law is not the sole factor motivating the dispersion of ownership, functionally good law is also not the sole determinant of efficient *versus* inefficient controlling shareholder systems.

5.5.3. *Inferences for Corporate Governance Reform in Sri Lanka by Examination of the Controlling Shareholder Trade-off*

The trade-off thesis articulated by this study implies a varying relationship not only between functionally good law and efficient controlling shareholders, and functionally bad law and inefficient controlling shareholders, but also between market forces coupled with the size of the economic stake of the controlling shareholders and the ratio between the economic and control stakes of the controlling shareholders. The cost-benefit analysis in Sections 5.2 and 5.3 and the implications from such analysis in Section 5.4 of this chapter lend support to the framing of this thesis both generally and in the context of Sri Lanka.

The analysis of the trade-off thesis resulted in the discovery of the determinants that bring about efficient versus inefficient controlling shareholders. It now remains to draw implications for the reform of corporate governance in Sri Lanka by such findings.

The first inference drawn from the trade-off thesis for a corporate governance reform agenda in Sri Lanka is the need to enable access to finance to ensure that the economic stakes to control ratios of the controlling shareholders fall, thereby increasing the benefits of controlling shareholder systems (and also to some extent reduce its costs). Access to finance has a cyclical relationship with effective corporate governance.

The second inference drawn from the trade-off thesis for corporate governance reform in Sri Lanka is that a reform agenda need not be based on a move from one system to another, that is, controlling shareholder to widely held system. Rather, its focus should be on making the benefits of such a system outweigh its costs.

The third and most pertinent inference for corporate governance reform in Sri Lanka and for this study is that while the functionally good law is an important aspect in constraining controlling shareholders and making them efficient, law is not the sole factor that drives the wedge between efficient and inefficient controlling shareholders. Thus, an effective reform agenda must consider factors such as market forces that determine the point of trade-off and focus its attention on strengthening the most suitable of such factors.

CHAPTER 6

Controlling Shareholder Systems: The Search for Reform

6.1. Introduction

The governance of companies is a subject of increased scrutiny and evolving thought. There are few countries in the world not subject to a corporate governance reform agenda. The primary global drivers of corporate governance reform in the recent past are the financial crises and scandals in Asia, the US and Europe.[1]

For developing countries in particular, a driver of reforms is the need to demonstrate the commitment to the development of an effective corporate governance system to attract the increasing flows of global capital. There is also the need to emulate some of the reforms adopted in developed countries after corporate scandals, such as the Sarbanes-Oxley Act in the US.[2] International Financial Institutions such as the World Bank and the IMF influenced by the enormous output of research in the area of corporate governance,[3] the links between law and finance, and reoccurrence of financial scandals, habitually make financial sector and legal reforms a 'conditionality'[4] of their lending, thereby driving reforms in the area of corporate governance.

---

[1] G Hertig, On-going Board Reforms: One-size Fits-all and Regulatory Capture (2005), European Corporate Governance Institute Working Paper 25, http://ssrn.com/abstract=676417 [15 May 2006], claims that reformers battle past scandals rather than future market failures.

[2] 15 U.S.C.A. §7201–7266 (2003).

[3] Search of the Social Science Research Network Abstract database brings up over 500 entries for the words 'corporate governance'. Social Science Research Network, http://www.ssrn.com [9 September 2006].

[4] World Bank, *Review of World Bank Conditionality* (Washington DC 2005), defines conditionality as where the bank makes its resources available to the borrower, if the borrower (a) maintains an adequate macroeconomic framework, (b) implements its overall programme in a manner satisfactory to the bank and (c) complies with the policy and institutional actions that are deemed critical for the implementation and expected results of the supported programme.

6.1.1. *Corporate Governance Reforms in Sri Lanka*

Sri Lankan activism in corporate governance in the last decade was initially propelled by concern for numerous company failures, especially finance companies in the 1980s and 1990s. In the wake of these failures, the GOSL established the Presidential Commission on Finance and Banking to investigate the causes of such failures and recommend measures for strengthening the country's financial sector. Thus, the initial focus of the corporate governance reform agenda in Sri Lanka was on the financial aspects of corporate governance. The Institute of Chartered Accountants of Sri Lanka (ICASL) set up a task force in 1992 to enforce Sri Lankan Accounting Standards (SLAS)[5] and then extended this initiative in 1996 to set up a committee to make recommendations on the financial aspects of corporate governance.[6]

Like many countries around the world, much effort was devoted to the formulation of elaborate codes of practices and rules of corporate governance.[7] In the period after 1996, Sri Lanka adopted numerous voluntary codes and best practices for corporate governance codified as a *Handbook on Corporate Governance* by the Institute of Chartered Secretaries and Administrators (ICSA),[8] a booklet on *Corporate Governance* by the Ceylon Chamber of Commerce, an *Exposure Draft on Boardroom Governance*, and a *Code of Best Practices on Audit Committees* by the ICASL. In 2001, a National Task Force on Corporate Governance was set up to compile a *Code of Corporate Governance for Banks and other Financial Institutions*. In 2004, taking best practices further, the SEC and

---

[5] This initiative resulted in the Sri Lanka Accounting and Auditing Standards Act No. 15 of 1995, which set up Sri Lanka Accounting and Auditing Standards Monitoring Board (SLAASMB), and empowered the ICASL to adopt SLAS and Sri Lanka Auditing Standards (SLAuS) 1997 which required all specified business enterprises (on a definition based on turnover, share capital, net assets, number of employees etc.) to prepare financial statements in accordance with SLAS and have accounts audited in accordance with SLAuS.

[6] Institute of Chartered Accountants of Sri Lanka, *Code of Best Practice: Report of the Committee to make Recommendations on Matters Relating to Financial Aspects of Corporate Governance* (Colombo 1997).

[7] H Gregory-Weil and Gotshal and Manges LLP, *International Comparison of Corporate Governance: Guidelines and Codes of Best Practice in Developing and Developing Countries* (New York 2002), report the adoption of over 100 such codes and practices.

[8] Institute of Chartered Secretaries and Administrators, *Handbook on Corporate Governance: Principles & Guidelines to Best Practice in Sri Lanka* (Colombo).

the national accounting body, the ICASL, announced plans to introduce a mandatory corporate governance code for listed companies.[9]

The Companies Act[10] in Sri Lanka was also subject to a process of reform since 2001. A new Companies Bill made its way through the Cabinet in October 2005 and came into force in mid-2007.[11] It is a progressive piece of legislation to simplify and modernise company law and corporate governance in Sri Lanka.

Despite progressive measures to strengthen regulatory aspects of corporate governance, there was a notable failure of a savings and development bank in 2003 and the failure of a credit card company, a subsidiary of a significant corporate group.[12] Investor confidence is low,[13] resulting in the high cost of capital. An empirical study on corporate governance practices of 50 public listed companies in Sri Lanka finds no evidence to even weakly confirm that many of the corporate governance practices that corporate entities were publicly claiming to be following were being adhered to.[14] A compilation on regulation of securities markets focussing on how laws regulate the issuance of new equity to the public finds Sri Lanka scoring weakly in the public enforcement of securities laws.[15]

---

[9] SEC and National Accounting Body Brings a New Code for Listed Companies (19 September 2004), *Lanka Business Online*; SEC and ICASL Rules on Corporate Governance for Listed Companies 2008. The rules are formulated in the areas of non-executive directors, independent directors, remuneration and audit committees and are incorporated into the CSE Listing Rules. The code was subsequently jointly issued by the SEC and ICASL on 1 July 2008 and is available on the SEC website.

[10] No. 17 of 1982.

11 The Bill was presented for its second reading in Parliament on 19 October 2006. P'ment Talks Biz with New Company Law (20 October 2006), *Daily Mirror*. The new Companies Act No. 7 of 2007 came into force on 3 May 2007.

[12] The Pramuka Savings and Development Bank in 2003 and the Golden Key Credit Card Company Limited in 2008.

[13] Exclusion from CalPERS Permissible Equity Markets List, Wilshire Consulting, *CalPERS Permissible Equity Markets Investment Analysis: Final Report* (California 2007).

[14] A Cabraal, Corporate Governance in Sri Lanka Fast Off the Tracks: But is the Progress Real Progress?, in F Sobhan and W Werner (eds.), *A Comparative Analysis of Corporate Governance in South Asia: Charting a Road Map for Bangladesh* (Bangladesh Enterprise Institute Dhaka 2003).

[15] R La-Porta, F Lopez-de-Silanes and A Shleifer, What Works in Securities Laws? (2004), National Bureau of Economic Research Working Paper 9882, http://papers.nber.org/papers/w9882.pdf [20 May 2006]. The index of public enforcement equals the arithmetic mean of: (1) supervisor characteristics index; (2) investigative powers index; (3) orders index and (4) criminal index. Sri Lanka scores 0.33 with 1.00 being a perfect score.

A primary reason for the ineffectiveness of the ad hoc compilations of best practices and legal reforms in Sri Lanka is a lack of understanding that corporate governance systems across the countries are different, while global best practices and legal reforms are remarkably similar. Another reason for such ineffectiveness is the overwhelming reliance on voluntary best practices and law-on-the-books as effective corporate governance mechanisms.

The bias towards legal reforms and corporate governance best practices as the panacea for all corporate governance problems does not bode well for Sri Lanka. For example, reform of the Companies Act was undertaken in the mistaken belief that the Act is the single most important obstacle to effective corporate governance. However, the Companies Act No. 17 of 1982, (which replaced the Ceylon Companies Ordinance[16]) is based on the Companies Act 1948 (United Kingdom) and while some provisions of the Act are archaic and unsuitable for modern commercial practices, a study by Franks *et al.*[17] argues that despite weaknesses in regulation, capital markets flourished in the UK in the post-1948 period under a similar legal regime.[18] Their arguments illustrate that the regulatory regime under the 1948 Act in the UK was not per se weak and lends support to the view taken in this study that improvements to law-on-the books is not necessarily the universal remedy.

6.1.2. *The Literature on Corporate Governance Reform*

The literature on corporate governance reform has two primary characteristics: (a) its emphasis on law as the primary mechanism of corporate

---

[16] No. 51 of 1938, which was based on the Companies Act 1929 (UK).

[17] J Franks, C Mayer and S Rossi, Ownership: Evolution and Regulation (2003), European Corporate Governance Institute Finance Working Paper 92, http://ssrn.com/abstract=35438 [10 January 2006]. Improvements illustrated by LLSV indexes on anti-director rights, disclosure requirements and liability standards; Similarly, B Cheffins, Law as Bedrock: The Foundations of an Economy Dominated by Widely Held Public Companies (2003), 23 *Oxford Journal of Legal Studies*, 1–13 quotes a financial journalist in 1929 *Economist* to support the view that UK company law offered investors little protection.

[18] ibid. Franks, Mayer and Rossi (2003), 37, attribute this to informal relations of trust rather than any formal system of regulation; ibid, Cheffins (2003) to market oriented factors such as reputation and LSE regulations.

governance reform and (b) its preoccupation with negating the costs arising from the conflict between managers and shareholders in dispersed shareholder systems.

While the second characteristic is losing its prominence due to findings that much of the world except the US and UK have concentrated shareholder systems,[19] scholars and policy makers are slow to realise that law-on-the-books by itself is inadequate within a reform agenda. This is largely due to a misreading of the influential body of 'law and finance' literature,[20] which reveals empirical links between the quality of a jurisdiction's legal rules and the prevalence of controlling shareholders, assumed to reflect poor corporate governance. The inference drawn from the literature is that weak law is associated with weak corporate governance and controlling shareholders,[21] and law reform is the viable solution. The literature is misread in that reform spurred by the literature has targeted the reform of law-on-the-books,[22] although the studies focus on the quality of law.[23]

6.1.3. *The Framework of the Chapter*

The challenge facing Sri Lanka and other developing countries is to devise a corporate governance reform agenda successful in bringing about

---

[19] Chapter 3.

[20] LLSV, Legal Determinants of External Finance (1997), 52 *Journal of Finance*, 1131; LLSV, Investor Protection and Corporate Governance (2000), 58 *Journal of Financial Economics*, 3.

[21] R Gilson, Corporate Governance, the Equity Contract and the Cost of Capital: Incremental and Accretive Reform Strategies (2004), http://www.oecd.org/dataoecd/19/58/34081304.pdf [10 January 2005], 5.

[22] K Pistor, M Raiser and S Gelfer, Law and Finance in Transition Economies (2000), European Bank for Reconstruction and Development Working Paper 48, http://www.ebrd.com/pubs/econo/wp0048.pdf [5 November 2004]. Effectiveness of legal institutions has a stronger impact on transition economies than law-on-the-books. K Pistor, Patterns of Legal Change: Shareholder and Creditor Rights in Transition Economies (2000), European Bank for Reconstruction and Development Working Paper 49, http://www.ebrd.com/pubs/econo/wp0049.pdf [13 November 2004], documents the retroactive pattern of legal reforms.

[23] LLSV 1997 (n. 20). While importance is placed on legal rules, other variables include measurement of the rule of law; LLSV, Law and Finance (1998), 106 *Journal of Political Economy*, 1113. Variables include efficiency of the legal systems, rule of law and corruption.

investor confidence and the development of capital markets. Such reform agenda must address the specific corporate governance issues prevalent within corporate governance systems in developing countries to promote economic growth and development.

Devising a corporate governance reform agenda for Sri Lanka entails consideration of the trade-off between the costs and benefits of controlling shareholder systems. The primary inference for corporate governance reform in Sri Lanka drawn by the Chapter 5 analysis of the trade-off thesis is that, while the functionally good law is an important aspect in constraining controlling shareholders and making them efficient, law is not the sole factor that drives the wedge between efficient and inefficient controlling shareholders. Thus, an effective reform agenda must consider factors, such as market forces, that determine the trade-off (i.e., between the costs and benefits of a particular shareholder system) and focus its attention on strengthening the most suitable of such factors.

In devising a corporate governance reform agenda for Sri Lanka, this study is also informed by the hypothesis in Chapter 4, that lack of financing is the primary reason for the existence of concentrated ownership and controlling shareholders in Sri Lanka. The lack of financing and resultant weak capital markets in Sri Lanka has important inferences for a corporate governance reform agenda in that: (a) if capital is made available or a source of capital identified, then the competition for capital will be an important driver of a corporate governance reform agenda and (b) it illuminates the potential of market forces (i.e., equity and debt capital markets) as a mechanism for constraining the costs of controlling shareholders.

The objective of this chapter is to develop a framework for the reform of corporate governance in Sri Lanka, which increases the benefits inherent in controlling shareholder systems and curbs the costs of controlling shareholders, that is, tilts the trade-off balance and creates efficiency among controlling shareholders. To achieve this objective, the focus of this chapter is on (a) devising mechanisms to constrain controlling shareholders and (b) enabling access to finance for investors, to ensure that the economic stakes to control ratios of the controlling shareholders fall. The framework for reform should evaluate the advantages and disadvantages of the different governance mechanisms available to control the costs of controlling shareholders, and also identify the most suitable among such mechanisms for a developing country such as Sri Lanka.

A critical precondition to enabling the benefits of the controlling shareholder system in Sri Lanka lies in increasing the economic stakes of controlling shareholders. Short of outlawing the mechanisms used by controlling shareholders to increase control stakes in excess of economic stakes,[24] an increase in the economic stakes of controlling shareholders requires the infusion of new equity capital. However, the infusion of equity capital into controlling shareholder systems is constrained due to the costs of controlling shareholder systems and weak capital markets. Controlling shareholders will also be hostile to fresh infusions of capital, which dilute their controlling stakes.[25]

An alternative solution is to first, focus on controlling the costs of controlling shareholder systems. Minimal costs should increase investor confidence and result in healthy capital markets. The increased capital flows should in turn, result in an increase in shareholders holding large economic stakes or at a minimum in a decrease in the control rights of controlling shareholders enabling increased benefits of controlling shareholder systems. Thus, the crucial issue in devising a corporate governance reform agenda for Sri Lanka is to control the costs of its controlling shareholder system.

The chapter is structured as follows. Section 6.2 proposes a corporate governance reform framework focussed on controlling the costs of controlling shareholders. Section 6.3 analyses the effectiveness and suitability of the three external governance mechanisms (law, norms and market forces) within the corporate governance framework deemed suitable to control the costs of the controlling shareholder system, generally and in the context of Sri Lanka. The analytical foundation in Section 6.3 results in a framework for reform in Section 6.4.

---

[24] This is a possibility. However only a weak effort is made by the Companies Act 2007 (n. 11) s. 72, which attempts to regulate cross-holdings by restricting a subsidiary holding shares in a holding company. In contrast, in the US, the Public Utility Holding Company Act of 1935 (subsequently repealed) which proscribed pyramiding beyond the second degree among public utility companies was successful in outlawing mechanisms used by controlling shareholders to increase control stakes in excess of economic stakes among public utility companies. R Larner, Ownership and Control in the 200 Largest Nonfinancial Corporations, 1929 and 1963 (1966), 56 *American Economic Review,* 777–785.

[25] Controlling shareholders typically ensure that large stakes are not sold via the exchange, by arranging for private sales, or by restricting the initial market float of the company to meeting the legal minimum.

6.2. Controlling the Costs of Controlling Shareholder Systems

6.2.1. *A Framework for Controlling the Costs of Controlling Shareholder Systems*

The agency problem in companies manifests itself in two ways. In dispersed ownership systems, the decision makers (i.e., the managers) manage the company poorly, reducing returns to outsiders. In controlling shareholder systems, the decision makers (i.e., the controlling shareholders) make decisions with their own interests in mind. While distinct, both categories of behaviour are discernible in controlling shareholder systems. To illustrate, if the decision maker's focus is on diverting resources for personal interest, facilitating such transfer must necessarily lead to poor management decisions. This distinction although blurred in controlling shareholder systems, is of relevance in the context of a reform agenda because mechanisms targeting the ability of the controlling shareholders to make decisions in their own interests may not always solve the poor management problem, which arises in consequence. Further, both costs and benefits of controlling shareholder systems emanate from the fact that controlling shareholders are in positions of control and make corporate decisions, which can be both beneficial and damaging.

The framework for controlling the costs of controlling shareholders proposed in this section of the chapter, identify the mechanisms capable of influencing and disciplining corporate decision making. Common corporate governance mechanisms are the board of directors, proxy fights, monitoring by large and institutional shareholders, the market for corporate control, executive compensation and incentive packages, and litigation. These mechanisms are categorised according to the actors or environment in which they are exercised: those internal to companies, such as the board of directors and shareholders, and those external to companies which arise due to a company's need to raise capital (e.g., creditors and capital markets), recruit workers and engage in corporate activities (e.g., product market competition, corporate norms, laws and regulations). In designing a framework for reform, it is useful to refer to the corporate governance framework set out in Chapter 1,[26] adopted with modification (Fig. 6.1).

---

[26] Fig. 1.3.

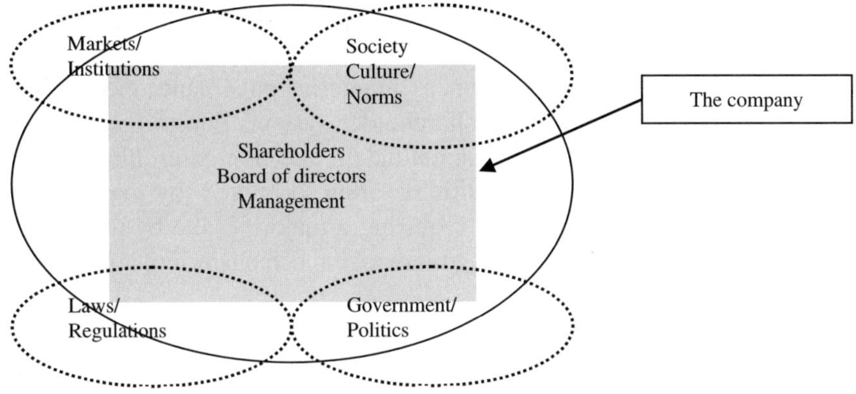

Figure 6.1: Corporate Governance Framework.

The agency problem in dispersed shareholder systems due to the conflict of interest between managers and shareholders and the resultant poor management is tackled with varying success through internal governance mechanisms, such as independent directors on corporate boards, stock options for managers, capital maintenance rules and specific provisions in the articles of association requiring majority vote of the shareholders.

However, internal governance mechanisms are unlikely to be effective in curbing the costs of controlling shareholders for two reasons. First, internal governance mechanisms are designed to prevent poor management decision making, not decisions made in the interests of one group of shareholders in positions of control. Second, the effectiveness of internal governance mechanisms may be compromised by prevailing local conditions. For example, in a controlling shareholder system with family connections, cross-holdings and pyramid corporate structures, finding a truly 'independent' director is a difficult task.[27] Once found, their

---

[27] While global independent directors are a possible solution, not all developing country companies can afford the associated costs. There is also a lack of willingness from within companies given the ability to influence such adoption through the use of political influence.

independence can be compromised, as their paymasters are the controlling shareholders.

Further, the role of shareholders as an internal governance mechanism is not significant in controlling shareholder systems due to the conflict of interest between controlling shareholders and non-controlling shareholders, with management positions often occupied by controlling shareholders. Similarly, any rule requiring a majority vote by the shareholders is an ineffective internal governance mechanism in a controlling shareholder system.

In the light of the limited use of the internal mechanisms of governance in controlling shareholder systems, notably the board of directors and shareholders, it is necessary to focus the corporate governance reform agenda of controlling shareholder systems on the external mechanisms of governance.

External governance mechanisms can be classified into three categories: (i) Law, specifically laws and regulations affecting companies and the corporate environment; (ii) Norms (standards, voluntary codes, corporate reputation and social norms with a bearing on corporate practices) and (iii) Market forces, including capital markets (potential shareholders and potential and present creditors), the market for corporate control, labour markets (potential and existing employees), product markets, the providers of capital market information (analysts, rating agencies, media), the markets for accounting, financial and legal services.

6.3. External Governance Mechanisms and Controlling the Costs of Controlling Shareholder Systems

Companies are subject to legal, regulatory, market and social constraints, (i.e., the external governance mechanisms), identified as most suitable for controlling the costs of controlling shareholder systems. To determine the most effective external governance mechanism among these, it is necessary to evaluate the three external governance mechanisms with respect to (a) their effectiveness as portrayed by literature and (b) their application and suitability in controlling the costs of the controlling shareholder system in Sri Lanka, a representative developing country.

6.3.1. *Law as an External Governance Mechanism*

The success of law as an external governance mechanism has received the most support from contemporary law and finance scholarship,[28] raising important questions on the interaction between law and finance with potential policy implications. These studies are based on the premise that legal reforms are the most straightforward and simplest method of controlling the costs of controlling shareholders as evidenced by corporate law reform programmes undertaken in Eastern Europe and Asia. Deficiencies in the findings of the law and finance scholarship (i.e., first, that countries with stronger legal protections have deeper and highly valued capital markets,[29] and second, that common law systems provide shareholders with stronger legal protections[30]) are that it does not provide a satisfactory explanation as to why some countries with poor legal protection of investors are able to attract capital (e.g., Thailand, India, China), nor does it explain why controlling shareholders appear to be more efficient in some jurisdictions than in others, irrespective of the system of law (e.g., Sweden (civil law) and Sri Lanka (common law)).[31]

It is undoubted that strong corporate law builds investor confidence.[32] The 'law matters thesis' is straightforward. From the point of view of an

---

[28] LLSV (1997) (n. 20). Countries with poorer investor protection measured by both the character of legal rules and the quality of law enforcement, have smaller and narrower capital markets; LLSV (2000) (n. 20) describes the legal protection of investors as a potentially useful way of approaching corporate governance and its reform; C Himmelberg, R Hubbard and I Love, Investor Protection, Ownership, and the Cost of Capital (2002), World Bank Working Paper 2834, http://econ.worldbank.org/files/34858_wps2834.pdf [12 April 2006], investigate the effect of investor protection (legal, institutional and regulatory environment) on the cost of capital and suggest that policies aimed at strengthening investor protection, law and enforcement improves capital allocation.

[29] LLSV (2000) (n. 20) 15–16; LLSV (1998) (n. 23) 1137–1139,1151–1152.

[30] LLSV (2000) (n. 20) 13–15; LLSV (1998) (n. 23) 1137–1139, 1151–1152.

[31] S Johnson *et al.*, Tunneling, in K Hopt and E Wymeersch (eds.), *Capital Markets and Company Law* (Oxford University Press Oxford 2003), make the argument that tunnelling takes place in countries with and without effective legal enforcement.

[32] B Black, The Legal and Institutional Preconditions for Strong Securities Markets (2001), 48 *University of Chicago Law Review*, 781. For alternative considerations of the importance of law in protecting investors, J Coffee, The Rise of Dispersed Ownership: The Role of Law in the Separation of Ownership and Control (2001), Columbia Law & Economics Working Paper 182, http://ssrn.com/abstract=254097 [20 February 2005], suggests functional substitutes for close governmental regulation such as self-regulation; Cheffins (n. 23), Law could 'jump start' a reform process although its success should not be taken for granted.

investor, a nation whose law[33] poorly protects minority shareholders against a controlling shareholder extracting value to the detriment of the minority shareholders is unappealing. From the perspective of a controlling shareholder weak law proffers large benefits from control.

While law reform and improvements to the legal systems appear the most straightforward and effective method of controlling the costs of controlling shareholders, it requires political will, lacking in controlling shareholder systems with politically influential controlling shareholders.

The reform efforts advocating law as an effective external mechanism of corporate governance, encourage legal reform either in the form of changes to (i) substantive law (i.e., legal rules); and/or (ii) enforcement mechanisms and/or (iii) judicial attitudes.

There is limited evidence on the effectiveness of legal rules in specifically controlling the costs of controlling shareholders. Dyck and Zingales[34] report a drop in the level of private benefits of control after Italy adopted legislation in 1998, which made it significantly easier for minority shareholders to pursue derivative litigation against management appointed by controlling shareholders ('Draghi' reforms). However, these results are only suggestive given the very small sample.[35]

In contrast, one of the propositions sought to be established by Johnson *et al.*,[36] in an article advocating the use of legal reforms to reduce tunnelling, is that tunnelling is not only limited to developing countries but also takes place in countries with effective legal enforcement. They attribute this to judicial attitudes and legal tradition (e.g., civil law, which emphasises predictability and rely on legal rules rather than concepts such as fairness). Their argument supports the view that changes to legal rules or enforcement mechanisms are insufficient in controlling the costs of controlling shareholders even within common law countries, if not accompanied by a change of judicial attitudes and legal culture.

It is further submitted that law as an external governance mechanism to curb the costs of controlling shareholder systems is not as straightforward

---

[33] That is, substantive corporate law.

[34] A Dyck and L Zingales, Private Benefits of Control: An International Comparison (2004), 59 *Journal of Finance*, 537, find that before reform the average value of private benefits of control are 47 percent, while after reform it is 6 percent.

[35] The sample contains only six (6) observations of a controlling shareholder block sale before the 1998 reforms and two (2) after the reforms.

[36] S Johnson *et al.* (n. 31), 617.

or simple. Law reform invariably involves an element of legal transplantation, which does not solve legal backwardness or the possibility that home grown institutions may marginalise the transplant and render it dysfunctional.[37] Further, legal reforms or legal transplantation invariably involves a choice of the optimal legal model, often dictated by political forces and not the local institutional environment.[38]

Law reform targeting law-on-the books without the necessary public and private mechanisms of enforcement is also unlikely to be optimal. The flip side of reliance on law as an external mechanism of governance with effective private enforcement mechanisms is the possibility of litigation abuse by minority shareholders. On the other hand, reforms aimed at strengthening public law enforcement mechanisms need active government and regulatory intervention such as empowering regulatory bodies.

The literature identifies another obstacle to legal reforms. While legal reforms backed by effective enforcement mechanisms and a proactive judiciary have the ability to control internal private benefits of control, such as outright theft, self-dealing, allocating business opportunities to related parties and use of insider information, legal rules are incapable of constraining specific controlling shareholder costs such as entrenchment and mismanagement.[39] For example, a related-party transaction or outright theft by a controlling shareholder can be attacked or prevented by effective corporate law, but an unprofitable transaction which arises due to mismanagement, entrenchment or political interference is unlikely to be within the purview of corporate law.[40]

It is submitted that Roe's[41] analysis deserves qualification in the context of controlling shareholder systems. Controlling shareholders if also large shareholders, unlike managers, bear the costs of their mismanagement, and

---

[37] K Pistor *et al.*, Evolution of Corporate Law and the Transplant Effect: Lessons from Six Countries (2003), 18 *World Bank Research Observer*, 89; D Berkowitz, K Pistor and J Richard, Economic Development, Legality, and the Transplant Effect (2003), 47 *European Economic Review*, 165, argue that transplanted legal systems stagnate for long periods of time.

[38] For example, Japan's post-war transplants of American institutions.

[39] M Roe, Corporate Law's Limits (2002), 33 *Journal of Legal Studies*, 233–234, identifies this as a conceptual problem and states 'The first, self-dealing, corporate law seeks to control directly; and the second, bad decision making that damages shareholders, it does not.'

[40] ibid 239–240, makes the point that in the US, the business-judgement rule ensures that legal scrutiny for mismanagement is avoided. The strongest argument in favour of the rule is that it is costly and inconvenient for judges to second-guess corporate managers.

[41] ibid.

therefore, it is likely that mismanagement in controlling shareholder systems will be minimal.[42] On the other hand, controlling shareholders are often without large economic stakes and while it is likely that mismanagement is likely to affect them,[43] it is unlikely to be large enough to curtail such actions.

6.3.2. *Law as an External Governance Mechanism in Sri Lanka*

It is unlikely that the costs of controlling shareholders can be curtailed by a reform agenda based solely on improvement to legal rules, enforcement mechanisms or judicial efficiency in Sri Lanka. There are five primary reasons for this.

First, as discussed in the introduction, Sri Lanka is a common law country with corporate laws based on English legal principles and English statutes. The legal system already has in place substantive law to control the costs of controlling shareholders.[44] A recent World Bank *Doing Business* survey on investor protection[45] gives Sri Lanka a score of 5.3 out of 10, based on the extent of substantive law in place on disclosure, director liability and ease of bringing a shareholder suit. In comparison, neighbouring India, sharing a common legal heritage with Sri Lanka, scores 6 and the UK scores 8. The above average score for Sri Lanka by this survey is misleading. As previously illustrated, the costs of the controlling shareholder systems in Sri Lanka is high.[46] This implies that within the institutional context of Sri Lanka, the existing law-on-the-books, is not an effective mechanism in curtailing the costs of its controlling shareholder system.

Second, it is unclear whether improvements to the legal system will curtail the costs of the controlling shareholder systems, as the effectiveness of a legal system is dependent not only on legal rules and standards,

---

[42] ibid 243. '…because the controlling stockholder owns a big block of the company's stock, it internalizes much of the cost of any mistake (unlike the unconstrained managers).'

[43] In the same manner as it affects managers with incentive compensation.

[44] For example, ability of minority shareholders to bring action against the majority shareholders, disclosure of related-party transactions.

[45] World Bank, Doing Business in 2006: Protecting Investors (2006), http://www.doingbusiness.org/ExploreTopics/ProtectingInvestors/ [5 June 2006].

[46] Chapter 5.

but also on effective enforcement,[47] judicial attitudes and judicial efficiency. Another World Bank *Doing Business* survey on enforcement of contracts,[48] indicative of enforcement mechanisms and judicial efficiency, cites the time required for resolution of dispute at 837 days (far above the OECD average of 351) and the costs involved as a percentage of debt at 21.3 percent (OECD average is 11.2 percent).[49] A related study on courts,[50] which attributes the efficiency of courts to characteristics of legal procedure, awards Sri Lanka a score of 3.78 on legal formalism[51] associated with the time it takes to collect a cheque and 3.89 on eviction of a tenant. This is among the highest for countries of English legal origin with countries such as Australia and New Zealand scoring 1.99 and 1.25 on the legal formalism index with respect to the eviction of a tenant.

A study undertaken by the Marga Institute[52] into the judicial system of Sri Lanka,[53] surveying judges, lawyers, court staff, civil litigants, remand prisoners and lawyers representing the corporate sector, finds that only 50 percent of the judges thought the judiciary as a whole deserve a high level of trust. Almost 84 percent of the respondents from within the legal community did not think that the judicial system of Sri Lanka was always fair and impartial, while 83.93 percent were of the view that the judicial system was corruptible. While the poor statistics for enforcement, judicial efficiency and attitudes demonstrate the need for improvement in the legal system, for purposes of this study, a reform agenda targeting only

---

[47] E Berglöf and S Claessens, Corporate Governance and Enforcement (2004), World Bank Policy Research Working Paper 3409, http://ssrn.com/abstract=625286 [5 May 2005], argue that enforcement is more important than the reform of legal rules in developing and transition countries.

[48] World Bank, Doing Business in 2006: Protecting Investors (2006), http://www.doing-business.org/ExploreTopics/EnforcingContracts/ [5 June 2006].

[49] Cost of recovering a debt through formal mechanisms is taken as illustrating the effectiveness of enforcement mechanisms and judicial efficiency.

[50] S Djankov *et al.*, Courts (2003), *Quarterly Journal of Economics*, 453.

[51] The legal formalism index measures substantive and procedural statutory intervention in judicial cases at lower-level civil trial courts, and is formed by adding up the following: (i) professionals *vs.* laymen, (ii) written *vs.* oral elements, (iii) legal justification, (iv) statutory regulation of evidence, (v) control of superior review, (vi) engagement formalities and (vii) independent procedural actions. The index ranges from 0–7, where 7 means a higher level of control in the judicial process.

[52] The Sri Lankan Centre for Development Studies.

[53] Marga Institute *A System Under Siege? An Inquiry into the Judicial System of Sri Lanka* (Marga Institute Colombo 2002).

enforcement mechanisms or judicial efficiency is unlikely to be effective in controlling the costs of controlling shareholders, who are likely to be wealthy individuals with political influence and social connections.

For law to be an effective mechanism in curbing the costs of controlling shareholders, it is necessary for legal reform to bring about changes to not only formal legal rules but also to the legal environment, including judicial attitudes and the quality of legal enforcement. While changes to legal rules are relatively straightforward with the necessary political will, changes to the legal environment require greater perseverance over a period of time, which may still be unsuccessful, if local conditions fail to embrace such a change.

Third, a reform agenda based on law as an external mechanism of governance is also unlikely to succeed in Sri Lanka as the corporate governance reform agenda is already changing without much success towards standard setting and improved disclosure as evidenced by the adoption of a number of best practices, voluntary codes and legal reforms.[54] Therefore, further standard setting or legal rules without adequate enforcement or monitoring mechanisms are unlikely to curb the costs of controlling shareholder systems.

Fourth, state-sanctioned law reform has the ability to favour certain industries or companies through various industrial policies. This is specially so in a country where political connections and businesses are entwined.[55] Therefore, impartiality in legal reforms is unlikely.

Fifth, the costs of controlling shareholders in Sri Lanka extend beyond outright theft or insider dealing by controlling shareholders. In fact, many of the costs involve mismanagement, entrenchment and external factors such as the use of political influence. Therefore, a reform agenda based solely on law reform is unlikely to be effective in minimising these particular costs of controlling shareholders in Sri Lanka.

However, regulations such as stock exchange regulations, when effective, do have the ability to impede controlling shareholders from diverting value for themselves (i.e., self-dealing). Further, the use of a regulatory agency can also to a large extent ameliorate the costs controlling shareholders, if such institution is independent, effective, with power to promulgate delegated legislation and effective enforcement powers. In the Sri Lankan context, the Securities and Exchange Commission is a regulatory

---

[54] Section 6.1.1.

[55] Chapter 5.

agency with the power to promulgate delegated legislation. However, its effectiveness in the area of enforcement in the recent past is questionable given the composition of its members.

The point here is not to reject the role of law as an external mechanism of corporate governance or doubt its effectiveness in constraining some of the costs of controlling shareholders. In fact, few would dispute the assertion that law is of utmost importance for corporate governance. Effective legal rules and enforcement mechanisms are fundamental institutions for any society and can lower the costs of controlling shareholders. However, in the context of Sri Lanka and other developing countries with controlling share-holder systems, its effectiveness as the most effective tool with which to successfully lower all the costs of controlling shareholders, is questionable.

6.3.3. *Norms as an External Governance Mechanism*

Norms guide behaviour and represent behavioural standards and rules that are often non-legally enforceable.[56] Definitions of norms in the corporate context have extended from socially accepted business practices, to 'soft law'[57] in the context of multinational corporations, to statements of best practices and codes of conduct. While the relationship between corporate law and norms is illuminating in explaining the manner in which corporate governance standards rather than rules work in a corporate setting, or why corporate attorneys are more deal makers than litigators,[58] the utility of norms for controlling the costs of controlling shareholders is ambiguous.

---

[56] P Mahoney and C Sanchirico, Competing Norms and Social Evolution: Is the Fittest Norm Efficient? (2001), 149 *University of Pennsylvania Law Review*, 2027–2030, define norms as ' … rules of conduct that constrain self-interested behaviour and that are adopted and enforced in an informal, decentralized setting.'; R Posner, Social Norms and the Law: An Economic Approach (1997), 87 *American Economic Review: Papers and Proceedings of the Hundred and Ninth Annual Meeting of the American Economic Association*, 365, defines a norm as a 'rule that is not promulgated by an official source, such as a court or a legislature, nor enforced by the threat of legal sanctions, yet is regularly complied with'. Norms may eventually give rise to principle-based regulation (legally enforceable).

[57] D Branson, Teaching Comparative Corporate Governance: The Significance of Soft Law and International Institutions (2000), 34 *Georgia Law Review*, 669–670, uses the term 'soft law' to refer to treaties, codes of conduct, draft company law directives, statements of best practices.

[58] E Rock and M Wachter, Symposium — Norms and Corporate Law: Introduction (2001). 149 *University of Pennsylvania Law Review*, 1607–1608.

Coffee,[59] in a study evaluating cross-country norms, argues that compliance with non-legally enforceable norms may significantly affect the market value of companies. Interpreting data in a study by an economist Nenova[60] on the value of corporate control, Coffee suggests that social norms regarding the behaviour of controlling shareholders may offer an explanation as to differences in private benefits of control across jurisdictions with relatively similar legal rules.[61] He goes on to state that norms may matter most when law is weak because they provide a functional substitute for law.[62]

Similarly, Black,[63] in a study questioning whether a firm's corporate governance behaviour (defined to include the governance rules that the firm adopts and the behaviour of its insiders along governance-related dimensions)[64] affects its market value, finds that in Russia, firm-level variation in governance behaviour appears to have an effect on market value,[65] although such effect is not found in developed countries. Again, the implication being that norms matter most when law is weak, which means that developing countries with weak legal systems may possibly improve firm value through a determined effort to improve their corporate governance practices.

In contrast, Milhaupt,[66] analysing the role of norms in Japanese corporate governance, hypotheses that one of the reasons some norms, such as the norm against hostile takeovers which emerged and persisted in Japan, despite evidence of its inefficiency, was that they provided private benefits to a small group. Milahaupt's analysis is important for this discussion in that it demonstrates: (i) the gap between law and practice may

---

[59] J Coffee, Do Norms Matter? A Cross-Country Evaluation (2001), 149 *University of Pennsylvania Law Review*, 2151. However, capital market forces and financing patterns can also explain this difference.

[60] T Nenova, The Value of Corporate Votes and Control Benefits: A Cross-Country Analysis (2003), 68 *Journal of Financial Economics*, 325.

[61] Coffee (n. 59) Part I.

[62] ibid 2175–2176.

[63] B Black, Does Corporate Governance Matter? A Crude Test Using Russian Data (2001), 149 *University of Pennsylvania Law Review*, 2131.

[64] ibid 2131.

[65] For example, when such firm-level variation of governance behaviour differentiates that firm from others, which are not so compliant.

[66] C Milhaupt, Creative Norm Destruction: The Evolution of Non-legal Rules in Japanese Corporate Governance (2001), 149 *University of Pennsylvania Law Review*, 2083.

sometimes be attributed to norms (e.g., Japanese boards are legally charged with monitoring corporate activity, however, in practice the boards have not traditionally emphasised their role)[67] resulting in the beneficial regulatory structure being overridden by a norm and (ii) that norms which develop through social and cultural influences may favour those in control, rather than curbing the costs arising from their control of companies within the jurisdiction.

In a similar vein, Roe,[68] examining the connection between a shareholder primacy norm, social wealth maximisation and the competitiveness of product markets, makes the argument that the 'shareholder wealth maximisation norm' is less effective in raising social wealth[69] in countries with weak product markets. While the specifics of Roe's argument are not relevant for purposes of this analysis, the general implication to be drawn is that the effectiveness of norms (in Roe's study, the shareholder primacy norm) is dependent on institutions within the jurisdiction.

Norms are unlikely to be an effective governance mechanism in controlling shareholder systems especially in developing countries, where institutional support is likely to be weak and corporate power in the hands of a few. Principally, 'norms work best when a party that would act opportunistically cannot do so without suffering a wealth or utility loss'.[70] Thus, it is questionable whether controlling shareholder systems will foster the development of institutions and norms, which restrict the ability of controlling shareholders to act opportunistically.

6.3.4. *Norms as an External Governance Mechanism in Sri Lanka*

Norms as an external mechanism of governance is of limited application to Sri Lanka. First, a recent empirical study on corporate governance practices or firm-level governance norms of 50 public listed companies in Sri Lanka[71] finds no evidence to even weakly confirm that many of the

---

[67] ibid 2091.

[68] M Roe, The Shareholder Wealth Maximization Norm and Industrial Organization (2001), 149 *University of Pennsylvania Law Review*, 2063.

[69] ibid 2065, the utilitarian, greatest-good-for-the-greatest number.

[70] Rock and Wachter (n. 58), 1615.

[71] Cabraal (n. 14). The governance norms analysed relate to the internal governance mechanism of the board of directors — that is, director training, audit committees.

non-legally enforceable standards based on OECD principles[72] that corporate entities in Sri Lanka are publicly claiming to be following are being adhered to. Thus, if the existing corporate norms are disregarded or paid lip service, it is unlikely that a reform agenda based primarily on norms as a mechanism to control the costs of controlling shareholders is likely to be successful.

Second, while there is little doubt that firm-level variation in governance behaviour will affect the market value of companies,[73] it is unlikely to have an effect in a market where nonadherence to norms is the accepted practice, and where deviation from adherence to norms is likely to be more costly than the value to be gained from the positive effect on market valuation of the company.

Third, as Milhaupt implies,[74] norms, which develop through social forces are more likely to favour those in control. For example, among Sri Lankan family controlled companies, it is a norm to ensure that board succession is passed on to the next generation within the family, directly favouring those in control. Therefore, a reform agenda based on norms is more likely to favour those in control than curb the costs of controlling shareholders.

Fourth, due to the self-enforcing nature of norms, norms are unlikely to be effective in curbing the costs of controlling shareholders within the Sri Lankan controlling shareholder system because the controlling shareholders themselves will be the biggest obstacles to the adoption of such norms. It is unlikely that controlling shareholders will voluntarily suffer loss by adoption of a practice or standard, which is not in their best interest, especially when the gain from such adoption (such as appreciation of market value or corporate recognition), is outweighed by the cost of such adoption. Further, in developing countries it is more likely for gains from market valuation to be lower due to lack of investor appreciation of the adopted norms.

Finally, and related to the self-enforcing nature of norms, norms are unlikely to be adhered to in a developing country such as Sri Lanka, where watch-dog market mechanisms such as a strong financial press and market for corporate control are weak. The market for corporate control is weak due to the presence of controlling shareholders and the financial

---

[72] OECD, *Principles of Corporate Governance: 2004* (Paris 2004).
[73] Contrast, Black (n. 63), 2148, firm-level variation in governance practices has a minor effect in developed countries, while its effect in developing countries is likely to be greater.
[74] Milhaupt (n. 66).

press is weak and biased due to the influences that controlling shareholders wield on the press. This has led many Sri Lankan companies to pay lip service to national and international codes and standards.

The weakness of norms is further exaggerated if the moral element as a compliance factor is weak. Two decades of ethnic war in the North and East of Sri Lanka and the resultant societal degeneration have weakened moral compulsion as a mechanism to ensure norm compliance. In effect, the cultural foundation for compliance with norms is fragmented.[75]

The point here is not to reject the role of norms as an external mechanism of governance effective in constraining the costs of controlling shareholders, but rather to analyse its suitability to the Sri Lankan context. The number of codes and practices adopted in Sri Lanka[76] demonstrates either its willingness to be guided by norms and standards in the area of corporate governance or conversely its reluctance to undertake changes in the legal system or a more complex agenda of reform. Norms can, in effect, be a 'kind of short cut'.[77]

In controlling shareholder systems, where the reputation of controlling shareholders is at stake, norms have the ability to act as an effective deterrent to the costs of such shareholders.[78] Further, norms as an alternative governance mechanism can work within a wider corporate governance agenda and may precede or supplement a reform agenda. However, in controlling shareholder systems given ineffective market mechanisms, strong controlling shareholders, poor record of norm compliance, the indifference of minority shareholders towards norm compliance and the self-serving nature of norms, norms can at best only supplement and provide an informative role with regard to the corporate governance environment than act as a mechanism of governance.[79]

---

[75] On cultural foundations that underlie laws. A Licht, C Goldschmidt and S Schwartz, Culture, Law, and Finance: Cultural Dimensions of Corporate Governance Laws (2004), http://ssrn.com/abstract=277613 [5 July 2005].

[76] Section 6.1.1.

[77] M Dzierzanowski and P Tamowicz, Setting Standards of Corporate Governance: A Polish Experience with Drafting Codes (2003), 4 *European Business Organization Law Review*, 273–285.

[78] F Allen, Corporate Governance in Emerging Economies (2005), 21 *Oxford Review of Economic Policy*, 164, argues that in developing countries it is not necessarily optimal to use law to ensure good corporate governance. Other mechanisms such as reputation may be preferable.

[79] N Cankar, Transition Economies and Corporate Governance Codes: Can Self-regulation of Corporate Governance Really Work? (2005), 5 *Journal of Corporate Law Studies*, 285, makes a similar argument with regard to corporate governance codes.

6.3.5. *Market Forces[80] as an External Governance Mechanism*

Market forces or market discipline as an external mechanism of corporate governance, first recognised in the context of dispersed shareholder systems, is primarily aimed at coping with the agency problem between shareholders and managers. Markets are broadly defined as including capital markets (potential and existing shareholders and creditors), the market for corporate control (mergers and acquisitions), labour markets (potential and existing employees), product markets, the providers of capital market information (such as those provided by analysts, rating agencies and the media), the markets for accounting, financial and legal services, among others. Market forces reduce agency costs in dispersed shareholder systems by punishing managers and boards for reduction in shareholder value by the loss of jobs, loss of customers, becoming takeover targets or being scorned in the financial press or being named-shamed by analysts.

Market forces must encompass not only the relevant market information or assessment but also its disciplinary effects. For example, if the market valuation of a company is to be an effective market force, it must necessarily affect the price of the company's shares or its managers' remuneration. Similarly, discontent among shareholders and the 'exit' option available to them is also a market-based disciplinary device. In essence, the disciplinary role of market forces is its ability to assess the adequacy of information and pressurise conformity of a company towards accepted corporate governance practices. For example, market discipline is the basis of the 'comply or explain' principles of the United Kingdom Combined Code on Corporate Governance.[81]

Finance literature for the most part, identifies market forces as a mechanism to meet corporate governance problems in market-oriented systems such as the UK or the US.[82] One factor in Cheffins' hypothesis on the separation of ownership and control in the UK was the need by British

---

[80] The terms 'market forces' or 'market discipline' in this study indicate the ability of market-based mechanisms to affect the behaviour of controlling shareholders and does not presume the existence of perfect markets or markets that function well.

[81] I MacNeil and X Li, Market Discipline and Non-compliance with the Combined Code (2006), 14 *Corporate Governance: An International Review*, 486.

[82] J Franks and C Mayer, Corporate Ownership and Control in the UK, Germany and France (1997), 9 *Journal of Applied Corporate Finance*, 30, identify the market for corporate control active in the UK and US, but not in France and Germany as such a mechanism.

industry to meet the superior organisational capabilities of foreign competitors.[83] This argument helps illustrate the evolutionary role of a market mechanism (i.e., competition) in meeting governance challenges. Increasingly, market forces are viewed as governance mechanisms in continental European countries, where the lower enforceability of norms in civil law affects the application of codes of good governance without the force of regulation.[84]

In a series of recent papers, Allen *et al.*[85] present the powerful argument that ferocious competition from both domestic and overseas companies in China as the reason for its successful growth despite an underdeveloped legal system. Allen then goes on to make the point that competition is one of the most important non-standard mechanisms that drives good management and corporate governance.[86] Implicit in the use of China as an example is the argument that it matters little if it is a market-oriented or bank-oriented system, since the competition is for finance in either event.

Market forces such as the market for corporate control and product market competition are at the forefront of market-based mechanisms,[87] while the role of debt or labour as disciplinary market forces have received little attention in the literature or reform programmes. This is primarily due to the focus of market-based mechanisms being on corporate control and managerial incentive compensation in the context of dispersed shareholder systems.

---

[83] B Cheffins, Putting Britain on the Roe Map: The Emergence of the Berle–Means Corporation in the United Kingdom, in J McCahery (ed.), *Corporate Governance Regimes: Convergence and Diversity* (Oxford University Press Oxford 2002), 147, citing A Chandler, The Growth of the Transnational Industrial Firm in the United States and United Kingdom: A Comparative Analysis (1980), 33 *Economic History Review*, 396.

[84] A Cuervo, Corporate Governance Mechanisms: A Plea for Less Code of Good Governance and More Market Control (2002), 10 *Corporate Governance: An International Review*, 84–91.

[85] Allen (n. 78), 174; F Allen, J Qian and M Qian Finance, Law and Economic Growth in China (2005), 77 *Journal of Financial Economics*, 57–97.

[86] F Allen and G Dale, Corporate Governance and Competition, in X Vives (ed.), *Corporate Governance: Theoretical and Empirical Perspectives* (Cambridge University Press Cambridge 2000), 23.

[87] J Franks, C Mayer and S Rossi, Spending Less Time with the Family: The Decline of Family Ownership in the UK (2004), European Corporate Governance Network Finance Working Paper 35, http://ssrn.com/abstract=493504 [25 July 2005].

However, market forces as an external governance mechanism have substantial defects. First, market discipline can be imperfect in that its effect is only felt in instances of wide deviations from accepted behaviour. For example, given the lack of full information and the effect of reputation in controlling shareholder systems, market forces may react to substantial mismanagement, but not to management oversight.

Second, market forces are affected by prevalent market conditions. For example, corporate mismanagement is overlooked in a market with rising share prices (i.e., 'bull' market).[88] This was the case with Enron, WorldCom and the 'dotcom' market.

Third, in many developing countries, markets and market forces are weak or underdeveloped. In such scenarios, market forces are unlikely to be effective external governance mechanisms. This in effect produces a 'Catch 22' situation, that is, good corporate governance induces efficient markets and vice versa. However, not all market forces in developing countries are at the same level of underdevelopment and therefore, it maybe possible to find a particular market force in a superior position.

The advantages of market forces are many. First, expanding the realm of market-based governance mechanisms ensures that controlling shareholder defences or influences are avoided. Second, market forces are not dependent on effective enforcement mechanisms, identified as a crucial lacuna in most developing countries. Third, market forces supplement and uphold corporate norms and standards, and pressurise conformity to legal rules and regulations without resort to litigation. In effect, market forces are themselves an enforcement mechanism. Fourth, strong market forces result in increased disclosure and transparency, one of the pillars of corporate governance.[89] Finally, given that corporate entities and markets are indispensable, market forces have the potential to be a driving force for improving corporate governance.

Promoting market forces as governance mechanisms does not devalue legal and regulatory structures or narrow the applicability of norms. In fact, the existence of an effective legal and regulatory infrastructure is essential for the effectiveness of market forces as an external governance

---

[88] MacNeil and Li (n. 81), 492–494, argue that investor's tolerance for noncompliance with the combined code in the UK is linked to some extent with superior financial performance and share price.

[89] OECD (n. 72) Part V.

mechanism. Further, companies acting under the pressure of market forces can bring about wide acceptance and legitimacy to norms.

6.3.6. *Market Forces an External Governance Mechanism in Sri Lanka*

In Sri Lanka, market forces are a potentially effective mechanism to curb the costs of controlling shareholders. The primary advantages of market forces in the context of controlling shareholder systems in Sri Lanka are threefold.

First, corporate entities and markets lead an existence of co-dependence. This is more so in developing countries like Sri Lanka. Companies are dependent on debt and labour markets, and to some extent on market intermediaries. This co-dependence makes market forces a formidable tool in curbing controlling shareholder costs.

Second, the vested interests of controlling shareholders are least likely to be felt among market forces, such as debt or labour markets or gatekeepers like auditors with their own standards of independence. In the case of legal reforms or the adoption of norms, controlling shareholders themselves are the biggest obstacle to the development or adoption of such reforms, while in the case of market forces their influence is more constrained.

Third, governments in many developing countries, in their move towards free markets and liberalisation, are unwilling to take corrective action by way of legal reforms, which effectively ban or curtail the activities of controlling shareholders. While market forces need some form of indirect legal propping and facilitation, they are unlikely to meet the same form of resistance or be perceived as being as restrictive as legal reforms. Further, while social and political forces are likely to favour those in control, market forces are more likely to be unbiased and independent.

There are also many obstacles to market forces as an external governance mechanism in Sri Lanka. First, it is questionable if market forces can have an impact in a developing country such as Sri Lanka, where most market forces (such as the market for corporate control) are in an embryonic stage of development.

Second, market forces without adequate legal and institutional preconditions are unlikely to curb the costs of controlling shareholders in many developing countries. For example, the debt market is unlikely to be an effective corporate monitor without lenders having potential resources, such as experienced bankers, to evaluate borrowers. This requires the flow of transparent and reliable information and experienced professionals competent to analyse such information, which is limited in many developing countries including Sri Lanka.

Third, while most market forces are likely to be beyond the reach of controlling shareholder influences, debt markets and labour markets are open to controlling shareholder and political pressures. For example, labour markets may be influenced by politically biased trade unions, or debt markets, especially bank lending, may be influenced by government policies.

However, market forces (especially product market competition) as an external mechanism of governance have significant advantages over the other mechanisms of governance in Sri Lanka. Primarily, the lack of political will power necessary to bring about changes in the legal and regulatory environment or the vested interests of controlling shareholders are unlikely to affect market forces. Poor enforcement mechanisms or the self-regulatory nature of norms or codes of practice based on compulsion brought about by the co-dependent nature of markets and companies, are also unlikely to affect market forces. These contribute towards making market forces an appealing external governance mechanism in Sri Lanka and other developing countries.

6.4. The Framework for Reform

The analysis in Section 6.3 above was conducted at a fairly high level of abstraction. This was necessary to broadly analyse and evaluate the three external governance mechanisms: (a) in the light of their effectiveness as portrayed by literature and (b) in their application and suitability to controlling the costs of the controlling shareholder system in Sri Lanka and other developing countries, to determine the most suitable external governance mechanism capable of controlling the costs of the controlling shareholder system.

Which of these external governance mechanisms should a developing country such as Sri Lanka empower? The answer to this question is critical to a framework for reform, as the development of capital markets and economic growth depends on an effective external governance mechanism able to control the costs of controlling shareholders.

The basic intuition is that the simplest mechanism to control the costs of controlling shareholders is a mandatory model of corporate law that will prevent private benefits of control and tunnelling. Law as an external mechanism of governance has its flaws, for example, in enforcement, in adequately dealing with the costs of controlling systems and in overcoming the vested interests of the controlling shareholders. So do norms and corporate codes of conduct, which are tried in various forms in Sri Lanka, often to keep up appearances among international organisations than with any commitment.

While market forces as governance mechanisms are not without their defects, their advantages far outweigh their disadvantages in developing countries such as Sri Lanka where enforcement mechanisms are weak, and vested interests of controlling shareholders are likely to influence any 'top-down' legal and regulatory reform. Critically, corporate entities even within controlling shareholder systems are exposed to markets, indirectly exposing controlling shareholders to market forces. However, not all market-based governance mechanisms are suitable in the context of developing countries.

Thus, the next stage of analysis in the proposed framework for reform of corporate governance in a developing country such as Sri Lanka is a brief evaluation of the most suitable market-based mechanism.

6.4.1. *Debt as an External Market-based Governance Mechanism in Sri Lanka*

The market discipline paradigm in controlling shareholder systems is distinct from the market discipline paradigm in dispersed shareholder systems. Importantly, the market discipline paradigm in controlling shareholder systems is unlikely to be of effective application among all market forces.

Competitive equity markets are necessarily abandoned in favour of bilateral negotiations and blockholder conflicts,[90] within controlling shareholder systems. It is also questionable whether controlling shareholders in weak equity markets respond to the discipline of equity markets when internal financing and debt financing within a closely controlled

---

[90] E Berglöf and E von-Thadden, The Changing Corporate Governance Paradigm: Implications for Transition and Developing Countries (1999), Annual World Bank Conference on Development Economics Working Paper 263, http://ssrn.com/abstract= 183708 [28 May 2004], 4.

structure keeps most external equity financing at a minimum. Similarly, markets for corporate control operate differently among concentrated or controlling shareholders. Outright hostile takeovers are impossible when one shareholder controls the majority of the shares and sale of control takes place outside official exchanges.[91] The market for corporate control is also unlikely to be successful in countries with underdeveloped mergers and acquisitions markets. Likewise, the disciplinary effect of product market competition, although an important market constraint on poor corporate governance, is nullified by the presence of monopolies or markets dominated by a small number of companies.[92] Thus, equity capital markets, the market for corporate control and product markets are unlikely to be effective in constraining controlling shareholders.

While the labour market's potential as a governance mechanism has received much attention in the 1990s,[93] its ability to meet the challenges of a controlling shareholder system are inhibited by the markets' political orientations, its lack of cohesion,[94] its inability to withstand threats to the livelihood of its members, especially in countries where the labour markets are less protective of employee rights.

Professional advisers (e.g., auditors, attorneys, investment bankers) and securities analysts, and credit-rating agencies, commonly referred to as 'gatekeepers',[95] are a potential market-based governance mechanism. However, a crucial problem with the gate-keeping professions as Coffee points out,[96] is that the party paying the gatekeeper is the party that the gatekeeper is expected to monitor. This has not prevented the recognition

---

[91] R Stulz, Managerial Control of Voting Rights, Financing Policies, and the Market for Corporate Control (1988), 20 *Journal of Financial Economics*, 25, states that in managerial ownership, increases in the fraction of voting rights controlled by managers decreases the probability of a successful tender offer.

[92] Product market competition as a mechanism of corporate governance works best in competitive markets, which are rare in developing countries.

[93] For example, M Blair and M Roe (eds.), *Employees and Corporate Governance* (Brookings Institute Washington DC 1999), highlight German co-determination, Japanese lifetime employment and employee share ownership schemes.

[94] Notably, a trade union at a Sri Lankan bank intervened in a recent dispute on shareholdings — Labour Chief Intervenes in COMBank Trade Union Dispute on Shareholding (26 September 2006), *Daily Mirror* — but this was alleged to be spurred by a backlash against a particular controlling shareholder.

[95] J Coffee, *Gatekeepers — The Professions and Corporate Governance* (Oxford University Press Oxford 2006), 2.

[96] ibid 3.

of the principle in the context of the US that professional gatekeepers owe a *'public* responsibility transcending any employment relationship with the client'[97] or the repeated failure of professional gatekeepers to discharge such responsibility evidenced by the well-publicised scandals such as Enron and WorldCom. Further, gatekeepers, pay a larger and more critical role in dispersed ownership systems than in controlling ownership systems such as in Sri Lanka, where the role of professional intermediaries is in its embryonic stages[98] and an ingrained sense of ethical concerns is lacking.

Debt markets as a potential market force in controlling the costs of controlling shareholder systems is often overlooked. The strongest factor in favour of debt as a governance mechanism especially in developing countries such as Sri Lanka is the lack of equity financing,[99] which makes debt an indispensable part of a corporate entity. Debt has an element of compulsion in it, which is appealing to the controlling shareholders, that is, the long-term benefits to controlling shareholders from their co-operation with debt holders, exceeds the short-term benefits from acting opportunistically.

There are two principal forms of debt, bank debt and market debt (i.e., corporate bonds). In Sri Lanka, the debt market is dominated by bank debt. Although a corporate bond market exists, it is thin.[100] Banks usually have larger stakes in companies than dispersed bondholders and therefore, have strong incentives to monitor corporate activities. Bank lending is also an importance source of funds to the corporate sector in Sri Lanka. Further, given the institutional context and costs and benefits of controlling shareholders in Sri Lanka, bank lending as a market-based governance mechanism has the potential to be most effective.

---

[97] *United States v. Arthur Young* 465 US 805 (1984), 817.

[98] The exception being auditors sufficiently guided by the SLAASMB and regulations made under Sri Lanka Accounting and Auditing Standards Act (n. 5). In contrast, corporate attorneys have no 'reporting up' or 'reporting out' duties as found in the US and there is only one local credit-rating agency established in June 2002.

[99] Chapter 4.

[100] Central Bank of Sri Lanka, *Annual Report 2005* (Colombo 2005), 135, attributes the underdeveloped nature of the private debt market, particularly the corporate bond market, to factors, such as 'a lack of institutional investor base, availability of bank credit at attractive rates for high net worth companies, high cost of debt issues, lack of investor awareness, lack of investor information on the quality of debt and nonavailability of a longer term bench mark yield curve.'

6.4.2. *The Hybrid Reform Agenda*

The framework that is proposed for adoption by Sri Lanka to constrain the costs of controlling shareholder systems must essentially be hybrid. It must overcome the biggest hurdle faced by law reform processes in Sri Lanka, that of ineffective enforcement; it must avoid the pitfall of setting up norms and standards which are only paid lip service; and it must avoid market forces which are embryonic and lacking effectiveness within controlling shareholder systems.

The framework that is proposed is hybrid in that it utilises an identified market force with the necessary legal and institutional preconditions to control the costs of controlling shareholders. It is necessary to confine the parameters of this framework to the most effective actor amongst the market forces, which have been subject to analysis, as this ensures the greatest impact and most success in developing a framework for corporate governance reform in Sri Lanka.

The framework that is proposed envisages the use of lenders, such as banks and financial institutions as a market force mechanism supported by legal and institutional structures to control the costs of controlling shareholder systems in Sri Lanka.

In the light of the primary thesis of this study that the reform of corporate governance in developing countries should begin with a focus on local market structures and institutions that define its adaptation, efficiency and effectiveness, this proposal is formulated after due evaluation of the corporate ownership structures in Sri Lanka,[101] the reasons for the existence of such ownership structures,[102] the costs and benefits of such structures[103] and an evaluation of the most effective and beneficial mechanism to approach such a reform agenda in the context of Sri Lanka. The proposed framework is also likely to be of relevance to other developing countries with controlling shareholder systems.

---

[101] Chapter 3.
[102] Chapter 4.
[103] Chapter 5.

CHAPTER 7

The Role of Lenders[1] in Controlling Shareholder Systems

7.1. Introduction

The important question facing with controlling shareholders is who (or what mechanism) can best control the controllers?[2] Are such control mechanisms effective and can they be made more effective? Chapter 6 concludes with the observation that controlling shareholders are best constrained by a hybrid reform agenda, which utilises lenders in the form of banks, supported by legal and institutional structures, to curb the costs of controlling shareholder systems.

Scholars of corporate governance promote various reform agendas for improving corporate governance in both developed and developing countries. Such agendas in dispersed ownership systems focus on the internal mechanisms of governance, such as the board of directors and shareholders, incentive compensation for managers, or the external mechanism of the takeover market. Reform agendas in concentrated or controlling shareholder systems focus on the legal system to constrain large or controlling shareholders (such as strengthening minority protection, voting caps, the imposition of one share-one vote, limits on the share of capital held by certain types of investors) or the imposition of codes of conduct or corporate norms.

Useful and necessary as these reform agendas are, they fail to effectively control the costs of controlling shareholders. Many reform agendas both ignore the institutional context of controlling shareholder systems, and are too broad and fail to adequately assess the suitability of such

---

[1] Title inspired by G Hertig, Lenders as a Force in Corporate Governance Criteria and Practical Examples for Switzerland, in KJ Hopt *et al.* (eds.), *Comparative Corporate Governance: The State of the Art and Emerging Research* (Oxford University Press Oxford 1998).

[2] Note effective control of controlling shareholders involves much more than simply preventing outright theft or fraud for which legal remedies are most effective.

reform. They also ignore the interdependence between corporate governance and corporate finance, and the role of debt finance in controlling shareholder systems. While the role of banks in corporate governance is the subject of much debate in the current context of the financial crisis, and in the past in the context of Japan and Germany,[3] the corporate governance role of debt, with institutional lenders such as banks utilising their positions as lenders to curb the costs of controlling shareholders has received little in-depth study in the context of developing countries.[4]

This chapter advances the hypothesis that lenders are an effective external corporate governance mechanism in controlling the costs of controlling shareholder systems in developing countries such as Sri Lanka. This chapter seeks to assess the suitability of lenders as a corporate governance mechanism both generally, and in the context of Sri Lanka as an illustrative developing country and thereafter, sets out a reform agenda based on the legal and institutional preconditions necessary for lenders to be an effective mechanism to control the costs of controlling shareholders in countries such as Sri Lanka.

Section 7.2 clarifies what is proposed by the reform agenda, explains the evolution of lenders and why they play a critical role in corporate governance. Section 7.3 examines the effectiveness of lenders as a corporate governance mechanism, generally and in the context of Sri Lanka. Section 7.4 sets out a reform agenda of policy options based on the legal and institutional preconditions necessary for lenders to be an effective mechanism to control the costs of controlling shareholders in Sri Lanka. Section 7.5 concludes.

7.2. Lenders as a Corporate Governance Mechanism

Corporate governance and corporate finance are intrinsically intertwined.[5] Consideration of how companies are governed must pay attention to the

---

[3] In both countries, banks have significant equity position in public companies. S Prowse, Institutional Investment Patterns and Corporate Financial Behaviour in the United States and Japan (1990), 27 *Journal of Financial Economics*, 43, argues that banks hold over 20 percent of all outstanding corporate equity in Japan, versus none in the US in 1984.

[4] A notable exception is M Aoki, H Patrick and P Sheard, The Japanese Main Bank System: An Introductory Overview, in M Aoki and H Patrick (eds.), *The Japanese Main Bank System* (Oxford University Press Oxford 1994), who suggest that developing countries should start off with Japanese-style bank finance, at least until their economies reach a point of maturity.

[5] Chapters 1 and 2.

financing structure of such companies. This is the crux of this study, with its focus on the implications of corporate ownership structures on corporate governance. In the light of this focus, it is appropriate that the answer to how best to control the costs of controlling shareholders in a developing country like Sri Lanka, also arises from corporate finance.

7.2.1. *Definitions*

Companies are financed by way of equity or debt capital. Loans and bonds are subcategories of debt. Put simply, debt is a contract in which the borrower promises to repay the loan over a specified period. Covenants or contractual promises are safeguards made by the borrower, such as restrictions on asset sales or a requirement to maintain certain financial ratios. The period of the debt is also a safeguard. In the event the borrower violates a covenant or fails to make timely repayments, the lender can make a claim on the security or force the borrower into insolvency.

The corporate governance role of debt depends to a great extent on the type of debt (i.e., loans or corporate bonds) and how closely it is held and the term of debt (whether short or long term). A corporate bond is issued by a company and is distinct from a loan, which is money lent on condition that it is repaid either in instalments or all at once, on agreed dates at an agreed rate of interest.[6] The focus of this chapter is on loans, and not corporate bonds held by the dispersed public for shorter periods of time and have fewer and less strict covenants and are therefore, ineffective as a monitoring mechanism.

The hypothesis that lenders are an effective external corporate governance mechanism in controlling the costs of controlling shareholders in Sri Lanka focuses on the corporate governance role of banks in their capacity as lenders.[7] Lenders are recognised to be an external corporate governance mechanism within the corporate governance framework referred to in Chapters 1 and 6.[8] Corporate governance mechanisms 'are economic and

---

[6] J Smullen and N Hand, *Dictionary of Finance and Banking* (Oxford University Press Oxford 2005).

[7] D Diamond, Financial Intermediation and Delegated Monitoring (1984), 51 *Review of Economic Studies*, 393, notes that banks are better monitors than public debt holders.

[8] Chapter 1, Fig. 1.3; Chapter 6, Fig. 6.1.

legal institutions that can be altered through the political process — sometimes for the better'.[9]

What is proposed by the reform agenda suggested by this chapter is facilitating the role of lenders as a corporate governance mechanism in controlling the costs of controlling shareholder systems by strengthening the legal framework and institutions associated with lenders both generally and in the context of Sri Lanka.

7.2.2. *Literature*

The early literature on corporate finance and corporate governance recognises debt as an important mechanism for solving agency problems in companies typically characterised by the separation of ownership and control.[10] The literature also recognises that debt and debt holders play a significant role in corporate governance and in shaping business strategy and performance.[11] Easterbrook[12] argues that debt forces managers to be accountable to the external capital market. Shleifer and Vishny[13] also emphasise debt as an effective contractual tool in contrast to equity.

However, it is argued that the role of debt as a potential corporate governance mechanism is weakened in the context of concentrated or controlling shareholder systems, where management is drawn from among the controlling shareholders, as it is likely that the controlling shareholders are also likely to control the lenders through a web of cross-holdings and

---

[9] A Shleifer and R Vishny, A Survey of Corporate Governance (1997), 52 *Journal of Finance*, 737–738.

[10] M Jensen and W Meckling, The Theory of the Firm: Managerial Behaviour, Agency Costs and Ownership Structure (1976), 3 *Journal of Financial Economics*, 305, emphasise the role played by debt in reducing agency conflicts between managers and shareholders by constraining managerial expropriation by imposing fixed obligations on the cash flow; M Jensen, Agency Costs of Free Cash Flow, Corporate Finance and Takeovers (1986), 76 *American Economic Review*, 323, refers to the benefits of debt in motivating managers and companies to be efficient and calls these effects the 'control hypothesis' for debt creation.

[11] O Hart, *Firms, Contracts, and Financial Structure* (Clarendon Oxford 1995) Chapter 6; S Myers, Capital Structure (2001), 15 *Journal of Economic Perspectives*, 81.

[12] F Easterbrook, Two-agency Cost Explanations of Dividends (1984), 74 *American Economic Review*, 650.

[13] Shleifer and Vishny (n. 9), 757.

pyramids.[14] Similarly, Faccio *et al.*,[15] suggest that the disciplinary effect of debt is limited and that debt acts more as an instrument for expropriation of minority shareholders than as an effective corporate governance mechanism within Asian corporate pyramids. While it is correct that the 'role of debt depends on how governance is exercised, that is, on the structure of corporate ownership and control',[16] it is also acceptable to say that the effectiveness of debt as a mechanism of corporate governance further depends on the institutional framework within a country. The quality of monitoring and disciplinary role of debt should not be overlooked even in countries with controlling shareholder systems, if the necessary legal and institutional requirements for effective monitoring of controlling shareholders by lenders are available.

While the legal form of the company vests the responsibility of running the company in the hands of the holders of equity, controlling shareholders make a mockery of this legal responsibility. While shareholders other than controlling shareholders, if large, have the capacity to constrain and curb the costs of controlling shareholders,[17] their very existence and survival can be threatened by controlling shareholders who may force them out of the company. However, this does not mean that controlling shareholders' control rights are unfettered. If the company is dependent on debt finance, especially bank lending, the suppliers of such debt capital are vested with rights and capabilities to exert control over the governance of the companies,[18] and the controlling shareholders of such companies.

The theoretical foundations for monitoring and intervention by creditors, typically banks, are found in theories of financial intermediation.[19]

---

[14] Similarly, S Prowse, Corporate Governance: Emerging Issues and Lessons from East Asia (1999), World Bank mimeo, http://www1.worldbank.org/finance/assets/images/prowse.pdf [10 May 2006], 17, argues that debt is a weak mechanism of governance in East Asia due to government interference in lending.

[15] M Faccio, L Lang and L Young, Debt and Corporate Governance (2001), www2.owen. vanderbilt.edu/fmrc/Activity/paper/Faccio_Paper_Debt.pdf [7 July 2005].

[16] ibid 1.

[17] Shleifer and Vishny (n. 9); A Shleifer and R Vishny, Large Shareholders and Corporate Control (1986), 94 *Journal of Political Economy*, 461.

[18] J Stiglitz, Credit Markets and the Control of Capital (1985), 17 *Journal of Money, Credit and Banking*, 132, 140, claims that concentration of a company's claims either in equity or debt is an important corporate governance mechanism.

[19] D Diamond (n. 7).

In practice, monitoring and intervention by banks or the main bank,[20] is most famous in Japanese-style corporate governance.[21] Much was written about the Japanese model of corporate governance in the 1990s, and at one point of time it was touted as an alternative corporate governance mechanism to American style corporate governance in which hostile takeovers and managerial incentive schemes were important governance mechanisms.[22] In the traditional Japanese system, the main bank was the principal supplier of funds to the company. Japanese banks were both creditors and shareholders. Other financial institutions and investors expected the main bank to be the principal monitor of the company ('delegated monitoring'). There was no direct intervention by the banks in the management of companies when company performance was satisfactory. When performance is poor, creditors and especially the main bank intervenes, decides whether to bail out and restructure, and also discipline poorly performing management (the so-called 'contingent governance').[23]

However, the Japanese style of corporate governance, which lost its appeal during the Japanese banking crisis, is now thought to be unsuitable. Some commentators have argued that the Japanese system of bank-centred corporate governance was a cause of the financial crisis in Japan.[24] The future prospects for the Japanese style of corporate governance are predicted to be dim.[25]

---

[20] Aoki *et al.* (n. 4), 3, claim that there is no legal definition of a main bank and that its definition should include not only the 'long-term relationship between a firm and a particular bank from which the firm obtains its largest share of borrowings' but also its role in monitoring and governance.

[21] ibid; Y Yafeh, Corporate Governance in Japan: Past Performance and Future Prospects (2000), 16 *Oxford Review of Economic Policy*, 74.

[22] Aoki *et al.* (n. 4) and M Aoki, Monitoring Characteristics of the Main Bank System: An Analytical and Developmental View, in M Aoki and H Patrick (eds.), *The Japanese Main Bank System: Its Relevance for Developing and Transforming Economies* (Oxford University Press Oxford 1995).

[23] Aoki *et al.* (n. 4), 16, refer to this as 'State-Contingent Nature of Relationships'. Also see, M Aoki, Controlling Insider Control: Issues of Corporate Governance in Transition Economies, in M Aoki and H Kim (eds.), *Corporate Governance in Transitional Economies: Insider Control and the Role of Banks* (World Bank Washington DC 1995), 18.

[24] R Morck and M Nakamura, Japanese Corporate Governance and Macroeconomic Problems (2000), Harvard Institute of Economic Research Discussion Paper 1893, http://ssrn.com/abstract=235758 [5 June 2005].

[25] Yafeh (n. 21).

In contrast, Germany has had greater success with a system in which banks have a monitoring role.[26] Morck and Nakamura[27] attribute factors such as German bank's equity stakes being uncapped, German banks being subsidiaries of insurance companies and financial firms, the role of employees in German corporate governance and the existence of German families owning large blocks of equity which acts as a counter-weight, to the success of the banks' corporate governance monitoring role in Germany. The German position is similar in many respects to the corporate ownership and debt finance environment in Sri Lanka. Sri Lankan banks are often subsidiaries of other financial conglomerates and characterised by families and individuals owning large blocks of equity and exerting control over companies in which they could obtain controlling stakes.[28]

What is proposed in the context of Sri Lanka is not the adoption of the Japanese or German style of corporate governance. Nor is it envisaged to create a new class of lenders or increase the debt–equity ratios of Sri Lankan companies. What is proposed is the empowering of banks and financial institutions as lenders to control the costs incurred by controlling shareholders. The analysis in Chapter 4 illustrates that lack of equity finance in capital markets contributed to the prevalence of a controlling shareholder system in Sri Lanka. Chapter 4 also highlights the preference of the public to invest their savings in banks.[29] This resulted in the concentration of corporate ownership and the rise of debt as a dominant source of financing for companies in Sri Lanka. The hypothesis presented in this chapter, is that debt in the form of lenders, is a corporate governance mechanism by which to ensure that the costs of controlling shareholders in Sri Lanka are curtailed. This follows from the discussion in Chapter 6 establishing debt as the most effective mechanism of corporate governance in the context of Sri Lanka with a controlling shareholder system, where other internal and external mechanisms are less useful and ineffective.

7.2.3. *Conventional Role of Lenders*

A serious impediment to the development of the limited liability company is that when a company defaults, part of the cost of the mistakes made by

---

[26] Morck and Nakamura (n. 24), 13–15.
[27] ibid.
[28] Chapter 3.
[29] Chapter 4, Section 4.3.2(e).

the individual making the decision are borne not by such individual alone, but also by the creditors. The fact that the individual making the corporate decision (i.e., the controlling shareholder in controlling shareholder systems) is not solely responsible for the costs of the decision generates two important implications. First, the decision-making individual has the incentive to undertake riskier actions than if the full cost was to be borne individually. Second, the creditor has the incentive to control the decision-making individual.[30]

However, according to the conventional account of corporate control, lenders as creditors receive no special rights against a company. The legal form of the company vests the running of the company in the hands of its equity holders, (i.e., the shareholders and their agents). In controlling shareholder systems, this power is concentrated in the hands of the controlling shareholders. The lender's power is limited to suing the debtor when the debtor fails to pay. According to the conventional view, lenders do not have any control rights until the company is in financial distress.[31] Accordingly, lenders protect themselves by contractual means, by setting out specific covenants in their loan agreements and by means of security interests in the company's property.

However, this conventional view neglects the role of lenders in corporate finance. Banks are more than passive lenders. Loan covenants have the ability to wrest control of the company from the shareholders and the board of directors. Lenders with revolving credit facilities and short-term debt possess the ability to demand compliance to accepted practices when corporate managers or controlling shareholders revisit to refresh facilities. The conventional view of lenders also overlooks the disciplinary effect of debt with its focus on the bottom line due to the obligation to make repayments.

Further, the conventional view of lenders crucially ignores the corporate finance reality in most controlling shareholder systems, which is that controlling shareholders loath to relinquish control, are more likely to raise capital through banks with what they perceive as more effective control over capital, than through equity markets.

The strongest theoretical argument against the monitoring role of lenders is that contractual claimants, such as creditors with a fixed or prearranged

---

[30] Stiglitz (n. 18), 135.

[31] It is at this point that the director's duties shift from shareholders to creditors. *West Mercia Safetywear Ltd v. Dodd* [1988] BCLC 250 (CA).

claim against the company's assets, should not be assigned with any control rights (in contrast to its residual claimants, i.e., the shareholders), because contractual claimants will in general, seek to minimise the probability of the company defaulting before their contractual claims are paid, while the residual claimants will seek to maximise the value of their residual claims.[32] While this is largely correct, the fact that a lender as a contractual claimant will seek to minimise the probability of corporate failure is in the interests of the shareholders.

7.2.4. *The Governance Role of Lenders*

Debt is a contractual guarantee as to future cash flows, with an expectation of achieving a level of return specified at the beginning of the contract, including the repayment of the debt itself. This contractual guarantee constrains managerial discretion, and holders of debt are able to force liquidation or restructuring when a company is in distress. This is a critical control on managerial behaviour.[33] Further, in the context of dispersed ownership systems, high leverage is attributed to reducing managerial agency costs and improving corporate governance.[34] There is no reason for the exclusion of the same argument in controlling shareholder systems. In fact, further analysis demonstrates that lenders are most effective within controlling shareholder systems.[35]

The popular view is that lenders are often constrained in exerting any form of control over controlling shareholders until the company defaults on its debt repayments. In practice, the negotiation of the initial debt provides the first opportunity for the exertion of influence. Thereafter, once a debt contract is entered into, large lenders such as banks and financial institutions are often unwilling to allow controlling shareholders or management a free reign, and engage in monitoring which provides for interactions between lenders, managers and controlling shareholders. Where there are repeated interactions, a relationship develops between lenders and borrowers, and lenders become directly involved in the governance and management of the

---

[32] Morck and Nakamura (n. 24), 10.

[33] F Modigliani and M Miller, The Cost of Capital, Corporate Finance, and the Theory of Investment (1958), 48 *American Economic Review*, 261 and Hart (n. 11).

[34] Jensen and Meckling (n. 10).

[35] To be discussed in Sections 7.3.1 and 7.3.2.

borrower companies.[36] This can lead to interlocking directorships, where an officer of the lender sits on the board of directors of a borrower company. Another form of control likely to influence lenders is credit ratings, which signal the financial health of the company to all other creditors and investors.

The principal methods used by lenders to monitor borrowers including controlling shareholders are (a) the use of debt covenants; (b) direct involvement in the management of the borrowers; (c) the use of asset-based lending; (d) the threat of insolvency and (e) the reduction of free cash flows.[37]

(a) *Debt Covenants*

The monitoring role of lenders is aided by the basic structure of the debt contract, which gives managers and controlling shareholders a strong incentive to ensure the company's success and ability to meet repayment requirements. As default on repayment will eventually deprive the controlling shareholders and managers of control, debt covenants are a disciplining device to align the interests of the controlling shareholders and managers with general shareholder interests.[38] Debt covenants serve as both bonding and monitoring mechanisms and are essentially 'trip wires' for lenders and violations do not necessarily mean that the borrower is facing any financial distress. Debt covenants can stipulate requirements such as the timely submission of audited accounts, the replacement or rotation of management,[39] access to books of account, a fundamental overhaul of the methods of business etc. The violation of any one of the debt covenants may vest control of the borrower company in

---

[36] Stiglitz (n. 18), 140–150. J Franks and C Mayer, Corporate Ownership and Control in the UK, Germany and France (1997), 9 *Journal of Applied Corporate Finance*, 30, provide empirical evidence of how these relationships can work.

[37] Cash flow remaining after all expenditures required for maintenance or expansion of business are paid off (cash available for distribution). J Pallister and J Daintith, *Dictionary of Business and Management* (Oxford University Press Oxford 2006).

[38] D Baird and R Rasmussen, Private Debt and the Missing Lever of Corporate Governance (2005), University of Chicago Law & Economics Working Paper 247, http://ssrn.com/abstract=692023 [5 July 2006], identify loan covenants as the missing lever of corporate governance.

[39] Especially useful given entrenchment in controlling shareholder systems. Chapter 5 contains an analysis of entrenchment as a cost of controlling shareholder systems.

the hands of the lender. Debt covenants also have the ability to encompass mismanagement and not just fraudulent behaviour by controllers.

However, the debt-covenant hypothesis predicts that managers or controlling shareholders of companies will make accounting choices that reduce the likelihood that their companies will violate accounting-based debt covenants.[40] While this may adversely affect the effectiveness of accounting-based debt covenants, effective accounting standards and monitoring of such standards should overcome this. Another factor affecting the ultimate efficiency of debt covenants is effective contract enforcement within a country and this can only be overcome with the strengthening of contract enforcement mechanisms and institutions.

(b) *Direct Involvement in the Management of the Borrowers*

Direct involvement in the management of borrowers is another monitoring tool used by lenders to reduce information asymmetry and influence timely repayments. A lender joining the board of a borrower company signals to the market that the borrower company is unlikely to experience any financial difficulty due to its connections with a credible lender. Further, the participation of representatives of lenders on the board of directors of the borrower enables the vetoing of dysfunctional corporate decisions, which can harm the company and the shareholders.

However, a lender on the board of directors of a borrower company, unlike other outside directors, faces a conflict of duty, between a fiduciary duty to the shareholders and the duty to the lender, the ultimate employer. The divergent interests of shareholders, who may prefer high-risk investments, and debt holders who may prefer to maximise repayment, further complicates this duty. This is mitigated to some extent by lenders taking on equity stakes in the companies to which they lend. However, this in turn influences the corporate governance role of lenders, which operates on the assumption that lenders maintain arms-length relationship with the controlling shareholders and the companies they lend to.

However, arms-length transactions between the lender and borrower are not the norm, especially in the context of controlling shareholder systems with cross-shareholdings and pyramids encompassing not just among

---

[40] I Dichev and D Skinner, Large Sample Evidence on Debt Covenant Hypothesis (2002), 40 *Journal of Accounting Research*, 1091.

companies but also among banks and other financial institutions. This form of pervasive ownership structures often lead to a conflict of interest for the lenders and undermines the corporate governance role of lenders. Arguably, ownership structures within a country may not always adversely affect the role of lenders in corporate governance, as for example in the context of Germany, where universal banking is largely successful despite the presence of group structures.[41]

The conflict of interest that a lender faces as a member of the board of directors of a borrower company is constrained in countries such as the US which uses the concepts of equitable subordination[42] and lender liability, to prevent lender opportunism if the lender has overreached its role as a creditor and exercised some form of managerial control, which detrimentally affects the interests of the equity holders or other creditors. If a lender is found to be active in the management of the borrower company and have acted 'inequitably' prior to the borrower's bankruptcy, the lender may lose its seniority in its claims against the bankrupt company. Additionally, a lender involved in the management of a borrower may also face liability for losses to other claimants that may be attributed to its actions while in management.[43]

---

[41] T Baums, The German Banking System and Its Impact on Corporate Finance and Governance, in M Aoki and H Patrick (eds.), *The Japanese Main Bank System: Its Relevance for Developing and Transforming Economies* (Oxford University Press Oxford 1995).

[42] The judge made doctrine of equitable subordination predates US Congress's revision of the Bankruptcy Reform Act of 1978 11 U.S.C. § 101 et seq.; for example, *Pepper v. Litton* 308 US 295 (1939); *Taylor v. Standard Gas & Elec. Co.* 306 U.S. 307 (1939); the Fifth Circuit, in its influential opinion in *Benjamin v. Diamond (In re Mobile Steel Co.)*, 563 F. 2d 692, 700 (5th Cir 1977), observed that the application of the doctrine was generally triggered by a showing that the creditor had engaged in 'some type of inequitable conduct.' *Mobile Steel* discussed two further conditions relating to the application of the doctrine: that the misconduct has 'resulted in injury to the creditors of the bankrupt or conferred an unfair advantage on the claimant,' and that the subordination 'not be inconsistent with the provisions of the Bankruptcy Act.' In recent times, this was applied by the United States Bankruptcy Court for the Southern District of New York in *Enron Corp. v. Avenue Special Situations Fund II, LP (In re Enron Corp.)*, 333 B.R. 205 (Bankr. S.D.N.Y. 2005).

[43] There are no bright line rules on what would amount to an involvement in management. M Roe, *Strong Managers, Weak Owners: The Political Roots of American Corporate Finance* (Princeton University Press Princeton 1994), 98, suggests that the Banking Holding Company Act of 1956 12 U.S.C.§ 1841–1848 (Supp. 1958) which restricted the holding company's activities to those closely related to banking and banning it from holding more than 5 percent of a non-banking firm played a part in constraining the development of debt as a governance force in the US.

There is the relatively new and ill-defined tort or measure of damages known as 'deepening insolvency', which effectively holds a lender liable for prolongation of a company's life while it is insolvent, which damages a company by incurring additional debt obligations without any prospect or ability to repay.[44] While the concept of 'deepening insolvency' may prevent the propping of a financially distressed company and also restrain the direct involvement of lenders in the management of borrower companies, liability maybe avoided by debt contracts that set out explicit representations by the borrower company and also provide indemnity. Liability may also perhaps be avoided by being directly involved in the management of the companies in the role of professional advisers and not in any fiduciary capacity.

While the concepts of equitable subordination and lender liability may resolve the conflict between lenders and equity holders, it also potentially stifles the valuable monitoring role of lenders by direct involvement in the management of the borrower companies. In the US, this has meant that lenders or bankers in particular, are less likely to be on boards of firms that may benefit most from active monitoring, preferring instead, to be on the boards of large and stable companies with little risk of bankruptcy.[45] In contrast, in what can be termed as non-litigious countries such as Germany and Japan, lenders typically sit on the boards of their major borrowers.

(c) *Asset-based Lending*

Asset-based lending such as revolving credit facilities (better known as the 'revolver'), are a tool by which lenders monitor the activities of the

---

[44] *Official Committee of Unsecured Creditors v. Credit Suisse First Boston* (*In re Exide Technologies, Inc.*), 299 B.R. 732 (Bankr. D.Del. 2003), where a successful a claim for 'deepening insolvency' was asserted against a secured lender by a creditors committee. However, not all courts have been as quick to embrace 'deepening insolvency' as a new cause of action, for example, *Kittay v. Atlantic Bank of New York* (*In re Global Service Group LLC*), 316 B.R. 451 (Bankr. S.D.N.Y. 2004); *Bondi v. Bank of America* (*In re Parmalat Securities Litigation*), 383 F. Supp. 2d 587 (S.D.N.Y. 2005). In *Official Committee of Unsecured Creditors v. Rural Telephone Finance Cooperative* (*In re Vartec Telecom, Inc.*), 335 B.R. 631, (Bankr. N.D. Tex. 2005), 'deepening insolvency' was thought to be a measure of damages for other claims such as those alleging a breach of duty.

[45] R Kroszer and P Strahan, Bankers on Boards: Monitoring, Conflicts of Interest, and Lender Liability (1999), National Bureau of Economic Research Working Paper 7319, http://www.nber.org/papers/w7319.pdf [10 July 2005].

borrower company. A revolving credit facility enables a lender to actively manage a debtor's cash flow. These types of lending facilities are often of a shorter term and require the controllers of the borrower to go to the market repeatedly and be scrutinised on their management and corporate governance practices. Lenders are able to monitor the activities of a lender using the relationship between the value of the collateral and the actual balance of the loan, with the use of collateral reporting and ongoing audits.

It is suggested that less efficient monitors extend asset-based security to reduce monitoring burdens.[46] Scott[47] argues to the contrary, that secured credit can give a lender control rights that encourage the borrower company to pursue promising investments. Thus, secured credit, especially when such credit is short term is able to foster relationship lending and provide a monitoring tool for lenders.

The monitoring capacity of lenders is also aided by the fact that secured credit leaves few of the borrowers' assets unencumbered. The borrower is thus constrained in finding alternative financing and the lender has the ability to monitor the borrower more effectively. However, to be an effective monitoring tool and assist the governance role of lenders, asset-based lending needs to be accompanied by effective debt covenants and an effective secured credit and contract enforcement regime.

(d) *Threat of Insolvency by Lenders*

The threat of insolvency is a powerful disciplining device, especially since insolvency laws shift the control of the borrower company to lenders on insolvency. The threat of insolvency makes managers and controllers focus on the bottom line and avoid mismanagement or fraudulent practices, which may result in corporate failure. In informal credit markets, there is also the threat of ostracism, which is the loss of reputational capital.

---

[46] T Jackson and A Kronman, Secured Financing and Priority among Creditors (1979), 88 *Yale Law Journal*, 1143.

[47] R Scott, A Relational Theory of Secured Financing (1986), 86 *Columbia Law Review*, 901–904, states that 'The leverage obtained by holding the debtor's assets hostage empowers the secured creditor to influence the debtor's business decisions, thus ensuring that new projects are properly developed. More significantly, this relationship induces the creditor to provide valuable financial coordination and control ...'.

It is not only the mere threat of insolvency by a lender, which is an effective disciplinary device, but also the fact that a lender may effectively gain control of the company in the event of insolvency. Much of the literature on corporate governance is aimed at reducing agency costs when a company is a going concern. However, at the point of insolvency, controllers and managers have the incentive to pursue private benefits rather than maximise shareholder wealth. This can be effectively curtailed if the company is highly leveraged and lenders gain control of the company and are able to monitor the company during insolvency proceedings.

The effectiveness of the threat of insolvency as a disciplinary device requires an effective legal framework to provide procedures for secured lending, workouts, that is, creditor-mandated reorganisation of debtor companies and liquidation.

(e) *Reduction of Free Cash Flow*[48]

Shareholders face the danger that those in control of the company will fail to focus on maximising cash flows. Debt has the ability to constrain free cash flows. The creation of debt acts as a disciplinary mechanism by bonding the controllers and managers to make payments out of future cash flows and thereby, reduces cash flow available for spending at the discretion of the controllers.[49]

The reduction of free cash flow with short-term credit facilities such as the revolver requiring controllers to go to the market repeatedly, enable monitoring by lenders who are able to manage the borrowers' cash flow and participate in corporate decision making. With effective monitoring enhanced by the reduction in free cash flow, the lender is also less dependent on relying on the borrower for information.

To summarise, the above analysis illustrates that the ability of lenders to effectively act as a corporate monitor is affected by a number of factors. First, the lender must be in a position of control over the borrower company's finances. This would depend on whether the companies within the jurisdiction are dependent on debt finance and whether such lenders play a significant corporate governance role through board positions or

---

[48] J Pallister and J Daintith (n. 37).
[49] M Jensen (n. 10), Part I.

otherwise.[50] The significance of a lender's monitoring role is also affected by the credibility of the lender not only in the capacity of a lender, but also with regard to industry-specific knowledge and lending policies.[51]

Second, the lender must exercise such monitoring and control in a manner effectively enhancing the governance practices of the borrower,[52] and aimed at reducing the costs of controlling shareholders. Thus, the lender's legal status within a jurisdiction and its own corporate governance must not be at issue,[53] and an effective legal and institutional framework should support the lender's role. Further, the lender must not act in its own interest, especially in the light of the confidential information it possesses about its borrowers.

In theory, there is no mechanism to limit the monitoring role of debt,[54] once debt financing is taken on. It is of course possible for a company to replace a lender whose governance role is unappreciated by the management or the controllers, but the borrower must have the ability to settle such debt at short notice and on terms unfavourable to itself.

7.3. Lenders as a Corporate Governance Mechanism

7.3.1. *Evaluating Lenders as a Corporate Governance Mechanism*

Developing countries face the evolutionary tendency towards concentrated and controlling ownership structures. To cope with the costs and inefficiencies within controlling shareholder systems, this study submits that an external monitor must play an active monitoring role. This chapter proposes that lenders have the potential to be such external monitor and this section of the chapter evaluates the role of lenders as a corporate governance mechanism in the context of controlling shareholder systems.

---

[50] Hertig (n. 1), 810–835, argues that in the Swiss context lenders are a significant corporate governance force especially in the case of management buyout and workout situations. (A workout is when a lender confronts a situation in which the borrower is facing financial problems and the options are more financing, restructuring or liquidation).

[51] ibid 835.

[52] Baird and Rasmussen (n. 38).

[53] Asian Development Bank, *Corporate Governance and Finance in East Asia* (Manila 2000) Chapter 2.

[54] For example, such as the defensive mechanisms adopted in the corporate control market or the rotation of auditors.

(a) *Supply of Capital*

The company receives its capital in the form of equity and debt from shareholders, bondholders and lenders. In turn, the controllers of the company, managers or controlling shareholders do not have unfettered rights in the management of this capital. The providers of capital in supplying capital impose conditions on the controllers of the company and its resources. In the case of shareholders, the providers of equity finance, this is in the form of payment of dividends and the right to vote. Similarly, lenders the providers of debt finance, also impose conditions, often contractual in nature. However, unlike a shareholder, a lender has the ability to demand from the company the return of the loan with the threat of bankruptcy.[55] Therefore, a lender is in a better position than a minority shareholder to constrain and control the controllers of the company. Further, when a company is capitalised with debt and much of its expected cash flow is dedicated to repaying creditors, the discretion of managers or controlling shareholders in management positions declines.[56] This is supported by evidence that debt, especially syndicated term loans, creates shareholder value for companies that face agency costs such as those created by pyramid ownership structures.[57]

In controlling shareholder systems, the role of lenders is likely to be greater than in dispersed shareholder systems, as controlling shareholders are more likely to turn to debt markets for additional capital. There are two reasons for this. First, as previously noted, controlling shareholders are more willing to raise capital through a bank without relinquishing what they perceive to be effective control of the company.[58] Second, and this is equally applicable in dispersed shareholder systems, raising more capital through equity markets is likely to depress the price of the shares and send out wrong signals to equity markets.[59] Thus, raising additional

---

[55] The shareholder cannot demand the return of his her investment, although the possibility to sell the shares in the market exists. However, this right is curtailed in weak capital markets.

[56] M Roe, The Institutions of Corporate Governance (2004), Harvard Law and Economics Discussion Paper 488, http://ssrn.com/abstract=612362 [3 August 2005], 14.

[57] C Harvey, K Lins and A Roper, The Effect of Capital Structure When Expected Agency Costs are Extreme (2001), National Bureau of Economic Research Working Paper 8452, http://www.nber.org/papers/w8452.pdf [7 August 2006].

[58] Section 7.2(c).

[59] B Greenwald, J Stiglitz and A Weiss, Informational Imperfections in the Capital Market and Macro-economic Fluctuations (1984), 74 *American Economic Review*, 194.

capital through debt markets in controlling shareholder systems is preferred, enabling lenders to play a greater corporate governance role.

(b) *Access to Information and Ability to Monitor*

The strongest argument in favour of a greater corporate governance role for lenders is based on their ability to overcome problems arising from information asymmetries. Lenders' access to corporate information is likely to be greater than a shareholder's access to, or ability to analyse such information. Lenders' access to corporate information is greater because a controlling shareholder in the position of a borrower is more likely to disclose relevant financial information to a lender. The analysis of such information is also likely to be superior, as banks tend to employ people competent to analyse and evaluate such information. While it is possible for creditors to monitor passively,[60] the free flow of information makes the lenders' ability to monitor greater. The opportunity for a lender to monitor the activities of a company can arise *ex ante*: prior to the borrowing, it can be ongoing, and it can be *ex post*: where there is intervention in the event of difficulties or bankruptcy.

A further factor strengthening the argument in favour of lenders in a corporate governance role is that the relationship between lenders and companies tends to be stable and long standing, giving lenders more access to information and better capabilities to analyse such information over the long term, in contrast to short-term investors who are focussed on the price on the share market, rather than on long-term monitoring.

Lenders are also able to overcome a related issue connected to short-term outside investors who sometimes suffer from overoptimism and are insensitive to defects of controlling shareholder systems. Short-term investors rely on the shortterm appreciation of company shares than the long-term ability of the company to pay dividends. Therefore, the monitoring role played by lenders is indispensable to maintaining the long-term prospects of a company.

The disadvantages of lenders in a corporate governance role include the possibility that increased involvement in the borrower company's affairs may result in the lender's support of inefficient companies due to lender's

---

[60] The decision on active or passive management is often influenced by the security offered as collateral by the borrower company.

long-term interests and the increased monitoring costs. Further, lenders' interests may not always correlate to other stakeholders' interests. Companies may be forced to abandon certain projects, which require additional funding, or be forced to liquidate in the interests of the debt holders. However, while a general monitoring role by a lender may be biased, the ability of a lender to curb the costs of controlling shareholders is undoubted.

(c) *Incentive*

Monitoring and controlling the costs arising from controlling shareholder systems are costly. However, lenders have the incentive to monitor since their lending is at risk. Lenders are motivated to earnestly perform *ex ante* and ongoing interim monitoring to avoid the heavy costs of liquidation and restructuring. Further, lenders' commitment to *ex post* monitoring is also likely to be greater as once lending is made, the future success of the company is desirable from the point of view of the lender. Incentive led lenders, in contrast, for example, to a government regulatory authority, are in a better position to obtain information and exercise control and reduce some of the costs inherent in controlling shareholder systems.

From the point of view of the lender, the cost of monitoring and the incentive to monitor pose a trade-off as monitoring reduces the lending risk. While monitoring is likely to be costly to a lender, it is also likely to constrain the costs of controlling shareholders and minimise the risk of corporate failure.

From the point of view of the company, the debt contract (if obtained through an unaffiliated lender) gives the controlling shareholders or managers appointed by the controlling shareholders a strong incentive to ensure the company's success and ability to meet the repayment requirements. As default on repayment is likely to deprive the managers or controlling shareholders of control, debt is both a disciplining device and a device by which to align the interests of the controlling shareholders with minority shareholders.

(d) *Ability to Secure Compliance*

Market regulators such as securities and exchange commissions and banking and insurance regulators, secure compliance with laws aimed at controlling the costs of controlling shareholders, corporate governance best practices and norms with the threat of sanctions. However, such threat is only likely to be effective in an environment with successful enforcement mechanisms, which is rare in many developing countries. On the other hand, banks as lenders help control the costs of controlling shareholders among borrower companies by securing compliance as part of their risk assessment process.[61] The borrower is thus, incentivised into complying.

Further, the ability of lenders to secure compliance is strengthened by the long-term relationship between lenders and borrower companies and the future prospects of the borrower. Future prospects are of importance to the borrower as the company is likely to engage in a series of repeated transactions with the lender for which its' reputation for co-operation and honest dealing is essential. This ability of lenders to get borrowers to commit credibly by contract or otherwise to control the costs of controlling shareholders is valuable in weak enforcement environments.

(e) *Controlling Shareholders*

It is submitted that the system of controlling shareholders makes the position of lenders attractive as an external mechanism of corporate governance. The costs of controlling shareholders are unlikely to be curtailed by internal governance mechanisms and thus, there is a need for an external monitor. Lenders as an external monitor have the added advantage of being able to trigger a loss of control rights through the use of contractual terms and debt-equity swaps.[62] This ability to trigger a loss of control rights is a powerful disciplinary weapon and heightens the success of lenders as an external mechanism of governance in controlling shareholder systems.

(f) *Limitations on Equity Markets and Equity Finance in Developing Countries*

Equity markets in developing countries tend to be embryonic. Emphasis on equity finance in such countries requires the development of equity

---

[61] OECD, *Corporate Governance of Non-Listed Companies in Emerging Economies* (Paris 2006), 12, recognises the ability of debt to demand compliance with codes and norms in the context of non-listed companies.

[62] Aoki (n. 22), 18, calls this contingent governance, that is, insider control is maintained contingent on the financial viability of the company.

markets and the fostering of a particular culture of risk taking and savings. This places a heavy burden on policy makers to develop laws and institutions to change the behaviour of people instilled with a culture of savings placed in banks, to investing in equity markets and institutional investors such as pension funds. While such change is slow, the result of underdeveloped equity markets is such that equity and corporate bond markets are unlikely to play a major role in the provision of finance for companies. Many companies in developing countries do not have sufficient internal reserves, and outside financing by banks and other institutional lenders is the only viable alternative for raising finance. This critical need for finance, vests lenders with the ability to act as a corporate governance monitor and secure compliance in controlling the costs of controlling shareholders.

Weak equity markets also lack the necessary institutions to provide necessary monitoring. In market-oriented economies, *ex ante* monitoring would be provided by investment banks or venture capitalists, interim and on going monitoring by rating firms, commercial banks and *ex post* monitoring by accounting firms, corporate raiders and leveraged buyout specialists. Developing countries lack diverse financial intermediaries and the delegation of the above three phases of monitoring to lenders is, in fact, a technique by which such scarcity is overcome.[63]

(g) *Lenders' Ability to Overcome Weaknesses in Enforcement*

Lenders' corporate governance role is less dependent on the legal and institutional framework within a country than that of shareholders or regulators. This is because lenders are in the powerful position of being able to demand that borrowers adhere to their terms if the companies are to continue to have access to future financing. This makes the lenders' terms and conditions of a self-enforcing nature and is especially useful in the context of developing countries with deficient legal and institutional frameworks. It is recognised that lenders can help implement good corporate governance by demanding that companies comply with best practices as part of their risk assessment process.[64]

---

[63] ibid 22, makes this point in support of the reasons to develop banking institutions in transition economies.

[64] OECD (n. 61), 12, states the Basel II accord with its overriding aim of risk assessment procedures for individual banks could speed up this process.

Much scepticism is expressed about the binding nature of legal rules in the context of company law, since companies can opt out of these rules by their corporate charters.[65] However, in many developing countries, companies very rarely opt out of the applicable legal rules, which is both expensive and can result in a loss of confidence among investors. In such countries, the fundamental issue is enforcement of the rules, rather than the rules themselves.

In recent writings, Berglof and Claessens, make the argument that 'more than regulations, law on the books, or voluntary codes, enforcement is the key to creating an effective business environment and good corporate governance'.[66] In a similar vein, they argue that while monitoring by lenders relies to a great extent on the effectiveness of the regulatory framework and supervision in addition to public enforcement institutions that allow collateral to be collected, banks as lenders compensate for some weaknesses in the general enforcement environment, as 'lenders have repeated dealings, have a reputation to maintain in lending, and can economise on monitoring and enforcement technology'.[67] However, while reputation may be a powerful inducement to existing firms to pay their debts, a system relying primarily on reputation as a mechanism makes it difficult for new entrants, who have yet to develop a reputation, to secure finance.

(h) *Lenders Are Potentially Effective Resource Allocators*

Lenders, especially banks, have an influence on the allocation of resources, risk sharing and economic performance of a country. In addition to general payments, banks as lenders are involved in asset transformation, managing risk, monitoring and information processing and allocation of risk.[68] Banks in developing countries, although underdeveloped in comparison to banking

---

[65] F Easterbrook and D Fischel, *The Economic Structure of Corporate Law* (Harvard University Press Massachusetts 1991).

[66] E Berglof and S Claessens, Enforcement and Good Corporate Governance in Developing Countries and Transition Economies (2006), 21 *World Bank Research Observer*, 123.

[67] ibid 142.

[68] J Day and P Taylor, Institutional Change and Debt-based Corporate Governance: A Comparative Analysis of Four Transition Economies (2004), 8 *Journal of Management and Governance*, 73–79.

systems in developed economies, have a comparative advantage over securities markets in relation to information processing and monitoring, transforming assets into units acceptable to savers, assessing and managing risk.[69] They also have the ability to act as delegated monitors for other stakeholders. This makes them potentially effective resource allocators in assessing the health of the market and strengthens the argument in support of an increased corporate governance role for lenders.

(i) *Limited Liability*

The concept of a separate legal personality for companies and the related issue of limited liability move the risk of corporate failure from shareholders to creditors. As a result of the movement of risk to creditors, creditors especially institutional lenders with the capacity to monitor are forced into monitoring positions to protect against lending risk more effectively. Some of this is done by way of secured lending and risk premiums. Increasingly lenders are willing to take on board positions and monitor as they are aware that courts are reluctant to lift the veil of incorporation[70] or disregard the separate legal personality of the company and hold the shareholders liable for the debts of the company, except in exceptional circumstances.[71] Thus, the concept of a separate corporate personality and limited liability of companies encourages a governance role for lenders in borrower companies.

(j) *The Lending Bias*

The use of lenders as a corporate governance mechanism is not without its downside. Lenders are not charitable institutions and as such may require a company to take on projects, which are relatively low risk, even though

---

[69] ibid.

[70] *Salomon v. Salomon & Co Ltd* [1897], 1 AC 22 (HL); *Adams v. Cape Industries Plc* [1990], BCLC 479 (CA).

[71] *Adams* (n. 70), was an attempt to pierce the corporate veil by involuntary creditors. Court made clear that Cape could only be held liable for actions of subsidiary if the group arrangements were a 'façade'. The requirements for the satisfaction of this test were not explored in detail.

the expected return is significantly lower than other riskier ones. On the other hand, a greater degree of debt can distort the equity holders' incentives, pushing them towards unwarranted high risks. In this respect, the interests of the lenders and the shareholders are diametrically opposed.[72] Of course, reducing the probability of default ensures a guaranteed return for shareholders. Therefore, the lending bias has the ability to support the role of lenders as a corporate governance mechanism, though they may tilt towards less risky, lower return projects. However, debt can also hinder growth of a company where financing of future projects is limited due to the 'debt-overhang' effect which affects company valuation.[73]

Further, lenders in an increased monitoring role may support inefficient or insolvent companies, to recover monies due and protect their own interests. In some jurisdictions, activism by the judiciary in restraining this type of behaviour by lenders has forced lenders to exercise control over the borrowers in an indirect manner.[74] The propping of insolvent companies in their own self-interest means that lenders do not always act in ways consistent with the interests of all of the shareholders of the company, which is a negative characteristic inherent in the corporate governance role of lenders.

(k) *Contingent[75] or Conditional Governance*

Lenders tend to engage in what is termed contingent or conditional governance. When performance is good, company affairs are left to controlling shareholders but when it deteriorates, there is intervention by the banks in the management of the companies. This is a major drawback in the role of lenders as a corporate governance mechanism. The only way in which this can be overcome is by encouraging lenders to also take up equity positions in the companies that they lend to. However, holdings of

---

[72] Lenders by requiring companies to take on low-risk projects with guaranteed but low returns do safeguard shareholder value. However, this must be qualified by the fact that shareholders in highly leveraged companies are unlikely to bear the costs of failure of a high risk-, high-return investment.

[73] S Myers, Determinants of Corporate Borrowing (1976), Sloan School of Management Working Paper 875–876, http://dspace.mit.edu/bitstream/1721.1/1915/1/SWP-0875-02570768.pdf [15 September 2006].

[74] Section 7.2.4(b).

[75] Text at (n. 23).

equities in the borrowing company by lenders have both positive and negative features.[76]

To summarise, the above evaluation of the role of lenders as a corporate governance mechanism demonstrates that lenders are in strong position to influence the corporate governance of companies and control controlling shareholders. However, the role of lenders is dependent on a number of factors within the local environment in which the companies operate, such as the ownership structure of companies, potential access to other sources of financing such as capital markets and the ability of companies to generate their own funds. The next section evaluates the role of lenders as a corporate governance mechanism in the context of Sri Lanka.

7.3.2. *Evaluating Lenders as a Corporate Governance Mechanism in Sri Lanka*

In Sri Lanka, the debt market is dominated by bank lending. Although a corporate bond market exists, it is underdeveloped.[77] The principal financial sector lenders in Sri Lanka are commercial and specialised banks (e.g., development banks). Other financial sector lenders are non-bank deposit taking financial institutions, such as registered finance companies, co-operative rural banks, thrift and credit co-operative societies and other specialised financial institutions, such as leasing companies and merchant banks.

The focus of the study in the context of Sri Lanka is on licensed commercial and specialised banks (hereinafter 'banks') in the role of lenders due to their dominance in the lending market. Banks hold dominant positions in the financial sector contributing about 56 percent of financial assets.[78] Licensed commercial banks are also the largest mobilisers of

---

[76] Examined in the context of Sri Lanka, in Section 7.3.2(d).

[77] Central Bank of Sri Lanka, *Annual Report 2005* (Colombo 2005), 135, attributes the underdeveloped nature of the private debt market, particularly the corporate bond market, to several factors, such as 'a lack of institutional investor base, availability of bank credit at attractive rates for high net worth companies, high cost of debt issues, lack of investor awareness, lack of investor information on the quality of debt and nonavailability of a longer term bench mark yield curve.'

[78] ibid 126, Table 8.1.

deposits.[79] Both categories of banks are under the direct supervision of the Central Bank of Sri Lanka. As at the end of 2005, Sri Lanka had 22 licensed commercial banks and 14 licensed specialised banks.[80]

This section evaluates the role of lenders, specifically licensed commercial and specialised banks, as a corporate governance mechanism in Sri Lanka. Such analysis highlights both the strengths and weaknesses inherent in relying on lenders as a corporate governance mechanism and thereby, helps formulate a hybrid reform agenda to enable and strengthen the role of lenders as a corporate governance mechanism in Sri Lanka.

(a) *The Importance of Bank Lending in Sri Lanka*

While the Sri Lankan financial system is not recognised as being a predominantly bank based, bank loans are a primary source of finance in the corporate sector. Financial sector assets are over 130 percent of GDP at current market prices.[81] Banks in Sri Lanka perform investment-banking functions, often through a subsidiary, as well as commercial banking functions. The reliance on debt markets (corporate bonds and bank lending) is demonstrated by the high debt–equity ratios among many listed companies.[82]

Bank loans are a main source of financing in Sri Lanka due to the lack of access to other sources of finance (i.e., weak capital markets and a lack of other sources of non-bank lending such as private capital). Further, while controlling shareholders are reticent in using equity markets to raise additional capital due to a perceived loss of control, the use of debt markets, especially bank lending is preferred and widespread. Credit to the private sector extended by the domestic private banks was 48 percent of the total credit extended by licensed commercial banks.[83] In a comparative analysis

---

[79] ibid 126.

[80] ibid 125, Table 8.2.

[81] ibid 125, this is the sum of assets of the banking sector, non-bank deposit taking financial institutions, other specialised financial institutions and contractual financial institutions divided by the GDP at current market prices for 2005. The sum of assets of the banking sector plus non-bank deposit taking financial institutions amount to around 98 percent of the GDP.

[82] Debt ratios of Sri Lankan non-financial companies (1998–2001) are a median of 47.94 percent. S Cheng and C Shiu, Investor Protection and Capital Structure: International Evidence (2007), 17 *Journal of Multinational Financial Management*, 30–33.

[83] Central Bank of Sri Lanka (n. 77), 127–128.

Table 7.1: Comparative Distributions of Financial Markets (2002).

	Sri Lanka (in %)	Malaysia (in %)	India (in %)
Bank lending	**57**	36	35
Equity	**22**	47	37
Government bonds	**20**	9	22
Corporate bonds	**1**	7	6

of bank lending among Sri Lanka, Malaysia and India in 2002, bank lending was highest in Sri Lanka amounting to 57 percent (Table 7.1).[84]

As illustrated, due to the importance of bank lending in Sri Lanka, the use of lenders, as a mechanism to curb the costs of controlling shareholders is likely to be successful, especially as such governance mechanism is arising from the market and is likely to receive a degree of deference from controlling shareholders.

(b) *Availability of Funds for Lending by Banks and other Financial Institutions*

The high rates of deposit interest[85] coupled with public perception of shares as high risk, low liquidity investments is successful in diverting private savings from equity markets into the banking sector in Sri Lanka. The high rates of interest have attracted demand and savings deposits into banks,[86] which provided banks the capital base for their lending activities. The lending activities of banks is reflected in the use of funds of commercial banks as at the end of 2005, where loans and advances constitute 53 percent.[87]

---

[84] ibid Table 6.1. Reproduced from Asian Development Bank, *Sri Lanka: Financial Sector Assessment* (Manila 2005), 101.

[85] Commercial banks' weighted average deposit rate, which was at 12 percent in 1990, was reduced to a more realistic 7.6 percent in 2006. Central Bank of Sri Lanka, *Annual Report 2006* (Colombo 2006) Key Economic Indicators.

[86] Central Bank of Sri Lanka, *Bulletin-January 2005* (Colombo 2005), Table 71, reports that as on September 2004, over 75.7 percent of demand and savings deposits with commercial banks are owned by individuals.

[87] Central Bank of Sri Lanka (n. 86), 129, Chart 8.1.

This heavy reliance on interest-bearing activities as a major source of income by banks can, among other reasons, be attributed to the high interest rate spread.[88] In a regional comparison of interest spreads in 2004, Sri Lanka was highest at 4.2 percent, in comparison to India at 2.9 percent, Pakistan at 2.1 percent and Bangladesh at 1.2 percent.[89]

A high interest rate spread and heavy reliance on interest-bearing activities has meant that the banking sector as a key financial intermediary is ineffective in channelling funds from the banking sector into equity markets, and has contributed to the persistence of concentrated ownership among companies in Sri Lanka.[90] However, the heavy reliance by the banking sector on interest-bearing activities, such as loans and advances, has meant that banks are a primary source of funds for the corporate sector, placing them in a strong position from which to act as a corporate governance mechanism within a controlling shareholder system.

(c) *Creditor Rights Are Stronger Than Shareholder Rights*

Creditor rights in Sri Lanka are reported to be stronger than shareholder rights and therefore, banks[91] as creditors with better rights are in a stronger position to act as corporate monitors. LLSV,[92] in their study advancing the hypothesis that companies in countries with poor investor protection have more concentrated ownership of their shares, engage in an analysis of shareholder rights and creditor rights of 49 countries. The analysis covers Sri Lanka and is useful in demonstrating the argument that creditor rights in Sri Lanka are stronger than shareholder rights.

The LLSV analysis covers four creditor rights variables: (i) whether reorganisation procedure imposes an automatic stay on the assets; (ii) whether secured creditors are assured a right to collateral in reorganisation; (iii) whether management can seek protection from creditors

---

[88] ibid Key Economic Indicators. Difference between weighted average lending rate and borrowing rate, was a high six (6) percent in 2005.

[89] ibid 130, Box 16.

[90] Chapter 4.

[91] The studies examining creditor rights focus on senior secured creditors, encompassing banks.

[92] LLSV, Law and Finance (1998), 106 *Journal of Political Economy*, 1113; Oxford Analytica, *Shareholder & Creditor Rights in Key Developing Countries 2005: A Study Prepared for CalPERS* (Oxford 2006).

unilaterally by filing for reorganisation without creditor consent and (iv) whether management stays pending the resolution of the reorganisation procedure. In the creditor rights index aggregating these four variables, Sri Lanka scores 3 out of 4 or 75 percent.[93] The same analysis also covers shareholder rights. These include: (i) whether the one-share-one-vote principle applies; (ii) whether proxy by mail is allowed; (iii) whether shares are blocked (i.e., deposited with the company or a financial intermediary) before a shareholder meeting; (iv) whether cumulative voting for directors is allowed and whether mechanisms of proportional representation on the board are available; (v) whether oppressed minority shareholders have legal mechanisms available; (vi) whether pre-emptive rights are available to buy new issues of stock and (vii) whether percentage of share capital needed to call an extraordinary shareholders' meeting is below or above the world median of 10 percent. In the anti-director rights measure comprising variables (ii)–(vii), Sri Lanka scores 3 out of 6 or 50 percent,[94] while it scores a zero on the one-share-one vote variable.[95] While by no means conclusive, the LLSV analysis seems to suggest that creditor rights in Sri Lanka are marginally stronger than shareholder rights.

Table 7.2 is a comparative analysis of investor protection, creditor protection and judicial enforcement in several Asian economies. Sri Lanka scores marginally better in creditor protection in this analysis as well.

Banks as creditors are also subject to a tighter regime of regulation, while at the same time being given the necessary rights to collect their debts, as in a wider context dependable debt collection is the key to making banks and the financial sector run efficiently. Banks in Sri Lanka are subject to supervision by the Central Bank of Sri Lanka through its bank supervision department. The regulation and supervision of banks is governed by the

---

[93] LLSV (n. 92), 1136. A score of 1 = creditor protection is in the law. Sri Lanka scores a zero in (ii) as non-secured creditors, such as the government and workers, are given priority in proceeds in bankruptcy.

[94] LLSV (n. 92), 1130. 1 = investor protection is in the law. Sri Lanka scores a zero in category numbers (i), (iii) and (v).

[95] ibid 1130. Further, it should also be noted that other studies such as the World Bank, Doing Business in 2008: Comparing Regulation in 178 Economies (2008), http://www. doingbusiness.org/documents/fullreport/2008/DB08_Indicator_Tables_Country_Tables. pdf [5 May 2009], demonstrate better results for Sri Lanka with respect to creditor rights than other similarly situated countries.

Table 7.2[96]: Comparative Analysis of Creditor and Investor Protection.

	Investor protection[a]	Creditor protection[b]	Judicial enforcement[c]
India	2.0	4.0	6.1
Indonesia	2.0	4.0	4.4
Malaysia	4.0	4.0	7.7
Pakistan	5.0	4.0	4.3
Philippines	4.0	0.0	4.1
Sri Lanka	2.0	3.0	5.0
Thailand	3.0	3.0	5.9
Average	3.1	3.1	5.3

[a] An index of how well the legal framework protects equity investors. It will equal six when (i) shareholders are allowed to vote by mail; (ii) shareholders are not required to deposit share in advance of meeting; (iii) cumulative voting is allowed; (iv) when the minimum percentage of share capital required to call a meeting is less than 10 percent; (v) an oppressed minority mechanism is in place and (vi) legislation mandates one-vote per share for all shares (or equivalent).

[b] An index of how well the legal framework protects secured creditors. It will equal four when (i) there are minimum restrictions (e.g., creditor consent) for companies to file for reorganisation; (ii) there is no automatic stay on collateral; (iii) debtor loses control of company during reorganisation and (iv) secured creditors are given priority during a reorganisation.

[c] Measures quality of judicial enforcement equal to an average of five subclasses measuring (i) efficiency of judicial system; (ii) rule of law; (iii) corruption; (iv) risk of expropriation and (v) risk of contract repudiation.

Banking Act[97] and the Monetary Law Act[98] and is based on internationally accepted standards for bank supervision set by the Basel Committee for Banking Supervision.[99] This gives banks as lenders a certain degree of legitimacy in the collection of debts and in acting as a corporate governance

---

[96] *Source*: LLSV, Legal Determinants of External Finance (1997), 52 *Journal of Finance*, 1131; ibid.

[97] No. 30 of 1988.

[98] No. 58 of 1949.

[99] Basel Committee on Banking Supervision, *Basel II: International Convergence of Capital Measurement and Capital Standards: A Revised Framework-Comprehensive Version* (Basel 2006).

mechanism in controlling the costs of controlling shareholders, as they are themselves have mechanisms in place to ensure their own governance is regulated.

(d) *Banks as Equity Holders of the Borrowing Companies: Relationship Banking*

The fact that banks in Sri Lanka are also equity holders of borrowing companies or controlled by the borrowing companies significantly affects the corporate governance role of banks. Sri Lankan banks have economic stakes in nearly every single one of the 20 largest companies listed on the CSE and are among the 20 largest shareholders in over 12 of the 20.[100] Controlling shareholders, in turn, control many of these banks.[101]

Relationship banks provide both equity and debt financing to their clients, have strong ties with them and serve on the boards of directors of the companies. Transactional banks primarily provide short-term bank loans but not equity financing, monitor loan covenants and have limited interference on corporate management.[102] Many Sri Lankan banks are relationship banks by virtue of their subsidiary investment companies and interlocking ownership structures with the borrowing companies.

On the one hand, relationship banks have closer ties with their clients than transactional banks, better information about borrowing companies, help constrain the costs of controlling shareholder systems and enhance financial sector stability. On the other hand, relationship banks' close ties with their clients lead to conflict of interest situations and decrease the role of bank debt in controlling the costs of controlling shareholder systems.[103] Relationship banking also allows the possibility of government

---

[100] *Source*: Annual reports.

[101] Reforms are being enacted restricting controlling shareholders' excessive control of financial institutions in Sri Lanka, at Section 7.4.

[102] F Allen and D Gale, A Welfare Comparison of Intermediaries and Financial Markets in Germany and the US (1995), 39 *European Economic Review*, 179, distinguish between relationship banking and transactional banking.

[103] Asian Development Bank (n. 53), Chapter 2, recognises that interlocking ownership arrangements between creditors and borrowers compromise the role of creditors as external agents monitoring and disciplining borrowers.

influence due to the government holding a significant percentage of equity in state banks.[104]

It is argued that in the context of controlling shareholder systems with cross-holdings extending to banks, debt cannot play a corporate governance role.[105] This is primarily attributed to two reasons. First, default on debt extended by a group bank is likely to take the form of propping and unlikely to constrain the actions of a controlling shareholder.[106] Second, debt could facilitate the expropriation of minority shareholders,[107] for example, through related-party transactions.

A Faccio *et al.* study[108] which tests data for ownership, control and leverage of all listed companies with 'credible accounting data' in five European economies and nine Asian economies report that, in their sample of Asian countries, group affiliates are more leveraged giving controlling shareholders resources to expropriate without direct liability for debt, and that there is evidence to demonstrate that European capital markets are more effective in containing the abuse of debt.[109] This is attributed to the legal and regulatory framework within European capital markets for lenders to be an effective corporate governance force.

Further, while expropriation via debt in Asia is obscured by weak capital market institutions, pyramids, related-party lending and the perception of endless growth opportunities that seemed to justify high leverage,[110] the

---

[104] J Solomon, A Solomon and C Park, A Conceptual Framework for Corporate Governance Reform in South Korea (2002), 10 *Corporate Governance: An International Review*, 29–31, cite the entry of the Korean *chaebol* in the 1970s into the steel, petrochemical and steel-building industries as a direct result of government influence due to significant government holdings in debt finance.

[105] Faccio *et al.* (n. 15).

[106] E Friedman, S Johnson and T Mitton, Propping and Tunneling (2003), 31 *Journal of Comparative Economics*, 732–734, suggest that the 'possibility of propping makes issuing debt attractive to entrepreneurs and investors when courts cannot enforce contracts.

[107] M Backman, *Asian Eclipse: Exposing the Dark Side of Business in Asia* (Wiley Singapore 1999), attributes debt-facilitated expropriation as a cause of the Asian financial crisis. In contrast, J Sarkar and S Sarkar, Debt and Corporate Governance in Developing Countries: Evidence from India (2005), Indira Gandhi Institute of Development Research Working Paper 7, http://econpapers.repec.org/paper/indigiwpp/2005-007.htm [10 August 2006], find only limited evidence of debt being used as a mechanism for expropriation in group-affiliated firms in India.

[108] Faccio *et al.* (n. 15).

[109] ibid 1, 22–23, Table 7.

[110] ibid 17–21, Tables 7 and 8.

findings suggest that if these hurdles are overcome or if the institutional framework for debt is different to the analysis offered, it is likely that debt can be an effective corporate governance mechanism even within controlling shareholder systems as demonstrated by the sample of European countries.

While relationship banking does have its benefits, the presence of cross-holdings and pyramids which encompass borrower companies and lender banks, detracts from its benefits and gives rise to fears of expropriation via debt and the ineffectiveness of debt as a corporate governance mechanism within controlling shareholder systems. If the full benefits of debt as a corporate governance mechanism are to be obtained, a reform agenda will need to address the conflict of interest resulting from cross-shareholdings and pyramids encompassing both borrowers and lenders.

(e) *Lenders Are Strictly Regulated and Less Likely to Suffer from Own Corporate Governance Issues*

Lenders' own corporate governance structures, including regulations and supervision of lending institutions determine to a large extent their ability to act as monitors and play an effective corporate governance role. Generally, lenders are strictly regulated by a financial services authority or a central bank and are less likely to be vulnerable to expropriation by controlling shareholders or management entrenchment or tunnelling.

However, lenders may suffer from their own corporate governance and corporate control issues due to state intervention or due to failures in their risk assessment strategies. Thus, lenders may have motives other than timely debt repayment or monitoring of debt when there is government-directed lending, which channels bank lending, especially by state-controlled banks into small and medium industries.[111] Politically misdirected lending has resulted in the two state-controlled banks in Sri Lanka facing financial difficulties,[112] with corporate governance concerns due to allegations of

---

[111] Bank of Ceylon, *Annual Report 2005* (Colombo 2005), 29, reports that 57 percent of its loan portfolio comprised of loans made to small and medium enterprises and consumer loans.

[112] Pramuka to Get Treasury Money through Rs. 2.2 Billion Restructuring Bond (22 February 2006), *Lanka Business Online*, reports that although the government has injected nearly SLRS 30 billion into the state banks through restructuring, the banks fell into financial difficulties due to politically directed lending turning bad; International Monetary Fund, *IMF Country Report No. 6/446* (Washington DC 2006), 14, reports that the low capital adequacy of the state-controlled People's Bank is a risk to financial sector stability in Sri Lanka.

corruption and lending bias. As the financial crisis has demonstrated lenders may also face difficulties due to poor credit risk analysis.

Lenders may also face corporate governance and control problems due to controlling shareholder systems such as cross-holdings and pyramids. In Sri Lanka, the concentration of ownership and cross-holding among banks is recognised as hindering financial sector stability and undermining investor confidence.[113]

Despite Sri Lanka's first post-independence banking failure occurring only in the recent past,[114] efforts have been made in Sri Lanka to improve the regulation and corporate governance of banks under supervision of the Central Bank of Sri Lanka.[115] The Central Bank of Sri Lanka has expanded its reporting system to monitor compliance. Strengthening banking and financial regulations and making bank supervision effective enables banks to overcome their own corporate governance problems and play a significant role in monitoring and controlling, controlling shareholders.

To recapitulate, banks in Sri Lanka have access to a large reserve of funds for lending than equity markets and are dominant financiers to companies in Sri Lanka, increasing their potential as a corporate governance mechanism. Creditor rights in Sri Lanka are reportedly stronger than shareholder rights also strengthening the role of banks as monitors. While concentrated ownership structures within banks and cross-holdings between banks and the borrowing companies coupled with weaknesses in corporate governance practices among banks may detract from the overall ability of lenders to act as monitors, prudent regulation and supervision by the Central Bank of Sri Lanka and the adoption of international banking standards have alleviated some of these obstacles.

The monitoring potential of Sri Lankan banks is similar to the German banking system where external sources of funds illustrate that banks in Germany provide about twice the financing as direct securities markets.[116] It is also similar in many respects to the German system of banking where

---

[113] Central Bank of Sri Lanka (n. 77), 126.

[114] The failure of Pramuka Savings and Development Bank was attributed to almost 80 percent non-performing loans (NPLs) by the Director of Banking Supervision, Central Bank of Sri Lanka. J Zilva, Regulation of the Banking and the Related Sectors in Sri Lanka (2004), http://www.ips.lk/events/workshops/22_07_2004_ria/papers/joan_de_zilva_banking_supervision.pdf [5 January 2007].

[115] Implementing Basel II, Central Bank of Sri Lanka (n. 77), 125.

[116] 1965–1989, Baums (n. 41), Table 12.1.

banks because of specific institutional arrangements like owning equity in the companies they lend to, have interlocking directorates and control of proxies, and are able to play a role in the corporate governance of the borrower companies.[117] However, the above analysis demonstrates that if lenders in Sri Lanka are to become an effective corporate governance mechanism in controlling the costs of controlling shareholder systems, the necessary legal and institutional preconditions must support their monitoring potential.

7.4. Legal and Institutional Preconditions Necessary for Lenders to Be an Effective Corporate Governance Mechanism to Control the Costs of Controlling Shareholders in Sri Lanka

Thus far, this chapter has evaluated the suitability of lenders as a corporate governance mechanism in controlling the costs of controlling shareholder systems and proposed that lenders with their enhanced abilities to monitor are best suited to control the costs of controlling shareholder systems.

Chapter 6 proposed that the framework for reform to constrain the costs of controlling shareholder systems must essentially be hybrid, that is, it must utilise the identified market force (i.e., identified as lenders) with the necessary legal and institutional preconditions.[118] This section of the chapter sets out a reform agenda of policy options based on the legal and institutional preconditions necessary for lenders to be an effective mechanism to control the costs of controlling shareholders in Sri Lanka.

In setting out the reform agenda of policy options, the legal, regulatory and institutional environment in Sri Lanka is also subject to analysis and evaluation to determine its effectiveness in assisting lenders to control the costs of controlling shareholders.

The basic inventory of legal, regulatory and institutional preconditions necessary for lenders to be an effective corporate governance mechanism is surveyed under the heads of: (i) Regulating conflicts of interest: Independence of lenders; (ii) Improving accountability: Disclosure and transparency; (iii) Improving rights of lenders; (iv) Fiduciary duties owed to lenders; (v) Enabling an internal management role for lenders; (vi) Enhancing lenders' own corporate governance; (vii) Credit ratings and credit bureaus and (viii) Encouraging competition.

---

[117] ibid 423–433.
[118] Chapter 6, Section 6.4.

A note of clarification is necessary with respect to the law of partnerships, corporations, banks and banking in Sri Lanka, which is subject to the application of the Civil Law Ordinance.[119] Section 3 of the Act sets out that '… with respect to the law of Partnerships, Corporations, Banks and Banking …the law to be administered shall be the same as would be administered in England in the like case, at the corresponding period, if such question or issue had arisen or had to be decided in England, unless in any case other provision is or shall be made by any enactment now in force in Ceylon or hereafter to be enacted.' The statute thus paved the way for the introduction of English law, which was adopted by Sri Lankan courts most recently in the areas of principal and agent,[120] and derivative actions.[121] While it is clear that it is the substantive law and not procedural law that is of application,[122] and not only law in force at the time of the enactment but also any subsequent statute,[123] inadequate case law on the introduction of English law principles has raised a number of issues as to the extent of its application.[124] For purposes of this study, it is suffice to take the position that where there is no substantive enactment in the areas of law stated in Section 3 of the Civil Law Ordinance 1852, the corresponding English law is deemed to apply to Sri Lanka.[125]

7.4.1. *Regulating Conflicts of Interest: Independence of Lenders*

If lenders are to be effective corporate governance monitors, it is important that they engage in arms-length transactions with their borrowers or

---

[119] No. 5 of 1852.

[120] *Wright and Three Others v. People's Bank* [1985] 2 SLLR 292.

[121] *Amarasekere v. Mitsui and Company and others* [1992] 1 SLLR 22.

[122] *Oretra Enterprises and Others v. Wijekoon* [2003] 3 SLLR 1.

[123] *Usman v. Rahim* [1930] 32 NLR 259 (n. 120).

[124] Namely, as to whether English law principles (again is it limited to English common law or does it include English statutes?) of wider scope will be of application, if the local enactment on the question is narrower? Although, the courts in Sri Lanka did not address this issue, the recognition of the English common law derivative action in *Amarasekere* (n. 121), does seem to answer this in the affirmative. In this instance, while ss. 210, 211 of the Companies Act No. 17 of 1982 were the principal shareholder remedy, the courts allowed an action to be brought on the basis of the English common law derivative action.

[125] *MA Razak & Company Ltd v. Lanka Walltiles Ltd* [2000] 1 SLLR 1. Contrast, C Weeramantry *The Law of Contracts being a Comparative Study of the Roman–Dutch, English and Customary Laws of Contract in Ceylon* (HW Cave Colombo 1967), 44 — 'Adoption of English law in matters governed by the common law is now at an ebb'.

alternatively, ensure that any conflict of interest transaction with borrowers is properly disclosed and authorised.

Banking laws and regulations that set limits on equity ownership of banks and regulate cross-holdings between banks and companies, related-party banking transactions and conflict of interest transactions, serve to strengthen the position of lenders as a corporate governance mechanism by attempting to vest a degree of independence for lenders. Further, strengthening the monitoring capabilities of lender by tighter legal and regulatory controls also indirectly serves to limit the costs of controlling shareholder systems such as private benefits of control and tunnelling among companies with cross-holdings in banks.

(a) *Restrictions on Shareholdings in Lenders*

Controlling shareholder systems are widespread among commercial banks in Sri Lanka with many non-financial companies owning controlling stakes in banks,[126] raising the potential for undue influence in the manner banks conduct business and negatively affecting the governance role these institutions as lenders may have with respect to related companies.

Banks should not be a captive source of finance for its controlling shareholders. Therefore, tightening control on shareholdings in banks in Sri Lanka is critical if lenders are to be an effective corporate governance mechanism.

Under section 12 of the Banking Act,[127] 'an individual, partnership or corporate body shall not either directly or indirectly or through a nominee or 'acting in concert',[128] with any other individual, partnership or corporate body acquire a material interest in a licensed commercial bank without the prior written approval of the Monetary Board of Sri Lanka'.[129] Material interest is defined to be 10 percent of the issued capital of the licensed commercial bank carrying voting rights. Under section 46(1) (d) of the Banking Act, the maximum percentage of shares held by a group of companies is restricted to 20 percent.

---

[126] Chapter 3; D Edirimuni, Curtains for Major Players in Banks (7 January 2007), *The Sunday Times*, reports that over 10 commercial banks are controlled by a few wealthy individuals and their associates.

[127] Banking Act (n. 97) as amended by Act No. 2 of 2005.

[128] ibid s. 12 is restrictive in that it applies only when acquisitions take place, although this was probably not the intention of the legislature.

[129] ibid s. 12(1C).

The conflicting statutory provisions have resulted in a number of disputes concerning share ownership concentration in banks in Sri Lanka. The first, concerned the increased shareholding in National Development Bank Limited (now known as National Development Bank Plc), (NDB Bank)[130] by Janashakthi Insurance Company Limited.[131] NDB Bank sought an interim injunction against Janashakthi Insurance Company Limited, preventing interference by Janashakthi Insurance Company Limited to NDB Bank giving effect to the provisions of its memorandum and articles of association. The lawyers for Janashakthi Insurance Company Limited argued that the Banking Act refers only to an acquisition and not the holding of shares and that Janashakthi Insurance Company Limited did not acquire a material interest within the meaning of section 12(1C) on or after the date of the Banking Amendment Act.[132] The lawyers for the Janashakthi Insurance Company Limited also claimed that the maximum percentage for the purpose of s 46(1)(d) of the Act as applicable to Janashakthi Insurance Company Limited is 20 percent. In a controversial judgement, the District Judge of Colombo refused the interim injunction sought by NDB Bank and held that Janashakthi Insurance Company Limited and related parties were not in violation of the Banking Act by its shareholding in NDB Bank.[133] The situation was eventually resolved after Janashakthi Insurance Company Limited was pressurised by the insurance regulator[134] to reduce its excessive shareholding in NDB Bank.

In the light of the difficulties in enforcement due to the contradictory statutory provisions, the Central Bank of Sri Lanka in early 2007 proposed new guidelines on share ownership in banks,[135] by which the maximum percentage of ownership permitted in the issued share capital carrying voting rights in a bank will be 15 percent of the issued share capital carrying

---

[130] The NDB was formed in 1979 as a government-owned development financing institution, which was privatised in 1993. In 2001, it added commercial banking to its portfolio with the acquisition of ABN Amro Bank, Sri Lanka.

[131] An insurance company whose interest in NDB Bank was fuelled by the possible synergies with Eagle Insurance Company Limited, a subsidiary of NDB.

[132] Banking Amendment Act 2005 (n. 127).

[133] NDB Bank's Plea for an Injunction against Janashakthi Refused (20 December 2005), *Daily Mirror*.

[134] The Insurance Board of Sri Lanka created in 2001.

[135] Central Bank of Sri Lanka, *Press Release: New Policy on Share Ownership in Banks* (19 January 2007) and Banking Act (Ownership of Issued Capital Carrying Voting Rights) Directions No. 1 of 2007.

voting rights. This limit will apply to acquisition or holding of shares by all categories of shareholders whether individually or in a group. In the case of licensed commercial banks, the acquisition of shares carrying voting rights in excess of 10 percent requires the prior approval of the Monetary Board.

It is submitted that relaxing the restrictions on ownership limits from 10 percent to 15 percent is a step in the wrong direction. The debate on share ownership concentration in banks in Sri Lanka is clouded by confusion regarding the concentration of shareholdings in banks and the need for banking sector consolidation. In terms of restrictions on ownership of banks Sri Lanka scores 2 out of 4^{136} in a World Bank study, along with countries such as Philippines, Spain, Canada and Argentina. Many developed markets do not impose specific regulatory limits on the ownership of banks, primarily because large market capitalisation of banks acts as an effective deterrent against single ownership. In contrast, in Sri Lanka, market capitalisation of banks is comparatively low making them easy targets for those who seek to acquire control. Therefore, restrictions on ownership of banks are appropriate due to low market capitalisation.

Increased concentration of ownership in banks affects financial sector stability and the potential corporate governance role of banks as lenders. As a matter of arithmetic, raising the limit from 10 percent to 15 percent will enable fewer shareholders to obtain control of a bank. Conversely, raising such limit should achieve banking sector consolidation. If lenders are to realise their full potential as corporate governance monitors, tightening of control on shareholdings in banks is essential to place them in positions of independence. It is suggested that the maximum percentage of ownership permitted in the issued share capital carrying voting rights in a bank should remain at 10 percent, while the ambiguity surrounding the provisions be clarified.

(b) *Lenders' Ownership in Non-Financial Companies*

An attempt to limit or regulate lenders' equity ownership of companies is a double-edged sword. On the one hand, large blockholders are inherently

---

[136] The higher the value the higher, the restrictions. J Barth, G Caprio and R Levine, The Regulation and Supervision of Banks Around the World (2001), World Bank Policy Research Working Paper 2588, http://papers.ssrn.com/sol3/papers.cfm?abstract_id=262317 [14 August 2006], 55, Fig. 6.

superior monitors and if lenders are to engage in a monitoring role, large equity blocks in the borrower companies serve to align the interests of the lenders with those of other shareholders consistent with a positive incentive effect.[137] Other benefits are better risk management, better information gathering and diversified income streams. It is further suggested that regulatory restrictions on bank's equity ownership of non-financial companies promote government power and encourage corruption through the granting of exceptions.[138] However, large equity ownership by lenders in the companies they lend to create conflict of interest situations and result in propping.[139] It also creates financial sector instability and creates financial conglomerates that are difficult to monitor.

While a great deal is written on the entry of commercial banks into merchant banking after the introduction of the Gramm–Leach–Bliley Act[140] in the US, surprisingly few studies comment on whether such amalgamation resulted in any monitoring role being assumed by the financial holding companies.

Most countries do limit bank ownership in non-financial companies. In a survey of OECD countries,[141] it was found that banks may own up to 50 percent of a company's voting stock in Denmark and Norway, 25 percent in Portugal, 10 percent in Finland and Ireland, and up to 5 percent in Belgium, Japan and Sweden. Germany, Austria, Greece, Spain and Turkey (and more recently Italy) have no general restrictions on the percentage of a company that a bank may own.

In Sri Lanka, the Banking Act specifically prohibits a licensed commercial bank having as its subsidiary a company, which is not a licensed commercial bank.[142] Further, a licensed commercial bank shall not acquire or hold shares in any company other than a listed public company[143] in excess

---

[137] S Claessens *et al.*, Disentangling the Incentive and Entrenchment Effects of Large Shareholdings (2002), 57 *Journal of Finance*, 2741.

[138] A Shleifer and R Vishny, Corruption (1993), 108 *Quarterly Journal of Economics*, 599.

[139] Use private funds to benefit minority shareholders. Friedman *et al.* (n. 106), suggest that issuing debt may commit an institution to propping.

[140] Pub. L. No. 106–102, 113 Stat. 1338 (November 12, 1999), which repealed the Glass–Steagall Act (1933).

[141] OECD, *Banks Under Stress* (Paris 1992).

[142] Banking Act (n. 97), s. 17(1). s. 17(3) defines a subsidiary.

[143] The proviso to this section provides for the acquisition of shares in a public company that is unlisted if such acquisition is necessary for purpose of rehabilitation of such company to make it financially viable.

of such percentage of its capital funds[144] as determined by the Monetary Board.[145] By determination of the Monetary Board such percentage is set at 10 percent of its capital funds,[146] provided that such acquisition or holding of shares shall not exceed 20 percent of the paid up capital of such listed public company. The determination also provides that the aggregate amount invested in the shares of listed public companies excluding companies which are subsidiaries of the bank, shall not exceed 30 percent of its capital funds.[147]

It is submitted that while some form of restriction is necessary with regard to banks holding shares in non-financial companies to protect financial sector stability, mitigate risk and diversify investments, low threshold restrictions with regard to the percentage of paid up capital of a company a commercial bank can hold or acquire, restricts equity investments that commercial banks may make in the companies they extend credit to, and affect the monitoring incentive of the lender. The way forward may be to retain restrictions with respect to capital funds, but not with regard to the paid up capital of a company. This has the advantage of mitigating risk and concurrently leaving it within the discretion of the bank as to the exact amount of paid up capital in a company it may wish to invest in.[148] The bank can exercise its discretion according to the ownership structures (i.e., the controlling shareholder's interests) and lending risk.

This is also prudent due to the predominance of cross-holdings and pyramids in Sri Lanka, and the likelihood that banks may hold controlling shareholdings in listed companies through equity shareholdings in holding companies, nullifying the effect of the regulation.

(c) *Single-Borrower Limit (Large Exposure Limit)*

A single-borrower limit is essential for the avoidance of conflict of interest transactions in countries such as Sri Lanka, where collusive

---

[144] Equity capital and reserve fund as set out in the Banking Act 1988 (n. 97).

[145] ibid s. 17A.

[146] In Singapore it is 20 percent of the capital base, in Taiwan 15 percent and in Hong Kong 25 percent. In Thailand, a bank may hold up to 10 percent of the equity capital of a non-financial company.

[147] Determination made by the Monetary Board of the Central Bank of Sri Lanka under section 17A(1)(a) and (1)(b) of the Banking Act No. 30 of 1988 (22 August 1997).

[148] This discretion is limited as a commercial bank cannot have as its subsidiary a company, which is not another financial institution.

connections exist between borrowers and lenders. Stringent requirements as to single-borrower limits reduce the credit risk of banks, prevent expropriation by way of private benefits of control, and tunnelling by controlling shareholders. It is one of the many firewalls to prevent self-dealing and conflict of interest transactions while at the same time vesting in lenders a degree of detachment from their borrowers.

Single-borrower limits for commercial banks in Sri Lanka are set out by directions issued by the Monetary Board under section 46(1) of the Banking Act. The single-borrower limit is set at 30 percent of the capital funds of the bank for any single company, public corporation, firm, association of persons or an individual or in the aggregate to customers such as 'an individual, his close relations or to a company ... in which he has a substantial interest'[149] or to a company and its subsidiaries or its holding company.[150] This is a sufficiently stringent limit as generally accepted international practices prescribe a ceiling of 25 percent.[151] However, given the prevalence of pyramids and cross-holdings involving banks in Sri Lanka, it is submitted that a lower limit on a single borrower (e.g., 25 percent) is likely to provide a degree of independence to the banking sector and strengthen their monitoring capabilities.

Further, the effectiveness of the requirement is diluted by permitting accommodations in excess of specified limits for certain named government undertakings and for purposes of infrastructure development projects.[152] A potential loophole for exceeding the single-borrower limit and thereby, engaging in tunnelling activities for financial conglomerates is also the exclusion from the computation of the single-borrower limit, accommodations granted against certain types of security including accommodations granted against the security of a guarantee or similar instrument issued by a licensed commercial bank or licensed specialised bank incorporated in Sri Lanka.[153]

While the single-borrower limit in Sri Lanka assists the monitoring role of lenders by its focus on credit allocation, there is the potential to strengthen the role and independence of lenders by more stringent requirements in relation to single-borrower limits.

---

[149] Banking Act (n. 97), s. 46(1) (c) (ii) (a).

[150] ibid s. 46(1) (c) (ii) (b).

[151] OECD, *Policy Brief on Corporate Governance in Banks in Asia* (Paris 2006), 27.

[152] Banking Act (Single-Borrower Limit) Directions No. 2 of 2005 as amended by Direction Nos. 3 and 5 of 2005.

[153] ibid as amended by Direction Nos. 3, 4 and 5 of 2005.

(d) *Rules on Related-Party Transactions between Lenders and Borrowers*

For lenders to be an effective corporate governance monitor, it is necessary that related-party transactions between lenders and borrowers be made at arms-length on market terms. The presence of controlling shareholders within lending institutions and the pyramid and cross-shareholding structures in Sri Lanka reinforce the argument for effective related-party rules on transactions between lenders and borrower companies. Related-party transactions made at arms-length on market terms prevent self-dealing in the form of private benefits of control or tunnelling and achieve for lenders a degree of independence to engage in monitoring.

The Banking Act by amendment in 2005 provides that a licensed commercial bank shall not grant an accommodation to a director of a licensed commercial bank or close relation of such director or to a concern in which any director has a substantial interest unless such accommodation is sanctioned at a meeting of the board of directors of the bank by the votes of not less than two-thirds of the number of its directors other than the director concerned.[154]

In principle, related-party transactions with directors should be reviewed by a sufficient number of independent directors capable of exercising independent judgement. Given that control of banks in Sri Lanka is associated with voting rights in excess of equity stakes, it is doubtful whether independent directors capable of exercising independent judgement exist. One alternative for the Central Bank of Sri Lanka, as an effective regulator, is to require mandatory voting caps on controlling shareholders in banks during election of independent directors or for directors to serve on certain committees such as a committee to review related-party transactions. The other option is for the Central Bank of Sri Lanka as regulator to consider the option of outright prohibition of certain types of related-party transactions between licensed commercial banks and directors.[155]

---

[154] Banking Act (n. 97), s. 47(3) and (5). An exception is given for an accommodation by credit card.

[155] Most jurisdictions by their companies acts prohibit loans by companies to their directors, with an exception for a company whose ordinary business includes the lending of money, Companies Act No. 7 of 2007 s. 217 restricts loans to director with an exception for private companies with unanimous approval of members.

Interestingly, while the granting of accommodations to directors or close relations of such director or to a concern in which any director has a substantial interest is regulated under the Banking Act, the granting of accommodations to a substantial shareholder (i.e., a shareholder who controls or controlled within the last 12 months 10 percent or more of the voting shares) is unregulated. This lacuna must be rectified if lenders are to effectively control the costs of controlling shareholders.

Rules on related-party transactions must also encompass public disclosure of such transactions. In the light of the Basel Committee's core principles,[156] it is desirable to set out guidelines with respect to the reporting of 'any transactions with related parties that pose special risk to the bank', which would encompass a wider range of transactions. This will undoubtedly require clear and defined criteria of what may consist of special risks.

(e) *Minimising Government Interference in the Banking Sector*

La Porta *et al.* in a study on government ownership of banks[157] reports that in 1995, 71.39 percent of the assets of the top 10 banks were owned and controlled by the GOSL. A study by the World Bank reports that 55 percent of the total bank assets in Sri Lanka are government owned.[158] While government ownership of banks is likely to affect a country's development, more relevantly, it affects lending practices of banks[159] and importantly the monitoring role of lenders. Government ownership of banks is also likely to propagate political influence among the financial and corporate sectors, which is a significant cost of the controlling shareholder system in Sri Lanka.[160]

---

[156] Basel Committee on Banking Supervision, *Core Principles for Effective Banking Supervision* (Basel 1997).

[157] R La-Porta, F Silanes and A Shleifer, Government Ownership of Banks (2002), 57 *Journal of Finance*, 265. The percentage of the assets owned by the government in a given bank is calculated by multiplying the share of each shareholder in that bank by the share the government owns in that shareholder, and then summing the resulting shares.

[158] Barth *et al.* (n. 136), Fig. 4. Other countries with over 60 percent of banks assets owned by the government are Bhutan, Egypt, Russia and Bangladesh.

[159] P Sapienza, The Effects of Government Ownership on Bank Lending (2004), 72 *Journal of Financial Economics*, 357.

[160] Chapter 5, Section 5.2.

It is recommended that government ownership of banks and bank assets be reduced by way of privatisation.[161] This will remove the role of the government in the banking sector[162] and also reduce the budget deficit financing by banks, a serious impediment to financial sector development and a direct cause of ownership concentration in Sri Lanka.[163]

While privatistion was actively pursued in Sri Lanka and six financial sector institutions were privatised in the past,[164] there is criticism of its process, the lack of transparency and lack of technical knowledge by evaluation committees. A study on the distributional effects of privatisation in Sri Lanka reports that more than 60 percent of the respondents opposed the privatisation of banks and ports.[165] This is disturbing in the light of the need to divest government ownership of banks and make future privatisation processes work.

7.4.2. *Improving Accountability of Borrowers: Disclosure and Transparency*

Disclosure is the classic answer to many conflicts of interest transactions. Lenders' effectiveness as a corporate governance monitor is affected by the disclosure and transparency regime within the country. Increased disclosure, which leads to transparency, has moved away from the traditional questioning of its role in monitoring corporate management to becoming a fundamental principle of corporate governance.[166]

There is recent evidence that an increase in mandatory disclosure requirements in a country is associated with a substantially lower level of

---

[161] International Monetary Fund, Summary and Policy Recommendations (2002), http://www.imf.org/external/country/lka/rr/pdf/031802.pdf [10 January 2006].

[162] For example, a reduction in NPLs. Bank NPLs to total loans is at 9.6 percent in 2005. In India it is 5.2 percent, Bangladesh 10.5 percent and Hong Kong 1.5 percent for the same period. International Monetary Fund, *Global Financial Stability Report: Market Developments and Issues* (Washington DC 2006) Table 24.

[163] Chapter 4.

[164] World Bank, Privatization Database (1998–2003), http://rru.worldbank.org/Privatization/ [10 February 2007].

[165] M Knight-John and P Athukorala, Assessing Privatization in Sri Lanka: Distribution and Governance, in J Nellis and N Birdsall (eds.), *Reality Check: The Distributional Impact of Privatization in Developing Countries* (Center for Global Development Washington DC 2005), 419.

[166] OECD, *OECD Principles of Corporate Governance: 2004* (Paris 2004).

private benefits of control for companies in that country.[167] In the light of this evidence, one would anticipate general acceptance that a mandatory disclosure regime is the most effective means to bring about capital market transparency.[168] But alternative views exist. Romano makes the controversial argument that mandatory disclosure is unnecessary and harmful,[169] as market forces ensure that companies disclose the optimal level of information.[170] More recently, a study in behavioural science[171] makes the claim that disclosure can have perverse effects. First, because people do not discount advice from biased advisors even when such advisors' conflicts of interest are disclosed and second, disclosure can encourage bias in advice because advisors feel morally licensed after disclosure has been made.[172]

Proponents of mandatory disclosure argue that mandatory or required disclosure has a useful function by its influence on corporate governance,[173] due to its value to potential and existing shareholders, but more importantly as it results in transparency, which assists monitoring.

The flip side of mandatory disclosure is that it raises contracting costs and invites interference in capital markets by politicians. Comparative corporate governance literature implies that optimal disclosure regimes differ among countries. While much of the literature in the past focused on mandatory disclosure in the US, the role of mandatory disclosure in countries with concentrated ownership patterns is gaining prominence.

---

[167] R La-Porta, F Lopez-de-Silanes and A Shleifer, What Works in Securities Laws? (2004), National Bureau of Economic Research Working Paper 9882, http://papers.nber.org/papers/w9882.pdf [20 May 2006], 16, Table III.

[168] Asian Development Bank (n. 53); EU Transparency Directive 2004/109/EC; A Ferrell, The Case for Mandatory Disclosure in Securities Regulation Around the World (2004), Harvard Law & Economics Discussion Paper 492, http://ssrn.com/abstract=631221 [10 July 2006].

[169] R Romano, Empowering Investors: A Market Approach to Securities Regulation (1998), 107 *Yale Law Journal*, 2359; R Romano, The Need for Competition in International Securities Regulation (2001), Yale International Center for Finance Working Paper 00–49, http://ssrn.com/abstract=278728 [25 July 2006].

[170] This goes back to the 'null hypothesis' (i.e., optimal government policy is to do nothing) associated with R Coase, The Problem of Social Cost (1960), 3 *Journal of Law and Economics*, 1.

[171] D Cain, G Lowenstein and D Moore, The Dirt on Coming Clean: Perverse Effects of Disclosing Conflicts of Interest (2005), 34 *Journal of Legal Studies*, 1.

[172] ibid 4–8.

[173] L Lowenstein, Financial Transparency and Corporate Governance: You Manage What You Measure (1996), 96 *Columbia Law Review*, 1335; M Fox, Required Disclosure and Corporate Governance (1999), 62(3) *Law and Contemporary Problems*, 113.

Ferrell makes the powerful argument supported by empirical research that 'a mandatory disclosure regime can reduce the level of diversion of corporate resources by controlling shareholders and promote competition (both for capital and in the product market)'.[174]

The case for mandatory disclosure is stronger in the context of developing countries. While self-regulatory corporate governance codes with voluntary disclosure are popular in developing countries, self-regulation depends on the efficiency of the system, the goodwill of the controlling shareholders and the voluntary compliance environment. In developing countries, underdeveloped capital markets make minimal or no disclosure demands on companies due to their inability to discipline. Further, the presence of controlling shareholders obstructs any voluntary disclosure detrimental to their interests. Therefore, mandatory disclosure provisions are prima facie desirable in developing countries and strengthen the role of lenders as corporate governance monitors.

It is also necessary to ensure that some of the benefits of controlling shareholder systems, such as monitoring and planning by controlling shareholders, are not stifled by increased disclosure standards. Controlling shareholders prefer imperfect disclosure to protect their private benefits of control.[175] Therefore, a balance needs to be achieved between prevention of private benefits of control, an increase in transparency to assist lenders in their role as corporate monitors, and the monitoring role of controlling shareholders.

The disclosure regime in Sri Lanka is examined under three heads: (a) financial disclosure, (b) disclosure on corporate governance practices and (c) disclosure with respect to material information and related-party transactions.

(a) *Financial Disclosure*

Financial disclosure serves as an assessment of management and share value.[176] It increases competition in capital and product markets due to

---

[174] Ferrell (n. 168), 5.

[175] ibid.

[176] K Hofstetter, One Size Does Not Fit All: Corporate Governance for "Controlled Companies" (2005), http://www.hertig.ethz.ch/LE_200506_files/Papers/Hofstetter_Corporate_Governance_2005.pdf [10 February 2006].

higher credibility levels[177] and also mitigates the potential for insider trading and the extraction of private benefits of control. However, financial disclosure regimes can be burdensome, costly both in terms of money and result in the loss of competitive advantage by the disclosure of proprietary information.

The regulatory framework for financial disclosure in Sri Lanka is contained in the Companies Act[178] and the Listing Rules[179] of the CSE, which enumerate disclosures in annual financial statements to be made by private and public companies and companies listed on the CSE. As the quality of financial transparency and disclosure depends on accounting and auditing standards and the financial reporting system, the regulatory regime also encompasses SLAS promulgated by the ICASL and monitored by the SLAASMB, which are mostly in line with internationally accepted accounting and auditing rules.[180]

In controlling shareholder systems where corporate groups are mechanisms to leverage control in excess of ownership, financial disclosure with respect to group accounts is a primary mechanism to curb private benefits of control by making the market aware of the financial standing of the corporate group as a whole. This is achieved by consolidation of the accounts of a parent and its subsidiaries, which eliminates intergroup transactions and treats the entities as a single company.

The Companies Act requires that proper books of account are kept[181] and also mandates that if a company has subsidiaries, such company prepare group accounts consisting of consolidated accounts dealing with the profit or loss and state of affairs of itself and its subsidiaries.[182]

Publicly traded companies and specified business enterprises are rightly compelled by virtue of the listing rules of the CSE and the

---

[177] Ferrell (n. 168).

[178] Companies Act 2007 (n. 155), ss. 148–169.

[179] Colombo Stock Exchange, Listing Rules 2004, requires listed companies to present interim financial reports (r. 8.3) and for audited accounts to be prepared in accordance with Sri Lanka Accounting Standards (r. 8.6).

[180] For a comparison of SLAS with International Accounting Standards (IAS) and the more recent International Financial Reporting Standards (IFRS) — Deloitte Financial Reporting Framework in Sri Lanka (2006), http://www.iasplus.com/country/srilanka.htm [10 June 2006]. The growing gap between SLAS and IFRS is due to the slow pace at which the standards are adopted in Sri Lanka.

[181] Companies Act 2007 (n. 155), s. 148.

[182] ibid ss. 152–153.

Sri Lanka Accounting and Auditing Standards Act, to adhere to SLAS which has promulgated accounting standards in respect of 'consolidated and separate financial statements' for group companies, 'investments in associates', 'revenue recognition and disclosures in the financial statements of banks'[183] and 'revenue recognition and disclosures in the financial statements of finance companies'.[184]

The frequency of disclosure mandated for companies listed on the CSE and required to present interim financial reports is quarterly or half-yearly,[185] while all other companies are expected to prepare their financial statements 6 months after balance sheet date[186] and public companies need to ensure their registration at the company registry within 20 working days.[187] The Companies Act also mandates that shareholders be entitled to receive a copy of the balance sheet and annual report 15 working days before the date of the annual general meeting.[188] Additionally, Specified Business Enterprises and listed companies under the Sri Lanka Accounting and Auditing Standards Act 1995 are required to submit their annual reports to the SLAASMB for regular review.

In the light of the above, it appears that the legal and regulatory framework in Sri Lanka provides for sufficiently stringent mandatory financial disclosure. In practice, it is far from flawless. It is submitted that financial disclosure with respect to group accounts can be improved by broadening the definitions of holding and subsidiary companies and ensuring effective monitoring of corporate groups by lenders. For example, financial disclosure with respect to group accounts is invariably linked to definitions of a holding and subsidiary company.[189] The Companies Act definition[190] is limited to the parent company being (a) a member of its subsidiary and controlling the composition of its board of directors or (b) holding more than half the nominal value of the subsidiary's equity share capital (voting

---

[183] Sri Lanka Accounting Standards 2006, Standard 23.

[184] For which there is no corresponding IAS (n. 180).

[185] For entities listed on main board (equities) this will be quarterly, while entities on second board (equities) and debt securities board this will be half-yearly. Colombo Stock Exchange, Listing Rules 2004 (n. 179), r. 8.3.

[186] Companies Act 2007 (n. 155), s. 150.

[187] ibid s. 170.

[188] ibid s. 167.

[189] Also of importance in areas other than financial disclosure.

[190] Companies Act 1982 (n. 124), s. 150. Progressive change has been brought about by the Companies Act 2007 (n. 155), s. 529.

or nonvoting) or (c) such subsidiary being a subsubsidiary. The focus on majority shareholding and not necessarily 'control' (i.e., voting control) means that some entities which are de facto controlled by another entity but not coming within the above definition, would not be part of the consolidated financial statements of the group and in consequence not present a true reflection of the group's financial standing.

It is submitted that at a minimum, the definition of subsidiary and holding company should be pegged to the ability of the holding company to control more than half the voting rights of its subsidiary. In the context of controlling shareholder systems utilising group mechanisms, it is prudent, at least from a financial disclosure perspective to use a definition which encompasses the ability of one entity to exert a 'dominant influence' over another by the use of shareholder agreements or the memorandum and articles of association[191] or alternatively to control the composition of the board of directors without necessarily being a member of such subsidiary,[192] as in the case of pyramids. Further, the failure of the Companies Act definition to encompass entities such as partnerships and associated companies in its definition of a holding company and subsidiary for purposes of group accounts is clearly in conflict with SLAS and IAS/IFRS and provides a loophole for public companies with regard to consolidation of group accounts and enables the extraction of private benefits of control through the use of off-balance sheet transactions.[193]

In contrast, the SLAS in setting out requirements with regard to 'consolidated and separate financial statements' for group companies, defines a 'subsidiary' as an entity, including an unincorporated entity such as a partnership, that is controlled by another entity, and 'control' is broadly defined as the power to govern the financial and operating policies of an entity so as to obtain benefit from its activities.[194] Further, SLAS provides

---

[191] Companies Act 2006 (UK) s. 1162 and Schedule 7; Sri Lankan Companies Act 2007 (n. 155), s. 529 has significantly improved the definition of a subsidiary company; however, there is a lacuna with respect to voting arrangements.

[192] New Zealand Companies Act 1993, s. 5.

[193] T Hadden, Regulating Corporate Groups: An International Perspective, in J McCahery, S Picciotto and C Scott (eds.), *Corporate Control and Accountability* (Clarendon Oxford 1993), 360, associated companies not technically regarded as subsidiaries for purposes of consolidated accounts may be used as 'off balance sheet' vehicles to conceal significant transactions.

[194] Sri Lanka Accounting Standards 2006 (n. 183), Standard 26(4). Also Standard 26 (13) for presumptions of control.

for an accounting standard for 'investments in associates',[195] and defines an 'associate' as an entity including an unincorporated entity such as a partnership over which the investor has significant influence (presumed to be 20 percent or more of the voting power of the investee) and that is neither a subsidiary nor an interest in a joint venture.[196] The SLAS definitions with respect to subsidiary, control and associate are sufficiently broad and capable of encompassing a broader range of controlling shareholder systems than those envisaged by the legislation. This is welcome especially in the light of the financial disclosures being regulated and their application to listed public companies by virtue of the listing rules of the CSE and the Sri Lanka Accounting and Auditing Standards Act[197] and facilitates the monitoring by lenders of public companies listed on the CSE and other specified business enterprises.

A further regulatory change that may be adopted in respect of financial disclosure is with regard to methods of valuation. In the light of the prevalence of controlling shareholders, it is prudent to require the adoption of a market value method with respect to investments in associates instead of allowing a choice between the equity method[198] and the cost method of valuation. This is in line with IFRS and is also less likely to be subject to manipulation by the parent company or controlling shareholders who may choose to use a method of valuation best suited to their interests. Other regulatory changes can encompass the disclosure of audit and non-audit services fees separately, and mandate the use of IAS/IFRS without modification amidst strengthened enforcement.

While considerable efforts are made in aligning accounting and auditing practices with international standards to establish high-quality corporate financial reporting, there is a certain degree of noncompliance in both accounting and auditing practices, resulting mainly from weak enforcement. The weakness is primarily attributed to inadequate regulatory

---

[195] ibid Standard 27.

[196] ibid Standard 27(2) and (4).

[197] Sri Lanka Accounting and Auditing Standards Act No. 15 of 1995, supplemented by Sri Lanka Accounting and Auditing Standards Monitoring Board, *Information of Importance to Companies, Public Corporations, Directors, Managers, Secretaries and other Officers, and Auditors* (2001).

[198] The equity method is a method of accounting whereby the investment is initially recorded at cost and adjusted thereafter for the post acquisition change in the investor's share of net assets of the investee. Sri Lanka Accounting Standards 2006, Standard 27(2).

capacity.[199] Lenders in a monitoring capacity may to a certain extent overcome this deficiency in enforcement by demanding compliance with the regulatory framework as a condition to lending. This should not be misunderstood as advocating that lenders should in any way replace an independent financial standards monitor.

The monitoring role of lenders can also be strengthened in the area of financial disclosure by the Central Bank of Sri Lanka setting out directions that lenders extend credit facilities beyond a stipulated amount only after ensuring that borrowers comply with the auditing and accounting standards.

(b) *Disclosures with regard to Corporate Governance Practices*

There is importance placed on corporate governance disclosures due to various international corporate governance codes, such as the OECD Principles of Corporate Governance 2004[200] and Commonwealth Association for Corporate Governance Principles of Corporate Governance and national codes such as the Combined Code adopted in the UK and the American Legal Institute (ALI) Principles of Corporate Governance.[201] The downside of the availability of a large number of corporate governance codes for guidance is that many developing countries have found it convenient to adopt these principles without reference to the prevailing local governance issues such as entrenchment or the extraction of private benefits of control.

If lenders are to be an effective corporate governance monitor and ensure that the costs of controlling shareholders are curbed, it is necessary for an effective framework to be in place whereby companies are required to make adequate disclosure with regard to their adherence to corporate governance practices. While it is submitted that disclosure of corporate governance practices are of importance not only for controlling shareholder systems, the importance attached to the information differs according to the ownership structure (e.g., the actual control exerted by controlling shareholders).

---

[199] World Bank, *Report on the Observance of Standards and Codes Sri Lanka: Accounting and Auditing* (Washington DC 2004).

[200] OECD (n. 166).

[201] American Law Institute, *Principles of Corporate Governance: Analysis and Recommendations* (Philadelphia 1994).

Disclosures of importance to a corporate monitor in controlling shareholder systems are (i) disclosure with regard to shareholdings; (ii) disclosure with regard to shareholdings by directors and (iii) disclosure with respect to board composition and board committees.

(i) *Disclosure with regard to shareholdings*

The Companies Act[202] mandates that companies registered under the Act file an annual return, containing a list of members together with a list of those who have ceased to be members since the last return date, together with holdings of each class of share and particulars of any transfers. While the 1982 Act obliged any person who became owner of more than one-tenth of the issued share capital of the company, to inform the company of this fact,[203] this provision is removed from the 2007 Act. This has taken away an important alerting mechanism on substantial acquisition of shares.

The Listing Rules of the CSE applicable to listed companies mandate the disclosure in annual reports the number of holders in each class of equity securities and the percentage of their total holdings, the names of the 20 largest holders of equity and the number of securities and percentage of capital held by them.[204] It also mandates the disclosure of the percentage of shares held by the public.[205] Public holdings are defined as excluding holdings by parent, subsidiaries and associate companies, directors, CEOs and their spouses and children or companies in which a director's holdings exceed 50 percent of the equity or where the director controls the composition of the board of directors of such other company or any shareholder holding in excess of 10 percent of the issued share capital.

Although both the Companies Act 2007 and the CSE listing rules mandate periodic disclosure with regard to equity ownership, there is no provision for disclosure to encompass beneficial ownership of shares. Thus, it is possible for the *names* of beneficial owners to be outside the public domain where nominees are used or inadequate disclosure made where control rights attached to shares are separated from legal ownership.

---

[202] Companies Act 2007 (n. 155), s. 131.

[203] No. 17 of 1982 (n. 124), s. 199.

[204] Colombo Stock Exchange, Listing Rules, June 2001 (n. 179), r. 8.7 (f) and (g).

[205] ibid r. 8.7 (h).

In Sri Lanka with controlling shareholder systems, the focus of disclosure with regard to shareholdings should be on control rights. This will serve to inform both lenders as monitors of borrower companies and shareholders of the identity of the controlling shareholders thereby, bring about a greater degree of transparency and act as a deterrent to insider trading and related-party transactions. Thus, it is useful to mandate the disclosure of 'control over voting rights'[206] in listed companies in the interests of transparency with a starting threshold of at least 10 percent. This threshold must not be set too low since it may further stifle the already nearly nonexistent market for takeovers. However, setting a threshold helps identify shareholders with the ability to influence or control the company. It is also prudent to incorporate such requirement in the listing rules,[207] as is the practice in other jurisdictions.

It is useful to avoid the circumvention of these rules by the division of 'control over voting rights' between a number of subsidiaries or associates by requiring parties who can be labelled as 'acting in concert' to amalgamate their interests for purposes of disclosure and by requiring the disclosure of family and corporate interests.[208] It is also useful to mandate disclosure in the event 'control over voting rights' exceed certain thresholds, such as 20 percent, 25 percent, 50 percent and 75 percent, making shareholders aware of the exact amount of influence or control exerted by the controlling shareholders. Disclosure of 'control over voting rights' must ensure that the disclosure is a useful signal to the market, especially to a corporate monitor and is effective in bringing about greater transparency and

---

[206] There is a choice of terminology available with regard to the nature of interest requiring disclosure. The English Companies Act 1985 and 2006 uses the terminology 'interest in shares'. This may in some circumstances be more stringent and extensive-Financial Services Authority Implementation of the Transparency Directive, Investment Entities, Listing Review (2006), Part 1, Chapter 3.

Further, the Rules Governing Substantial Acquisitions of Shares (SARs) issued by the Panel on Takeovers and Mergers and applicable to companies listed on the LSE uses the terminology 'rights over shares'.

An alternative terminology was suggested by the Department of Trade and Industry (UK), *Proposals for Reform of Part VI of the Companies Act 1985* (April 1995), 16 — 'control, possession of and the right to acquire voting rights, and the right to dispose of vote-carrying shares'. This definition would encompass voting arrangements not involving the acquisition of shares.

[207] Colombo Stock Exchange, Listing Rules, r. 9.1 (iv) 8, requires prompt announcement of a change in control. However, as to what would amount to 'control' is not defined.

[208] Companies Act 2006 (UK) (n. 191), s. 82, 823 and 832.

curbing private benefits of control, rather than the mere provision of more information.

Enforcements mechanisms must be in place to ensure timely disclosure. It is suggested that public companies be given a self-help remedy in the form of a right to demand information on beneficial ownership of shares, to avoid companies shying away from their duty of disclosure on the basis of lack of information as to shareholdings.

(ii) *Disclosure with respect to shareholdings by directors*

The risk of directors extracting private benefits of control or making decisions detrimental to the company or its members is greater due to the relationship that exists between them and the company. There is also the likelihood of misuse of non-public inside information.

As reflected in the empirical data,[209] controlling shareholders in Sri Lanka use management positions to strengthen their positions of control within companies. While effective disclosure with regard to shareholdings by directors is pertinent even in circumstances where directors are not controlling shareholders, it is of far greater importance in controlling shareholder systems where controlling shareholders occupy management positions. Disclosure with regard to directors' shareholdings enable lenders to monitor the activities of the directors with greater transparency and therefore, acts as a deterrent to the extraction of private benefits of control or entrenchment.

The Companies Act 2007[210] requires every company to maintain a register of directors' shareholdings. This register showed the number, description and amount of shares or debentures held by each director (and director's spouse, child and corporate body controlled by such director) of the company or company's subsidiary or holding company or a subsidiary of the holding company. The register also included information of shares held in trust and information of any shares in respect of which the director, spouse or child has the right to become holder. The CSE listing rules also mandate the disclosure of a statement of each director's holdings (including spouse, children and nominees) in securities of the entity at the beginning and end of each financial year in the company's annual report.[211]

---

[209] Chapter 3.

[210] Companies Act 2007 (n. 155), s. 198.

[211] Colombo Stock Exchange, Listing Rules, r. 8.7 (c) (June 2001).

The disclosure of holdings in securities as mandated by the Companies Act 1982 and the CSE listing rules, did not encompass the element of 'control' until the introduction of the 2007 Act.[212] The 2007 Act also requires the immediate disclosure of director's dealings of 'relevant interests in shares'.[213] Immediate disclosure of a director's dealings with 'control over voting rights' of the company is important for two reasons. First, increased disclosure of the exact amount of control exerted on the company by a director can act as a deterrent to the extraction of private benefits of control. Second, it can act as a deterrent to insider trading of securities by directors.

Regulatory reform must focus on effective enforcement of automatic disclosure of director's dealings with 'control over voting rights' to ensure greater transparency. Unlike disclosure of shareholdings by controlling shareholders, it is not necessary to set minimum thresholds to trigger disclosure, as directors are in positions of management and therefore, even the smallest interest in the shares of the company (or debentures)[214] is sufficient to create conflicts of interest. It is also necessary to ensure that a person who becomes a director makes such disclosure on taking up appointment. To deter insider trading by directors, it is necessary to mandate the disclosure of the consideration paid or received by directors.

(iii) *Disclosure with respect to board composition and board committees*

The Companies Act 2007 mandates the filing with the Registrar of Companies within 21 days of the appointment of a director information about the director such as name, address, occupation, etc.[215] The CSE listing rules also mandate that the annual report of the company include details of the persons who were directors of the company during the year.[216]

However, there is no requirement for the register to contain any information with regard to directorships in other companies of which such company is a subsidiary or such other companies are the subsidiaries of either

---

[212] Companies Act 2007 (n. 155), ss. 198–200.

[213] ibid s. 200.

[214] Directors can engage in private benefit extraction to the detriment of the creditors as well as shareholders.

[215] Companies Act 2007 (n. 155), s. 223.

[216] Colombo Stock Exchange, Listing Rules (n. 179), r. 8.7 (a) (June 2001).

such company or of another company of which such company is a subsidiary, to ensure greater transparency especially in the event of a conflict of interest transaction. As controlling shareholders are likely to occupy management positions to strengthen their control, mandating the disclosure of board composition (between executive and nonexecutive) and information with regard to directorships in companies within pyramids or cross-holdings is prudent. Such disclosure can also help avoid conflict of interest transactions.

The ICASL Exposure Draft on Boardroom Governance envisages the presence of a remuneration committee and audit committee and the SEC/ICASL code of best practices on corporate governance provides for the voluntary disclosure of the composition by name of the audit committee, the work undertaken by the audit committee during the financial year, the number of times that the audit committee met during the year and significant issues addressed by the audit committee including review of financial reports and internal controls.[217]

In controlling shareholder systems disclosure on the balance between executive and non-executive directors on corporate boards, transparency with regard to remuneration and audit can curb the extraction of private benefits of control. Further, within controlling shareholder systems, non-executive directors can play a significant role as watchdogs on behalf of the minority shareholders and build lender confidence. Therefore, disclosure with regard to their presence on the board and board committees is significant.

(c) *Disclosure of Material Information*

Public disclosure of material information is fuelled by the old adage that 'sunshine is the best disinfectant'. In controlling shareholder systems, disclosure of material information curtails tunnelling and extraction of private benefits of control, and assists the monitoring role of lenders by giving lenders access to relevant information. Material information is information not in the public domain but likely to impact on the price of a company's securities.[218]

---

[217] Securities and Exchange Commission of Sri Lanka and Institute of Chartered Accountants of Sri Lanka Rules on Corporate Governance for Listed Companies 2008.

[218] Colombo Stock Exchange, Listing Rules (n. 179), r. 9.1 (ii), defines 'material information' as 'information of a factual nature that has a bearing on the value of an Entity's securities or on investor decisions as to whether or not to invest or trade in such securities'.

Public companies listed on the CSE in Sri Lanka are required by the listing rules[219] to make immediate disclosure of material information, such as a change in control or resignation of a CEO or change in directors. However, the disclosure obligations contained in the CSE listing rules are inadequate. First, some of these obligations are of a subjective nature with regard to transactions by listed companies and hinder the monitoring ability of a lender, for example, information with regard to the borrowing of funds[220] requires a prompt announcement if considered material in the opinion of the board of directors. It is similar with regard to the purchase or sale of an asset or even an investment with a material impact on the entity.[221] It is submitted that the subjectivity of the disclosure obligations must be removed and prompt disclosure mandated for transactions of the company according to the comparative size of the transaction.[222] It is also prudent to require significant transactions, to be approved by shareholders in general meeting. Second, the effectiveness of the disclosure obligations is impeded by the lack of effective information dissemination. There is no primary information provider such as the Regulatory Information Service in the UK and as a result disclosure of material information is made to the CSE. While commercial information services are expensive, it is essential that an effective mechanism be used to ensure that disclosures made by listed companies are publicly disseminated. This would be in the interests of both investors and a credible monitor.

Companies not listed on the CSE are not under any continuing obligation to make disclosures with regard to developments in the company's business likely to affect the price of a company's securities. Extension of the rules of the duty to make an immediate disclosure to shareholders with regard to transactions likely to affect the company may be too onerous a requirement for all companies, but it may be useful to extend the rule to large public companies (i.e., based on turnover).

(d) *Disclosure and Approval of Related-Party Transactions*

A related party is a substantial shareholder, a director or any individual or entity connected to such shareholder or director. In controlling shareholder

---

[219] ibid r. 9 (iv), requires immediate disclosure of information likely to have a significant effect on the price of any of the entities equities.

[220] ibid r. 9(v) 3.

[221] ibid r. 9(v) 5, 9.

[222] Similar to the 'class tests' under the London Stock Exchange, Listing Rules 2003 (UK).

systems, the disclosure and approval of related-party transactions is of utmost importance, and is likely to preclude the extraction of private benefits of control or tunnelling.

The Sri Lankan Companies Act 2007 requires that a director directly or indirectly interested in a contract or a proposed contract disclose the nature of his/her interest forthwith to the board.[223] However, there is no statutory requirement to obtain the approval of a disinterested board for such transactions.[224] In fact, it is expressly stated that a director may vote on a matter relating to the transaction in which he/she is interested.[225] While the requirement of approval by a disinterested board is unlikely to be as effective in controlling shareholder systems, a requirement that a director obtains approval from a disinterested board strengthens the monitoring role of lenders in companies with interlocking directorships with lenders.

There are no provisions in the Companies Act 2007 or the CSE listing rules, dealing with transactions with a substantial shareholder or any person or entity exerting significant influence over the company. This lacunae is a significant drawback to the monitoring role of lenders and is likely to permit the extraction of private benefits of control and tunnelling. If lenders are to play an effective corporate governance role in Sri Lanka, it is essential that the disclosure regime with regard to related-party transactions be extended to the disclosure of transactions with persons able to exert a significant influence over the company. For listed companies, it is prudent to require the approval of the company in general meeting for certain specified transactions classified by their size relative to the company's assets, profits or turnover or gross capital.[226]

To summarise, regulatory reform in the area of disclosure and transparency in Sri Lanka is of utmost importance. First, disclosure of financial information, corporate governance practices, material information or related-party transactions strengthen the monitoring role of lenders by making information about borrower companies accessible. It can be argued that lenders do not need the protection of a specific disclosure and transparency regime, as they are able to demand disclosures through debt covenants. While this is largely correct, a disclosure and transparency regime augments any specific rights. The only drawback is the need to process the volume of

---

[223] Companies Act 2007 (n. 155), s. 192.

[224] As required by Companies Act 2006 (UK) (n. 191), s. 175.

[225] Companies Act 2007 (n. 155), ss. 191, 192 and 196.

[226] 'Class tests' under the London Stock Exchange, Listing Rules 2003 (UK) (n. 222), Chapters 10 and 11.

information. Second, an effective disclosure and transparency regime can curtail some of the costs of controlling shareholder systems such as private benefits of control, tunnelling, entrenchment and abuse of market power.

While regulatory reform in the area of disclosure is a first step, disclosure is likely to be more effective and transparent if market institutions are likely to demand it. Therefore, lenders can also self-empower themselves as a corporate governance mechanism by demanding such disclosures prior to lending decisions.

7.4.3. *Improving Rights of Lenders*

The effectiveness of lenders as a mechanism to control the costs of controlling shareholder systems is linked to the protection of creditor rights. Creditor rights must be guaranteed if a jurisdiction is to obtain the disciplining effect of debt. However, strengthening creditor rights must be tempered with incentivising the monitoring role of lenders. If creditor rights are unduly strengthened, especially with regard to requirements of collateral, it is likely that creditors are unlikely to engage in any *ex ante* or *ex post* monitoring of the borrowers.

Rights of lenders encompass mechanisms in place to secure lenders' rights in (a) Creation and enforcement of security in real property, (b) Creation and enforcement of security in personal property and (c) Mechanisms to align rights of creditors with management in the event of insolvency.

(a) *Lenders' Rights in the Creation of Real and Personal Property*

The Roman-Dutch law[227] and the Mortgage Act 1949[228] govern mortgages over real and personal property in Sri Lanka.

---

[227] Under Roman-Dutch law, the mortgagor does not transfer title of the property to the mortgagee, but continues to retain title. Thus, the mortgagee does not have a right of ownership to the property but only the right to recover payment of the debt. This is different to the English common law mortgage where ownership of the mortgaged property is transferred to the lender but possession retained by mortgagor until repayment or default. S Abeyratne, *Banking and Debt Recovery in Developing Countries: The Law Reform Context* (Ashgate London 2001), 119.

[228] No. 6 of 1949.

A significant obstacle previously faced by lenders in the creation of security over real property was the limitation in the meaning of 'mortgaged property', which is now overcome by way of an amendment[229] allowing lending institutions which lend in excess of a defined monetary amount[230] to be able to proceed against any other property belonging to the mortgagor, in addition to the property mortgaged. However, no process for the sale or seizure of such other property shall be issued until the mortgaged property is sold and the proceeds applied in satisfaction of the order.[231] Effective recording and registration procedures for securities taken on real property are also in place. However, registration by itself does not confer validity, only priority.[232]

The law relating to the creation of security in personal property recognises security over movables in the form of a pledge or a mortgage created by way of registration.[233] Mortgage of movable property without registration, must be accompanied by actual delivery of the movable property.[234] A mortgage without actual delivery to the lender only confers validity but not priority.[235] While the Sri Lankan Companies Act recognises a floating charge as a valid charge,[236] very few if any floating charges are created. This is attributed to ignorance or fear of enforcement of such charge.[237]

There is in an overall reluctance on the part of lenders to lend to companies on flexible terms, which affects their ability to become a corporate governance mechanism. If lenders are to become an effective corporate governance mechanism, they must be inspired by a flexible collateral regime. For this purpose it is essential to enact clear laws relating to secured transactions and to encourage the use of personal property as collateral. It is also necessary to establish a separate and computerised system of registering movables, capable of conferring a degree of priority by registration.

---

[229] Mortgage Amendment Act No. 3 of 1990, amended s. 46 of the Mortgage Act 1949 (n. 228), and introduced s. 47A.

[230] Presently SLRS 150,000.

[231] Mortgage Act 1949 (n. 228), s. 47A(2).

[232] Registration of Documents Ordinance No. 23 of 1927 s. 7.

[233] Registration of Documents Ordinance 1927; Prevention of Frauds Ordinance 1840.

[234] Registration of Documents Ordinance 1927 (n. 233), ss. 17, 18 and Prevention of Frauds Ordinance 1840 (n. 233), s. 18.

[235] Registration of Documents Ordinance 1927 (n. 233), s. 7.

[236] Companies Act 2007 (n. 155), ss. 427–433, the new Act has detailed provisions relating to floating charges, which were absent from the previous Act.

[237] Abeyratne (n. 227), 124.

There is also the need to establish a system of checks on the registration system, to minimise interference and alteration of such records.

(b) *Lenders' Rights in the Enforcement of Real and Personal Property*

While the statutory provisions for the enforcement of security in Sri Lanka are sufficiently stringent,[238] lenders face a serious handicap due to inordinate delays when recovering through the court process.[239]

Lenders realise security under the Mortgage Act 1949[240] or by way of *parate*[241] execution. Enforcement of security by way of *parate* action which was previously exercisable by a few state banks,[242] was extended to all licensed commercial banks by the Recovery of Loans by Banks (Special Provisions) Act.[243] Despite the stringent statutory provisions available to banks to dispose of collateral both movable and immovable under the *parate* system, the level of actual realisations is low as *parate* execution is obstructed by injunctions that cause significant delays.[244] There is also reluctance on the part of the courts to enforce this remedy, which is viewed as deplorable and harsh. The rights of lenders in enforcement of security by way of *parate* executions is also constrained by the recent landmark case of *Ramachandran and another v. Anandasiva.*[245] where the Sri Lanka Supreme Court held that a mortgaged property which belonged to a guarantor or to another third party other than a borrower cannot be subject to *parate* execution. It is also unclear if *parate* execution is available to a

---

[238] After enactment of 14 laws relating to debt recovery in 1990.

[239] It is not possible to state with accuracy the number of cases pending before courts due to the lack of statistical data but it is estimated that the average delay is about 6 years.

[240] Mortgage Act 1949 (n. 228).

[241] *Parate executie* in Roman-Dutch law allows a creditor to realise the property of its debtor without first obtaining court sanction.

[242] There are also specific provisions in the Bank of Ceylon Act Ordinance No. 53 of 1938, People's Bank Act No. 29 of 1961 and State Mortgage Bank Act No. 16 of 1956.

[243] No. 4 of 1990 and Recovery of Loans by Banks (Amendment)(Special Provisions) Act No. 24 of 1995 extended the definition of a 'bank' in terms of s. 22.

[244] S Kelegama and K Parikh, Political Economy of Growth and Reforms in South Asia, in I Ahluwalia and J Williamson (eds.), *South Asian Experience with Growth* (Oxford University Press New Delhi 2003), report that a backlog of 15,000 debt recovery cases are pending in Sri Lankan courts.

[245] [SC Appeal No. 05/2004] Justice Bandaranayake in dissenting attempted to determine the intention of the legislature in enacting this legislation.

bank in a syndicate of banks who have obtained concurrent security in the property.[246]

A crucial issue facing lenders in developing countries including Sri Lanka is the efficiency of enforcement procedures. This results in the denial of credit to many borrowers, and lenders becoming risk averse and unwilling to lend to borrowers without adequate security.[247] The taking of security over and above the risk incurred makes lenders lazy and unwilling to monitor. This impedes their ability to become an effective corporate governance mechanism.

Enforcement of security is by way of civil actions according to the provisions of the Civil Procedure Code of 1890.[248] A lender may institute action by way of ordinary procedure or summary procedure,[249] (to recover debts in certain types of commercial actions, namely, recovery of dues on negotiable instruments, liquidated demands under a written contract and under an enactment or guarantee) where the defendant is not entitled to defend the claim against him as of right, but can apply to court for leave to defend. Summary procedure in Sri Lanka is also of limited application due to a misconception of the term 'debt or a liquidated demand in money' narrowly interpreted as applicable to documents referred to immediately before the expression, that is, bill of exchange, promissory note or cheque.[250] It is necessary for reforms to enlarge the scope of this procedure to enable its application to the recovery of monies arising out of all contractual obligations.

With the enactment of the Debt Recovery (Special Provisions) Act,[251] a change was brought about in debt recovery procedure for lending institutions, enabling the issue of decree *nisi* at the outset of the action.[252] Despite the availability of additional powers to recover debts due to lenders, in

---

[246] Although a Bill amending the Act No. 4 of 1990 (n. 240), and clarifying this issue was proposed, the constitutionality of such Bill was successfully challenged as inconsistent with Article 12(1) of the constitution, SC Special Determination 22/03.

[247] Poor debt recovery has a wider impact on economic growth by impeding investment, the denial of borrowings to those without security perpetuating inequalities in society. It also encourages dishonest borrowers to abuse the system.

[248] Both under regular procedure and summary procedure on liquid claims under Chapter LIII. A major concern was the inevitable delay in taking the steps stipulated by the code.

[249] Civil Procedure Code 1890, ss. 703–711.

[250] *Sabapatipillai v. Jaffna Trading Co* 4 Ceylon Recorder 210.

[251] No. 2 of 1990.

[252] ibid ss. 4, 5A.

practice, these procedures are not as effective as anticipated. There is judicial indifference with judges treating all cases whether under regular procedure or newer procedures similarly.[253] There is also unfamiliarity with the new procedures and lack of infrastructure for enforcement.[254] Therefore, the reform process must focus on clinical legal education and judicial training.

There is also political and social pressure, especially on state-owned banks, to refrain from auctioning collateral. Further, banks selling foreclosed property are required by the terms of the Banking Act 1988[255] to obtain Monetary Board approval of the sale price. This prevents banks from selling at a price that is lower than the market value set by the authorities and acts as a considerable impediment to the realisation of collateral. Banks are also reluctant to write off loans even if fully provisioned due to fear that this will weaken their ability to collect through legal action.

If lenders are to be an effective corporate governance mechanism in Sri Lanka, it is necessary that steps be taken to protect their rights especially in the creation and enforcement of security in real and personal property. Delays encountered by lenders in the enforcement of security must be minimised by the enactment of provisions to curtail the powers of borrowers to file enjoining orders or interim injunctions restraining lenders from taking steps pursuant to a *parate* execution resolution after a specified period of time. While *parate* execution is a powerful enforcement tool in the hands of lenders, it should be tempered in its use by lenders especially with regard to companies which are in need of restructuring.[256] A further factor, which inhibits lenders' rights in the enforcement of security over real property, is the costs payable in court proceedings. Taxed costs under the Civil Procedure Code 1890[257] are not sufficiently commensurate with the actual expenses incurred in legal proceedings.

To incentivise lenders and reduce the cost of credit, it is also necessary to have in place effective rules on repossession of collateral. However, effective creditor rights encompassing repossession of collateral and enabling effective enforcement of creditor rights while resulting

---

[253] Abeyratne (n. 227), 179.

[254] ibid 180.

[255] Banking Act 1988 (n. 97), s. 49.

[256] As successful restructuring can result in assets remaining for utilisation by a company unlike *parate* execution (i.e., like Chapter 11 in the US); Institute of Policy Studies, *Parate Execution in Sri Lanka: Necessity, Impact & Prospects* (Colombo 2001).

[257] Costs (Regulations) 1997 made under s. 214 Civil Procedure Code 1890 (n. 249).

in cheap credit may inhibit the monitoring function of creditors, if the collateral provided by the borrower is valued in excess of the debt and may make creditors lazy especially with regard to *ex ante* monitoring of borrowers. While strong rights to repossess collateral give lenders an essential threat to ensure that borrowers do not use the money borrowed unproductively or hide the proceeds of the project from their creditors and default on their repayment obligations, it can also be a substitute for screening of projects.[258] Therefore, protection of creditor rights to repossess collateral while undoubtedly important to ensure that creditors engage in lending must be tempered with limits on requirements for collateral. This is of importance in Sri Lanka, where banks have been criticised for their focus on collateral rather than the cash flow of their corporate borrowers.[259]

(c) *Rights of Creditors in the Event of Insolvency*

The ability of banks to effectively collect bad debts strengthens the role of lenders as a corporate governance mechanism. Insolvency laws need to effectively signal not only insolvency but also corporate distress and the need for restructuring; any creditor should be able to start the process; there must be accountability for wrongful depletion of assets which adversely affects creditors, and there must be recognition in certain circumstances of a duty on directors to consider or act in the interests of creditors of a company.

Under the provisions of the Companies Act 2007,[260] and the Winding Up Rules,[261] a creditor may bring an action for a compulsory winding up if the company is deemed unable to pay its debts,[262] or pass a resolution for a creditor's voluntary winding up.[263] In the event of a voluntary winding up, court may order such winding up to continue subject to supervision of the court.[264] The provisions for compulsory winding up available to a creditor

---

[258] M Marove, A Padilla and M Pagon, Collateral versus Project Screening: A Model of Lazy Banks (2001), 32 *RAND Journal of Economics*, 726–728.

[259] Asian Development Bank (n. 84), 21.

[260] Companies Act 2007 (n. 155), Part XII.

[261] Promulgated under the Companies Ordinance No. 51 of 1938.

[262] Companies Act 2007 (n. 155), ss. 270(e) and 271.

[263] ibid s. 322.

[264] ibid s. 351. Creditors have no entitlement to this order as a right.

are far from satisfactory. While it is only right that an application by a creditor for a winding up of a company with knowledge of a bona fide dispute regarding the debt is considered as an abuse of process of court, it is unfortunate that this has given rise to a suggestion that where a debt is disputed, a winding up application can only proceed if the debt has been determined as due in ordinary proceedings.[265] While most debts subject to winding up proceedings are likely to be disputed, the above suggestion takes away the ease of this remedy.

It is submitted that winding up of a debtor company is of little use to an unsecured lender due to the application of the *pari passu*[266] treatment. However, it is specially beneficial procedure to a lender in circumstances where the debtor company has diminished its assets by committing fraud in anticipation of winding up,[267] as winding up allows a lender to increase the assets available for distribution by having these transactions set aside.

The laws governing insolvent companies in Sri Lanka in addition to being inefficient[268] do little to align the rights of creditors with managerial incentives in corporate restructuring. While companies that are hopelessly insolvent must be wound up, it is also necessary that an alternative to the drastic measure of winding up should be available.[269] Resuscitation of ailing companies provides an opportunity to a creditor to recover their debt and for the companies to remain in existence. It also provides lenders with opportunities to monitor and acts as an effective corporate governance mechanism if they are involved in the resuscitation process. Thus, there is the urgent need in Sri Lanka for a procedure, which allows for the reconstruction of a company with minimal court intervention and also binds creditors to such arrangement, ensuring *ex post* monitoring by creditors and enabling creditors an opportunity to be an effective corporate

---

[265] H Cabral, Corporate Collapses and Insolvency Regimes: The Sri Lankan Experience (2007), http://www.lawnet.lk/docs/articles/inter_legal_articles/HTML/CV10.html [1 March 2007]. This suggestion in fact requires a two-stage process of first proving the debt and then petitioning for a winding up order on the basis of such debt.

[266] Ranking equally.

[267] Companies Act 2007 (n. 155), ss. 374–375.

[268] It takes 2.2 years and costs 18 percent of the estate. World Bank and International Finance Corporation, *Doing Business in 2006: Creating Jobs* (Washington DC 2006).

[269] There is provision for arrangements and reconstructions under Companies Act 2007 (n. 155), ss. 255–259. However, these cumbersome provisions are not expressly for purposes of enabling an insolvent company to restructure itself and involve court involvement at every stage.

governance mechanism.[270] Further, future reforms should encompass changes to labour laws[271] and enable restructuring.[272]

Another possible reform likely to align the rights of lenders with the management in insolvency is the provision of a creditors committee in insolvency and in restructuring to monitor and supervise the proceedings. The Companies Act 2007 provides for a committee of inspections[273] in liquidations, which is rarely used. While the timely filing for insolvency or restructuring will result by following the US or Japanese practice and allowing the incumbent board of directors to remain during attempts at restructuring rather than having a court appointed or creditor appointed board,[274] such practice in the context of a controlling shareholder systems is likely to result in asset stripping. Therefore, reforms must also encompass provision for a creditors committee independent of the board.

7.4.4. *Fiduciary Duties Owed to Lenders*

The legal and institutional preconditions necessary for lenders to be an effective corporate governance mechanism in controlling the costs of controlling shareholder systems extend to the recognition of a fiduciary duty in certain circumstances towards creditors by a company's directors, professional agents and controlling shareholders, (if such controlling agents are actively involved in the management of the company).[275]

---

[270] Companies Act 2007 (n. 155), s. 401. The board may resolve to appoint an administrator where the company is or is likely to become unable to pay its debts. However, provision for court to intervene in the process is likely to lead to delays. s. 408, 416(2).

[271] Termination of Employment of Workmen Act No. 45 of 1971 as amended prohibits employers from dismissing workers even on the grounds of inefficiency. While the Act was recently revised to facilitate retrenchment, the compensation formula for retrenched workers is excessive.

[272] The Central Bank of Sri Lanka has set up a committee to review the laws for the recovery of loans due to banking institutions and Business Recovery and Insolvency Practitioners Association of Sri Lanka (BRIPASL) is attempting to propose draft legislation for the revival of sick industries.

[273] Companies Act 2007 (n. 155), ss. 299–301.

[274] R Kraakman *et al.*, *The Anatomy of Corporate Law: A Comparative and Functional Approach* (Oxford University Press Oxford 2004), 74, make reference to this practice, which leaves incumbent board in place and acts as an incentive to enter bankruptcy proceedings.

[275] ibid 88–96. Courts in UK have traditionally used the problematic concept of 'in the interests of a company' to extend director liability towards lenders.

The imposition of a fiduciary duty on the company's directors, controlling shareholders and professional agents achieves two important goals. First, it provides lenders with an additional remedy against those directing, providing information and responsible for the affairs of the company, which strengthens their ability to lend and monitor the activities of the company. Second, the imposition of additional liability on directors and professional agents indirectly deters some of the costs of controlling shareholder systems, such as private benefits of control, tunnelling and entrenchment.

(a) *The Liability of Directors*

While many jurisdictions appear to recognise some form of personal liability of directors to creditors when a company is nearing insolvency, these provisions face difficulties in courts, which attempt to determine a fiduciary duty different to a director's fiduciary duty to shareholders.[276] It is in recognition of these inherent difficulties that recent statutory reforms to company law in the UK provide that the duties imposed by the statement of director's duties in the Companies Act 2006 has effect 'subject to any enactment or rule of law requiring directors, in certain circumstances, to consider or act in the interests of creditors of the company'.[277]

However, in many jurisdictions directors are held personally liable for damages to creditors resulting from a board negligently trading when the company is not in a position to pay its debts.[278] The Sri Lankan Companies Act 2007 imposes personal liability on directors for fraud in anticipation of winding up and fraudulent trading during the course of

---

[276] ibid 66–67. A key difficulty is that a lender is constrained in bringing an action against a director, except when the company is in insolvency when action can be brought via a liquidator.

[277] Companies Act 2006 (UK) (n. 191), s. 172(3). Also, the Company Law Review Steering Group *Modern Company Law for a Competitive Economy-Final Report* (2001) paras 3.12–3.20.

[278] English common law has used the concept of 'interests of the company' in expanding director liability to lenders — *West Mercia Safetywear* (n. 31), where in insolvency the 'company' encompassed the creditors. By statute, the Insolvency Act 1986 (UK), ss. 213–214.

winding up.[279] However, due to the requirement of proving that such transactions were 'fraudulent', the fraudulent trading provision was rarely used in the past and is inadequate in dealing with directors who have negligently allowed companies hopelessly insolvent to trade, thereby, reducing the ability of creditors' to recover their debts.

In the light of controlling shareholders and group structures in Sri Lanka, which make creditors especially vulnerable to intergroup transactions and the blurring of the divisions between the assets of the companies within a group, two matters are of importance for a reform agenda. First, liability must move from fraudulent standard to a negligence standard. Second, the definition of a 'director' must be expanded to include 'shadow directors'[280] and 'de facto' directors.[281] This includes a parent company, a controlling shareholder or even a lender, who exercises control over a company's affairs.[282] The expansion of liability must encompass instances when a parent company causes a subsidiary to act contrary to its own interests.

The imposition of personal liability on directors whether by statutory provision or by way of judicial pronouncements protects the rights of lenders by way of deterring opportunistic behaviour of directors and increasing the chances of recovery on default.[283] It is the concept of director liability that ensured some degree of director accountability for depositors and shareholders during the spate of financial company collapses in Sri Lanka in the

---

[279] Companies Act 2007 (n. 155), s. 374–375. Fraudulent trading is similar to Companies Act 1948 (UK), s. 332 which the Department of Trade and Industry (UK), *Report of the Review Committee on Insolvency Law and Practice (Cmnd 8558)* (1982), found not to be particularly effective due to the requirement to show dishonesty on the part of those responsible for the management of the company.

[280] Shadow directors are persons on whose instructions the directors of a company are accustomed to act and are a legislative category.

[281] De facto directors are persons who act as directors and are held out by a company as directors but are not formally appointed as directors.

[282] In *Ultraframe (UK) Ltd v. Fielding* [2005] EWHC 1638 (Ch) para 1267, Lewison J stated that '…where the alleged shadow director is also a creditor of the company, he is entitled to protect his own interests as creditor without necessarily becoming a shadow director.' There are good reasons for such a distinction as lenders are likely to be reluctant to engage in monitoring if liability is likely to attach. Conversely, there is no reason for lenders to escape liability if similar to a director, they exercised control over the company's affairs, *Re a company (no 005009 of 1987), ex parte Copp* [1989] BCLC 13; D Prentice, Creditor's Interests and Director's Duties (1990), 10 *Oxford Journal of Legal Studies*, 265, 268.

[283] B Cheffins, *Company Law, Theory, Structure and Operation* (Oxford University Press Oxford 1997), 537–548, supports the public interest element in regulating director conduct.

late 1980s and the more recent collapse of the Pramuka Savings & Development Bank.

The Companies Act 2007 in Sri Lanka imposes a duty on directors operating at a point before insolvency who believe that the company is unable to pay its debts as they fall due to call a meeting of the board and consider whether the board should apply to court for a winding up order.[284] Such a rule is of considerable merit in principle. In practice, it requires the directors to make a judgement on the ability of the company to pay its debts and due to the personal liability attached to such judgement, may result in directors initiating winding up proceedings at the first hint of trouble. Personal liability is also likely to result in directors seeking expensive professional advice.[285] From a lender's perspective, liquidation can be harmful if there are other means of rescuing the company, and can lead to an increase in corporate insolvencies. There is also no positive duty imposed on a director to take into account the interests of lenders in determining such 'belief',[286] and provides directors with inadequate guidance on reaching such belief.

Standards of director liability whether leading to insolvency or in insolvency must strike the right balance between affording creditor protection and personal liability of directors or the ultimate beneficiaries will be the indemnity insurance sector. Its utility must also be questioned in the light of a director's financial ability to satisfy personal liability claims and the constraints it imposes on their duties towards shareholders. A worthy alternative that may help achieve a balance, are provisions that disqualify directors instead of holding them personally liable,[287] and is an effective remedy where the loss of reputation is an effective deterrent.

(b) *The Liability of Controlling Shareholders*

Kraakman *et al.* identify (i) the doctrine of de facto or shadow directors; (ii) equitable subordination and (iii) piercing the corporate veil; as the

---

[284] Companies Act 2007 (n. 155), s. 219. There is an additional duty on directors to call an extraordinary general meeting of the shareholders on a serious loss of capital. s. 220.

[285] The Company Law Review Steering Group (n. 277), para 3.19.

[286] It is questionable if such belief is to be based on an objective or subjective standard.

[287] The Company Directors Disqualification Act 1986 (UK) allows courts to disqualify unfit directors of insolvent companies. The matters for determining the unfitness of directors include *inter alia* a director's responsibility for the causes of the company becoming insolvent.

principal tools for holding controlling shareholders liable for debts of an insolvent company.[288] Controlling shareholder liability raises difficult issues. In particular, determining when liability should attach and the likelihood that controlling shareholder liability is likely to increase costs of lending, as a lender is likely to be interested in the financial health of an individual rather than the company.[289]

Under the doctrine of de facto or shadow directors, a controlling shareholder who directs a company to divert assets or directs directors to violate fiduciary duties is held liable for losses of the company if insolvency follows.[290] In fact, such doctrine may extend by application to lenders as shadow directors. While there is no judicial recognition of the doctrine of de facto directors or statutory recognition of shadow directors in Sri Lanka, rectification of this position by a reform agenda will ensure that controlling shareholders assume greater responsibility for their corporate actions and minimise the extraction of private benefits of control.

The doctrine of equitable subordination[291] is not recognised in Sri Lanka either judicially or by statute. The doctrine in its application to controlling shareholders requires that the courts subordinate the claims of the controlling shareholders against the insolvent company. While the doctrine if applied equitably deters the extraction of private benefits of control, it can also curtail the incidence of propping[292] by controlling shareholders.[293] Therefore, a reform agenda must incorporate this doctrine only in limited circumstances and not as an arbitrary solution.

Another useful weapon in the hands of lenders is the ability to hold controlling shareholders' liable for the debts of the company by lifting the corporate veil. Lifting of the corporate veil of incorporation is a direct response to an abuse of limited liability and is achieved by express statutory

---

[288] Kraakman *et al.* (n. 274), 92.

[289] D Prentice, Some Comments on the Law Relating to Corporate Groups, in J McCahery, S Picciotto and C Scott (eds.), *Corporate Control and Accountability* (Clarendon Oxford 1993), 372, raises similar concerns regarding corporate groups.

[290] While the statutory definition of a director is capable of encompassing a de facto director (s. 250), the UK courts have drawn a distinction between de facto directors and shadow directors in *Ultraframe* (n. 282), paras 1279–1291 where it was stated that while a shadow director will owe duties imposed by law, such director will not owe the full range of duties owed by a de facto director.

[291] Section 7.2.4(b).

[292] A benefit of controlling shareholder systems, Chapter 5.

[293] Kraakman *et al.* (n. 274), 93.

provisions[294] or by judicial intervention. From the point of view of lenders, limited liability restricts lenders claims' to company assets, especially in the light of controlling shareholder systems of pyramids and cross-holdings which can intermingle assets between a group.

In Sri Lanka, there is statutory[295] and judicial[296] recognition that a company is a separate legal entity distinct from its members. Courts are yet to make any judicial pronouncements in this area, especially with regard to the use of veil piercing in protecting lenders within corporate groups. In what can be seen as a reaffirmation of the concept that a company is a separate legal entity distinct from its members, the Court of Appeal in *Samaraweera and another v. Sunpower Systems (Private) Limited*[297] set out that a holding company is a separate and distinct entity from its subsidiary company and therefore, a holding company is not liable for any obligations incurred by the subsidiary companies. While it is only right that courts should not set aside the corporate form easily, limited liability must not be allowed to be abused by controlling shareholders and directors, especially in groups to the detriment of a company's lenders.

A reform strategy in a controlling shareholder system aimed at strengthening lenders as a corporate governance mechanism must recognise that limited liability should not shield the intermingling of company assets to the detriment of shareholders or lenders, or perpetrate fraud. A strategy suggested by Davies in the context of group companies is to confine the claims of lenders to the assets of the subsidiary company while making the holding company liable for harm caused to the lenders of the subsidiary company by the shifting of assets.[298]

---

[294] For example, wrongful or fraudulent trading, that is, by holding directors personally liable for debts of a company.

[295] For example, Companies Act 2007 (n. 155), s. 152, requires holding and subsidiary companies to prepare group accounts.

[296] *Trade Exchange (Ceylon) Ltd v. Asian Hotels Corporation* (1981) 1 SLLR 67; *Visuvalingam and others v. Liyanage and others* (1983) 2 SLLR 311, upheld a right to information within the right of free speech, and upheld the principle of the separate legal personality of the seventh respondent company and by such treatment denied it *locus standi* under the constitutionally protected fundamental rights which were interpreted as being available only to 'citizens'.

[297] [1996] 1 SLLR 284.

[298] P Davies, *Introduction to Company Law* (Clarendon Law Series Oxford University Press Oxford 2002), 106–107.

(c) *The Liability of Professional Advisers*

The investor reaction to Enron and worldwide accounting scandals has brought the gate-keeping professions (i.e., auditors, attorneys and securities analysts) to the forefront. Coffee recognises that '[N]o board of directors — no matter how able and well intentioned its members — can outperform its professional advisers.'[299] Increasingly lenders to large public companies are relying on auditors to verify the financial statements of companies, corporate attorneys to ensure that legal obligations of the company are met and securities analysts to credibly signal the health of companies. While professional advisers have a larger role to play in dispersed ownership systems than in controlling shareholder systems, many jurisdictions have not extended statutory liabilities to professional advisers who fail to report managerial misconduct to creditors. However, courts have not been so constrained and have extended a duty of care to professional advisers when the party seeking the information from a professional adviser possessed of a special skill, trusts such adviser to exercise due care, and such adviser knew or ought to have known that reliance was being placed on such skills and judgement.[300] While the UK courts in particular are constrained by the dicta in *Caparo Industries Plc v. Dickman*[301] which firmly rejected the proposition that professional advisers were liable to those who are likely to be foreseeable users of such advice, cases after *Caparo* have focused on establishing whether there was an 'assumption of responsibility' on the part of the advisers.[302] While liability of professional advisers in many jurisdictions is likely to be extended in the light of the accounting scandals, it is also likely that there will be lobbying for capping of such liability, counter claims for contributory negligence and a rise in indemnity insurance.

There is no express statutory provision or a decision of the courts in Sri Lanka, which imposes liability on professional advisers such as auditors or attorneys who fail to report breaches of managerial duty to

---

[299] J Coffee, Gatekeepers: The Professions and Corporate Governance (Oxford University Press Oxford 2006), 1; Also, R Smith and I Walter, *Governing the Modern Corporation* (Oxford University Press New York 2006), 172, suggest that 'The auditor, in becoming more dependent on *all* its clients, becomes more independent of *any* one'.

[300] *Hedley Byrne & Co. v. Heller & Partners* [1964] AC. 465 (HL) 486, 502, 514.

[301] [1990] 2 AC 605 (HL).

[302] P Davies, *Gower and Davies' Principles of Modern Company Law* (Seventh edn., Sweet & Maxwell London 2003), 584–585.

creditors.[303] In the light of the application of the common law of Sri Lanka,[304] the Roman-Dutch law, it is likely that an argument can be made for liability of a professional adviser in delict. However, such liability to be actionable in Roman-Dutch law, if of a non-defamatory nature, must be made with the intention of causing damage and damage must be done as a result.[305] Thus, while it is likely that a professional adviser may incur liability for fraudulent conduct, negligent conduct is likely to escape liability. This unfortunate state of affairs is made worse by the Sri Lanka courts' inflexibility in developing the Roman-Dutch law to extend to professional advisers' liability in negligence.[306]

If lenders are to be an effective corporate governance mechanism in Sri Lanka, it is necessary that professional advisers, who have assumed responsibility, especially in respect of lenders who are foreseeable users of the information produced by such professional adviser, be held liable not only for fraud but also for negligence. If lender confidence and monitoring is to be inspired it is essential that either legislation be passed encompassing liability to third parties such as lenders, by professional advisers to companies, or alternatively the judiciary adopt a flexible approach in its application of Roman-Dutch law principles, especially post-Enron.

The imposition of liability on directors, controlling shareholders and professional advisers must be tempered by the wider picture of increasing costs of indemnity insurance, the effect of such liability on lenders' involvement in corporate management, controlling shareholders' propping of failing companies, and the fact that directors and controlling shareholders within controlling shareholder systems are likely to benefit most at the expense of creditors.[307]

---

[303] There is the imposition of liability by professional codes of conduct, but the Companies Act 2007 (n. 155), is silent on liability of professional advisers.

[304] The term 'common law' is used in different senses — A Smith (ed.), *Glanville Williams: Learning the Law* (Sweet & Maxwell London 2002). In Sri Lanka, it is most commonly used to denote a residuary law, filling in the gaps in the legal system. Contrast, approach of Lord Diplock in *Kodeesweran v. Attorney General* [1969] 72 NLR 337.

[305] *Chissel v. Chapman* [1954] 56 NLR 121.

[306] 'I think we are not entitled, as judges, to change the material of the Roman-Dutch Law, but are only permitted to iron out its creases, whenever the necessity arises. Effecting structural alterations to the Common Law should be the exclusive preserve of the Legislature …' — Justice Dheeraratne, in *Prof. Priyani Soysa v. Rienzie Arsacularatne* [2001] 2 SLLR 293, 306; R Dheeraratne, Liability of an Auditor in Delict (2006), http://webtest.cisworld.net/lawnet/docs/articles/inter_legal_articles/HTML/CV3.html [29 March 2007].

[307] Kraakman *et al.* (n. 274), 95–96.

7.4.5. *Internal Management Role for Lenders*

One important measure by which lenders can influence managerial decisions and become an effective corporate governance monitor is by becoming involved in the internal management of the debtor company. Such involvement is either by way of making such position a condition of their lending or by taking an equity interest in the debtor company. It is also possible for a substantial lender to acquire an informal voice in management decisions and the fact that a lender has an interest in the performance of a company over a long period of time may facilitate such relationship.[308]

There are obvious trade-offs between lender monitoring and the costs of such active involvement in internal management from the perspective of a company. Conflicting interests between the lenders and shareholders exacerbate this position. While volatile companies are likely to benefit most from providing for an internal management role for lenders, lenders may in fact be reluctant to lend to or be involved in the governance of such companies.[309] On the other hand, lenders may be keen to take up an internal management role in companies facing financial distress to protect their interests in insolvency, especially in countries with weak creditor rights.

Direct involvement in the management of borrower companies is a governance tool of lenders and has several benefits.[310] First, a close bank relationship formalised through board representation improves the flow of information between a bank and a company and facilitates lending. Such involvement increases the potential for monitoring, reduces information asymmetries and increases the lender's ability to influence repayment.[311] Second, if lender liability is high, the presence of a banker on the board signals to the market the stability of a company. Lenders in internal management positions also have industry-specific knowledge. Third, the costs of lenders in internal management positions arise from the conflict of

---

[308] For example, Germany or Japan where long-term lending has facilitated relationship-based lending. Baums (n. 41), states that in Germany a major source of bank influence on boards lie in the banks position as proxy holders for shareholders.

[309] Kroszer and Strahan (n. 45), find that bankers tend to be represented on the boards of large stable companies in the US, which they attribute to strong creditor rights and the bankruptcy doctrines of equitable subordination and lender liability.

[310] Section 7.2.4(b).

[311] Day and Taylor (n. 68), 80–81.

interests between a lender's fiduciary duty to shareholders of the borrower company and from the fiduciary duty owed to shareholders of the lender. It is suggested that if a lender takes an equity position in a company, in principle, it may mitigate the conflict.[312] Other methods by which the conflicting interests are mitigated, especially in the US, are by way of equitable subordination of debts and the imposition of lender liability.[313] Given the ability of these doctrines to negatively affect lender involvement in the management of its borrowers, they must be used with caution.

It is essential that if lenders are to be in effective internal management positions, the conflict of interest that lenders face on the borrower company boards be reduced, by encouraging the holding of both equity and debt of a company by lenders, subject to certain restrictions. This objective can be achieved by relaxing rules on lenders' equity stakes in borrower companies, by encouraging leveraged buyouts and transactions requiring a mix of debt and equity, and encouraging the development of venture capital.

(a) *Lenders' Equity Stakes in Borrower Companies*

In Sri Lanka, lenders do not face any legal restriction on their executives sitting on the boards of non-financial companies. However, restrictions are in place on lender's equity stakes in non-financial companies.[314] While restrictions with regard to the percentage of capital funds that a lender may invest in the equity stakes of a non-financial company can mitigate risk, a maximum investment limit of 20 percent with respect to the paid up capital of a company does little to merit lender involvement in the management of borrower companies.

Similarly, while stringent capital adequacy ratios (CARs) are an essential feature of prudent credit regulations, care must be taken not to set such CAR at excessive levels as this could result in lenders seeking to

---

[312] R Rajan, A Theory of the Costs and Benefits of Universal Banking (1992), Center for Research on Security Prices University of Chicago Working Paper 346, http://www. crsp.com/resources/papers.html [15 November 2004].

[313] Section 7.2.4(b); D Fischel, The Economics of Lender Liability (1989), 99 *Yale Law Journal*, 131.

[314] Section 7.4.1(b). Lenders may invest up to 20 percent of the paid of capital and not exceeding 10 percent of its own capital funds in one company (a maximum of 30 percent in aggregate).

reduce equity holdings in non-financial companies to maintain the CAR. All licensed banks in Sri Lanka are required to maintain a CAR of 10 percent at minimum in relation to risk-weighted assets covering both credit and market risk.[315] While this requirement at 2 percent above the minimum Basel[316] requirement is prudent from a banking sector risk mitigation point of view, any further increase to this requirement is likely to adversely affect lenders' equity holdings in borrower companies and any likelihood of an unbiased internal management role by lenders.

(b) *Leveraged Buyouts*[317]

In a leveraged buyout transaction the shareholders of a public company are bought out by a new group of investors, (i.e., managers, a specialised buy-out firm, banks). Most of the financing comes from banks and public debt holders. While there are costs to taking companies private, encouraging leveraged buyout transactions often financed through a combination of debt and equity encourages lenders to take up debt and equity stakes in the borrower companies and thus, mitigates the potential conflict of interest that lenders face.

While the previous Sri Lankan Companies Act 1982 did not have any provisions that enable or facilitate leveraged buyouts,[318] the new Companies Act 2007 envisage the giving of financial assistance by a company, if it is in the interests of the company and if the company is able to satisfy the solvency test immediately after the giving of such assistance.[319] It is hoped that this will enable the growth of the leveraged buyout activity. The importance of leveraged buyout activity from the perspective of this study is, its substitution of debt for equity, which if large, will result

---

[315] Determination made by the Monetary Board of the Central Bank of Sri Lanka under Section 76J(1) of the Banking Act No. 30 of 1988 (2006).

[316] Basel Committee on Banking Supervision (n. 156), sets the CAR at 8 percent. This is expected to remain in Basel II.

[317] The acquisition of one company by another through the use of borrowed funds. The intention is that the loans will be repaid from the cash flow of the acquired company. J Pallister and J Daintith (n. 37).

[318] Companies Act 1982 (n. 124), s. 55 prohibited the giving of financial assistance for the purchase of a company's own share and effectively barred leveraged buyout transactions. Transactions were, thus, rather onerously undertaken by creation of special purpose vehicles.

[319] Companies Act 2007 (n. 155), s. 70.

in greater lender involvement in the management of companies and also encourage lenders to take up equity stakes or seek the conversion of debt into equity. This argument is supported by evidence of the predicted efficiencies of leveraged buyouts.[320]

(c) *Venture Capital*

Usually underdeveloped capital markets also have limited venture capital and private equity markets. Specialist venture capital companies in Sri Lanka have failed due to a lack of understanding by entrepreneurs who view it as a form of cheap capital that does not have to be repaid.[321] Unlike in Germany and Japan, lenders in Sri Lanka are reluctant to provide venture capital due to the difficulties in exiting companies through the illiquid CSE and the prevailing tax structure.

Venture capital investments must be encouraged if lenders are to take on active roles in the management of companies. For this purpose, financial sector reforms must extend to development of the CSE and improvements to the prevailing tax structure to prevent double taxation of profits and dividends.

7.4.6. *Enhancing Lenders' Corporate Governance*

The corporate governance practices of lenders must be beyond reproach if they are to be effective corporate governance monitors of their borrowers. Shortcomings in the corporate governance of lenders are of importance not only due to their role as monitors but also because of the larger threat to the stability of the financial system posed by bad governance among lenders.[322] This is of importance in the Asian region and in Sri Lanka due to the dominant role of lenders in external finance. Some of the suggested reforms of corporate governance of banks, especially in Asia,[323] include

---

[320] Shleifer and Vishny (n. 9), 766.

[321] Asian Development Bank (n. 84), 75–76.

[322] OECD, *OECD White Paper on Corporate Governance Reform in Asia 2003* (Paris 2003).

[323] Basel Committee on Banking Supervision, *Enhancing Corporate Governance for Banking Organizations* (Basel 2006) and OECD (n. 166).

recognition of fiduciary duties of individual board members in banks, the role and functions of boards of directors in banks, preventing abusive related-party transactions, firewalls in the event of banks being part of a group structure, disclosure, autonomy in relation to the State and engaging in the monitoring of borrower companies.[324]

The Basel Committee on Bank Supervision recently revised the 1998 Basel Accord.[325] The new recommendations develop procedures for computing minimum capital requirements, enhancing supervisory practices and adoption of market discipline policies that will force banks to make greater disclosure of information.[326] Undoubtedly, these requirements are designed to bring about a degree of stability to the banking industry.

While the Basel accord is meant to cover internationally active banks, the Central Bank of Sri Lanka has decided to adopt Basel II for all banks in Sri Lanka with effect from January 2008.[327] While prudent banking regulation is likely to improve the governance practices of lenders and improve the ability of banks to develop active monitoring of their borrower companies, banking regulation must not be used as a tool by weak governments to promote their own interests or encourage corruption.[328] This is not to say that banking regulation and supervision is unnecessary.[329] In fact, for many developing countries banking regulation in the form of an international accord is an effective guideline to improving financial sector stability. Further, international regulation also leads to harmonisation of markets and develops disciplining market forces.

However, the political economy of many developing countries is also a cause of concern. There is likely to be crony capitalism, a feature of the Asian financial crisis. Those in government are likely to be connected to

---

[324] OECD (n. 166), paras 13–39.

[325] Basel Committee (n. 99).

[326] The three pillars of Basel II.

[327] Central Bank of Sri Lanka (n. 86), 139, Box 17.

[328] J Barth, G Caprio and R Levine, *Rethinking Banking Regulation: Till Angels Govern* (Cambridge University Press Cambridge 2006), exploring banking regulation and the three pillars of Basel II, argue that governments choose banking regulation based on the role of government in economy (i.e., based on a public interest and the private interest approach). Thus, greater regulation and supervision is likely to result in banking sector corruption and intensify banking system fragility.

[329] ibid 1, 9, recognises this by quoting James Madison, *Federalist Papers* Number 51, 'If men were angels, no government would be necessary. If angels were to govern men, neither external nor internal controls would be necessary'.

families controlling companies, banks. Thus, the institutional framework to ensure implementation of banking regulations is weak. Therefore, Sri Lankan regulators must ensure that the implementation of Basel II empowers fair and transparent supervision and regulation of the banking industry and does not breed crony capitalism giving controlling shareholders even greater access to financial sector resources. International market forces are likely to be a disciplining force in this respect.

It is laudable that Sri Lankan regulators are recognising the need to make modifications in the implementation of the accord to suit local conditions.[330] Imposing quantitative restrictions on lenders by way of banking regulations such as portfolio concentration limits by sector and type of borrower, minimum capital requirements for banks, risk adjusted CARs limit on exposure to different types of risks with respect to liquidity will promote sound financial policies. However, these requirements must not be too stringent so as to stifle competition among lenders.

In June 2002, the Central Bank of Sri Lanka issued a voluntary code of corporate governance for banks.[331] The two principal issues in this regard are first, the contents of the guidelines and second, their voluntary nature. The guidelines focus on the boards of directors, board committees, senior management of banks, transparency, external auditors of banks, risk management and prudent regulation by regulators.[332] While the initiative is laudable, the lack of understanding of the ownership structure of banks in Sri Lanka and resulting agency costs, has resulted in insufficient attention being paid to related-party transactions, the stresses caused to management due to group ownership structures and government interference. Further, the voluntary nature of the guidelines makes them superfluous. It is suggested that plans by the Central Bank of Sri Lanka to make the guidelines mandatory in the near future,[333] must be accompanied by changes encompassing the stresses placed on the board and senior management of banks by prevailing ownership structures. This is now of paramount importance given the current financial crisis encompassing banks and financial institutions.

---

[330] R Jayamaha, Basel II: A Roadmap for Sri Lankan Banking System with International Comparisons (2006), https://www.cbsl.lk/cbsl/Speech_181206.doc [5 May 2007].
[331] Central Bank of Sri Lanka, *Code of Corporate Governance for Banks and Other Financial Institutions* (Colombo 2002).
[332] ibid guidelines 1–12.
[333] N Cabraal, Road Map for Monetary and Financial Sector Policies in 2007 and Beyond (2007), https://www.cbsl.lk/cbsl/speech-020107.pdf [30 January 2007].

While improving lenders own corporate governance is a positive step towards improving the monitoring abilities of lenders, regulation of lenders must be undertaken with care. Effective regulation ensures that lenders are stable and ready to undertake lending risks, monitor and be effective corporate governance mechanisms. However, regulations and lender supervision determined by factors other than financial sector stability are likely to perpetuate crony capitalism.

7.4.7. *Credit Ratings and Credit Bureaus*

Most developing countries are characterised by poor information sharing among lenders. The availability of a system of credit ratings for companies, and effective credit bureaus with credit histories of individuals (linked to an individual's ability to become a company director) is a precondition to make lenders an effective corporate governance mechanism.

Credit ratings signal to the market and lenders the creditworthiness of borrowers,[334] and encourage lending, facilitating the ability of lenders to become effective corporate governance mechanisms. Credit rating agencies have the necessary leverage required to obtain the voluntary disclosure of company information. They also have access to other sources of information such as newspapers, databases and industry sources, to produce credible information.

Fitch Ratings Lanka Limited, a joint venture between the International Finance Corporation, Central Bank of Sri Lanka and Fitch Ratings Inc.,[335] pioneered credit ratings in Sri Lanka and has issued entity ratings for over 50 listed, unlisted companies and financial institutions.[336] There are moves underway for insurer ratings. However, it is necessary that more listed companies in Sri Lanka are encouraged to obtain ratings. This can be helped by a reduction in the costs involved in obtaining credit ratings.

Further, if credit ratings are to be an effective market-based corporate governance tool for lenders, such ratings must play a role in borrower companies gaining access to financing. If lenders do not place emphasis

---

[334] The signal is useful not only to lenders but also investors and corporate debt markets.

[335] As many as 14 leading financial institutions hold 25 percent of the shareholding, raising concerns with regard to their own ratings.

[336] Credit ratings were made mandatory for all debt instruments over SLRS 100 million and deposit taking institutions from 2003.

on credit ratings, the most sophisticated systems of ratings is of no avail. Lenders can encourage the obtaining of ratings by requiring that listed companies seeking financing over a specific monetary amount obtain an entity rating. This will automatically raise the number of large borrowers obtaining ratings and make ratings a 'passport'[337] for obtaining credit and encourage good governance.

Credit information bureaus if effectively used by lenders are a strong governance tool due to their ability to name and shame corporate loan defaulters and effectively bar future access to financing.[338] Further, credit information bureaus enable information sharing and can overcome information asymmetries.

Sri Lanka's Credit Information Bureau ('CRIB'),[339] a public-private partnership between the Central Bank of Sri Lanka and several banks, leasing companies and finance companies, is empowered to collect credit information, both positive and negative on borrowers and prospective borrowers, both individuals and companies, and provide such information to lending institutions.

However, given the high rate of non-performing loans in Sri Lanka, it is suggested that to be an effective disciplinary force, the credit information bureau should consider lowering the minimum loan amount below which loans are excluded from the database effectively expanding coverage of borrowers.[340] It is submitted that there is a need to expand the users and shareholders of the credit information bureau, collect, update and disseminate information electronically and facilitate information sharing based on international standards. Therefore, it is suggested that the bureau considers expanding its ownership to include an international credit information bureau.[341] There is also a need to move away from significant

---

[337] R Abeysuriya, Credit Rating a Catalyst in Fortifying Sri Lanka's Capital Market, *Business Today* (2000).

[338] World Bank and International Finance Corporation, *Doing Business in 2005: Removing Obstacles to Growth* (Washington DC 2005), state that credit bureaus are associated with higher credit.

[339] This is the oldest bureau in the South Asian region established under the Credit Information Bureau of Sri Lanka Act No. 18 of 1990 amended by Credit Information Bureau of Sri Lanka (Amendment) Act No. 8 of 1995).

[340] The minimum amounts are presently SLRS 500,000 and over for positive information and SLRS 100,000 and over for negative information: World Bank *Analysis Report on Credit Bureau Development in South Asia* (Washington DC 2004), Table 1.

[341] ibid 35.

Central Bank of Sri Lanka ownership, especially given the environment of political cronyism. It is also suggested that the bureau collect information from more public sources such as data from the Registrar of Companies, court judgements and payments of public utilities to supplement existing information.[342]

Measures are proposed to modernise and expand the scope of the credit information bureau by providing online access to credit information bureau reports. Amendments are also proposed to the Credit Information Bureau Act 1990 to enable the credit information bureau to provide other services such as credit scoring and fraud prevention.[343]

7.4.8. *Competition*

Another important precondition in facilitating the role of lenders as a corporate governance mechanism lies in encouraging a competitive lending market. The Sri Lankan lending industry suffers from lack of competition. This amply demonstrated the interest rate spread in Sri Lanka, which is among the highest in the region.[344] There is also state control of and entrenchment within the financial sector.[345]

If lenders are to be an effective corporate governance mechanism, government interference in the financial system, especially in lending decisions must be eliminated.[346] A process of financial liberalisation coupled with privatisation of state-controlled financial institutions should achieve this.

Rigid regulation of banking viewed as essential in some respects, does not promote entry and competition among lenders. In fact, viewed from

---

[342] ibid.

[343] Central Bank of Sri Lanka (n. 77), 137.

[344] In 2000, it is 9.63 percent. Neighbouring India is at 5.76 percent and Bangladesh at 8.97 percent, World Bank, *2003 World Development Indicators* (Washington DC 2003). This also demonstrates the high level of NPLs and the legal impediments to the recovery of loans; Chapter 4, Table 4.8.

[345] The two state-controlled banks control 45 percent of the banking assets. T Kane *et al.*, *2001 Index of Economic Freedom* (The Heritage Foundation and *Wall Street Journal* Washington 2007). Sri Lanka scores 40 percent on financial freedom. This is below the average of other Asian countries such as Hong Kong (80 percent), Singapore (50 Percent), Thailand (50 percent) and Taiwan (50 percent).

[346] Section 7.4.1(e).

the perspective of encouraging competition, reforms must include the abolition of rigid banking supervision, interest rate restrictions and increased minimum capital requirements.[347] Financial sector supervision and regulation must move towards disclosure and transparency rather than restrictions[348] and entry barriers, if competition among lenders is to be encouraged. Increases in minimum capital reserve requirements[349] have resulted in consolidation within the banking sector and stifled competition. It is arguable whether the banking sector needs high minimum capital requirements in addition to a CAR. Further, foreign banks and financial intermediaries must be encouraged to take up venture capital investments through a permissible tax regime.

Competition in lending exposes lenders to market discipline and encourages monitoring of their borrowers. If lenders are to become an effective corporate governance mechanism, it is essential that healthy competition among lenders be encouraged.

7.5. Conclusion

Section 7.4 of this chapter has proposed and analysed the legal and institutional preconditions necessary for lenders to be an effective corporate governance mechanism to control the costs of controlling shareholders in Sri Lanka. These preconditions have ranged from the specific such as regulating conflicts of interests among lenders and borrowers, to the more general reforms aimed at encouraging competition and enhancing lenders own corporate governance. Many of the suggested reform options are not independent of each other (i.e., lender's ownership in non-financial companies and related-party transactions). Some are based on conflicting goals (i.e., independence of lenders and the internal management role for lenders). However, the overall impact is to ensure that lenders gain the corporate governance capacities to control the costs of controlling shareholder systems.

---

[347] Central Bank of Sri Lanka is significantly enhancing the minimum capital requirement of banks to promote consolidation in the banking sector. Central Bank of Sri Lanka (n. 77), 134. In 2005 the minimum equity capital requirement for licensed commercial banks rose to SLRS 2500 million from SLRS 500 million.

[348] Section 7.4.7.

[349] Banking Act 2005 (n. 127), (Enhancement of Minimum Capital Requirements of Banks).

Most importantly, the proposed reforms recommended above take into account the institutional context of the controlling shareholder system in Sri Lanka, the interdependence between corporate governance and corporate finance and identifies lenders as the most suitable mechanism to control the costs of controlling shareholder systems. Another benefit in using lenders as a corporate governance mechanism is that the identified benefits of controlling shareholder systems are not stifled.

Proposing a corporate governance reform agenda for a controlling shareholder system is a 'Sisyphean' challenge. Other costs related to the lenders' role as a corporate governance mechanism are likely to arise. Reforms are likely to be of limited success, dependent upon political will and effective legal enforcement. However, what is proposed is what is perceived to be the most suitable starting point for a developing country such as Sri Lanka. While by no means comprehensive, the common denominator within the reform agenda is the recognition that lenders are capable of controlling the costs of controlling shareholders systems and becoming an effective corporate governance mechanism, if the necessary legal and institutional preconditions are in place.

Conclusion

The primary objective of this study was to discover the implications of corporate ownership and control structures on the governance of companies and thereafter, suggest an agenda of reform to meet the challenges posed by such structures to stimulate economic development. Sri Lanka was chosen as an illustrative example of a developing country to support the primary thesis of this study that an analysis into the reform of corporate governance in developing countries should begin with a focus on local market structures that define its adaptation and effectiveness.

The study provides an insight into the enlightening nexus between economic development and corporate governance and the correlation between corporate ownership, control and corporate governance. It scrutinises the corporate ownership and control structures in Sri Lanka, the determinants of such structures, their costs and benefits and thereafter, suggests a viable reform agenda. The analysis is used to both, understand the impact of ownership and control structures on corporate governance, and achieve resolution of corporate governance issues arising from such structures.

Chapter 1 provided the foundation for the study by an investigation of the nexus between economic development and corporate governance. Chapter 2 examined the correlation between corporate ownership, control and corporate governance. Chapters 3 and 4 provided insight into corporate ownership and control structures in Sri Lanka by an empirical examination of the ownership structures of its companies and an enquiry into the causes and determinants of such structures. The focus of Chapter 5 was on the identification of the corporate governance challenge by an examination of the costs and benefits of controlling shareholder systems. Chapter 6 applies the findings of the study and the corporate governance framework to formulate a reform agenda to meet the corporate governance challenges of a controlling shareholder system. Chapter 7 submits that it is vital to empower a market-based governance mechanism such as a lender, to control the costs of controlling shareholders in controlling shareholder systems.

Bibliography Acts, Statutes and Rules

Sri Lanka

Bank of Ceylon Act Ordinance No. 53 of 1938.

Banking Act (Single Borrower Limit) Directions No. 2 of 2005 as amended by Direction Nos. 3, 4 and 5 of 2005.

Banking Act (Ownership of Issued Capital Carrying Voting Rights) Directions No. 1 of 2007.

Banking Act No. 30 of 1988.

Banking Amendment Act No. 2 of 2005.

Business Undertakings Acquisition Act No. 35 of 1971.

Civil Law Ordinance No. 5 of 1852.

Civil Procedure Code 1890.

Companies Act No. 17 of 1982.

Companies Act No. 7 of 2007.

Companies Ordinance No. 51 of 1938.

Constitution of the Democratic Socialist Republic of Sri Lanka 1978.

Conversion of Government Owned Business Undertakings into Public Corporations Act No. 22 of 1987.

Conversion of Public Corporations or Government Owned Business Undertakings into Public Companies Act No. 23 of 1987.

Costs (Regulations) 1997.

Credit Information Bureau of Sri Lanka (Amendment) Act No. 8 of 1995.

Credit Information Bureau of Sri Lanka Act No. 18 of 1990.

Colombo Stock Exchange Listing Rules 2004.

Debt Recovery (Special Provisions) Act No. 2 of 1990.

Determination made by the Monetary Board of the Central Bank of Sri Lanka under Section 76J(1) of the Banking Act No. 30 of 1988 [2006].

Determination made by the Monetary Board of the Central Bank of Sri Lanka under section 17A(1)(a) and (1)(b) of the Banking Act No. 30 of 1988 [1997]

Government-Sponsored Corporations Act No. 19 of 1955.

Joint Stock Companies Ordinance No. 4 of 1861.

Land Reform Act No. 1 of 1972.

Monetary Law Act No. 58 of 1949.
Mortgage Act No. 6 of 1949.
Mortgage Amendment Act No. 3 of 1990.
National Savings Bank Act No. 30 of 1971.
National Development Bank of Sri Lanka (Consequential Provisions) Act No. 1 of 2005.
People's Bank Act No. 29 of 1961.
Public Enterprises Reform Act No. 1 of 1996.
Recovery of Loans by Banks (Amendment) (Special Provisions) Act No. 24 of 1995.
Recovery of Loans by Banks (Special Provisions) Act No. 4 of 1990.
Registration of Documents Ordinance No. 23 of 1927.
Securities and Exchange Commission of Sri Lanka and Institute of Chartered Accountants of Sri Lanka Rules on Corporate Governance for Listed Companies 2008.
Securities and Exchange Commission of Sri Lanka Act No. 36 of 1987.
Sri Lanka Accounting Standards 2006.
Sri Lanka Accounting and Auditing Standards Act No. 15 of 1995.
State Industrial Corporation Act No. 49 of 1957.
State Mortgage Bank Act No. 16 of 1956.
Takeovers and Mergers Code 1995 (amended 2003).
Termination of Employment of Workmen Act No. 45 of 1971.
Winding Up Rules.

India

Companies (Second Amendment) Act 2002.
Sick Industrial Companies (Special Provisions) Act 1985.

United Kingdom

Companies Act 1929 (United Kingdom).
Companies Act 1985 (United Kingdom).
Companies Act 2006 (United Kingdom).
Company Directors Disqualification Act 1986 (United Kingdom).
Insolvency Act 1986 (United Kingdom).
Joint Stock Companies Act 1856 (United Kingdom).
London Stock Exchange Listing Rules 2003 (United Kingdom).
Rules Governing Substantial Acquisitions of Shares.

United States of America

Banking Holding Company Act of 1956 12 U.S.C.§1841–48 (Supp.1958).
Bankruptcy Reform Act of 1978 11 U.S.C. §101 et seq.
Glass-Steagall Act (1933).
Gramm–Leach–Bliley Act Pub. L. No. 106–102, 113 Stat. 1338 (November 12, 1999).
Sarbanes-Oxley Act 15 U.S.C.A. §7201–7266 (2003).

New Zealand

Companies Act No. 23 of 1987 (NZ).

International

EU Transparency Directive 2004/109/EC.
International Accounting Standards (IAS).
International Financial Reporting Standards (IFRS).

Bibliography Cases

Sri Lanka

Al-Nakib v. E.B Creasy & Company Limited [Commercial HCC 9/2005].
Amarasekere v. Mitsui and Company and others [1992] 1 SLLR 22.
Chissel v. Chapman [1954] 56 NLR 121.
Kodeesweran v. Attorney General [1969] 72 NLR 337.
MA Razak & Company Limited v. Lanka Walltiles Limited [2000] 1 SLLR 1.
Oretra Enterprises and Others v. Wijekoon [2003] 3 SLLR 1.
Prof. Priyani Soysa v. Rienzie Arsacularatne [2001] 2 SLLR 293.
Ramachandran & another v. Anandasiva [SC Appeal No. 05/2004].
Ratnam and Others v. Jayatilake [2002] 1 SLLR 409.
Sabapatipillai v. Jaffna Trading Co. 4 Ceylon Recorder 210.
Samaraweera and another v. Sunpower Systems (Private) Limited [1996] 1 SLLR 284.
SC Special Determination 22/03.
Trade Exchange (Ceylon) Limited v. Asian Hotels Corporation [1981] 1 SLLR 67.
Usman v. Rahim [1930] 32 NLR 259.
Visuvalingam and others v. Liyanage and others [1983] 2 SLLR 311.
Wright and Three Others v. People's Bank [1985] 2 SLLR 292.

United Kingdom

Adams v. Cape Industries Plc [1990] BCLC 479 (CA).
Caparo Industries Plc v. Dickman [1990] 2 AC 605 (HL).
Hedley Byrne & Co. v. Heller & Partners [1964] AC 465 (HL).
Macaura v. Northern Assurance Co. Limited [1925] AC 619 (HL).
Re a company (no. 005009 of 1987), ex parte Copp [1989] BCLC 13.
Salomon v. Salomon & Co. Limited [1897] 1 AC 22 (HL).
Ultraframe (United Kingdom) Limited v. Fielding [2005] EWHC 1638 (Ch).
West Mercia Safetywear Limited v. Dodd [1988] BCLC 250 (CA).

United States of America

Benjamin v. Diamond (*In re Mobile Steel Co.*), 563 F. 2d 692, 700 [5th Cir 1977].

Bondi v. Bank of America (*In re Parmalat Securities Litigation*) 383 F. Supp. 2d 587 [S.D.N.Y. 2005].

Enron Corp. v. Avenue Special Situations Fund II, LP (*In re Enron Corp.*), 333 B.R. 205 [Bankr. S.D.N.Y. 2005].

Kittay v. Atlantic Bank of New York (*In re Global Service Group LLC*), 316 B.R. 451 [Bankr. S.D.N.Y. 2004].

Official Committee of Unsecured Creditors v. Credit Suisse First Boston (*In re Exide Technologies, Inc.*) 299 B.R. 732 [Bankr. D.Del. 2003].

Official Committee of Unsecured Creditors v. Rural Telephone Finance Cooperative (*In re Vartec Telecom,Inc.*) 335 B.R. 631, [Bankr. N.D. Tex. 2005].

Pepper v. Litton 308 US 295 [1939].

Taylor v. Standard Gas & Elec. Co. 306 US 307 [1939].

United States v. Arthur Young 465 US 805 [1984].

Bibliography Journals

Alchian, A and H Demsetz (1972). Production, Information Costs and Economic Organization. *American Economic Review*, 62, 777.

Allen, F (2005). Corporate Governance in Emerging Economies. *Oxford Review of Economic Policy*, 21, 164.

Allen, F and D Gale (1995). A Welfare Comparison of Intermediaries and Financial Markets in Germany and the US. *European Economic Review*, 39, 179.

Allen, F, J Qian and M Qian (2005). Finance, Law and Economic Growth in China. *Journal of Financial Economics*, 77, 57.

Anderlini, L and L Felli (1994). Incomplete Written Contracts: Undescribable States of Nature. *Quarterly Journal of Economics*, 109, 1085.

Anderson, R and D Reeb (2003). Founding Family Ownership and Firm Performance: Evidence from the S&P 500. *Journal of Finance*, 58, 1301.

Arunatilake, A, S Jayasuriya and S Kelegama (2001). The Economic Cost of the War in Sri Lanka. *World Development*, 29, 1483.

Bae, K, J Kang and J Kim (2002). Tunneling or Value Added: Evidence from Mergers by Korean Business Groups. *Journal of Finance*, 62, 2695.

Barclay, M and C Holderness (1989). Private Benefits from Control of Public Corporations. *Journal of Financial Economics*, 25, 371.

Bebchuk, L and A Cohen (2005). The Costs of Entrenched Boards. *Journal of Financial Economics*, 78, 409.

Bebchuk, L and M Roe (1999). A Theory of Path Dependence in Corporate Ownership and Governance. *Stanford Law Review*, 52, 127.

Becht, M and A Roell (1999). Blockholdings in Europe: An International Comparison. *European Economic Review*, 43, 1049.

Beck, T, R Levine and N Loayza (2000). Finance and Sources of Growth. *Journal of Financial Economics*, 58, 261.

Berglöf, E and S Claessens (2006). Enforcement and Good Corporate Governance in Developing Countries and Transition Economies. *World Bank Research Observer*, 21, 123.

Berglöf, E and E Perotti (1994). The Governance Structure of the Japanese Financial Keiretsu. *Journal of Financial Economics*, 36, 259.

Berkowitz, D, K Pistor and J Richard (2003). Economic Development, Legality, and the Transplant Effect. *European Economic Review*, 47, 165.

Berkowitz, D, K Pistor and J Richard (2003). The Transplant Effect. *American Journal of Comparative Law*, 51, 163.

Bertrand, M, P Meht and S Mullainthan (2002). Ferreting Out Tunneling: an Application to Indian Business Groups. *Quarterly Journal of Economics*, 117, 121.

Bhagat, S and B Black (1999). The Uncertain Relationship between Board Composition and Firm Performance. *Business Lawyer*, 55, 921.

Black, B (2001a). Does Corporate Governance Matter? A Crude Test Using Russian Data. *University of Pennsylvania Law Review*, 149, 2131.

Black, B (2001b). The Legal and Institutional Preconditions for Strong Securities Markets. *University of California Los Angeles Law Review*, 48, 781.

Black, B and J Coffee Jr. (1994). Hail Britannia? Institutional Investor Behavior Under Limited Regulation. *Michigan Law Review*, 92, 1997.

Boutchkova, M and W Megginson (2000). Privatization and the Rise of Global Capital Markets. *Financial Management*, 29, 31.

Branson, D (2000). Teaching Comparative Corporate Governance: The Significance of "Soft Law" and International Institutions. *Georgia Law Review*, 34, 669.

Bratton Jr., W and J McCahery (1999). Comparative Corporate Governance and the Theory of the Firm: The Case Against Global Cross-Reference. *Columbia Journal of Transnational Law*, 38, 213.

Brown, L and M Caylor (2006). Corporate Governance and Firm Valuation. *Journal of Accounting and Public Policy*, 25, 409.

Burkart, M, F Panunzi and A Shleifer (2003). Family Firms. *Journal of Finance*, 58, 2167.

Cain, D, G Lowenstein and D Moore (2005). The Dirt on Coming Clean: Perverse Effects of Disclosing Conflicts of Interest. *Journal of Legal Studies*, 34, 1.

Cankar, N (2005). Transition Economies and Corporate Governance Codes: Can Self-regulation of Corporate Governance Really Work? *Journal of Corporate Law Studies*, 5, 285.

Carlin, W and C Mayer (2003). Finance, Investment and Growth. *Journal of Financial Economics*, 69, 191.

Chandler, A (1980). The Growth of the Transnational Industrial Firm in the United States and United Kingdom: A Comparative Analysis. *Economic History Review*, 33, 396.

Cheffins, B (1999). Current Trends in Corporate Governance: Going from London to Milan via Toronto. *Duke Journal of Comparative and International Law*, 10, 5.

Cheffins, B (2003). Law as Bedrock: The Foundations of an Economy Dominated by Widely Held Public Companies. *Oxford Journal of Legal Studies*, 23, 1.

Cheng, S and C Shiu (2007). Investor Protection and Capital Structure: International Evidence. *Journal of Multinational Financial Management*, 17, 30.

Claessens, S and L Laeven (2002). Financial Development, Property Rights, and Growth. *Journal of Finance*, 58, 2401.

Claessens, S, S Djankov and L Lang (2000). The Separation of Ownership and Control in East Asian Corporations. *Journal of Financial Economics*, 58, 81.

Claessens, S *et al.* (2002). Disentangling the Incentive and Entrenchment Effects of Large Shareholdings. *Journal of Finance*, 57, 2741.

Coase, R (1937). The Nature of 'The Firm'. *Economica* (ns), 4, 386.

Coase, R (1960). The Problem of Social Cost. *Journal of Law and Economics*, 3, 1.

Coffee Jr., J (1991). Liquidity Versus Control: The Institutional Investor as a Corporate Monitor. *Columbia Law Review*, 91, 1277.

Coffee Jr., J (1999). The Future as History: The Prospects for Global Convergence in Corporate Governance and Its Implications. *Northwestern University Law Review*, 93, 641.

Coffee Jr., J (2001). Do Norms Matter? A Cross-Country Evaluation. *University of Pennsylvania Law Review*, 149, 2151.

Cuervo, A (2002). Corporate Governance Mechanisms: A Plea for Less Code of Good Governance and More Market Control. *Corporate Governance: An International Review*, 10, 84.

Cunningham, L (1999). Commonalities and Prescriptions in the Vertical Dimension of Global Corporate Governance. *Cornell Law Review*, 84, 1133.

Day, J and P Taylor (2004). Institutional Change and Debt-based Corporate Governance: A Comparative Analysis of Four Transition Economies. *Journal of Management and Governance*, 8, 73.

De Silva, G (1982). Development of Entrepreneurship in Sri Lanka. *Central Bank of Sri Lanka Staff Studies*, 12, 45.

Demirag, I and M Serter (2003). Ownership Patterns and Control in Turkish Listed Companies. *Corporate Governance: An International Review*, 11, 40.

Demirguc-Kunt, A and R Levine (1996). Stock Markets, Corporate Finance, and Economic Growth: An Overview. *World Bank Economic Review*, 10, 223.

Demsetz, H (1967). Towards a Theory of Property Rights. *American Economic Review*, 57, 347.

Diamond, D (1984). Financial Intermediation and Delegated Monitoring. *Review of Economic Studies*, 51, 393.

Dichev, I and D Skinner (2002). Large Sample Evidence on Debt Covenant Hypothesis. *Journal of Accounting Research*, 40, 1091.

Djankov, S *et al.* (2003). Courts. *Quarterly Journal of Economics* 453.

Dyck, A and L Zingales (2004). Private Benefits of Control: An International Comparison. *Journal of Finance*, 59, 537.

Dzierzanowski, M and P Tamowicz (2003). Setting Standards of Corporate Governance: A Polish Experience with Drafting Codes. *European Business Organization Law Review*, 4, 273.

Easterbrook, F (1984). Two-agency Cost Explanations of Dividends. *American Economic Review*, 74, 650.

Faccio, M (2006). Politically Connected Firms. *American Economic Review*, 96, 369.

Faccio, M and L Lang (2002). The Ultimate Ownership of Western European Corporations. *Journal of Financial Economics*, 65, 365.

Fama, E and M Jensen (1983). Separation of Ownership and Control. *Journal of Law and Economics*, 26, 301.

Fischel, D (1989). The Economics of Lender Liability. *Yale Law Journal*, 99, 131.

Fox, M (1999). Required Disclosure and Corporate Governance. *Law and Contemporary Problems*, 62(3), 113.

Fox, M and M Heller (2000). Corporate Governance Lessons from Russian Enterprise Fiascoes. *New York University Law Review*, 75, 1720.

Franks, J and C Mayer (1990). Capital Markets and Corporate Control: A Study of France, Germany and the UK. *Economic Policy*, 5, 189.

Franks, J and C Mayer (1997). Corporate Ownership and Control in the U.K., Germany and France. *Journal of Applied Corporate Finance*, 9, 30.

Franks, J and C Mayer (2001). Ownership and Control of German Corporations. *Review of Financial Studies*, 14, 943.

Friedman, E, S Johnson and T Mitton (2003). Propping and Tunneling. *Journal of Comparative Economics*, 31, 732.

Gilson, R and J Gordon (2003). Doctrines and Markets: Controlling Controlling Shareholders. *University of Pennsylvania Law Review*, 152, 785.

Gomes, A (2000). Going Public without Governance: Managerial Reputation Effects. *Journal of Finance*, 55, 615.

Gompers, P, L Ishii and A Metrick (2003). Corporate Governance and Equity Prices. *Quarterly Journal of Economics*, 118, 107.

Gordon, J (1997). The Shaping Force of Corporate Law in the New Economic Order. *University of Richmond Law Review*, 31, 1473.

Gordon, J (1999). Pathways to Corporate Convergence? Two Steps on the Road to Shareholder Capitalism in Germany. *Columbia Journal of European Law*, 5, 219.

Greenwald, B, J Stiglitz and A Weiss (1984). Informational Imperfections in the Capital Market and Macro-economic Fluctuations. *American Economic Review*, 74, 194.

Greif, A (1993). Contract Enforceability and Economic Institutions in Early Trade: The Maghribi Traders' Coalition. *American Economic Review*, 83, 525.

Grossman, S and O Hart (1980). Take Over Bids, the Free-rider Problem, and the Theory of the Corporation. *Bell Journal of Economics*, 11, 42.

Grossman, S and O Hart (1986). The Costs and Benefits of Ownership: A Theory of Vertical and Lateral Integration. *Journal of Political Economy*, 94, 691.

Grossman, S and O Hart (1988). One-share, One-vote, and the Market for Corporate Control. *Journal of Financial Economics*, 20, 175.

Hansmann, H and R Kraakman (2001). The End of History for Corporate Law. *Georgetown Law Journal*, 89, 439.

Harris, M and A Raviv (1988). Corporate Governance: Voting Rights and Majority Rules. *Journal of Financial Economics*, 20, 203.

Hart, O and J Moore (1990). Property Rights and the Nature of the Firm. *Journal of Political Economy*, 98, 1119.

Hu, H and B Black (2006). The New Vote Buying: Empty Voting and Hidden (Morphable) Ownership. *Southern California Law Review*, 79, 811.

Jackson, T and A Kronman (1979). Secured Financing and Priority Among Creditors. *Yale Law Journal*, 88, 1143.

Jensen, M (1986). Agency Costs of Free Cash Flow, Corporate Finance and Takeovers. *American Economic Review*, 76, 323.

Jensen, M and W Meckling (1976). The Theory of the Firm: Managerial Behaviour, Agency Costs and Ownership Structure. *Journal of Financial Economics*, 3, 305.

Johnson, S *et al.* (2000). Corporate Governance in the Asian Financial Crisis. *Journal of Financial Economics*, 58, 141.

Kang, J and A Shivdasani (1995). Firm Performance, Corporate Governance, and Top Executive Turnover in Japan. *Journal of Financial Economics*, 38, 29.

Khanna, T and K Palepu (1997). Why Focussed Strategies May Be Wrong for Emerging Markets. *Harvard Business Review*, 75(4), 41.

Khanna, T and K Palepu (2000a). Is Group Affiliation Profitable in Emerging Markets? An Analysis of Diversified Indian Business Groups. *Journal of Finance*, 15, 867.

Khanna, T and K Palepu (2000b). The Future of Business Groups in Emerging Markets: Long-run Evidence from Chile. *Academy of Management Journal*, 42, 268.

Khanna, T and Y Yafeh (2005). Business Groups and Risk Sharing Around the World. *Journal of Business*, 78, 301.

Kim, W, B Black and H Jang (2006). Does Corporate Governance Predict Firms' Market Values? Evidence from Korea. *Journal of Law, Economics, and Organization*, 22, 366.

King, R and R Levine (1993). Finance and Growth: Schumpeter Might Be Right. *Quarterly Journal of Economics*, 108, 717.

Krugman, P (1994). The Myth of Asia's Miracle. *Foreign Affairs*, 73, 62.

La-Porta, R, F Lopez-de-Silanes and A Shleifer (1999). Corporate Ownership Around the World. *Journal of Finance*, 54, 471.

La-Porta, R, F Lopez-de-Silanes and A Shleifer (2002). Government Ownership of Banks. *Journal of Finance*, 57, 265.

La-Porta, R, F Lopez-de-Silanes, A Shleifer and R Vishny (1997). Legal Determinants of External Finance. *Journal of Finance*, 52, 1131.

La-Porta, R, F Lopez-de-Silanes, A Shleifer and R Vishny (1998). Law and Finance. *Journal of Political Economy*, 106, 1113.

La-Porta, R, F Lopez-de-Silanes, A Shleifer and R Vishny (2000a). Agency Problems and Dividend Policies Around the World. *Journal of Finance*, 55, 1.

La-Porta, R, F Lopez-de-Silanes, A Shleifer and R Vishny (2000b). Investor Protection and Corporate Governance. *Journal of Financial Economics*, 58, 3.

La-Porta, R, F Lopez-de-Silanes, A Shleifer and R Vishny (2002). Investor Protection and Corporate Valuation. *Journal of Finance*, 57, 1147.

Larner, R (1966). Ownership and Control in the 200 Largest Nonfinancial Corporations, 1929 and 1963. *American Economic Review*, 56, 777.

Levine, R (1997). Financial Development and Economic Growth: Views and Agenda. *Journal of Economic Literature*, 35, 688.

Levine, R and S Zervos (1998). Stock Markets, Banks, and Economic Growth. *American Economic Review*, 88, 537.

Lins, K (2003). Equity Ownership and Firm Value in Emerging Markets. *Journal of Financial and Quantitative Analysis*, 38, 159.

Lowenstein, L (1996). Financial Transparency and Corporate Governance: You Manage What You Measure. *Columbia Law Review*, 96, 1335.

Lucas, R (1988). On the Mechanics of Economic Development. *Journal of Monetary Economics*, 22, 3.

MacNeil, I and X Li (2006). Market Discipline and Non-Compliance with the Combined Code. *Corporate Governance: An International Review*, 14, 486.

Mahoney, P and C Sanchirico (2001). Competing Norms and Social Evolution: Is the Fittest Norm Efficient? *University of Pennsylvania Law Review*, 149, 2027.

Marove, M, A Padilla and M Pagon (2001). Collateral versus Project Screening: A Model of Lazy Banks. *RAND Journal of Economics*, 32, 726.

Milhaupt, C (2001). Creative Norm Destruction: The Evolution of Nonlegal Rules in Japanese Corporate Governance. *University of Pennsylvania Law Review*, 149, 2083.

Mitton, T (2002). A Cross-firm Analysis of the Impact of Corporate Governance on the East Asian Financial Crisis. *Journal of Financial Economics*, 64, 215.

Modigliani, F and M Miller (1958). The Cost of Capital, Corporate Finance, and the Theory of Investment. *American Economic Review*, 48, 261.

Morck, R, A Shleifer and R Vishny (1988). Management Ownership and Market Valuation: An Empirical Analysis. *Journal of Financial Economics*, 20, 293.

Myers, S (2001). Capital Structure. *Journal of Economic Perspectives*, 15, 81.

Nenova, T (2003). The Value of Corporate Votes and Control Benefits: A Cross-Country Analysis. *Journal of Financial Economics*, 68, 325.

Pistor, K *et al.* (2003). Evolution of Corporate Law and the Transplant Effect: Lessons from Six Countries. *World Bank Research Observer*, 18, 89.

Pitt-Watson, D (2003). Why Corporate Governance is Important. *The Edge*, 14, 29.

Posner, R (1997). Social Norms and the Law: An Economic Approach. *American Economic Review: Papers and Proceedings of the Hundred and Ninth Annual Meeting of the American Economic Association*, 87, 365.

Prentice, D (1990). Creditor's Interests and Director's Duties. *Oxford Journal of Legal Studies*, 10, 265.

Prowse, S (1990). Institutional Investment Patterns and Corporate Financial Behaviour in the United States and Japan. *Journal of Financial Economics*, 27, 43.

Rajan, R and L Zingales (1995). What Do We Know about Capital Structure? Some Evidence from International Data. *Journal of Finance*, 50, 1421.

Reed, D (2002). Corporate Governance Reforms in Developing Countries. *Journal of Business Ethics*, 37, 223.

Rock, E (1996). America's Shifting Fascination with Comparative Corporate Governance. *Washington University Law Quarterly*, 74, 367.

Rock, E and M Wachter (2001). Symposium: Norms and Corporate Law: Introduction. *University of Pennsylvania Law Review*, 149, 1607.

Rodik, D (2000). Institutions for High Quality Growth: What They are and How to Acquire them. *Studies in Comparative International Development*, 35, 59.

Roe, M (2000). Political Preconditions to Separating Ownership from Corporate Control. *Stanford Law Review*, 53, 539.

Roe, M (2001). The Shareholder Wealth Maximization Norm and Industrial Organization. *University of Pennsylvania Law Review*, 149, 2063.

Roe, M (2002). Corporate Law's Limits. *Journal of Legal Studies*, 33, 233.

Romano, R (1993). A Cautionary Note on Drawing Lessons from Comparative Corporate Law. *Yale Law Journal*, 102, 2021.

Romano, R (1998). Empowering Investors: A Market Approach to Securities Regulation. *Yale Law Journal*, 107, 2359.

Sapienza, P (2004). The Effects of Government Ownership on Bank Lending. *Journal of Financial Economics*, 72, 357.

Scott, R (1986). A Relational Theory of Secured Financing. *Columbia Law Review*, 86, 901.

Shleifer, A and R Vishny (1986). Large Shareholders and Corporate Control. *Journal of Political Economy*, 94, 461.

Shleifer, A and R Vishny (1993). Corruption. *Quarterly Journal of Economics*, 108, 599.

Shleifer, A and R Vishny (1997). A Survey of Corporate Governance. *Journal of Finance*, 52, 737.

Soederberg, S (2002). On the Contradictions of the New International Financial Architecture: Another Procrustean Bed for Emerging Markets? *Third World Quarterly*, 23, 607.

Solomon, J., A Solomon and C Park (2002). A Conceptual Framework for Corporate Governance Reform in South Korea. *Corporate Governance: An International Review*, 10, 29.

Stiglitz, J (1985). Credit Markets and the Control of Capital. *Journal of Money, Credit and Banking*, 17, 132.

Stulz, R (1988). Managerial Control of Voting Rights, Financing Policies, and the Market for Corporate Control. *Journal of Financial Economics*, 20, 25.

Stultz, R (2005). Corporate Governance and Financial Globalization. *National Bureau of Economic Research Reporter*, 13.

Summers, L (2000). International Financial Crisis: Causes, Prevention, Cures. *American Economic Review Papers and Proceedings*, 90(2), 1.

Wymeersch, E (2006). The Enforcement of Corporate Governance Codes. *Journal of Corporate Law Studies*, 6, 113.

Yafeh, Y (2000). Corporate Governance in Japan: Past Performance and Future Prospects. *Oxford Review of Economic Policy*, 16, 74.

Yeh, Y (2005). Do Controlling Shareholders Enhance Corporate Value? *Corporate Governance: An International Review*, 13, 313.

Yeh, Y and T Woidtke (2005). Commitment or Entrenchment? Controlling Shareholders and Board Composition. *Journal of Banking & Finance*, 29, 1857.

Bibliography Books

Associated Newspapers of Ceylon (1930). *Ferguson's Ceylon Directory for 1930*. Colombo: Lake House.

Abeyratne, S. (2001). *Banking and Debt Recovery in Developing Countries: The Law Reform Context*. London: Ashgate.

Allen, F and G Dale (2000). Corporate Governance and Competition. In *Corporate Governance: Theoretical and Empirical Perspectives*, X Vives (ed.), pp. 23–83. Cambridge: Cambridge University Press.

Aoki, M (1995a). Controlling Insider Control: Issues of Corporate Governance in Transition Economies. In *Corporate Governance in Transitional Economies: Insider Control and the Role of Banks*, M Aoki and H Kim (eds.), pp. 3–30. Washington DC: World Bank.

Aoki, M (1995b). Monitoring Characteristics of the Main Bank System: An Analytical and Developmental View. In *The Japanese Main Bank System: Its Relevance for Developing and Transforming Economies*, M Aoki and H Patrick (eds.), pp. 109–141. Oxford: Oxford University Press.

Aoki, M (2001). *Toward a Comparative Institutional Analysis*. Massachusetts: Massachusetts Institute of Technology.

Aoki, M, H Patrick and P Sheard (1994). The Japanese Main Bank System: An Introductory Overview. In *The Japanese Main Bank System*, M Aoki and H Patrick (eds.), pp. 1–50. Oxford: Oxford University Press.

Athukorala, P and S Jayasuriya (1994). *Macroeconomic Policies, Crises, and Growth in Sri Lanka, 1969–90*. Washington DC: World Bank.

Athukorala, P and S Rajapathirana (2000). *Liberalization and Industrial Transformation: Sri Lanka in International Perspective*. New Delhi: Oxford University Press.

Athukorala, S and B Reid (2002). *Diagnostic Study of Accounting and Auditing Practices in Sri Lanka*. Manila: Asian Development Bank.

Backman, M (1999). *Asian Eclipse: Exposing the Dark Side of Business in Asia*. Singapore: Wiley.

Balasuriya, L (2004). The Impact of Corporate Governance on Productivity in Sri Lanka. In *Impact of Corporate Governance on Productivity: Asian Experience*, E Gonzalez (ed.), pp. 354–370. Tokyo: Asian Productivity Organisation.

Barca, F (1997). Alternative Models of Control: Efficiency, Accessibility and Market Failures. In *Property Relations, Incentives and Welfare*, J Roemer (ed.). New York and London: St. Martin's and Macmillan.

Barca, F and M Becht (eds.) (2001). *The Control of Corporate Europe.* Oxford: Oxford University Press.

Barth, J, G Caprio and R Levine (2006). *Rethinking Banking Regulation: Till Angels Govern.* Cambridge: Cambridge University Press.

Baums, T (1995). The German Banking System and Its Impact on Corporate Finance and Governance. In *The Japanese Main Bank System: Its Relevance for Developing and Transforming Economies*, M Aoki and H Patrick (eds.), 409–449. Oxford: Oxford University Press.

Bebchuk, L, R Kraakman and G Triantis (2000). Stock Pyramids, Cross-ownership and Dual Class Equity: The Mechanisms and Agency Costs of Separating Control from Cash-flow Rights. In *Concentrated Corporate Ownership*, R Morck (ed.), pp. 295–318. Chicago: University of Chicago Press.

Becht, M and C Mayer (2002). Introduction. In *The Control of Corporate Europe*, F Barca and M Becht (eds.), pp. 1–45. Oxford: Oxford University Press.

Becht, M and J De Long (2005). Why Has There Been So Little Block-holding in America? In *A History of Corporate Governance Around the World: Family Business Groups to Professional Managers*, R Morck (ed.), pp. 613–660. Chicago: University of Chicago Press.

Becht, M, A Chapelle and L Renneboog (2002). Shareholding Cascades: The Separation of Ownership and Control in Belgium. In *The Control of Corporate Europe.* F Barca and M Becht (eds.), pp. 71–105. Oxford: Oxford University Press.

Berglöf, E (1997). A Note on the Typology of Financial Systems. In *Comparative Corporate Governance Essays and Materials*, K Hopt and E Wymeersch (eds.), pp. 151–164. Berlin: Walter de Gruyter and Co.

Berglöf, E and A Pajuste (2003). Emerging Owners, Eclipsing Markets? Corporate Governance in Central and Eastern Markets. In *Corporate Governance and Capital Flows in a Global Economy*, PK Cornelius and B Kogut (eds.), pp. 267–304. New York: Oxford University Press.

Berle, A and G Means (1967). *The Modern Corporation and Private Property* (Revised edn.). New York: Harcourt, Brace and World Inc.

Blair, M (2003). Shareholder Value, Corporate Governance, and Corporate Performance: A Post-Enron Reassessment of the Conventional Wisdom. In *Corporate Governance and Capital Flows in a Global Economy*, P Cornelius and B Kogut (eds.), pp. 53–82. New York: Oxford University Press.

Blair, M and M Roe (eds.) (1999). *Employees and Corporate Governance.* Washington DC: Brookings Institute.

Bloch, L and E Kremp (2002). Ownership and Voting Power in France. In *The Control of Corporate Europe*, F Barca and M Becht (eds.), pp. 106–127. Oxford: Oxford University Press.

Cabraal, A (2003). Corporate Governance in Sri Lanka Fast Off the Tracks: But Is the Progress Real Progress? In *A Comparative Analysis of Corporate Governance in South Asia: Charting a Road Map for Bangladesh*, F Sobhan and W Werner (eds.) Dhaka: Bangladesh Enterprise Institute.

Capulong, V, D Edwards and J Zhuang (eds.) (2001). *Corporate Governance and Finance in East Asia: A Study of Indonesia, Republic of Korea, Malaysia, Philippines, and Thailand: Volume Two (Country Studies)*. Manila: Asian Development Bank.

Chang, S (2003). *Financial Crisis and Transformation of Korean Business Groups*. Cambridge: Cambridge University Press.

Cheffins, B (1997). *Company Law, Theory, Structure and Operation*. Oxford: Oxford University Press.

Cheffins, B (2002). Putting Britain on the Roe Map: The Emergence of the Berle–Means Corporation in the United Kingdom. In *Corporate Governance Regimes: Convergence and Diversity*, JA McCahery (ed.), pp. 147–174. Oxford: Oxford University Press.

Chung, K and Y Wang (2001). Republic of Korea. In *Corporate Governance and Finance in East Asia: A Study of Indonesia, Republic of Korea, Malaysia, Philippines and Thailand*, M Capulong, D Edwards and J Zhuang (eds.), pp. 53–154. Manila: Asian Development Bank.

Claessens, S (2003). *Focus 1: Corporate Governance and Development*. Washington DC: Global Corporate Governance Forum-World Bank.

Claessens, S, S Djankov and L Lang (1999). Corporate Ownership and Valuation: Evidence from East Asia. In *Financial Markets and Development: The Crisis in Emerging Markets*, A Harwood, R Litan and M Pomerleano (eds.), pp. 159–178. Washington: Brookings Institution.

Coffee Jr., J (2006). *Gatekeepers-The Professions and Corporate Governance*. Oxford: Oxford University Press.

Corley, T (2004). Cargill, David Sime (1826–1904). In *Oxford Dictionary of National Biography*, H Matthew and B Harrison (eds.). Oxford: Oxford University Press.

Cornelius, PK and B Kogut (2003). Introduction. In *Corporate Governance and Capital Flows in a Global Economy*, PK Cornelius and B Kogut (eds.), pp. 1–28. New York: Oxford University Press.

Crespi-Cladera, R and M Garcia-Cestona (2002). Ownership and Control of Spanish Listed Firms. In *The Control of Corporate Europe*, F Barca and M Becht (eds.), pp. 207–227. Oxford: Oxford University Press.

Dam, K (2006). *The Law-Growth Nexus: The Rule of Law and Economic Development*. Washington DC: Brookings Institution Press.

Davies, P (2002). *Introduction to Company Law*. Clarendon Law Series Oxford: Oxford University Press.

Davies, P (2003). *Gower and Davies' Principles of Modern Company Law* (7th edn.). Sweet & Maxwell.

De Soto, H (2001). *The Mystery of Capital: Why Capitalism Triumphs in the West and Fails Everywhere Else*. London: Transworld.

Dine, J (1998). Models of Companies and the Regulation of Groups. In *The Corporate Dimension: An Exploration of Developing Areas of Company and Commercial Law*, BAK Rider (ed.). Jordon Publishing Bristol.

Dine, J (2000). *The Governance of Corporate Groups*. Cambridge: Cambridge University Press.

Easterbrook, F and D Fischel (1991). *The Economic Structure of Corporate Law*. Massachusetts: Harvard University Press Cambridge.

Eells, R (1962). *The Government of Corporations*. New York: Free Press of Glencoe.

Eisenberg, M (1976). *The Structure of the Corporation: A Legal Analysis*. Little Brown and Company Boston.

Farrar, J (2005). *Corporate Governance: Theories, Principles and Practice* (2nd edn.). Oxford University Press Melbourne.

Goetzmann, W and E Koll (2005). The History of corporate Ownership in China: State Patronage, Company Legislation, and the Issue of Control. In *A History of Corporate Governance Around the World: Family Business Groups to Professional Managers*, R Morck (ed.), pp. 149–181. Chicago: University of Chicago Press.

Goodhand, J (2001). *Aid, Conflict, and Peacebuilding in Sri Lanka*. Center for Defense Studies, London: King's College.

Granovetter, M (2005). Business Groups and Social Organization. In *The Handbook of Economic Sociology*, N Semelser and R Swedberg (eds.), pp. 429–450 (2nd edn.). Princeton: Princcton University Press.

Hadden, T (1993). Regulating Corporate Groups: An International Perspective. In *Corporate Control and Accountability*, J McCahery, S Picciotto and C Scott (eds.), pp. 343–370. Clarendon Oxford.

Hart, O (1995). *Firms, Contracts, and Financial Structure*. Clarendon Oxford.

Hertig, G (1998). Lenders as a Force in Corporate Governance Criteria and Practical Examples for Switzerland. In *Comparative Corporate Governance: The State of the Art and Emerging Research*, KJ Hopt et al. (eds.), pp. 809–836. Oxford: Oxford University Press.

Honore, A (1961). Ownership. In *Oxford Essays in Jurisprudence*, A Guest (ed.). First Series Clarendon Oxford.

Hopt, K and S Prigge (1998). Preface. In *Comparative Corporate Governance-The State of the Art and Emerging Research*, K Hopt et al. (eds.), pp. v–xix. Oxford: Oxford University Press.

Jennings, Sir I (1951). *The Economy of Ceylon* (2nd edn.). Madras: Oxford University Press.

Johnson, S *et al.* (2003). Tunneling. In *Capital Markets and Company Law*, K Hopt and E Wymeersch (eds.), pp. 611–618. Oxford: Oxford University Press.

Karunatilake, H (1987a). *The Banking and Financial System of Sri Lanka.* Center for Demographic and Socio-Economic Studies Colombo.

Karunatilake, H (1987b). *The Economy of Sri Lanka.* Center for Demographic and Socio-Economic Studies Colombo.

Kelegama, S (1997). Privatisation in Sri Lanka: An Overview. In *How Does Privatisation Work? Essays on Privatisation in Honour of Professor V.V. Ramanadham*, A Bennett (ed.), pp. 163–203. Routledge London.

Kelegama, S and K Parikh (2003). Political Economy of Growth and Reforms in South Asia. In *South Asian Experience with Growth*, I Ahluwalia and J Williamson (eds.), pp. 80–145. New Delhi: Oxford University Press.

Khanna, T and K Palepu (2005). The Evolution of Concentrated Ownership in India: Broad Patterns and a History of the Indian Software Industry. In *The History of Corporate Governance Around the World: Family Groups to Professional Managers*, R Morck (ed.), pp. 283–320. Chicago: University of Chicago Press.

Kirkpatrick, G (2009). *Corporate Governance Lessons from the Financial Crisis.* OECD Paris.

Knight-John, M and P Athukorala (2005). Assessing Privatization in Sri Lanka: Distribution and Governance. In *Reality Check: The Distributional Impact of Privatization in Developing Countries*, J Nellis and N Birdsall (eds.), pp. 389–426. Washington DC: Center for Global Development.

Kotelawala, Sir J (1956). *An Asian Prime Minister's Story.* London: George Harrap.

Kraakman, R *et al.* (2004). *The Anatomy of Corporate Law: A Comparative and Functional Approach.* Oxford: Oxford University Press.

Lakshman, W (ed.) (1979). *Public Enterprises in the Economic Development of Sri Lanka.* National Institute of Business Management Colombo.

Levine, R (2004). Finance and Growth: Theory, Evidence and Mechanisms. In *Handbook of Economic Growth*, P Aghion and S Durlauf (eds.), pp. 865–920. Amsterdam: North-Holland Elsevier Publishers.

Madison, A (2001). *The World Economy: A Millennial Perspective.* OECD Washington.

Madison, A (2003). *The World Economy: Historical Statistics.* OECD Paris.

Madison, J. (2003). *Federalist Papers.* Number 51. New York: Penguin Publishing.

Maherbe, S and N Segal (2003). South Africa: After Apartheid. In *Corporate Governance in Development: The Experiences of Brazil, Chile, India and South Africa*, C Oman (ed.), pp. 161–233. OECD Paris.

Mallin, CA (2003). *Corporate Governance*. Oxford: Oxford University Press.

Meisel, N (2004). *Governance Culture and Development*. OECD Paris.

Moore, M (1998). Ethnicity, Caste and the Legitimacy of Capitalism. In *Sri Lanka-Collective Identities Revisited*, M Roberts (ed.) Colombo: Marga Institute-Sri Lanka Centre for Development Studies.

Morck, R (ed.) (2005). *A History of Corporate Governance Around the World: Family Business Groups to Professional Managers*. Chicago: University of Chicago Press.

Morck, R and M Nakamura (2005). A Frog in the Well Knows Nothing of the Ocean: A History of Corporate Ownership in Japan. In *The History of Corporate Governance around the World: Family Business Groups to Professional Managers*, R Morck (ed.), pp. 367–459. Chicago: University of Chicago Press.

Morck, R, A Shleifer and R Vishny (1988). Characteristics of Targets of Hostile and Friendly Takeovers. In *Corporate Takeover: Causes and Consequences*, A Auerbach (ed.), pp. 101–136. (National Bureau of Economic Research/University of Chicago Press Chicago.

Morck, R, D Stangeland and B Yeung (2000). Inherited Wealth, Corporate Control and Economic Growth: The Canadian Disease. In *Concentrated Corporate Ownership*, R Morck (ed.), pp. 319–372. Chicago: University of Chicago Press.

Morck, R *et al.* (2005). The Rise and Fall of the Widely Held Firm: A History of Corporate Ownership in Canada. In *A History of Corporate Governance Around the World: Family Business Groups to Professional Managers*, R Morck (ed.), pp. 65–140. Chicago: University of Chicago Press.

North, D (1990). *Institutions, Institutional Change and Economic Performance*. Cambridge: Cambridge University Press.

Pallister, J and J Daintith (2006). *Dictionary of Business and Management* etc. Oxford: Oxford University Press.

Pearsall, J (ed.) (2002) *Concise Oxford English Dictionary* (10th edn.). Oxford: Oxford University Press.

Prentice, D (1993a). A Survey of the Law Relating to Corporate Groups in the United Kingdom. In *Groups of Companies in the EEC: A Survey Report to the European Commission on the Law Relating to Corporate Groups in Various Member States*, E Wymeersch (ed.), pp. 279–295. Berlin: Walter De Gruyter.

Prentice, D (1993b). Some Comments on the Law Relating to Corporate Groups. In *Corporate Control and Accountability*, J McCahery, S Picciotto and C Scott (eds.), pp. 371–374. Clarendon Oxford.

Ranaraja, S (2001). *Case Study of Privatised Enterprises in Sri Lanka.* ILO Colombo.

Reed, D and S Mukherjee (eds.) (2004). *Corporate Governance, Economic Reforms and Development: The Indian Experience.* New Delhi: Oxford University Press.

Roberts, M (1982). *Caste, Conflict and Elite Formation: The Rise of a Karava Elite in Sri Lanka, 1500–1931.* Cambridge: Cambridge University Press.

Roberts, M (1997). Elite Formation and Elites, 1832–1931. In *Sri Lankan Collective Identities Revisited*, M Roberts (ed.), Colombo: Marga Institute.

Robinson, J (1952). *The Rate of Interest and Other Essays.* London: Macmillan.

Roe, M (1994). *Strong Managers, Weak Owners: The Political Roots of American Corporate Finance*, Princeton: Princeton University Press.

Roe, M (2002). *Political Determinants of Corporate Governance: Political Context, Corporate Impact*, Oxford: Oxford University Press.

Salih, R (2000). Privatisation in Sri Lanka. In *Privatisation in South Asia: Minimizing Negative Social Effects through Restructuring*, G Joshi (ed.), pp. 175–197. New Delhi: ILO.

Sen, A (1999). *Development as Freedom.* New York: Knopf.

Smith, A (1999). *An Inquiry into the Nature and Causes of the Wealth of Nations* (Regnery Washington DC reprinted).

Smith, A (ed.) (2002). *Glanville Williams: Learning the Law.* London: Sweet & Maxwell.

Smith, R and I Walter (2006). *Governing the Modern Corporation.* New York: Oxford University Press.

Smullen, J and N Hand (2005). *Dictionary of Finance and Banking.* Oxford: Oxford University Press.

Van den Berghe, L (2000). *Corporate Governance in a Globalising World: Convergence or Divergence? A European Perspective.* Boston: Kluwer.

Van den Berghe, L and S Carchon (2003). Redefining the Role and Content of Corporate Governance from the Perspective of Business in Society and Corporate Social Responsibility. In *Corporate Governance and Capital Flows in a Global Economy*, PK Cornelius and B Kogut (eds.), pp. 481–490. New York: Oxford University Press.

Villiers, S (1940). *Mercantile Lore.* Colombo: Ceylon Observer Press.

Weeramantry, C (1967). *The Law of Contracts being a Comparative Study of the Roman-Dutch, English and Customary Laws of Contract in Ceylon.* Colombo: HW Cave.

Wright, A (1907). *Twentieth Century Impressions of Ceylon.* London: Lloyd's Great Britain Publishing Company.

Wymeersch, E (2003). Do We Need a Law on Groups of Companies? In *Capital Markets and Company Law*, K Hopt and E Wymeersch (eds.), pp. 573–600. Oxford: Oxford University Press.

Zingales, L (1998). Corporate Governance. In *The New Palgrave Dictionary of Economics and the Law*, P Newman (ed.). New York: Macmillan.

Working Papers and Discussion Papers

Bai, C *et al.* (2003). Corporate Governance and Market Valuation in China, William Davidson Institute Working Paper 564. http://ssrn.com/abstract=393440 [20 July 2008].

Baird, D and R Rasmussen (2005). Private Debt and the Missing Lever of Corporate Governance, University of Chicago Law & Economics Working Paper 247. http://ssrn.com/abstract=692023 [5 July 2006].

Barth, J, G Caprio and R Levine (2001). The Regulation and Supervision of Banks around the World, World Bank Policy Research Working Paper 2588. http://papers.ssrn.com/sol3/papers.cfm?abstract_id=262317 [14 August 2006].

Bebchuck, L (1999). A Rent Protection Theory of Corporate Ownership and Control, National Bureau of Economic Research Working Paper 7203. http://www.nber.org/papers/w7203. [5 November 2005].

Bebchuck, L, A Cohen and A Ferrell (2005). What Matters in Corporate Governance?, Harvard Law School John M. Olin Center for Law, Economics and Business Discussion Paper 491.

Beck, T, A Demirguc-Kunt and R Levine (2004). Law and Firms' Access to Finance, World Bank Policy Research Working Paper 3194. http://papers.ssrn.com/sol3/papers.cfm?abstract_id=570365 [10 February 2005].

Bennedsen, M *et al.* (2005). Inside the Family Firm: The Role of Families in Succession Decisions and Performance (2005), Center of Industrial Economics University of Copenhagen Working Paper 13. http://www.econ.ku.dk/CIE/Discussion%20Papers/2005/2005-13.pdf [16 July 2006].

Berglöf, E and S Claessens (2004). Corporate Governance and Enforcement, World Bank Policy Research Working Paper. 3409. http://ssrn.com/abstract=625286 [5 May 2005].

Berglöf, E and E von-Thadden (1999). The Changing Corporate Governance Paradigm: Implications for Transition and Developing Countries, Annual World Bank Conference on Development Economics Working Paper 263. http://ssrn.com/abstract=183708 [28 May 2004].

Bloom, N and J Van-Reenen (2006). Measuring and Explaining Management Practices Across Firms and Countries, CEP Working Paper 716. http://cep.lse.ac.uk/pubs/download/dp0716.pdf [5 July 2007].

Claessens, S *et al.* (1999). Expropriation of Minority Shareholders: Evidence from East Asia, World Bank Policy Research Working Paper 2088. http://www.worldbank.org/html/dec/Publications/Workpapers/wps2000series/wps2088/wps2088.pdf [10 February 2005].

Coffee, J (2001). The Rise of Dispersed Ownership: The Role of Law in the Separation of Ownership and Control, Columbia Law & Economics Working Paper 182. http://ssrn.com/abstract=254097 [20 February 2005].

Demirguc-Kunt, A (2006). Finance and Economic Development: Policy Choices for Developing Countries (2006), World Bank Policy Research Working Paper 3955. http://ssrn.com/abstract=923262 [20 July 2008].

Dunham, D and S Jayasuriya (2001). Liberalisation and Political Decay: Sri Lanka's Journey from Welfare State to Brutalized Society, Institute of Social Studies Working Paper 352. http://adlib.iss.nl/adlib/uploads/wp/wp352.pdf [10 October 2007].

Ferrell, A (2004). The Case for Mandatory Disclosure in Securities Regulation Around the World, Harvard Law & Economics Discussion Paper 492. http://ssrn.com/abstract=631221 [10 July 2006].

Franks, J, C Mayer and S Rossi (2003). Ownership: Evolution and Regulation, European Corporate Governance Institute Finance Working Paper 92. http://ssrn.com/abstract=354381 [10 January 2006].

Franks, J, C Mayer and S Rossi (2004). Spending Less Time with the Family: The Decline of Family Ownership in the UK, European Corporate Governance Network Finance Working Paper 35. http://ssrn.com/abstract=493504 [25 July 2005].

Gilson, R (2005). Controlling Shareholders and Corporate Governance: Complicating the Comparative Taxonomy, European Corporate Governance Institute Law Working Paper 49. http://papers.ssrn.com/sol3/papers.cfm?abstract_id=784744 [8 January 2006].

Glen, J and A Singh (2004). Corporate Governance, Competition and Finance: Rethinking Lessons from the Asian Crisis, ESRC Centre for Business Research, University of Cambridge Working Paper 288. http://www.cbr.cam.ac.uk/pdf/wp288.pdf [14 April 2007].

Harvey, C, K Lins and A Roper (2001). The Effect of Capital Structure when Expected Agency Costs are Extreme, National Bureau of Economic Research Working Paper 8452. http://www.nber.org/papers/w8452.pdf [7 August 2006].

Hertig, G (2005). On-going Board Reforms: One-size Fits-all and Regulatory Capture, European Corporate Governance Institute Working Paper 25. http://ssrn.com/abstract=676417 [15 May 2006].

Himmelberg, C, R Hubbard and I Love (2002). Investor Protection, Ownership, and the Cost of Capital, World Bank Working Paper 2834. http://econ.worldbank.org/files/34858_wps2834.pdf [12 April 2006].

Jayasuriya, S and M Knight-John (2002). Sri Lanka's Telecommunications Industry: From Privatization to Anti-competition, University of Manchester Center on Regulation and Competition Working Paper 14. http://www.competitionregulation.org.uk/publications/working_papers/ wp14.pdf [14 August 2006].

Kaufmann, D and A Kraay (2002). Growth Without Governance, World Bank Policy Research Working Paper 2928. http://ssrn.com/ abstract=316861 [23 April 2009].

Kaufmann, D, A Kraay and M Mastruzzi (2005). Governance Matters IV: Governance indicators for 1996–2004, World Bank Policy Research Working Paper 3630. http://ssrn.com/abstract=718081 [5 March 2008].

Khanna, T and K Palepu (1999). Emerging Market Business Groups, Foreign Investors and Corporate Governance, National Bureau of Economic Research Working Paper 6955. http://papers.nber.org/papers/ w6955.pdf [29 April 2005].

Khanna, T and Y Yafeh (2005). Business Groups in Emerging Markets: Paragons or Parasites?, European Corporate Governance Institute Finance Working Paper 92. http://ssrn.com/abstract=787625 [10 January 2006].

Klapper, L and I Love (2002). Corporate Governance, Investor Protection, and Performance in Emerging Markets, World Bank Policy Research Working Paper 2818.

Kroszer, R and P Strahan (1999). Bankers on Boards: Monitoring, Conflicts of Interest, and Lender Liability, National Bureau of Economic Research Working Paper 7319. http://www.nber.org/papers/ w7319.pdf [10 July 2005].

La-Porta R, F Lopez-de-Silanes and A Shleifer (2004). What Works in Securities Laws?, National Bureau of Economic Research Working Paper 9882. http://papers.nber.org/papers/w9882.pdf [20 May 2006].

Morck, R (2004). How to Eliminate Pyramidal Business Groups: The Double Taxation of Inter-corporate Dividends and Other Incisive Uses of Tax Policy, National Bureau of Economic Research Working Paper 10944. http://papers.ssrn.com/sol3/papers.cfm?abstract_id=629586 [5 December 2005].

Morck, R and M Nakamura (2000). Japanese Corporate Governance and Macroeconomic Problems, Harvard Institute of Economic Research Discussion Paper 1893. http://ssrn.com/abstract=235758 [5 June 2005].

Morck, R and B Yeung (2004). Special Issues Relating to Corporate Governance and Family Control, World Bank Policy Research Working Paper 3406. http://econ.worldbank.org/files/38739_wps3406.pdf [10 May 2005].

Morck, R, D Wolfenzon and B Yeung (2004). Corporate Governance, Economic Entrenchment and Growth, National Bureau of Economic Research Working Paper 10692. http://papers.nber.org/papers/w10692.pdf [5 November 2005].

Murphy, A (2004). Corporate Ownership in France: The Importance of History (2004), National Bureau of Economic Research Working Paper 10716. http://www.nber.org/papers/W10716 [3 July 2005].

Myers, S (1976). Determinants of Corporate Borrowing, Sloan School of Management Working Paper 875–876. http://dspace.mit.edu/bitstream/1721.1/1915/1/SWP-0875-02570768.pdf [15 September 2006].

Pistor, K (2000). Patterns of Legal Change: Shareholder and Creditor Rights in Transition Economies, European Bank for Reconstruction and Development Working Paper 49. http://www.ebrd.com/pubs/econo/wp0049.pdf [13 November 2004].

Pistor, K, M Raiser and S Gelfer (2000). Law and Finance in Transition Economies, European Bank for Reconstruction and Development Working Paper 48. http://www.ebrd.com/pubs/econo/wp0048.pdf [5 November 2004].

Prowse, S (1999). Corporate Governance: Emerging Issues and Lessons from East Asia, World Bank mimeo. http://www1.worldbank.org/finance/assets/images/prowse.pdf [10 May 2006].

Rajan, R (1992). A Theory of the Costs and Benefits of Universal Banking, Center for Research on Security Prices University of Chicago Working Paper 346. http://www.crsp.com/resources/papers.html [15 November 2004].

Roe, M (2004). The Institutions of Corporate Governance, Harvard Law and Economics Discussion Paper 488. http://ssrn.com/abstract=612362 [3 August 2005].

Romano, R (2001). The Need for Competition in International Securities Regulation, Yale International Center for Finance Working Paper 00–49. http://ssrn.com/abstract=278728 [25 July 2006].

Samarajiva, R and A Dokeniya (2004). Regulation and Investment: Sri Lanka case Study, World Dialogue on Regulation Discussion Paper 303b. http://www.regulateonline.org/content/view/207/31/ [12 July 2006].

Sarkar, J and S Sarkar (2005). Debt and Corporate Governance in Emerging Economies: Evidence from India, Indira Gandhi Institute of Development Research Working Paper 7. http://econpapers.repec.org/paper/indigiwpp/2005-007.htm [10 August 2006].

Zhuang, J (1999). Some Conceptual Issues of Corporate Governance, Asian Development Bank Economics and Development Resource Centre Briefing Note 13. http://209.225.62.100/Documents/EDRC/Briefing_Notes/BN013.pdf [11 April 2007].

Bibliography Reports

Aitken Spence & Company Limited *Annual Report 2004–05* (Colombo 2005).

ALI *ALI Principles of Corporate Governance: Analysis and Recommendations* (Philadelphia 1994).

Asian Development Bank *Corporate Governance and Finance in East Asia* (Manila 2000).

Asian Development Bank *Key Indicators 2005: Labour Markets in Asia: Promoting Full, Productive and Decent Employment* (Manila 2005).

Asian Development Bank *Sri Lanka: Financial Sector Assessment* (Manila 2005).

Asian Hotels & Properties Limited *Annual Report 2004–05* (Colombo 2005).

Bank of Ceylon *Annual Report 2005* (Colombo 2005).

Basel Committee on Banking Supervision *Basel II: International Convergence of Capital Measurement and Capital Standards: A Revised Framework-Comprehensive Version* (Basel 2006).

Basel Committee on Banking Supervision *Core Principles for Effective Banking Supervision* (Basel 1997).

Basel Committee on Banking Supervision *Enhancing Corporate Governance for Banking Organizations* (Basel 2006).

Bukit Darah Company Limited *Annual Report 2004–05* (Colombo 2005).

Carson Cumberbatch & Company Limited *Annual Report 2003–04* (Colombo 2005).

Carson Cumberbatch & Company Limited *Annual Report 2004–05* (Colombo 2006).

Central Bank of Sri Lanka *A Guide to Financial Services in Sri Lanka* (Colombo 2004).

Central Bank of Sri Lanka *Annual Report 2002* (Colombo 2003).

Central Bank of Sri Lanka *Annual Report 2003* (Colombo 2004).

Central Bank of Sri Lanka *Annual Report 2006* (Colombo 2006).

Central Bank of Sri Lanka *Bulletin-January 2005* (Colombo 2005).

Central Bank of Sri Lanka *Code of Corporate Governance for Banks and Other Financial Institutions* (2002).

Central Bank of Sri Lanka *Press Release: New Policy on Share Ownership in Banks* (Colombo 19 January 2007).

Central Bank of Sri Lanka *Public Debt Management: Debt Profile of Sri Lanka* (Colombo 2004).

Ceylon Brokers' Association *Rupee Company Year Book* (Colombo 1977).

Ceylon Theatres Limited *Ceylon Theatres 2003* (Colombo 2005).

Ceylon Tobacco Company Limited *Annual Report 2004* (Colombo 2005).

Colombo Fort Land & Building Company Limited *Annual Report 2001–02* (Colombo 2002).

Colombo Stock Exchange *Annual Report 2004* (Colombo 2005).

Colombo Stock Exchange *Fact Book 2003* (Colombo 2004).

Colombo Stock Exchange *Handbook of Listed Companies 2004* (Colombo 2005).

Commercial Bank of Ceylon Limited *Annual Report 2005* (Colombo 2005).

Commonwealth Association for Corporate Governance *Corporate Governance Principles 1999* (Marlborough 1999).

Department of Trade and Industry (United Kingdom) *Report of the Review Committee on Insolvency Law and Practice (Cmnd 8558)* (1982).

DFCC Bank Limited *Annual Report 2005* (Colombo 2005).

Dialog Telekom Limited *Annual Report 2005* (Colombo 2005).

Dialog Telekom Limited *Initial Public Offering Prospectus 2005* (Colombo 2005).

Dipped Products Limited *Annual Report 2004–05* (Colombo 2005).

Distilleries Company of Sri Lanka Limited *Annual Report 2004* (Colombo 2004).

Distilleries Company of Sri Lanka Limited *Annual Report 2005* (Colombo 2005).

European Corporate Governance Network *The Separation of Ownership and Control: A Survey of 7 European Countries: Preliminary Report to the European Commission Volumes 1–4* (Brussels 1997).

H Gregory-Weil, Gotshal & Manges LLP *International Comparison of Corporate Governance: Guidelines and Codes of Best Practice in Developing and Emerging Markets* (New York 2002).

Hatton National Bank Limited *Annual Report 2005* (Colombo 2005).

Hemas Holdings Limited *Annual Report 2004–05* (Colombo 2005).

Human Rights Watch *Caste Discrimination: A Global Concern* (2001 London).

Institute of Chartered Accountants of Sri Lanka *Code of Best Practice: Report of the Committee to make Recommendations on Matters Relating to Financial Aspects of Corporate Governance* (Colombo 1997).

Institute of Chartered Secretaries and Administrators *Handbook on Corporate Governance: Principles and Guidelines to Best Practice in Sri Lanka* (Colombo _____).

Institute of Policy Studies *Parate Execution in Sri Lanka: Necessity, Impact and Prospects* (Colombo 2001).

Institute of Policy Studies *Sri Lanka: State of the Economy* (Colombo 2006).

Institute of Research for Development *Measurement of the Contribution of Informal Sector/Informal Employment to GDP in Developing Countries* (Paris 2006).

International Finance Corporation *A Corporate Governance Approach Statement by Development Finance Institutions* (Washington DC 2007).

International Monetary Fund *Global Financial Stability Report: Market Developments and Issues* (Washington DC 2002).

International Monetary Fund *Global Financial Stability Report: Market Developments and Issues* (Washington DC 2003).

International Monetary Fund *Global Financial Stability Report: Market Developments and Issues* (Washington DC 2006).

International Monetary Fund *IMF Country Report No. 05/337* (Washington DC 2005).

International Monetary Fund *IMF Country Report No. 6/446* (Washington DC 2006).

International Monetary Fund *World Economic Outlook: Housing and the Business Cycle* (Washington DC 2008).

International Organization of Securities Commissions *Report on the Subprime Crisis (Final Report)* (Madrid 2008).

James Finlay and Company (Colombo) Limited *Annual Report 2004* (Colombo 2005).

Jenkins Committee, *Report of the Company Law Committee* (Cmnd 1749, 1962).

John Keells Holdings Limited *Annual Report 2003–04* (Colombo 2004).

John Keells Holdings Limited *Annual Report 2004–05* (Colombo 2005).

Lanka IOC Limited *Annual Report 2004–05* (Colombo 2005).

Lankem Ceylon Limited *Annual Report 2004–05* (Colombo 2005).

Marga Institute *A System Under Siege? An Inquiry into the Judicial System of Sri Lanka* (Colombo 2002).

National Savings Bank *Annual Report 2004* (Colombo 2005).

NDB Bank *Annual Report 2004* (Colombo 2005).

NDB Bank *Annual Report 2005* (Colombo 2006).

Nestle Lanka Limited *Annual Report 2004* (Colombo 2004).

OECD *Banks Under Stress* (Paris 1992).

OECD *Corporate Governance of Non-Listed Companies in Emerging Economies* (Paris 2006).

OECD *Principles of Corporate Governance: 2004* (Paris 2004).

OECD *White Paper on Corporate Governance Reform in Asia 2003* (Paris 2003).

OECD *Policy Brief on Corporate Governance in Banks in Asia* (Paris 2006).

Oxford Analytica *Shareholder and Creditor Rights in Key Emerging Markets 2005: A Study Prepared for CalPERS ('California Public Employees' Retirement System')* (Oxford 2006).

Richard Pieris *Annual Report 2004–05* (Colombo 2005).

Securities and Exchange Commission of Sri Lanka *Report on the Capital Market Advancement Workshop* (Colombo 1999).

Sri Lanka Telecom *Annual Report 2005* (Colombo 2005).

T Kane *et al. 2001 Index of Economic Freedom* (The Heritage Foundation and *Wall Street Journal* Washington 2007).

The Committee on the Financial Aspects of Corporate Governance *The Financial Aspects of Corporate Governance* (London 1992).

The Company Law Review Steering Group *Modern Company Law for a Competitive Economy-Final Report* (London 2001).

Transparency International *Transparency International Corruption Perception Index 2002* (Berlin 2002).

UNDP *Human Development Report 2007/2008 Fighting Climate Change: Human Solidarity in a Divided World* (New York 2007).

Wilshire Consulting *CalPERS Permissible Equity Markets Investment Analysis: Final Report* (California 2006).

Wilshire Consulting *CalPERS Permissible Equity Markets Investment Analysis: Final Report* (California 2007).

World Bank *Analysis Report on Credit Bureau Development in South Asia* (Washington DC 2004).

World Bank and International Finance Corporation *Doing Business in 2005: Removing Obstacles to Growth* (Washington DC 2005).

World Bank and International Finance Corporation *Doing Business in 2006: Creating Jobs* (Washington DC 2006).

World Bank and International Finance Corporation *Doing Business in 2008: Comparing Regulation in 178 Economies* (Washington DC 2008).

World Bank *Finance for Growth: Policy Choices in a Volatile World* (Washington DC 2001).

World Bank *Report on the Observance of Standards and Codes (ROSC) Sri Lanka: Accounting and Auditing* (Washington DC 2004).

World Bank *Review of World Bank Conditionality* (Washington DC 2005).

World Bank Sri Lanka Development Forum: *The Economy, Regional Disparities and Global Opportunities* (Washington DC 2007).

World Bank *Sri Lanka: Recapturing Missed Opportunities* (Washington DC 2000).

World Bank *Lending Instruments: Resources for Development Impact* (Washington DC 2001).

World Bank *World Development Indicators 2002* (Washington DC 2002).

World Bank *World Development Indicators 2003* (Washington DC 2003).

World Bank *World Development Indicators 2006* (Washington DC 2006).

World Bank *World Development Report 2005: A Better Investment Climate for Everyone* (New York 2004).

Bibliography Electronic Sources

———— Colombo Stock Exchange. http://www.cse.lk/home/main.jsp [5 December 2004].

———— History of Ceylon Tea: Foundation Laid for a Plantation Enterprise. http://www.historyofceylontea.com/Tea_Feature/Foundation_%20Laid_for_a_Plantation_Enterprise.htm [20 April 2009].

———— Registrar of Companies (2004). http://www.drc.gov.lk [5 December 2004].

———— Securities and Exchange Commission of Sri Lanka. http://www.sec.gov.lk/ [5 December 2004].

Board of Investment Indian Investments http://www.boi.lk/InvestorSite/content.asp?content=india&SubMenuID=59#4 [10 March 2005].

Board of Investment Japanese Investments. http://www.boi.lk/InvestorSite/content.asp?content=japan&SubMenuID=58#5 [25 July 2005].

Central Bank of Sri Lanka Historical Information on Treasury Bill Auctions. http://www.lanka.net/centralbank/billdata.xls [5 February 2005].

Colombo Dockyard Limited Our Partners. http://www.cdl.lk/Our%20Partner.htm [15 July 2005].

Colombo Stock Exchange Introduction to the CSE. http://www.cse.lk/static/introduction_to_the_cse.htm [20 April 2009].

Colombo Stock Exchange Colombo Stock Exchange Glossary. http://www.cse.lk/static/Glossary.htm [20 April 2009].

Colombo Stock Exchange EB Creasy High-Low Prices Quarterly. http://www.cse.lk/listings/highlowprices_table.jsp?symbol=EBCR [10 January 2006].

Colombo Stock Exchange Historical Milestones. http://www.cse.lk/home/main.jsp [3 June 2005].

Colombo Stock Exchange Market Capitalization of Listed Companies. http://www.cse.lk/marketinfo/print/marketcap.jsp [24 April 2006].

Colombo Stock Exchange Year-to-Date Listings. http://www.cse.lk/home/main.jsp [10 July 2006].

Commercial Bank of Ceylon Limited Best Bank in Sri Lanka. http://www.combank.net/newweb/ [1 April 2006].

Dankotuwa Porcelain Limited Who We Are. http://www.dankotuwa.com/about_us.htm [10 March 2005].

Deloitte Financial Reporting Framework in Sri Lanka. http://www.iasplus.com/country/srilanka.htm [10 June 2006].

Employees' Provident Fund EPF Investments. http://www.epf-cbsl.lk/ [5 July 2005].

Employees' Trust Fund ETF Investments. http://www.lanka.net/etf/investment.html [5 July 2005].

Heston, A, R Summers and B Aten Penn World Table (version 6.2). http://pwt.econ.upenn.edu/php_site/pwt_index.php [13 January 2007].

International Monetary Fund Word Economic Outlook Database WEO Groups and Aggregates Information-April 2009. http://www.imf.org/external/pubs/ft/weo/2009/01/weodata/groups.htm#oem [5 May 2009].

International Monetary Fund Reports on the Observance of Standards and Codes. http://www.imf.org/external/standards/index.htm [15 June 2007].

Jet-Wing About Us http://www.jetwing.com/about_us.html [19 March 2005].

Lanka Milk Foods Limited About Us. http://www.lankamilkfoods.com/lmf/about_lmf.htm [25 March 2005].

McKinsey and Company McKinsey Global Investor Opinion Survey on Corporate Governance 2002: Key Findings. http://www.mckinsey.com/clientservice/organizationleadership/service/corpgovernance/pdf/globalinvestoropinionsurvey2002.pdf [5 July 2008].

Nortrade Norsk Hydro. http://www.nortrade.com/Companies/ShowCompany.aspx?id=1827&p=5 [7 July 2005].

Public Enterprises Reform Commission Past Divestitures. http://www.perc.gov.lk/pastdivt.html [5 June 2005].

Securities and Exchange Commission of Sri Lanka Market Intermediaries. http://www.sec.gov.lk/ [12 September 2005].

Social Science Research Network Social Science Research Network. http://www.ssrn.com [9 September 2006].

UN Adoption of 2005 World Summit Outcome (2005) A/RES/60/1. http://unpan1.un.org/intradoc/groups/public/documents/UN/UNPAN021752.pdf [15 April 2009].

World Bank 1988–1999 Privatization Transaction Data: Sri Lanka. http://rru.worldbank.org/Documents/Privatization/PrivatizationData.xls [10 July 2006].

World Bank Doing Business in 2006: Protecting Investors. http://www.doingbusiness.org/ExploreTopics/ProtectingInvestors/ [5 June 2006].

World Bank Governance and Anti-Corruption. www.worldbank.org/wbi/governance [25 July 2008].

World Bank Governance Matters 2008: Worldwide Governance Indicators 1996–2008 http://info.worldbank.org/governance/wgi/index.asp [5 July 2008].

World Bank Privatization Database (1998–2003). http://rru.worldbank.org/Privatization/ [10 February 2007].

Bibliography Conference and other Papers

Amit, R and B Villalong (2004). How Do Family Ownership, Control, and Management Affect Firm Value? http://wgfa.wharton.upenn.edu/VillalongaAmit121004.pdf [20 July 2006].

Bhagat, S and B Bolton (2007). Corporate Governance and Firm Performance. http://w4.stern.nyu.edu/emplibrary/Bhagat_paper_revised.pdf [21 July 2008].

Bianchi, M, M Bianco and L Enriques (1999). Pyramidal Groups and the Separation between Ownership and Control in Italy. http://ssrn.com/abstract=293882 [15 March 2006].

Block, B and K Forbes (2004). Capital Flows to Emerging Markets: The Myths and Realities. Myths and Realities of Globalization. http://web.mit.edu/kjforbes/www/Shorter%20Articles/CapitalFlowsTo EmergingMarkets-Myths&Realities.pdf [21 April 2009].

Boubaker, S (2005). Ownership-Control Discrepancy and Firm-Value: Evidence from France. http://ssrn.com/abstract=740756 [10 March 2006].

Brady, L (2005). Colonials, Bourgeoisies and Media Dynasties: A Case Study of Sri Lankan Media. http://www.ejournalism.au.com/ejournalist/brady2521.pdf [5 November 2005].

Brown, L and M Caylor (2004). Corporate Governance and Firm Performance. http://ssrn.com/abstract=586423 [21 July 2008].

Cabraal, N (2007). Road Map for Monetary and Financial Sector Policies in 2007 and Beyond. https://www.cbsl.lk/cbsl/speech-020107.pdf [30 January 2007].

Cabral, H (2007). Corporate Collapses and Insolvency Regimes-The Sri Lankan Experience. http://www.lawnet.lk/docs/articles/inter_legal_articles/HTML/CV10.html [1 March 2007].

Central Bank of Sri Lanka-J. Zilva (2004). Regulation of the Banking and the Related Sectors in Sri Lanka. http://www.ips.lk/events/workshops/22_07_2004_ria/papers/joan_de_zilva_banking_supervision.pdf [5 January 2007].

Dheeraratne, R (2006). Liability of an Auditor in Delict. http://webtest.cisworld.net/lawnet/docs/articles/inter_legal_articles/HTML/CV3.html [29 March 2007].

Faccio, M (2006). The Characteristices of Politically Connected Firms. http://ssrn.com/abstract=918244 [18 August 2006].

Faccio, M, L Lang and L Young (2001) Debt and Corporate Governance. www2.owen.vanderbilt.edu/fmrc/Activity/paper/Faccio_Paper_Debt.pdf [7 July 2005].

Gilson, R (2004). Corporate Governance, the Equity Contract and the Cost of Capital: Incremental and Accretive Reform Strategies. http://www.oecd.org/dataoecd/19/58/34081304.pdf [10 January 2005].

Grant, J and T Kirchmaier (2004). Who Governs? Corporate Ownership and Control Structures in Europe. http://ssrn.com/abstract=555877 [15 March 2006].

Hofstetter, K (2005). One Size Does Not Fit All: Corporate Governance for Controlled Companies. http://www.hertig.ethz.ch/LE_2005–06_files/Papers/Hofstetter_Corporate_Governance_2005.pdf [10 February 2006].

International Monetary Fund (2002). Summary and Policy Recommendations. http://www.imf.org/external/country/lka/rr/pdf/031802.pdf [10 January 2006].

Jayamaha, R (2006). Basel II - A Roadmap for Sri Lankan Banking System with International Comparisons. https://www.cbsl.lk/cbsl/Speech_181206.doc [5 May 2007].

Krueger, A (2004). Lessons from the East Asian Crisis. http://www.imf.org/external/np/speeches/2004/021204.htm [26 April 2009].

Licht, A, C Goldschmidt and S Schwartz (2004). Culture, Law, and Finance: Cultural Dimensions of Corporate Governance Laws. http://ssrn.com/abstract=277613 [5 July 2005].

Maher, M and T Anderson (1999). Corporate Governance: Effects on Firm Performance and Economic Growth. http://www.ecgi.de/research/accession/cgeu.pdf [20 July 2008].

Messick, M (2005). What Governments Can Do to Facilitate the Enforcement of Contracts. Public Sector Group World Bank. http://siteresources.worldbank.org/INTLAWJUSTINST/Resources/ContractEnforcementCairo.pdf [10 February 2008].

Prowse, S (1999). Corporate Governance: Emerging Issues and Lessons from East Asia. World Bank mimeo. http://www1.worldbank.org/finance/assets/images/prowse.pdf [10 May 2006].

Valaderes, S and R Leal (2000). Ownership and Control Structure of Brazilian Companies. http://ssrn.com/abstract=213409 [5 March 2006].

Wiwattanakantang, Y (2001). The Equity Ownership Structure of Thai Firms. http://papers.ssrn.com/sol3/papers.cfm?abstract_id=271358 [5 March 2006].

Bibliography Newspapers

2003 — one of the best years for Trans Asia Hotel (8 June 2004). *Daily News.*

Abeysuriya, R (2000). Credit rating a catalyst in fortifying Sri Lanka's capital market (2000). *Business Today.*

Actis takes Sri Lanka gas-maker private signifying the end of an era (4 June 2007). *Lanka Business Online.*

Bank of Ceylon plans to sell off stakes in Ceylon Hotels Corp. (6 July 2005). *Lanka Business Online.*

BOI says any new owners of Apollo will lose special benefits (9 August 2006). *Daily Mirror.*

Colombo Stock Exchange Stock Market Statistics 07-04-2006 (8 April 2006). *Daily News.*

Colombo Stock Exchange Stock Market Statistics 11-07-2005 (12 July 2005). *Daily News.*

EB Creasy says shareholders should not abuse AGMS (18 December 2005). *Sunday Times.*

Edirimuni, D (2005). EB Creasy AGM turns Stormy (04 December 2005). *Sunday Times.*

Edirimuni, D (2007). Curtains for major players in banks (7 January 2007). *Sunday Times.*

Galle Face Hotels Group takes control of Ceylon Hotels Corp (8 July 2005). *Lanka Business Online.*

Harry Jayawardene now eyes Apollo Hospital (21 July 2006). *Daily Mirror.*

Hunas Falls – a paradise on the misty mountains (13 January 2002). *Daily News.*

Labour chief intervenes in COMBank trade union dispute on shareholding (26 September 2006). *Daily Mirror.*

Minority shareholders of Maskeliya Plantations threaten court action (8 July 2007). *Sunday Times.*

NDB Bank's plea for an injunction against Janashakthi refused (20 December 2005). *Daily Mirror.*

P'ment talks biz with new Company Law (20 October 2006). *Daily Mirror.*

Pramuka to get treasury money through Rs. 2.2 billion restructuring bond (22 February 2006). *Lanka Business Online.*

Rohitha to save Apollo from Harry (7 August 2006). *Daily Mirror.*
SEC and national accounting body brings a new code for listed companies (19 September 2004). *Lanka Business Online.*
Sri Lanka's Janashakthi Group agrees to buy Central Securities Limited (4 April 2006). *Lanka Business Online.*
The LMD 50 Share Profile *The Lanka Monthly Digest's 50 Sri Lanka's Leading Listed Companies (Special Issue)* (December 2005).
Under the Influence (17 November 2001). *Economist.*

Author Index

Company Index